Explorations in Maximizing Syntactic Minimization

This volume presents a series of papers written by Epstein, Kitahara and Seely, each of which explores fundamental linguistic questions and analytical mechanisms proposed in recent minimalist work, specifically concerning recent analyses by Noam Chomsky. The collection includes eight papers by the collaborators (one with Miki Obata), plus three additional papers, each individually authored by Epstein, Kitahara and Seely, that cover a range of related topics including the minimalist commitment to explanation via simplification; the Strong Minimalist Thesis; strict adherence to simplest Merge, Merge $(X, Y) = \{X, Y\}$, subject to 3rd factor constraints; and state-of-the-art concepts and consequences of Chomsky's most recent proposals. For instance, the volume clarifies and explores the properties of Merge, feature-inheritance, and Agree; the nature of phases, cyclicity and counter-cyclicity; the properties of Transfer; the interpretation of features and their values and the role formal features play in the form and function of syntactic operations; and the specific properties of derivations, partially ordered rule application and the nature of interface representations. At the cutting edge of scholarship in generative syntax, this volume will be an essential resource for syntax researchers seeking to better understand the Minimalist Program.

Samuel D. Epstein is Professor of Linguistics at the University of Michigan, USA. He is an Arthur F. Thurnau Professor and Director of the Weinberg Institute for Cognitive Science.

Hisatsugu Kitahara is Professor at the Institute of Cultural and Linguistic Studies, Keio University, Japan.

T. Daniel Seely is Professor in the Linguistics Program of the Department of English Language and Literature at Eastern Michigan University, USA.

Routledge Leading Linguists

Edited by Carlos P. Otero, *University of California, Los Angeles, USA*

Explorations in Maximizing Syntactic Minimization

Samuel D. Epstein, Hisatsugu Kitahara, and T. Daniel Seely

Routledge
Taylor & Francis Group

NEW YORK AND LONDON

First published 2015
by Routledge
711 Third Avenue, New York, NY 10017

and by Routledge
2 Park Square, Milton Park, Abingdon, Oxon OX14 4RN

*Routledge is an imprint of the Taylor & Francis Group,
an informa business*

Library of Congress Cataloging-in-Publication Data
Explorations in maximizing syntactic minimization / By Samuel D.
   Epstein, Hisatsugu Kitahara, and T. Daniel Seely.
      pages cm. — (Routledge Leading Linguists)
   Includes bibliographical references and index.
   1. Minimalist theory (Linguistics)   2. Generative grammar.
3. Explanation (Linguistics)   I. Kitahara, Hisatsugu editor.   II. Seely,
T. Daniel.   III. Title.
   P158.28.E68 2015
   415'.0182—dc23
   2014040303

ISBN: 978-1-138-85312-6 (hbk)
ISBN: 978-1-315-72276-4 (ebk)

Typeset in Sabon
by Apex CoVantage, LLC

Printed and bound in the United States of America by Publishers Graphics,
LLC on sustainably sourced paper.

We dedicate this volume to Noam Chomsky, to whom we are indebted not only for his many years of support and discussion of our (joint and individual) work but for his creation of a revolutionary framework of rational formal scientific inquiry within which we have been very fortunate to conduct our research.

Contents

Acknowledgments

We thank Noam Chomsky for his continued interest in our work and his absolutely invaluable input. We thank Carlos P. Otero, series editor, for his interest in our research, as well as Margo Irvin, Associate Editor, Routledge Research, for her kindness, professionalism and patience. Thanks are also due to a Routledge reviewer for insightful comments, including those concerning the overall organization of this book. We also thank our co-author (of Chapter 2), Miki Obata. The following people have all contributed by reading or discussing or supporting or influencing, in one way or another, our research: Marlyse Baptista, Stefanie Bode, Vicki Carstens, Chris Collins, Erich Groat, Norbert Hornstein, Rick Lewis, Yohei Oseki and Acrisio Pires; the students in our 2013 Linguistic Society of America (LSA) Summer Institute course at the University of Michigan, "Derivations in Minimalism"; and the syntax students at our respective schools who have read and commented on or discussed many of the chapters included here. In particular, we thank Marcus Berger, Tomislava Dragicevic, Sujeewa Hettiarachchi, Hezoa (Alan) Ke, Will Nediger and Jae-Young Shim.

We are also indebted to Will Nediger for his editorial assistance with the preparation of this manuscript.

Formal acknowledgment of editors and publishers granting us reprint permissions:

We thank Cedric Boeckx, the editor of *The Oxford Handbook of Linguistic Minimalism*, where Chapter 1 ("Derivation(s)") first appeared, as well as Oxford University Press for granting permission for it to be reprinted. We thank Marcel den Dikken, the editor of *The Cambridge Handbook of Generative Syntax*, where Chapter 2 ("Economy of Derivation and Representation") first appeared, as well as Cambridge University Press for granting permission for it to be reprinted. We also thank our co-author of this chapter, Miki Obata, for granting us permission to reprint it here. We thank Angel Gallego, the editor of *Phases: Developing the Framework*, where Chapter 3 ("Exploring Phase-Based Implications Regarding Clausal Architecture. A Case Study: Why Structural Case Cannot Precede Theta") first appeared, as well as Mouton de Gruyter for granting permission for it to be reprinted. We thank *Linguistic Analysis* for granting permission for Chapter 4 ("On

I(nternalist)-Functional Explanation in Minimalism") to be reprinted, as well as David Winningham, the editor of *Linguistic Analysis*, and Kleanthes Grohmann, the guest editor of the issue in which the paper appeared. We thank Michael Putnam, the editor of *Exploring Crash Proof Grammars*, where Chapter 5 ("Uninterpretable Features: What Are They and What Do They Do?") first appeared, as well as John Benjamins Publishers for granting permission for it to be reprinted. We thank Cedric Boeckx, the editor of *Minimalist Essays*, where Chapter 6 ("Merge, Derivational C-Command, and Subcategorization in a Label-Free Syntax") first appeared, as well as John Benjamins Publishers for granting permission to reprint the paper. We thank Myriam Uribe-etxebarria and Vidal Valmala, the editors of *Ways of Structure Building*, where Chapter 7 ("Structure Building That Can't Be!") first appeared, as well as Oxford University Press for granting permission for it to be reprinted. We thank Nobu Goto, Koichi Otaki, Atsushi Sato and Kensuke Takita, the editors of *The Proceedings of GLOW in Asia IX*, where Chapter 8 ("Simplest Merge Generates Set Intersection: Implications for Complementizer-Trace Explanation") first appeared, and we also thank them for granting permission for it to be reprinted. We also thank Miki Obata, who was on the local organizing committee of GLOW in Asia IX at Mie University. We thank the editors of *Reports of the Keio Institute of Cultural and Linguistic Studies* 43, for printing Chapter 9 ("External Merge of Internal Argument DP to VP and Its Theoretical Implications") and for granting permission for it to be reprinted. We thank *Linguistic Inquiry* for granting permission for Chapter 10 ("Labeling by Minimal Search: Implications for Successive-Cyclic A-movement and the Conception of the Postulate 'Phase'") to be reprinted, as well as Samuel Jay Keyser, Sheelah Ward and Anne Mark.

Formalities aside, we are very grateful to each of the above-mentioned people for their interest in and support of our work.

Finally, we would like to thank each other. EKS have spent countless hours together and have generated literally thousands of emails working through every idea and every word of the articles included here. We can't imagine a better working relationship; it is one with deep mutual respect and admiration, and despite its complex, hence unattractive, trinarity (see especially Chapter 7), we have had an amazing amount of fun.

Introduction

Explorations in Maximizing Syntactic Minimization

Samuel D. Epstein, Hisatsugu Kitahara and T. Daniel Seely

This volume contains a series of papers written by Epstein, Kitahara and Seely (EKS), and one paper co-authored with Miki Obata, over the last six years, each of which explores fundamental questions and analytical mechanisms proposed in recent minimalist work specifically concerning leading ideas and analyses proposed by Noam Chomsky. Eight EKS co-authored papers—one previously unpublished and written for this volume, Chapter 11—and three papers, each individually authored by Epstein, by Kitahara or by Seely, are included. The volume covers a range of related central topics, all of which center on:

- The minimalist commitment to explanation via simplification
- The Strong Minimalist Thesis
- Strict adherence to simplest Merge, Merge (X, Y) = {X, Y}
- The role of 3rd factor constraints in explanation
- State-of-the-art concepts and consequences of Chomsky's recent proposals, including those of Chomsky (2013).

More specifically, the volume clarifies and explores:

- The properties of Merge, feature-inheritance and Agree
- The nature of constraints on the application of operations, and the nature of "computational efficiency"; e.g. are narrow syntax (NS) operations applied only "in order to" satisfy the interfaces, or are they "freely applied" subject only to 3rd factor constraints?
- The nature of derivations, including phases, cyclicity and counter-cyclicity
- The properties of Transfer
- The interpretation of features and their values and the role formal features play in the form and function of syntactic operations
- The specific properties of interface legibility requirements and interface representations.

The first two chapters are introductory and first appeared in an Oxford (2011) and a Cambridge (2013) handbook. Each provides detailed background regarding core concepts of the Minimalist Program (MP) concerning principles of derivational and representational "economy." The book therefore also meets pedagogical needs and is accessible to a larger audience, including those interested, but not well versed, in minimalist foundational goals, framework and analysis.

The book is organized as follows:

Chapter 1. Epstein, S. D., Kitahara, H., and Seely, T. D. 2011. Derivation(s). In Boeckx, C. (ed.), *The Oxford Handbook of Linguistic Minimalism*, 291–310. Oxford: Oxford University Press.

Chapter 2. Epstein, S. D., Kitahara, H., Obata, M., and Seely, T. D. 2013. Economy of Derivation and Representation. In den Dikken, M. (ed.), *The Cambridge Handbook of Generative Syntax*, 487–514. Cambridge: Cambridge University Press.

Chapters 1 and 2 provide an accessible overview of the nature of the minimalist enterprise, the re-emergence of (simplified) rule-based systems, and continue with an introduction to the computational component addressing key issues regarding the nature of (the single, unified) primary structure building operation, Merge, and the nature of derivations in the optimal creation of interface representations.

Having set the stage with Chapters 1 and 2, we move on to Chapter 3:

Chapter 3. Epstein, S. D., Kitahara, H., and Seely, T. D. 2012. Exploring Phase-Based Implications Regarding Clausal Architecture. A Case Study: Why Structural Case Cannot Precede Theta. In Gallego, A. (ed.), *Phases: Developing the Framework*, 103–123. Berlin: Mouton de Gruyter (Studies in Generative Grammar 109).

This chapter explores the widely held central hypothesis that syntactic representations of sentential phenomena exhibit an invariant hierarchically organized clausal architecture: there is the theta domain, above that the Case domain and finally the scope domain. Within Government and Binding, this hierarchy reflected unexplained aspects of the very architecture of the system, given its incorporation of ordered syntax-internal levels of representation, specifically the ordered mapping from D-structure to S-structure to LF representation. By definition, D-structure was the "theta domain," while S-structure concerned Case/agree, and LF represented scope. But from what does the clausal hierarchy follow in the MP, given its elimination of syntax-internal levels? The chapter suggests that at least some properties of clausal architecture may be deducible within the MP, specifically from the analysis of Chomsky (2007, 2008). We explore the idea that Case before theta invariably results in crashing and/or interface gibberish (a violation of Full Interpretation at the conceptual-intentional (CI) interface) even within the level-less, optimality-seeking filter free minimalist system of Chomsky (2007, 2008). One central aspect of clausal architecture is shown to be deducible from Chomsky's current analysis, following strict minimalist tenets, positing nothing beyond irreducible lexical features, natural (and independently motivated) Interface Conditions, and 3rd factor considerations expressing optimality-seeking minimalist design. If on track, this provides another deep explanatory improvement over the level-ordered Government and Binding system, within which clausal architecture follows only from stipulated aspects of level ordering (D-structure precedes S-structure) and unexplained stipulated asymmetries regarding which filters apply at which levels and which do not (e.g. the Theta Criterion, but not the Case Filter, applies at D-structure).

Chapter 4. Epstein, S.D. 2007. On I(nternalist)-Functional Explanation in Minimalism. *Linguistic Analysis* 33:20–54.

This chapter suggests that the Strong Minimalist Thesis (SMT), encapsulated as "computationally efficient satisfaction of the interface conditions," represents a form of functionalist (internalist) explanation, whereby the NS is by hypothesis optimally designed to function in such a way as to satisfy the interface conditions. However, it is noted that under unconstrained Merge and in successive cyclic phase-based *wh*-movement there is crashing at the interface; that is, the NS as formulated does indeed "send" non-convergent representations to the interfaces. But if the system is not crash-proof, the following central argument seems unmaintainable: "If language is to be usable at all, its design must satisfy an interface condition IC; the information in the expressions generated by L must be accessible to other systems including the SM (sensorimotor) and CI systems." However, with crash existing, it is not the case that "the expressions are interpretable at the interface." But if they are not all interpretable, then by the above central assumption of the SMT, language is not usable at all. Two approaches to the problem are outlined: The first conjectures that the expressions (all of them) *are* interpretable, as in Frampton and Gutmann's 2002 "Crash-Proof Syntax" (Merge is not free, and successive cyclic *wh*-movement does not yield intermediate crashes). The second approach hypothesizes that for language to be usable at all, (only) some expressions must be interpretable at the interface. If this is so, one cannot explain rule application by saying rules apply in order to satisfy the bare output conditions (BOCs); e.g. one cannot say, "Agree applies in this derivation since uninterpretable features are barred at the interface," because in fact they are not barred; that is, the system, as proposed, delivers uninterpretable features to the interface. Hence, there is no explanatory answer to questions of the form: "Why did Agree apply in this derivation?" (other than "because it can apply"). Nonetheless, maybe with Chomsky (2000:112–113), we can instead ask why the rules have the form they have—and answer by saying,

"The NS provides only machinery needed to satisfy requirements of legibility and functions as simply as possible." By hypothesis, the (or one) simplest way possible of satisfying the interface conditions would then be unconstrained Merge and derivation by phase—which happen to (also) induce an infinite number of failures to satisfy these minimal requirements of legibility at the interface. From this counter-intuitive, but perfectly sound, perspective, optimal efficiency in the system induces "infinite failure" in its output.

Chapter 5. Epstein, S.D., Kitahara, H., and Seely, T.D. 2010. Uninterpretable Features: What Are They and What Do They Do? In Putnam, M. (ed.), *Exploring Crash Proof Grammars*, 125–142. Philadelphia: John Benjamins.

This chapter provides a careful examination of one of the central concepts of the MP, namely "crash" and the role that various formal crash-inducing features play in the form and function of the operations of the NS. The chapter first details certain unclarities regarding the concept "crash," suggesting that there is some confusion between crash as a formal property of interface representations containing certain individual features versus the distinct notion "gibberish," i.e. a convergent object that results in some semantically anomalous interpretation. The NS is by hypothesis designed to avoid crash, not gibberish; as detailed in Chapter 1 ("Derivation(s)") the SMT states that the syntax optimally builds convergent (non-crashing) objects for use by the interfaces. The NS is not designed to avoid gibberish; i.e. the quest for "convergence" and not for "coherence" is the engine driving the form and function of syntactic operations. However, at least with respect to certain lexical items (e.g. Tense, bearing valued phi features), the claim is that crashing would result from their appearance in a CI representation. However, we argue that, according to the theory, in fact it's gibberish, not crashing, that in fact results. The paper then details a possible problem with the Chomsky–Richards attempt to explain feature-inheritance and the timing of phasal Spell Out, which makes crucial use of "crashing" (Richards 2007; Chomsky 2007, 2008). The basic idea is that since formal features (like phi of C/T and Case) must be valued before Transfer (otherwise, they could cause crash at the interface), and since after valuation these features would be indistinguishable from the phi features of D/N (which do not induce crashing), then Transfer must apply during the valuation operation (Epstein and Seely 2002); that is, Transfer must be able to "see" the formal features change from unvalued to valued, and thus Transfer can "know" to remove just these features from the CI-bound object. Phasal Spell Out for Chomsky–Richards results since the NS must prevent crash-causing features from appearing at the phase-edge. However, EKS argue that in fact such features *do* occur at the edge, resulting in massive undergeneration for the Chomsky–Richards system. The paper then presents a solution providing a simple statement of the nature of features as CI interpretable or not. Phonological and formal features (phi of C/T and Case) are unvalued in the lexicon and hence are (naturally enough) –CI. Given conservation of features (a feature can't change its nature in the course of a derivation), such features remain –CI even after valuation. Thus, Transfer can "know" to spell out all and only the –CI features. This is a radical reformulation of the mechanics of the operation of Transfer.

Chapter 6. Seely, T.D. 2006. Merge, Derivational C-Command, and Sub-categorization in a Label-Free Syntax. In Boeckx, C. (ed.), *Minimalist Essays*, 182–217. Amsterdam: John Benjamins.

This chapter contains a foundational analysis seeking to explain or deduce the representational label-free syntax as proposed by Collins (2002) by appeal to the independently motivated derivational approach to syntactic relations. A central argument is that representational label-lessness follows from the simplification of Merge, eliminating the "projection phase" from Merge, thereby reducing it to a primitive operation. This elimination of the projection phase of Merge application is directly relevant to Chomsky's (2013) labeling analysis.

Chapter 7. Epstein, S.D., Kitahara, H., and Seely, T.D. 2012. Structure Building That Can't Be! In Uribe-etxebarria, M. and Valmala, V. (eds.), *Ways of Structure Building*, 253–270. Oxford: Oxford University Press.

It's argued that syntactically valued features are CI illegible and are in fact recognized as such by Transfer. How then is cyclic/phasal Spell Out induced? If Transfer does not have to apply during valuation, as for Chomsky–Richards (as detailed in Chapter 2), Chapter 5 provides a detailed argument that counter-cyclic Internal Merge to Spec of TP (and to Spec of VP) results in the "double peak" ("multidominance") representation (formally, a set-intersection syntactic representation, in bare phrase structure), and as a result one peak (one set) must be removed, and this removal is achieved by Transfer. We propose that even though Merge is in its simplest, strictly binary form, it is nonetheless the case that a category can have more than one sister (i.e. more than one element that it was merged with). The multiple sisters of a given category arise at different derivational points, generating a "two-peaked" structure or, more formally, intersecting sets, neither of which is a term of the other, and one of the sets must then be removed (= Transfer). The paper provides a careful deduction of the timing and nature of phasal Spell Out, adopting strict adherence to the simplest form of Merge, namely Merge $(X, Y) = \{X, Y\}$. This deduction of Transfer is argued to have important conceptual and empirical advantages over the Chomsky–Richards model.

Chapter 8. Epstein, S. D., Kitahara, H., and Seely, T. D. 2013. Simplest Merge Generates Set Intersection: Implications for Complementizer-Trace Explanation. In Goto, N., Otaki, K., Sato, A. and Takita, K. (eds.), *The Proceedings of GLOW in Asia IX*, 77–92. Mie, Japan: Mie University.

This chapter provides further exploration of the "double peak" representation postulated in Chapter 7 and simplest Merge, presenting an entirely novel account of core *that*-trace effects. We argue that our proposed simplest formulation of Merge (generating set intersection when applied, allowably, "counter-cyclically") coupled with the very general laws of Minimal Computation (informally, forcing features to be interpreted at most once) and Recoverability (informally, forcing features to be interpreted at least once) allows us to deduce core complementizer-trace phenomena with no further mechanisms required. Complementizer-trace effects turn out to be an immediate consequence of these arguably quite natural and general principles, having no *ad hoc* language-specific, construction-specific or operation-specific properties reflecting complementizer-trace configurations.

Chapter 9. Kitahara, H. 2012. External Merge of Internal Argument DP to VP and Its Theoretical Implications. *Reports of the Keio Institute of Cultural and Linguistic Studies* 43:241–248.

This chapter concerns External Merge of internal argument DP to VP and its theoretical implications. It shows that External Merge of the internal argument DP to VP poses a problem not only for Chomsky's (2008) labeling algorithm but also for the Case-theoretic analysis of feature-inheritance, developed by Richards (2007) and Chomsky (2007, 2008). A unified solution to these problems in which head-movement plays a crucial role is then outlined, and some of the implications of the proposed head-movement analysis concerning the notion "Spec" are explored.

Chapter 10. Epstein, S. D., Kitahara, H., and Seely, T. D. 2014. Labeling by Minimal Search: Implications for Successive Cyclic A-movement and the Conception of the Postulate "Phase." *Linguistic Inquiry* 45: 463–481.

This chapter elucidates the fundamental mechanics of Chomsky's elimination of explicitly represented phrase structure projections and his reduction of label identification to Minimal Search. We show that the analysis readily generalizes to A-movement cases not discussed by Chomsky (2013). The generalization of the labeling analysis to these cases has a potentially profound impact on current theory. The A-movement cases we reduce to Chomsky's (2013) labeling principles were precisely the original empirical motivation for phases defined in terms of lexical arrays and subarrays. If the proposed reduction to labeling is viable, the original empirical motivation for phase-based derivation dissolves. If "cyclicity" is a property of Merge application in NS, it must be captured differently. We suggest that the analysis presented in Chapter 7 above may provide one avenue to doing so.

Chapter 11. Epstein, S. D., Kitahara, H., and Seely, T. D. *What Do We Wonder Is Not Syntactic? [A previously unpublished paper, written for this volume.]

This chapter examines criterial freezing phenomena (earlier analyzed by Epstein (1992) as evidence for the SMT (computationally efficient satisfaction of the interface conditions)) re-analyzed by Rizzi (1997, 2006, 2011, 2014). Rizzi (2014) seeks to elegantly deduce freezing effects from his formalization of Chomsky's (2013) labeling-by-minimal-search analysis. We provide empirical and conceptual arguments against this analysis, based on its (implicit, entailed) departure from simplest Merge and from a single unified Merge. We argue that syntactic freezing is an illusion. Movement can in fact continue (via application of freely applied simplest Merge) from a criterial position. However, the result of such allowable movement invariably violates independently necessary morpho-phonological, CI interpretive requirements. This analysis allows broader empirical coverage by a simpler theory. This represents an illustrative contemporary case study of the always difficult question concerning the division of labor between syntax and the two interface systems. The argumentation is particularly relevant to the contemporary minimalist method of maximally simplifying NS and reassigning what were hypothesized to be specifically syntactic principles to 3rd factor and/or natural interface requirements concerning "sound"/"sign" (i.e. externalization) and "meaning."

REFERENCES

Chomsky, N. 2000. Minimalist Inquiries: The Framework. In Martin, R., Michaels, D. and Uriagereka, J. (eds.), *Step by Step: Essays on Minimalist Syntax in Honor of Howard Lasnik*, 89–155. Cambridge, MA: MIT Press.

Chomsky, N. 2007. Approaching UG from Below. In Sauerland, U. and Gärtner, H.-M. (eds.), *Interfaces + Recursion = Language?*, 1–29. Berlin: Mouton de Gruyter.

Chomsky, N. 2008. On Phases. In Freidin, R., Otero, C. P. and Zubizarreta, M. L. (eds.), *Foundational Issues in Linguistic Theory: Essays in Honor of Jean-Roger Vergnaud*, 133–166. Cambridge, MA: MIT Press.

Chomsky, N. 2013. Problems of Projection. *Lingua* 130:33–49.

Collins, C. 2002. Eliminating Labels. In Epstein, S. D. and Seely, T. D. (eds.), *Derivation and Explanation in the Minimalist Program*, 42–64. Oxford: Blackwell.

Epstein, S. D. 1992. Derivational Constraints on A´-Chain Formation. *Linguistic Inquiry* 23:235–259.

Epstein, S. D. and Seely, T. D. 2002. Rule Applications as Cycles in a Level-Free Syntax. In Epstein, S. D. and Seely, T. D. (eds.), *Derivation and Explanation in the Minimalist Program*, 65–89. Oxford: Blackwell.

Frampton, J. and Gutmann, S. 2002. Crash-Proof Syntax. In Epstein, S. D. and Seely, T. D. (eds.), *Derivation and Explanation in the Minimalist Program*, 90–105. Oxford Blackwell.

Richards, M. 2007. On Feature Inheritance: An Argument from the Phase Impenetrability Condition. *Linguistic Inquiry* 38:563–572.

Rizzi, L. 1997. The Fine Structure of the Left Periphery. In Haegeman, L. (ed.), *Elements of Grammar*, 281–337. Dordrecht: Kluwer.

Rizzi, L. 2006. On the Form of Chains: Criterial Positions and ECP Effects. In Cheng, L. and Corver, N. (eds.), *Wh-Movement on the Move*, 97–134. Cambridge, MA: MIT Press.

Rizzi, L. 2011. On Some Properties of Criterial Freezing. In Panagiotidis, E. P. (ed.), *The Complementizer Phrase*, 17–32. Oxford: Oxford University Press.

Rizzi, L. 2014. Cartography, Criteria and Labeling. Unpublished manuscript, University of Geneva, Geneva, Switzerland.

1 Derivation(s)

Samuel D. Epstein, Hisatsugu Kitahara, and T. Daniel Seely

1 INTRODUCTION

1.1 Human Knowledge of Language

The human capacity to acquire knowledge of language and to use it in speaking, understanding and thinking distinguishes us from all other members of the animal kingdom. What is this uniquely human, virtually defining capacity? It is a biologically determined, genetically endowed cognitive capacity present in each individual, barring pathology. "Language study" in this biological sense was introduced by Chomsky in 1955 and has revolutionized the field of "language" study as a branch of human bio-cognitive psychology or "Biolinguistics."

Seemingly paradoxical is the fact that an individual's knowledge of language is infinite yet is acquired on the basis of only finite exposure to "the language" (see below) spoken in the community. That is, we are not like parrots or tape-recorders capable only of mimicking or recording and playing back the sound strings we have been exposed to; rather, we can create and understand novel stimuli like this sentence, which you have probably never encountered before, and which was perhaps never produced before in the history of humankind. Thus, knowledge of language is knowledge, by a non-infinite organism, of an infinite domain, acquired on exposure to finite environmentally provided inputs. In addition to being infinite, the knowledge (by virtue of being knowledge) is entirely different from the environmental input to the organism. Contra standard presentations, the input to the child is not "the language" or even "parts of the language"; it is not, for example, "sentences" or "noun phrases" or "morphemes" or "phonemes" or "meanings," but rather consists of acoustic disturbances (of a particular kind, to be determined and characterized by a theory of human language acoustic phonetics), literally nothing more than perturbations of molecules in space hitting the eardrum, in contexts. Or, for signed languages, the input is visually perceived hand shapes in motion (again of a particular kind, not those of someone washing their hands). Thus, the input itself, the acoustic disturbances or (moving) hand shapes the child is exposed to, must somehow be separated out by the child and analyzed as linguistic unlike other non-linguistic acoustic disturbances/visual stimuli. Entities defined by Linguistic Theory as in fact linguistic, thus sentences, noun phrases, morphemes, phonemes, meanings, are part of your unconscious knowledge of language and do not propagate through air when I speak to you, or when we speak to our young children; e.g. no meaning floats from my lips to your ears, or from a signer's hands to a child's eyes. Thus, we have at least two fundamental bio-psychological mysteries (if not paradoxes) traditionally overlooked but revealed by Chomsky's revolutionary insights and reorientation: (i) How can any organism have knowledge over an infinite domain? and (ii) How can a being have knowledge not present in the input (e.g. knowledge of meanings, words, prefixes, suffixes, syntactic constituents, phonemes, etc.)?

Chomsky not only reveals these questions (not part of the traditional study of languages, e.g. Latin) but answers them. As for the first question, a (finite) being or entity can indeed have knowledge over an infinite domain. There is no paradox here, but rather the empirical scientific motivation for the assumption that humans have finite yet *recursive symbolic rule* systems. For example, a phrase structure rule such as "X→X (optional)" is itself finite, but since it can re-apply to its own output, it has infinite generative capacity. To determine the nature of such rule systems has been and remains the goal of syntactic research throughout the modern era; rule systems provide the basis for the notion "derivation," which it is the goal of this chapter to explore. As for the second question, how can an organism develop knowledge which is not in the input? Chomsky "solves" this problem by identifying it as "nothing other than" the central problem presented by all cases of biological growth: How is it that e.g. a tadpole develops into a frog, yet I am not inputting frog(ness) into the tadpole? How can an acorn develop into an oak tree, even though I am not giving the acorn an oak tree but rather dirt, water, light, etc.?

Knowledge, like any other property of an organism, develops as a result of an organism's genetically determined properties interacting with environmental inputs of a particular kind. Crucially, what can be an input (perhaps more accurately, "intake") is in fact *determined* by the organism's genetic endowment (UV light is not input to my visual system, nor can I use bat-emitted return echoes to construct an exquisitely precise sonar-determined mental map of my surroundings). Thus, for Chomsky there is a "mental organ," a faculty of language in humans. It grows with variation—arguably slight variation, under formal analysis—determined by varied input. Like biological growth in other domains, the input (French "noises" vs. visual perception of hand shapes in motion) can in fact exert only very limited influence on the outcome. An adult frog's size might depend on food given to the tadpole, but a tadpole has the capacity to develop only into a frog; no variation of the input can induce the tadpole to become a horse. Similarly, humans develop only human language, so the differences (though seemingly vast) between them must be in fact minor, a criterion for a successful theory (the quest for unifying generalizations, as sought in any science).

Part of the human capacity for developing language knowledge is then the innate capacity to formulate recursive (linguistic) symbolic rules, operating on a predetermined inventory of linguistic entities (phonemes, meanings, etc.) which the child brings to the grammar-growth task and "superimposes on the input" patently lacking these properties. Thus, a syntactic analysis is imposed on the acoustic disturbances, as is a meaning, even though the input—an acoustic disturbance—contains neither.

1.2 What Exactly Is Knowledge of Language?
A Seemingly "Simple" Case

No data or evidence in e.g. physics is "simply explained." Rather, explanation invariably requires a sufficiently explicit and articulated theory. If we postulate rules and entities upon which the rules operate, we need to specify the form of the rules and the class of entities. How do we go about doing this? Let's begin with a seemingly simple case. We ask: What does someone know exactly when someone knows a particular language? We proceed to construct a theory—the course of all rational scientific inquiry. We then hope to understand our theories, which, as a defining characteristic, elude common-sense intuition. Someone who knows "English" (but not a monolingual Hindi knower) knows something about e.g. an acoustic disturbance of the form:

(1) CATS

But formal analysis leads us to apparent paradoxes. We can ask: What do you know about "it"? How many entities does the sound CATS consist of? Contradictory answers all seem true: "There is one thing, the word *cats.*" "No, what is (or was) here is, as you said, an acoustic disturbance." "Yes, but I know that it is a noun, not a preposition, and hence word-class analysis is imposed." "No, there are two things here: the word *cat* and the plural suffix *s.*" "No, there are four things, the word cat, its meaning, the plural suffix and its meaning." "Nope, there are five things; you forgot the combined meaning of *cat* and of *s.*" "No, there are four things here, not five (the sounds C, A, T and S in that order)." None of these percepts (determined by our knowledge) are in fact present in the continuous non-phonemic acoustic signal, yet all seem roughly true. If not present in the input, nor "taught," then it must be imposed by the organism. Thus, the child comes to the language learning task pre-equipped with an inventory of uniquely linguistic analytical entities: phonemes, words, meanings and recursive symbolic rules for combining them, and these constructs are analytically imposed on the raw data input and thereby determine the linguistic percept. To overcome the apparent contradictions regarding *cats*, we assume everyone is in fact right—there is no contradiction, but rather human knowledge of language; i.e. my linguistic module is itself modularized and imposes *multiple levels and kinds of analysis.*

Cat is indeed a single word: More specifically, I analyze an acoustic disturbance of this sort as a noun, and it is also known by me to be a subpart of the noun *cats* (thus words can contain words, again suggesting recursive properties). The morpheme -*s* is known by me to be capable of functioning as the plural suffix, attached only to (a subclass of) nouns. The meaning of the word *cats* is determined by the meaning of its subparts (i.e. the meaning of *cat* and the meaning of -*s*) and the mode of combination that created them. (Although "I saw a **cat** and some dogs" contains both *cat* and -*s*, there is no plural meaning *cats* imposed here, because cat and -*s* do not "go together here"—they were not assembled together— no rule applied concatenating *cat* and *s*.) *Cats* means "greater than one cat." (We leave aside your knowledge of the confounding generic interpretation, as in "Cats meow," which you know is not synonymous with "Greater than one cat meows.") *Cats* consists of four (abstract) sound units, in a specific order.

Returning now to the infinitude problem, if I tell you there is a thing called a "plog" and ask you for the plural, you do not say, "I don't know, I have never encountered *plog* before, so how can I know anything about its plural form?"[1] Rather, you say "plogs" (and, interestingly, you seem to know the plural form even though I didn't tell you what *plog* means). How can you possibly have such knowledge regarding properties (its plural form) of a previously unencountered stimulus?[2] The hypothesis is that you know abstract symbolic algebraic rules that can apply to new data.

(2) If x = count NOUN, then plural = count NOUN + S

Attributing the *rule* to you, however much the attribution of abstract mental rules might offend common-sense, as the postulation of gravitational forces offended Newton himself,[3] explains the experimental result indicating that you do know the plural of *plog*—and hence could readily pluralize any of the infinite number of nonsense syllables I could give you. These plural forms cannot possibly be a memorized infinite list, since lists are by definition finite, but rather are by hypothesis generated by finite rules, with an infinite domain of application (algebra).

In addition, you know the plural of *plog* is pronounced plogZ while the plural of *cat* is pronounced catS. We therefore confront another paradoxical question. Is the *s* at the end of *cats* the same as the *z* sound at the end of *plogs*? More paradoxes: Yes—they are each the plural suffix and are identical in this regard. No—one is an *s*-sound, the other *z*, and *s* ≠ *z*. The solution again leads us to levels, and rules mapping one to the other: "a derivation." You know the *s* in *cats* and *z* in *plogs* are the same—each is the plural suffix, and thus you have mental representations of the form:

(3) a. cats = CAT + PLURAL
     b. plogs = PLOG + PLURAL

Is the plural suffix pronounced *s* or *z*? Neither is correct for all cases, and as just noted we cannot store the plural form for each (one of an infinite number of) possible nouns, but a rule can capture this, explaining the ability to know the plural of an unencountered case. Suppose then that we say the stored finite form of the plural that you know is:

(4) PLURAL suffix = ½ s, ½ z

This suffix, of course, is abstract, i.e. is not pronounceable—i.e. if we are on track, human phonological knowledge is not entirely knowledge of "pronounceable things." Whether the plural suffix surfaces as *s* (cats) or *z* (dogz) is determined by rule, by the voicing feature of the noun-final consonant (so-called voicing assimilation). Everything you seem to know about an acoustic disturbance like *cats* can then be captured in a derivation mapping one representation to another representation by algebraic rule application. All terms appearing in this analysis (noun, voicing, consonant, etc.) refer not to properties of the acoustic disturbance but to an innate analytical apparatus imposed upon it (by humans). Nor are rules part of the input; hence, their specific form (English rules) and general format (for any human linguistic rules) are also by hypothesis innately determined. Assuming there are such rules, then a new question emerges. Do the rules apply in any particular order, or are they unordered? If ordered, then there exists a specifiable assembly procedure: "a derivation."

What could the different assembly procedures possibly be? Here are two, for example:

(A) (1st) Choose CAT from the lexicon, (2nd) interpret its meaning, (3rd) add the plural suffix s/z, (4th) interpret N + s/z (plural) meaning, (5th) apply voicing assimilation, e.g. s/z → s.

What is another possible ordering?

(B) (1st) Choose plural suffix s/z, (2nd) add CAT to it yielding CAT + s/z, (3rd) apply voicing assimilation, (4th) interpret the meaning of subpart CAT, (5th) interpret the meaning of subpart -s, (6th) interpret the meaning of CATS, given the meanings of each subpart.

As concerns (A), we might observe that there is no empirical motivation for its applying Meaning interpretation before voicing assimilation. Voicing assimilation does not need to know the meaning in order to apply correctly (as we saw above with *plogs*). Similarly, in (B), there is no reason to apply the opposite order, in which voicing assimilation applies before semantics. The semantics ("of plurality") seems to be insensitive to the *s/z* distinction. Assuming that both parsimony and empirical motivation matter to the central goal, in all science, of explanation, the sound and meaning systems are by hypothesis "divorced"—in the sense that there are separate phonological and semantic systems operating on disjoint sets of primitives. Another question: Is it odd in (B) to build CATS, and then go back and interpret just CAT, *as if* CATS had not yet been assembled—even though it had been? (B) exhibits two independent cycles: Build X and Y, then interpret X alone and interpret Y alone, then interpret {X + Y}. Is this oddity worth eliminating—by integrating or intertwining structure building and interpretation of structures thus far built?

Note, in addition, that some orderings are *logically* impossible, so should not be excluded by specifically Linguistic Laws/Universal Grammar (UG), but rather are rightly excluded by more general factors, in this case, *logic*, e.g. all the orderings that begin with (1st) apply voicing assimilation between the final consonant of the noun and the *s/z* suffix (an impossibility, before "previously" selecting a noun). It would be wrong to exclude such derivations by specifically linguistic principles. Rather, here, we would appeal to a more general non-linguistic principle: No rule R can operate on X and Y, unless X and Y are present to be operated on by R. Voicing assimilation cannot (possibly) apply until I have "in hand" at least two consonants that can undergo the rule. Similarly, any order in which CATS is interpreted before CATS is constructed/assembled is excluded.[4]

Thus, as concerns rules and their possible order of application we have illustrated a number of questions with our seemingly simple example:

(5) a. Does the order of rule application matter empirically; i.e. do certain orders make the right predictions while others don't?

b. Assuming (with for example Newton and Einstein and countless others) that simplicity matters in depth of explanation, is rule ordering itself "simpler" or more illuminating than unordered-rule approaches?

c. If it is, then among the logically possible orderings, which ones seem to provide the most insight or illumination (and suffice empirically)?

d. If ordering has empirical consequences, are some non-existent orderings in fact excluded by, hence explained by, logic or over-arching, domain-general bio-cognitive or physical principles not specific to the human language faculty (this latter class is what Chomsky 2005 would call "the 3rd factor")?

1.3 Syntactic Derivation

Specific to syntax, Chomsky distinguishes derivational (rule-ordering) procedures from representational (unordered) ones as follows:

By a "derivational" approach, I mean one that takes the recursive procedure literally, assuming that one (abstract) property of the language faculty is that it forms expressions step-by-step by applying its operations to the pool of features: . . . it assembles features into lexical items, then forms syntactic objects from these items by recursive operations to yield an LF representation λ, at some point applying SPELL-OUT and the operations of PHON to form the PF representation π. By a "representational" approach I mean one that takes the recursive procedure to be nothing more than a convention for enumerating a set of expressions, replaceable without loss, by an explicit *definition* [our emphasis] in a standard way.

(Chomsky 1998:126)

As concerns (5b), does ordering versus non-ordering have any effect on explanation? That of course depends on what constitutes an explanation, always an extremely vexing question. As discussed by Epstein (1999) and Epstein and Seely (2002a), definitions are not explanatory and invariably prompt the question: Why do we find *this* definition, and not some other definable notion? Syntactic filters, the central Government and Binding (GB) theoretical construct in the "virtually rule free" (but not rule free, argue Epstein and Seely 2002a) GB system, are axiomatic. Vergnaud's Case Filter (though undeniably a major breakthrough) is axiomatic. We invariably confront the question: Why this filter—and not some other equally definable one? One answer is to derive the filter's "truth" by formulating an underlying generative procedure that yields the macro-configurations satisfying or described by the filter. The question "Why this filter?" is then answered as follows: This descriptive generalization obtains precisely because the rules are formulated in such a way that we generate representations satisfying this generalization—this is generative explanation (see J. M. Epstein 1999 for its application to what he calls "Generative social science").

The macroscopic syntactic regularities, macro tree structures or set representations are explained by appeal to simple local rules the iterated application of which—the derivation—grows the macrostructure phrase structure tree, or assembles step-by-step the set (of sets). But, with such rule systems, and generative explanation, we conversely confront the question: Why do we find *these* rules and not other definable rules? If the rules are axiomatic, we have no answer. The minimalist program recognizes and engages this apparent explanatory barrier, namely that if we have a filter-based GB-type system, the filters are unexplained, but if we have instead a rule-based system, then we might explain the filters but the rules themselves are unexplained. If there are both rules (assembly) and representations (the objects assembled by the assembly routine)—as we think there must in fact be (i.e. no system can be "purely representational, nor purely derivational," and it's not clear anyone has ever proposed such a system[5])—then how can we maximize explanation?

Suppose we have maximally simple rules and maximally simple (so-called bare) output conditions. The Strong Minimalist Thesis (SMT) regarding the human language faculty can then be succinctly stated as "computationally efficient satisfaction of the bare output conditions" by such maximally simple rules. This arguably maximizes explanation. Why these rules? Because they are maximally simple, neither construction-specific nor language-specific nor incorporating non-explanatory technicalia (as Chomsky notes—see below—the stipulation-free formulations of External and Internal Merge, in essence, come for free). Why these bare output conditions? Because they are maximally simple (e.g. a semantic representation contains only semantic entities, which follows from an even deeper not specifically linguistic general law that e.g. a color representation contains only color, not shape). In addition, not only is the format of the rules themselves maximally simple, but *the rule applications* (i.e. the nature of derivation) is reduced to 3rd factor constraints (e.g. minimal search, no-tampering, binary merger) along with the overarching (inter-modular) hypothesis that rules apply *so as to* satisfy the bare output conditions. This, we believe, extends Chomsky's "language faculty as a mental organ" hypothesis to embrace also inter-organ function; i.e. the narrow syntax (NS) interacts with other systems (conceptual-intentional and sensorimotor) and operates to produce outputs that are interpretable inputs to these NS-external systems. This approach includes not only formal specifications of single organ properties (e.g. the anatomy of the NS) but also inter-organ function or physiology.[6]

2   DERIVATIONS AND THE SMT

Derivation plays a critical role in minimalist inquiry, as outlined above. But what is the nature of syntactic derivation, and specifically of operations? Just how is the form and application of derivational operations determined? And what criteria can be used in formulating the "right" type of derivation? For the minimalist program, the SMT plays a central role in formulating and evaluating derivation.

2.1   Basic Statement of the SMT: Syntax Looking Outward

The SMT, a defining tenet of the minimalist program, can be characterized as:

> . . . to what extent is the human faculty of language FL an optimal solution to minimal design specifications, conditions that must be satisfied for language to be usable at all? We may think of these specifications as "legibility conditions": for each language L (a state of FL), the expressions generated by L must be "legible" to systems that access these objects at the interface between FL and external systems—external to FL, internal to the person. *The strongest minimalist thesis SMT would hold that language is an optimal solution to such conditions* [our emphasis]. The SMT, or a weaker version, becomes an empirical thesis

insofar as we are able to determine interface conditions and to clarify notions of "good design."

(Chomsky 2001:1)

The human faculty of language (FL) does not operate in a vacuum. Rather, it produces (syntactic) objects that are delivered to the phonological and semantic components, PHON and SEM respectively, and ultimately to performance systems, sensorimotor (SM) and conceptual-intentional (CI). Crucially FL then *interacts* with these external systems. The minimalist program puts a premium on the relation between FL and the external systems, and what emerges is a central role for derivation. Think of FL as an input-output device, and then ask: What is the nature of the input? What is the nature of the output? What is the nature of the mechanisms of FL producing that output from the given input? Throughout, the minimalist approach asks one additional question: And why does FL take the form that it does?

2.2   The SMT and the Nature of the Derivation: The Input

The minimum design requirement is that FL produces objects that the external systems can in fact use—thus, parts of at least some of those objects must be legible to the interfaces. But the SMT requires much more than that *some* objects (or *some* parts of objects) are legible to external systems:

> Suppose that a super-engineer were given design specifications for language: "Here are the conditions that FL must satisfy; your task is to design a device that satisfies these conditions in some *optimal* manner (the solution might not be unique)." The question is, how close does language come to such optimal design?
>
> (Chomsky 2000:92)

The hypothesis is that FL *optimally* meets conditions imposed on it from outside. An infinite number of mechanisms could produce legible objects. The minimalist hypothesis, however, is that FL is "perfectly designed" to meet these conditions, and this obviously puts important design constraints on the form and function of the mechanisms of FL producing objects for the interfaces. And this, in turn, determines the nature of derivations.

The atomic units of FL are the arguably ineliminable and irreducible properties of sound and meaning, i.e. linguistic features. If the products of FL are to be usable to the external systems, these products must *at least* contain some interface-legible features; if there were no legible features at all, then they would be useless since they would be "unreadable" by the interfaces. Minimalism takes an even stronger view, however: *Each and every element of the products of FL must be legible to one or the other interface*; if *any* feature of the input to the interfaces is illegible to either SM or CI, then the input crashes. This follows from Full Interpretation (FI), a principle carried over from the GB predecessor of Minimalism, proposed in Chomsky (1986b). FI requires that every element of a semantic representation and every element of a phonological representation receive an appropriate interpretation; elements cannot simply be disregarded. FI is the "convergence condition" of more recent minimalist literature; Chomsky (1995), for example, states that a phonological representation must be constituted entirely of elements that are legitimate to SM; similarly for a semantic representation at CI.

The initial point of the optimization of derivation required by the SMT, then, is the postulation of a set of linguistic features each of which is "usable" by one or the other interface, and a set of features that operations can access to generate expressions. The computational procedure doesn't operate directly on these features, however, since the SMT demands "optimization" of the derivation. Interestingly, and perhaps counter-intuitively at first glance, relative to the linguistic features of sound and meaning, the reduction of formal complexity involves the establishment of a lexicon: A set of lexical items is created out of the full set of linguistic features. Moreover, the derivation proceeds by making a "one-time selection of a lexical array" from the lexicon, namely the lexical materials to be used in the derivation "at hand." The atomic units of FL are linguistic features; the atomic units of the NS are presumed to be lexical items. The SMT determines that the relation between the NS and linguistic features be mediated by the lexicon containing lexical items (i.e. assemblages of linguistic features) and that a derivation selects an "array" of lexical items, from which the derivation builds an expression whose destination is the interfaces, where it serves as "a set of instructions" to the language-external systems.

2.3   The SMT and the Nature of Derivation: The Output

What about the *output* of FL? The output is an infinite set of syntactic objects. The relation between a lexical array and the interfaces of sound and meaning is mediated by the NS. The SMT hypothesizes that this mediation is carried out in an *optimal* way. Thus, it is not the case that "anything goes" in building syntactic objects. Although there is an infinite set of alternative mechanisms one could posit to "cover the data," the minimalist approach, with the SMT at its heart, seeks a far more difficult goal (one of explanation, as in other sciences):

> Tenable or not, the SMT sets an appropriate standard for true explanation: anything that falls short is to that extent descriptive, introducing mechanisms that would not be found in a "more perfect" system satisfying only legibility conditions.
>
> (Chomsky 2001:2)

The questions remain: (i) What does "optimal" mean exactly? and (ii) How is derivation involved? A linguistic expression is not just the pairing of a phonological representation and a semantic representation, each formed by a convergent derivation, but rather the derivation of this pairing must be optimal (Chomsky 1995). Note first (and crucially for present purposes) that if the *derivation* of an expression must be optimal for the SMT to be met, then *there must be a derivation* (contra, for example, the letter or at least spirit of the "rule free" GB theory). Meeting the condition of "good design" determines, in large part, the nature of the mechanisms of the derivation.

Clearly, some mechanism is required to form lexical items into phrases, as in fact there is an infinite set of linguistic expressions (i.e. phrases):

> The simplest such system is based on an operation that takes *n* syntactic objects (SOs) already formed, and constructs from them a new SO. Call the operation *Merge*. Unbounded Merge or some equivalent (or more complex variant) is unavoidable in a system of hierarchic discrete infinity, so we can assume that it "comes free" in the present context.
>
> (Chomsky 2008:137)

The simplest form of Merge, consistent with the SMT, is as an operation that puts two, and no more nor less than two, elements into a relation; less than two will not create an expression at all (beyond a lexical item itself), and more than two is beyond what is minimally required to create an expression (larger than a single lexical item). In large part, then, the form and the function of this "free" operation, essential for a derivation, is determined by the SMT.

2.4 Minimal Derivations

So far, a derivation is a partially ordered set of applications of the simple, binary operation Merge. Another property of I-language at the center of linguistic research since the inception of generative grammar is displacement: a single category, in one position for meaning but pronounced in a different position. The operation of movement has long been the primary mechanism by which displacement phenomena have been captured, and the seeming paradox that it raises (a single element in two places at once) resolved.

The initial merger of two elements is generally considered unconstrained. But a particularly intriguing domain of derivation involves the merger of categories X and Y, where X is an element properly contained within Y, referred to as "Internal Merge" (IM). IM is involved in such classic instances of movement as passive (e.g. *John was arrested*) and *wh*-movement (e.g. *Who did Sue arrest?*). Research questions regarding IM include (i) What are the constraints on IM? (ii) What features factor into IM, and why? and (iii) What are the structural consequences of IM? This is a robust area of current research, and current literature provides various answers. One of the enduring hypotheses regarding IM is that it obeys the principles of "least effort," seeking to eliminate anything unnecessary: superfluous elements in representations, and to do so without any superfluous steps in derivations; in short, to simplify and reduce formal complexity as much as possible (see Chomsky 1991).

Derivation is a fundamental property of current Minimalism. At the most general level, Minimalism is nothing more than a willingness to seek scientific explanation, not just description. A research goal is to determine the exact nature of derivation, at a deep, explanatory level, and not to describe data using whatever stipulated technicalia seem to do the job, nor are convenient (non-explanatory) definitions over representations allowed even if they seem to do the trick. Rather, we try to explain the properties of FL, by deducing whatever defined stipulations promise empirical coverage.[7] For example, structure building is the core of a derivation. Merge is thus "required." The SMT determines that we posit as little beyond Merge as possible, while still maintaining "empirical coverage." Epstein et al. (1998) and Epstein (1999) for example, seek compliance with the SMT in trying to maximize the explanatory impact of Merge and its iterative application, by deducing from it the relation of c-command. C-command is not stipulatively defined over representation but instead falls out of the derivation, i.e. the independently necessary, and maximally simple, iterative application of the structure building operation, Merge. Research on the nature of derivation within the minimalist program then goes hand in hand with criteria for evaluation, and this in turn entails taking the SMT and various 3rd factor constraints (common to all sciences) very seriously, and it raises the bar for what counts as an explanatory analysis.

3   THE MECHANISMS OF MINIMALIST DERIVATION

3.1   Introduction

As discussed in the preceding sections, generative grammar has long recognized that the human FL is recursive, and the minimalist program has advanced a derivational approach under the SMT by taking the recursive part of FL to be "a step-by-step procedure for constructing Exp[ression]s, suggesting that this is how things work as a real property of the brain, not temporally but as part of its structural design" (Chomsky 2000:98). In this section, couched within the framework of Chomsky (2007, 2008), we ask: (i) What is the minimum machinery specific to this recursive system (the genetic endowment for FL, the topic of UG)? and (ii) How does such machinery generate a stepwise derivation, in accord with the principles of efficient computation (the subcategory of what Chomsky 2005 calls "the 3rd factor" that enters into the design of any biological system)? The answers we give constitute current (minimalist) hypotheses regarding the structure and operation of the human FL.

3.2   Minimum Machinery

The recursive system allows FL to yield a discrete infinity of structured expressions, and "the simplest such system is based on an operation that takes *n* syntactic objects (SOs) already formed, and constructs from them a new SO" (Chomsky 2008:137). This elementary operation is called Merge. SOs not constructed by Merge are lexical items (LIs) (= heads), provided by the lexicon. For an LI to be able to permit Merge, it must have some "mergeability" property. This property is called the edge feature (EF) of the LI. In the simplest case, this EF either always deletes when used or never deletes. The empirical facts suggest the latter case, which allows an LI to have both a complement (a result of first Merge) and a specifier (a result of second Merge). As the SO retains EF, Merge can iterate (in principle) without limit (= unbounded Merge). The minimum machinery, therefore, includes (at least) Merge and (mergeable) LIs each bearing an undeletable EF.

3.3   Computational Efficiency

Under the SMT, the minimum machinery equipped with Merge generates a derivation, in accord with the principles of efficient computation. Let us then ask what these principles are (or might be) and how they operate in this Merge-based system.

3.3.1   Merge and Its Applications

Recall the operation Merge. In the simplest case, Merge takes two SOs already formed and constructs from them a new SO. The limitation "*n* = 2" yields Kayne's (1981) unambiguous paths—the binary structures that Chomsky's (2000) minimal search and Kayne's (1995) Linear Correspondence Axiom–based linearization operate on.[8] Unless shown otherwise, we assume this limitation (= the simplest binary operation) to be on the right track. Another principle of efficient computation is the No-Tampering Condition (NTC): "Merge of X and Y leaves the two SOs unchanged" (Chomsky 2008:138). Intuitively, Merge of X and Y does not alter X or Y but places the two SOs in a set. That is, Merge of X and Y results in "syntactic extension" (forming a new SO = {X, Y}), not "syntactic infixation" (embedding X within Y, for example). Thus, Merge invariably applies to the edge,[9] and the effects of Chomsky's (1993) extension condition (largely) follow from NTC.[10] We also assume the inclusiveness condition: "No new objects are added in the course of computation apart from rearrangements of lexical properties" (Chomsky 1995:228). It is a natural principle of efficient computation, which eliminates bar levels, traces, indices, and any similar non-explanatory encoding technicalia introduced by NS. Under these three conditions, NS takes two SOs, X, Y (keeping to the simplest binary operation), and merges X and Y to form a new SO, leaving them unchanged (satisfying NTC) and adding no new features to them (satisfying the inclusiveness condition).

Suppose X is merged to Y (introducing the asymmetry only for expository purposes). Then, either X originates external to Y, call it "External Merge" (EM); or X originates internal to Y, call it IM. Under NTC, IM yields two copies of X: one external to Y and the other within Y (as in [X [Y . . . X . . .]]). There is no need to stipulate a rule of formation of copies (or remerge), and Chomsky's (1993) copy theory of movement follows from "just IM applying in the optimal way, satisfying NTC" (Chomsky 2007:10).

How does Merge get access to SOs? In the simplest case, only the label (i.e. head) of the full SO—either the "root" SO thus far constructed or the "atomic" SO (= LI) not yet merged—can be accessed to drive further operations. If X and Y are two separate full SOs, then their labels x and y can be accessed with minimal search. But if X is internal to Y (where Y is the "root" SO thus far constructed), then the accessed label y of Y carries out the task of finding X; specifically, y probes into the complement of y (= the smallest searchable domain of y) and finds X as a goal of the probe.[11] We assume this probe-goal analysis to be part of minimal search.

Minimal search reduces operative complexity by infinitely restricting the searchable domain of the probe to just its complement domain. But complements can (in principle) be unbounded due to recursion. A further restriction (see below) rendering the search domain not only finite but quite small is then implemented to limit the smallest searchable domain to a more localized sub-domain of the complement domain of the probe—this is the general property of strict cyclicity.

3.3.2   *Phase-Based Cyclicity*

In the advent of the minimalist program, postulation of linguistic levels beyond conceptual necessity was taken to be a departure from the SMT. There were two linguistic levels assumed to be indispensable: the levels accessed by the two distinct interface systems: SM and CI. In versions of the Extended Standard Theory (EST)/Y-model, however, five linguistic levels had been postulated along with five separate cycles (taking LF to be the output of narrow-syntactic operations and the input of the mapping to CI, as originally defined in EST). In the past two decades, the multiplicity of levels has been subject to a minimalist critique,[12] and our conception of the architecture of FL has undergone a series of changes with some remarkable results. Chomsky writes:

> Optimally, there should be only a single cycle of operations. EST postulated five separate cycles: X-bar theory projecting D-structure, overt operations yielding S-structure, covert operations yielding LF, and compositional mappings to the SM and CI interfaces. With the elimination of D- and S-structure, what remains are three cycles: the narrow-syntactic operation Merge (now with overt and covert operations intermingled),

and the mappings to the interfaces. As noted earlier, optimal computation requires some version of strict cyclicity. That will follow if at certain stages of generation by repeated Merge, the syntactic object constructed [or some subpart of it] is sent to the two interfaces by an operation Transfer, and what has been transferred is no longer accessible to later mappings to the interfaces (the phase-impenetrability condition PIC). Call such stages *phases*. Optimally, they should be the same for both subcases of Transfer, so until shown otherwise, we assume so (the mapping to the SM interface is sometimes called "Spell-Out"). LF is now eliminated, and there is only a single cycle of operations. The cyclic character of the mappings to the interfaces is largely captured, but not completely: there may be—and almost certainly are—phase-internal compositional operations within the mappings to the interfaces.

(Chomsky 2007:16)

There is only a single cycle of the operations in NS: one cycle per phase, where CP and v*P each count as a phase (the smallest possible working domain).[13] As NS completes each phase, Transfer reduces the phase-head complement (PHC) to PHC* by deleting all CI-offending features (such as unvalued features and phonological features) from PHC. Then, NS sends the PHC* (lacking CI-offending features) to the semantic component SEM. PHC itself (with those CI-offending features to be replaced by some phonetic features, each receiving in principle some interpretation at SM) is sent to the phonological component PHON.[14] The subsequent mappings to the CI and SM interfaces by SEM and PHON proceed in parallel, and the Phase Impenetrability Condition (PIC) makes the "transferred" PHC inaccessible to any syntactic operations in later phases. Intuitively, PIC explains "syntactic inertness" and locality as deeply as possible by simply saying that the "transferred" PHC is gone (from the working domain of NS). Thus, no minimal search can probe into the complement of any earlier phase-head, predicting that there is no inter-phasal agreement.[15] Although there are still phase-internal compositional operations within the mappings to the CI and SM interfaces by SEM and PHON, phase-based cyclicity has contributed significantly to the reduction of computational load by restricting the working cycle to the size of the phase (minus the PHC of any lower phase).[16]

3.3.3 Phase-Level Operations

Every time NS reaches a phase level—where the values of uninterpretable features (such as structural Case and redundant verbal agreement) can be determined by context—it executes a series of operations, and one such operation is called Agree. Chomsky (2007:18) argues that "the simplest assumption is that they [uninterpretable features] are unvalued in the lexicon, thus properly distinguished from interpretable features, and assigned their values in syntactic configurations, hence necessarily by probe-goal relations." Specifically, a phi-probing head H and a nominal goal N (the latter bearing inherently valued phi and unvalued Case) match in feature-type (namely phi), and they undergo Agree, which values phi on H and Case on N. To be visible for Agree, SOs must be active, bearing at least one unvalued feature (e.g. if structural Case of N has been valued, then N is "frozen in place," unable to implement an operation).[17] Chomsky (2008:150) then extends this activity condition to syntactic operations generally (in effect strengthening the principle of last resort).[18] Under this generalized activity condition, once N is assigned a Case-value, it becomes invisible for operations such as Agree and Merge; hence, it no longer participates in valuation or movement.[19]

Prior to Agree, such unvalued features are (by definition) offending features at the two interfaces; hence, they cannot be transferred before they are valued. Once valued, however, they may yield a phonetic interpretation (e.g. present singular "be" = IS, present plural "be" = ARE), but they will never yield a semantic interpretation (i.e. IS and ARE are otherwise synonymous). Thus, even if they are valued, they must be deleted when transferred to SEM. But such deletion cannot take place after they are valued, since, once valued, they are (by definition) indistinguishable from those interpretable features with which they agreed. Thus, Chomsky (2007:19) concludes that they must be valued at the phase level where they are transferred, and such derivationally valued features are deleted when transferred to SEM, but they remain intact when transferred to PHON.[20]

Still keeping to the phase level, T exhibits a phonetic reflex of redundant (syntactic) agreement (vacuously in some cases) if and only if T is selected by C. With this observation, Chomsky (2007:20) proposes T's inheritance of such agreement features (and possibly some other inflectional features) from C, and he assigns this feature-transmitting property to phase heads generally: C and v*.[21] Furthermore, Richards (2007) deduces that feature-transmission exists and precedes probe-goal agreement; otherwise, a directly agreeing phase head PH retaining its phi features (and occupying the phase-edge) would come to bear derivationally valued features that would (by hypothesis) induce crash at the next phase level (given that PIC makes inaccessible any historical record of their "once unvalued" status). If probe-goal agreement is accompanied by IM, then a goal of the probe moves to the specifier of the probing head with which it agreed.[22] A-movement is then derivationally defined as IM contingent on probe by uninterpretable inflectional features, and A′-movement as IM driven solely by the EF of PH.[23,24]

3.4   Sample Derivations

With this much as background, let us examine how exactly the Merge-based system generates a stepwise derivation for a transitive *wh*-interrogative like (6):

(6) Who saw John?

In the first phase cycle, repeated EM has constructed the v*P phase as follows:

(7) a. EM merges V(see) to NP(John), forming [$_{VP}$ see John].
  b. EM merges v* to [$_{VP}$ see John], forming [$_{v*P}$ v* [$_{VP}$ see John]].
  c. EM merges NP(who) to [$_{v*P}$ v* [$_{VP}$ see John]], forming [$_{v*P}$ who [$_{v*P}$ v* [$_{VP}$ see John]]].

In each application of EM, NS takes two full SOs (keeping to the simplest binary operation) and merges them to form a new SO, leaving them unchanged (satisfying NTC) and adding no new features to them (satisfying the inclusiveness condition). Also, NS operates in a "bottom-up" fashion by the accessibility condition and merges to the edge by NTC. At the v*P phase level (constructed by EM(7c)), only the label v* of v*P can be accessed by the accessibility condition, and the label v* drives the following phase-level operations (where indices are introduced only for expository purposes):

(8) a. Feature-transmission transmits unvalued phi from v* to V(see).
  b. Agree values unvalued phi on V(see) and unvalued Case on NP(John).
  c. IM raises NP(John) to Spec, vP, forming [$_{v*P}$ who [$_{v*}$ v* [$_{VP}$ John$_2$ [$_{v'}$ see John$_1$]]]].
  d. Transfer reduces VP to VP* by deleting all CI-offending features and sends VP* to SEM and VP to PHON.

Under current assumptions, feature-transmission(8a) exists and precedes Agree(8b) and IM(8c). By the generalized activity condition, Agree(8b) cannot precede IM(8c), but IM(8c) also cannot precede Agree(8b) because this ordering would place NP(John) with unvalued Case out of the searchable domain of the phi-probe V(see), inducing a failure of phi-matching (hence, neither phi-valuation on V(see) nor Case-valuation on NP(John) would take place).[25] Thus, Agree(8b) and IM(8c) apply simultaneously,[26,27] and Transfer(8d) completes the v*P phase cycle.[28]

In the second phase cycle, repeated EM has constructed the CP phase as follows (where "—" is the site of the transferred VP, no longer accessible to any syntactic operations, given PIC):

(9) a. EM merges T to [$_{v*P}$ who [$_{v*}$ v* —]], forming [$_{TP}$ T [$_{v*P}$ who [$_{v*}$ v* —]]].
  b. EM merges C to [$_{TP}$ T [$_{v*P}$ who [$_{v*}$ v* —]]], forming [$_{CP}$ C [$_{TP}$ T [$_{v*P}$ who [$_{v*}$ v* —]]]].

Again, in each application of EM, NS takes two full SOs (keeping to the simplest binary operation) and merges them to form a new SO, leaving them unchanged (satisfying NTC) and adding no new features to them (satisfying the inclusiveness condition). At the CP phase level (constructed by EM(9b)), only the label C of CP can be accessed by the accessibility condition, and the label C drives the following phase-level operations:

(10) a. Feature-transmission transmits unvalued phi from C to T.
      b. Agree values unvalued phi on T and unvalued Case on NP(who).
      c. IM raises NP(who) to Spec, TP, forming $[_{CP}$ C $[_{TP}$ who_2 $[_{T'}$ T $[_{v*P}$ who_1 $[_{v*}$ v^* —]]]]].
      d. IM raises NP(who) to Spec, CP, forming $[_{CP}$ who_3 $[_{C'}$ C $[_{TP}$ who_2 $[_{T'}$ T $[_{v*P}$ who_1 $[_{v*}$ v^* —]]]]]].
      e. Transfer reduces CP to CP* by deleting all CI-offending features and sends CP* to SEM and CP to PHON.

Agree(10b) and IM(10c), just like Agree(8b) and IM(8c), carry out valuation and A-movement. At this CP phase level, however, there is an additional application of IM: IM(10d) raises the goal (= NP(who)) to the specifier of the EF-probing head (= C). IM(10d) is A'-movement, driven solely by the EF of C. Notice that Agree(10b) cannot precede or follow IM(10c), for the reason already discussed, and the same reasoning applies to the ordering between Agree(10b) and IM(10d). Thus, IM(10d) applies in parallel with Agree(10b) and IM(10c). As is generally assumed under the derivational approach, NS establishes syntactic relations in the course of a derivation, and (contra GB theory's unifying representationally defined concept "government") no syntactic relation can be arbitrarily defined on output structures.[29] It follows, then, that there is a direct relation between who_2 and who_1 (established by IM(10c)), and between who_3 and who_1 (established by IM(10d)), but there is no relation between who_3 and who_2 since no application of IM is involved in these two positions (i.e. there is no feeding relation between IM(10c) and IM(10d)).[30]

Finally, Transfer(10e) applies to the entire phase CP. Although how Transfer applies at the very final phase (= the root) remains to be spelled out, it is natural to assume, under the SMT, that Transfer sends the largest transferable domain to SEM and PHON, and the largest transferable domain may be the PHC when there is a continuation of the derivation but the phase itself when there is no continuation of the derivation. With this assumption, Transfer(10e) completes the CP phase cycle, and the derivation of (6) converges.[31]

3.5   Summary

Under the SMT, we expect the recursive part of FL to be a system that not only satisfies minimal requirements imposed by the interface systems but does so in accord with principles of efficient computation. Computational efficiency assumes computation, and we have seen how the computation equipped with Merge, as advanced by Chomsky (2007, 2008), goes some great distance in meeting this expectation, both identifying and satisfying the hypothesized (and arguably explanatory) 3rd factor principles (such as binary merger, no-tampering, inclusiveness, minimal search and phase-based cyclicity).

NOTES

We thank David Medeiros and Robin Queen for very helpful comments on an earlier version. We are indebted to Noam Chomsky and to Rick Lewis for discussions and comments that have significantly improved this chapter.

1. See Halle (1981) and Berko (1958).
2. This is Plato's problem; see Chomsky (1986b).
3. See e.g. Chomsky (2005) and Epstein (2000:3–5) for a brief explanation of Chomsky's mentalism and his rejection of "the mind-body problem."
4. More on this below: namely the search for overarching non-linguistic constraints that apply to human syntactic systems, not due to UG but to more general laws. See Chomsky (1965:59), cited by Chomsky (2007, 2008), and see also Chomsky (2005).
5. See Epstein and Seely (2002a) on derivations within the allegedly "rule free" GB theory.
6. As is standard in the biological sciences, physiological function to some extent explains anatomical properties of the individual interacting organs (e.g. the pump-like properties of the heart are to some extent explained by considering the larger circulatory system within which this single organ performs a function). See Hempel (1965) regarding the form of such explanation and Epstein (2007b) regarding its use within the SMT.
7. See Epstein and Seely (2002a) and the citations.
8. See also Barss and Lasnik (1986), Hale and Keyser (1993) and Larson (1988, 1990).
9. For discussion of other interpretations of "merge to the edge" (including local merge), see Chomsky (2000) and Richards (1997).
10. See Lasnik (2006) on the history of formulations of the cycle condition.
11. See Epstein et al. (1998) for an explanation of the choice of the complement (over e.g. Spec) as the sole search domain of the head.
12. See, among others, Epstein et al. (1998), Epstein and Seely (2002a, 2002b, 2006).
13. It is an active area of research to determine what are (and are not) phases and (of course) to explain why (see Epstein (2007a) for recent discussion). Whether DP should count as a phase is an open question.
14. For discussion of the operation Transfer and its application, see Chomsky (2004). See also Chomsky (1998) for discussion of assignment of phonetic features to a bundle of formal features (including CI-offending features).
15. It has been pointed out, however, that there seem to be cases of probe into a phase that has already been passed, as in Icelandic quirky case, with T agreeing in number with the embedded nominative nominal (e.g. me(dat) thought(pl) [t_{me} [they(pl, nom) be industrious]]). These properties remain to be explained. For relevant discussion, see Chomsky (2001) and Sigurðsson (1996).
16. For discussion of the notion phase and its comparison with the notion barrier (Chomsky 1986a), see Boeckx and Grohmann (2007).
17. The activity condition restricts the class of SOs eligible for Agree, thereby contributing to efficient computation in some natural sense, but it has been argued that it can be eliminated. See Nevins (2005) for critical discussion.

18. Chomsky (2008:150) notes, "[The] EF of C cannot extract the PP complement from within SPEC-T: if it could, the subject-condition effects [exhibited by (i) and (ii)] would be obviated."

   (i) a. it was the CAR (not the TRUCK) of which [they found the (driver, picture)]
        b. of which car did [they find the (driver, picture)]?
   (ii) a. *it was the CAR (not the TRUCK) of which [the (driver, picture) caused a scandal]
        b. *of which car did [the (driver, picture) cause a scandal]?

   He continues, "It must be, then, that the SPEC-T position is impenetrable to EF, and a far more natural principle would be that it is simply invisible to EF." The activity condition is then generalized to capture the observed subject-condition effects. For a different attempt to provide a derivational account of this invisibility, see Epstein, Kitahara and Seely (2008).

19. If the generalized activity condition does not apply to matching, such a nominal (with valued Case) may still match in phi, blocking any further searching by a phi-probe (i.e. once the probe matches in phi, it cannot search any deeper). This analysis receives support from Icelandic expletive constructions, in which dative NP blocks further search by phi-probe of matrix T (e.g. *expletive seem(pl) [some man(dat) [the-horses(pl, nom) be slow]]). For relevant discussion, see Chomsky (2008) and Holmberg and Hróarsdóttir (2003).

20. Epstein and Seely (2002b) suggest that Chomsky's analysis, under which Transfer neither before nor after valuation converges, leads to the hypothesis that Transfer operates derivationally, more specifically, inside the application of a single rule application, with Transfer thereby "seeing" the value change from minus (in the structural description) to plus (in the structural change). Another solution to this problem is to assume that all phase-internal operations apply simultaneously; hence, it is *as if* there is just one rule application within a phase, and Transfer can see any unvalued feature change to valued (its vision spanning the single rule application) and thereby knows to spell out the *just* valued feature.

21. In effect, feature-transmission renders an embedded head H accessible to NS by transmitting a feature from the accessed label of the phase head to H.

22. What forces IM to raise the goal to the specifier of the phi-probing head—the residue of Extended Projection Principle (EPP)—is still an open question.

23. For some potentially interesting consequences of these featural-derivational characterizations of movement types, as compared to previous representational definitions, see Obata and Epstein (2008).

24. The operation Agree would be dispensable if there were no unvalued features. But the empirical fact suggests that they do exist. Under the SMT, then, we seek some functional justification for the presence of such features (i.e. they are an inevitable part of efficient computation). For discussion of this issue, see Chomsky (2007).

25. See Chomsky (2000) for discussion of the "invisible" status of A-movement traces to the probe-goal relation.

26. Chomsky (2008) argues that movement to Spec-VP (e.g. IM (8c)) is obligatory, as in Exceptional Case Marking (ECM) constructions (e.g. "they believe him to be intelligent"). See also Lasnik and Saito (1991) and Koizumi (1995).

27. In addition to (8c), V(see) must adjoin to v* to restore the original VO order, thus head-movement must take place at the v*P phase level, but the nature

of head-movement and its exact mechanism (especially its relation to NTC) remain to be spelled out.

28. See Epstein and Seely (2002b) for discussion of problems regarding simultaneous rule application within a purportedly derivational theory. See also Grewendorf and Kremers (2009). Chomsky's (2007, 2008) analysis thus strikes a delicate balance between the derivational and representational approaches.

29. See, for example, Epstein et al. (1998), Epstein (1999), and Epstein and Seely (2002a, 2002b, 2006). For recent discussion on this issue, see also Epstein, Kitahara and Seely (2008).

30. The relation between who_2 and who_1 corresponds to an A-chain (who_2, who_1), and the relation between who_3 and who_1 corresponds to an operator-variable chain (who_3, who_1), though the notion chain need not be introduced, apart from expository reasons (cf. Chomsky 2007, 2008 and Epstein and Seely 2006 and the references cited therein).

31. If the derivation of simple sentences appears to be complex, that should not be taken as an argument against the SMT. A principled system—being explicit/falsifiable—may well yield intricate-looking derivations; i.e. simple (explanatory) laws can give rise to complex phenomena (= science).

REFERENCES

Barss, A. and Lasnik, H. 1986. A Note on Anaphora and Double Objects. *Linguistic Inquiry* 17:347–354.

Berko, J. 1958. The Child's Learning of English Morphology. *Word* 14:150–177.

Boeckx, C. and Grohmann, K. 2007. Putting Phases in Perspective. *Syntax* 10:204–222.

Chomsky, N. 1955. The Logical Structure of Linguistic Theory. Manuscript, Harvard University, Cambridge, MA. [Revised 1956 version published in part by New York: Plenum, 1975; Chicago: University of Chicago Press, 1985.]

Chomsky, N. 1965. *Aspects of the Theory of Syntax*. Cambridge, MA: MIT Press.

Chomsky, N. 1986a. *Barriers*. Cambridge, MA: MIT Press.

Chomsky, N. 1986b. *Knowledge of Language: Its Nature, Origin, and Use*. New York: Praeger.

Chomsky, N. 1991. Some Notes on Economy of Derivation and Representation. In Freidin, R. (ed.), *Principles and Parameters in Comparative Grammar*, 417–454. Cambridge, MA: MIT Press. [Reprinted in *The Minimalist Program*, 129–166. Cambridge, MA: MIT Press, 1995.]

Chomsky, N. 1993. A Minimalist Program for Linguistic Theory. In Hale, K. and Keyser, S. J. (eds.), *The View from Building 20: Essays in Linguistics in Honor of Sylvain Bromberger*, 1–52. Cambridge, MA: MIT Press. [Reprinted in *The Minimalist Program*, 167–217. Cambridge, MA: MIT Press, 1995.]

Chomsky, N. 1995. *The Minimalist Program*. Cambridge, MA: MIT Press.

Chomsky, N. 1998. Some Observations on Economy in Generative Grammar. In Barbosa, P., Fox, D., Hagstrom, P., McGinnis, M. and Pesetsky, D. (eds.), *Is the Best Good Enough?*, 115–127. Cambridge, MA: MIT Press.

Chomsky, N. 2000. Minimalist Inquiries: The Framework. In Martin, R., Michaels, D. and Uriagereka, J. (eds.), *Step by Step: Essays on Minimalist Syntax in Honor of Howard Lasnik*, 89–155. Cambridge, MA: MIT Press.

Chomsky, N. 2001. Derivation by Phase. In Kenstowicz, M. (ed.), *Ken Hale: A Life in Language*, 1–52. Cambridge, MA: MIT Press.

Chomsky, N. 2004. Beyond Explanatory Adequacy. In Belletti, A. (ed.), *Structures and Beyond*, 104–131. Oxford: Oxford University Press.

Chomsky, N. 2005. Three Factors in Language Design. *Linguistic Inquiry* 36:1–22.

Chomsky, N. 2007. Approaching UG from Below. In Sauerland, U. and Gärtner, H.-M. (eds.), *Interfaces + Recursion = Language?*, 1–29. Berlin: Mouton de Gruyter.

Chomsky, N. 2008. On Phases. In Freidin, R., Otero, C. P. and Zubizarreta, M. L. (eds.), *Foundational Issues in Linguistic Theory: Essays in Honor of Jean-Roger Vergnaud*, 133–166. Cambridge, MA: MIT Press.

Epstein, J. M. 1999. Agent-Based Computational Models and Generative Social Science. *Complexity* 4:41–60.

Epstein, S. D. 1999. Un-principled Syntax: The Derivation of Syntactic Relations. In Epstein, S. D. and Hornstein, N. (eds.), *Working Minimalism*, 317–345. Cambridge, MA: MIT Press. [Reprinted in *Essays in Syntactic Theory*, 183–210. New York: Routledge, 2000.]

Epstein, S. D. 2000. *Essays in Syntactic Theory*. New York: Routledge.

Epstein, S. D. 2007a. On I(nternalist)-Functional Explanation in Minimalism. *Linguistic Analysis* 33:20–53.

Epstein, S. D. 2007b. Physiological Linguistics, and Some Implications Regarding Disciplinary Autonomy and Unification. *Mind and Language* 22:44–67.

Epstein, S. D., Groat, E., Kawashima, R. and Kitahara, H. 1998. *A Derivational Approach to Syntactic Relations*. Oxford: Oxford University Press.

Epstein, S. D., Kitahara, H. and Seely, T. D. 2008. The "Value" of Phonological Underspecification in the Narrow Syntax. Manuscript, University of Michigan, Ann Arbor; Keio University, Tokyo; and Eastern Michigan University, Ypsilanti. [Presented at Carson-Newman College (Exploring Crash-Proof Grammars, February 29, 2008) and at Michigan State University (Linguistics Department Colloquium Series, February 7, 2008).]

Epstein, S. D. and Seely, T. D. 2002a. Introduction: On the Quest for Explanation. In Epstein, S. D. and Seely, T. D. (eds.), *Derivation and Explanation in the Minimalist Program*, 1–18. Oxford: Blackwell.

Epstein, S. D. and Seely, T. D. 2002b. Rule Applications as Cycles in a Level-Free Syntax. In Epstein, S. D. and Seely, T. D. (eds.), *Derivation and Explanation in the Minimalist Program*, 65–89. Oxford: Blackwell.

Epstein, S. D. and Seely, T. D. 2006. *Derivations in Minimalism*. Cambridge: Cambridge University Press.

Grewendorf, G. and Kremers, J. 2009. Phases and Cycles: Some Problems with Phase Theory. *The Linguistic Review* 26:385–430.

Hale, K. and Keyser, S. J. 1993. On Argument Structure and the Lexical Expression of Syntactic Relations. In Hale, K. and Keyser, S. J. (eds.), *The View from Building 20: Essays in Linguistics in Honor of Sylvain Bromberger*, 53–109. Cambridge, MA: MIT Press.

Halle, M. 1981. Knowledge Unlearned and Untaught: What Speakers Know about the Sounds of Their Language. In Halle, M., Bresnan, J. and Miller, G. A. (eds.), *Linguistic Theory and Psychological Reality*, 294–303. Cambridge, MA: MIT Press.

Hempel, C. 1965. The Logic of Functional Analysis. In *Aspects of Scientific Explanation and Other Essays*, 297–331. New York: Free Press.

Holmberg, A. and Hróarsdóttir, T. 2003. Agreement and Movement in Icelandic Raising Constructions. *Lingua* 113:997–1019.

Kayne, R. 1981. Unambiguous Paths. In May, R. and Koster, J. (eds.), *Levels of Syntactic Representation*, 143–185. New York: Mouton de Gruyter.

Kayne, R. 1995. *The Antisymmetry of Syntax*. Cambridge, MA: MIT Press.

Koizumi, M. 1995. Phrase Structure in Minimalist Syntax. Doctoral dissertation, MIT, Cambridge, MA.

Larson, R. 1988. On the Double Object Construction. *Linguistic Inquiry* 19:335–391.

Larson, R. 1990. Double Objects Revisited: Reply to Jackendoff. *Linguistic Inquiry* 21:589–632.

Lasnik, H. 2006. Conceptions of the Cycle. In Cheng, L. and Corver, N. (eds.), *Wh-Movement: Moving On*, 197–216. Cambridge, MA: MIT Press.

Lasnik, H. and Saito, M. 1991. On the Subject of Infinitives. In Dobrin, L., Nichols, L. and Rodriguez R. (eds.), *Proceedings of the Chicago Linguistics Society 27*, Vol. 1, 324–343. Chicago Linguistic Society, University of Chicago, Chicago, IL.

Nevins, A. 2005. Derivations without the Activity Condition. In McGinnis, M. and Richards, N. (eds.), *Perspectives on Phases (MIT Working Papers in Linguistics 49)*, 283–306. Cambridge, MA: MIT Press.

Obata, M. and Epstein, S. D. 2008. Deducing Improper Movement from Phase Based C-to-T Phi Transfer: Feature-Splitting Internal Merge. Manuscript, University of Michigan, Ann Arbor. [Presented at Carson-Newman College (Exploring Crash-Proof Grammars, February 29–March 1, 2008), at Newcastle University (the 31st GLOW, March 26–28, 2008), and at University of California, Los Angeles (the 27th WCCFL, May 16–18, 2008).]

Richards, M. 2007. On Feature Inheritance: An Argument from the Phase Impenetrability Condition. *Linguistic Inquiry* 38:563–572.

Richards, N. 1997. What Moves Where When in Which Language. Doctoral dissertation, MIT, Cambridge, MA.

Sigurðsson, H. A. 1996. Icelandic Finite Verb Agreement. *Working Papers in Scandinavian Syntax* 49:1–26.

2 Economy of Derivation and Representation

Samuel D. Epstein, Hisatsugu Kitahara,
Miki Obata, and T. Daniel Seely

1 BACKGROUND: GOVERNMENT AND BINDING THEORY, PRINCIPLES AND PARAMETERS

1.1 The Motivation for and the Beauty of Government and Binding Theory

Chomsky's Government and Binding (GB) theory (Chomsky 1980, 1981, 1982) is often and aptly characterized as a radical departure from pre-existing theories of the human capacity for acquiring knowledge of syntax.[1] Virtually all traditional approaches assume that languages are rule governed. The formal diversity of the rules postulated in order to capture the diverse set of cross-linguistic and cross-construction syntactic phenomena represented a serious impediment to the central goal of linguistic theory (as the Introduction of Chomsky 1955/1961 and subsequent work by Chomsky characterizes it), namely to explain the human capacity to acquire any possible human (I-)language on the basis of linguistic input consisting of continuous acoustic disturbances or (for signed languages) retinal images of hand shapes, locations, and orientations changing over time. That is, the quest for descriptive adequacy (in the sense of Chomsky 1964) precluded the construction of an explanatorily adequate theory.

This central problem was identified and addressed by the search for a more restricted unified, universal theory of the "possible human syntactic rule system." This was attained by determining and formulating general constraints on all rules (e.g. Ross 1967; Chomsky 1965, 1973). Another, slightly different approach was to impose constraints not on the formulations of rules themselves, or on their collective mode of application (e.g. rule ordering), but rather to formulate constraints on representations appearing at certain levels of representation.

This search for a more constrained explanatorily adequate and unified theory of syntax ultimately developed into what was the "radical departure" advanced by GB theory. The theory pursued the hypothesis that human knowledge of language (more specifically, syntax) consisted not of a system of rules but of constraints on output at one or another of the levels of representation postulated in GB (D-structure, DS; S-structure, SS; Phonetic Form, PF; Logical Form, LF). With such constraints on representation incorporated into the theory, the logic was that the diverse, unconstrained, language-specific, and construction-specific transformational rules could be significantly simplified. The transformational component of Universal Grammar (UG) was hypothesized to consist of Move α (Chomsky 1981, 1982) or Affect α (Lasnik and Saito 1992), and the set of phrase structure (PS) rules was simplified by the postulation of X-bar Theory (Jackendoff 1977), which in effect expressed a constrained theory of "possible PS rule" with X'-theory assumed to be expressed as a constraint on phrase structure representations, in part facilitating the wholesale elimination of PS rules. This shift from rules to principles (constraints on representation) was intended to overcome all the explanatory difficulty associated with the postulation of formally diverse, language-specific, and construction-specific rules. In addition, stipulated rule orderings were to be reducible to the more general, architectural, ordered set of levels of representation postulated in GB theory (the so-called T- or Y-model).

In postulating neither language-specific nor construction-specific rules, the theory no longer directly accounted for "sentence relatedness" (e.g. the relation between active and passive sentence) by a rule mapping the representation of one kind (actives) to the representation of the other kind (passives). Rather, the theory was attractively rendered far more distant from the data, with deeper deductive structure, more complex forms of argument, and more abstraction. That is, the GB theory was modularized, consisting of separate components and principles each dedicated to monitoring certain formal sub-properties of syntactic representations. Each of these modules contained an overarching constraint on a level of representation that ensured the well-formedness of certain sub-properties of each syntactic representation, despite the fact that the simplified rules massively overgenerate since they themselves incorporate no constraints and hence bear no empirical burden. Thus, "sentences" are analyzed as decomposable complex macrostructures, knowledge of which is the epiphenomenal manifestation of the satisfaction of the various dedicated principles. A sentence is what you get if and only if the unconstrained rules apply in such a way as to produce a representational output or outputs that satisfy each of the dedicated representational constraints of the theory as differentially applied to the various levels of representation (e.g. the Theta Criterion applying at DS, the Case Filter applying at SS).

This system of level-ordered filters and constraints also explained at a certain level why there existed transformational movement rules at all: They were necessitated because the demands of DS and the demands of SS were not simultaneously satisfiable, given the unification of theta and Case assignment under the single (binary local) relation government. That is, in order to satisfy theta theory at DS in [_____ *was believed John to steal*], *John* must, under government theory, be in the semantic position of subject of *steal*. But in order to satisfy Case Theory, with Case also assigned under government, *John* had to occupy the subject position of _____ *was believed*. Thus, the demands of theta and Case, both unified under government, required *John* to be in two different positions, thereby explaining the very existence of movement transformations such as these.

As Chomsky (1981:13) puts it, "[t]he objective of reducing the class of grammars compatible with primary linguistic data has served as a guiding principle in the study of generative grammar since virtually the outset, as it should, given the nature of the fundamental empirical problem to be faced—namely, accounting for the attainment of knowledge of grammar—and the closely related goal of enhancing explanatory power." Yet

> [e]arly work in transformational grammar permitted a very wide choice of base grammars and of transformations. Subsequent work attempted to reduce the class of permissible grammars by formulating general conditions on rule type, rule application, or output that would guarantee that much simpler rule systems, lacking detailed specification to indicate how and when rules apply, would nevertheless generate required structures properly. For example X-bar theory radically reduces the class of possible base components, various conditions on rules permit a reduction in the category of permitted movement rules and conditions on S-structure and LF allow still further simplification of rules and their organization.

However, as Chomsky warns from the very outset, "reduction in the variety of systems in one part of the grammar is no contribution to these ends if it is matched or exceeded by proliferation elsewhere."

1.2   Beauty and the Beast

Despite the logic and historical continuity underlying the birth of GB theory and despite its explanatory and empirical cross-linguistic successes, there were perceived to be problems, of perhaps a new kind, confronting the explanatory depth of this theory. Grappling with the specific problems perceived to be inherent in GB coupled with a continued commitment to explanation is what led to the transition to the Minimalist Program (see Chapter 4, and also the introduction to Epstein and Seely 2002 for discussion of the rationale for and—we believe—misplaced opposition to this program), aspects of which are discussed in the following subsections. For reasons of space, we will simply list some illustrative central problems confronted by GB theory, as were recognized by numerous researchers.

1.2.1   *The Theory of Syntactic Relations*

The single syntactic relation in GB theory, government, although unifying the modules and principles of UG, suffered from a number of potential problems. As Epstein (1999) observes, unification is in fact not attained, since the "is a" (immediate domination) relation is not subsumed under government. This problem relates to the levels postulated in GB. First, D-structures exhibiting the "is a" relation are built (all at once). Only then are government relations defined on these entirely built-up structures. This raises another problem. Since government is defined, it is unexplained—i.e. why is *this* definition on representations relevant and not other equally definable representational relations? Moreover, government is not primitive but (by the time of Chomsky 1986a) is a highly complex definition incorporating a number of (similarly unexplained) sub-definitions of more primitive concepts and relations, including m-command, maximal projection, "excludes," "(immediately) dominates," barrier, blocking category, L-marking, theta-marking, and sisterhood (see Epstein 1999:322 for discussion).

In addition, though theories of binding (Chomsky 1981) and the Empty Category Principle (ECP) (Lasnik and Saito 1984, 1992; Chomsky 1986b) were sought that appealed only to this single notion of government, it was arguably the case that the relations required by the principles of these modules had to be more permissive, allowing binary relations (e.g. binding relations and ECP-enforced antecedent–trace relations) to span larger domains that appeared irreducible to the very local relation of government. In addition, it was recognized that government in its initial form was a head to non-head relation, while the relations imposed by the theories of binding and ECP were seemingly relations between two maximal projections.

1.2.2   The Principles

Although Vergnaud's Case Filter and early formulations of the ECP represent pioneering improvements over the similarly pioneering generalized filters of Chomsky and Lasnik (1977) (e.g. the *that*-trace filter or the *for-to* filter), these filters, like the government relation, were nonetheless defined, hence not explained. As with the axioms of any theory, we must ask, "Why?": First, why is there a Case Filter at all? Second, why is the Case Filter an SS condition and not a DS, LF, or PF condition—or even an everywhere principle (as was the Theta Criterion, given the Projection Principle)? Why does it apply to NPs and not some other specific category? And why should (or how can) phonetic content be relevant to a non-PF, i.e. an SS (syntax-internal) condition? Finally, why should it apply to the non-natural class +phonetic NP and *wh*-trace (Freidin and Lasnik 1981)? This situation reflects precisely the concern to which Chomsky (1981:13) alluded, as noted at the end of Section 14.1.1 above: Simplification of one component (the rule system) is to some degree subverted by proliferation elsewhere, in the stipulative and diverse formalism incorporated into the output filters.

1.2.3   Technicalia

Since Fiengo (1977) and Chomsky (1973, 1975), there was another proliferation concern. The rules were simplified, but in order to feed the correct application of SS representational principles, traces, indexing on traces, and chains were proposed as representational constructs (see e.g. Sportiche 1983; Rizzi 1986). The concern then was that—to use Chomsky's (1995:224) term anachronistically—these kinds of postulates might constitute "coding tricks," non-explanatory technicalia that bear significant degrees of the empirical burden, thereby covering the data formally without providing the desired kind of explanatory insight regarding the phenomena under analysis.

1.2.4   Levels of Representation

As early as Chomsky (1986b) it was recognized that SS was a "suspect" level of representation since it was entirely internal to the syntax and, unlike DS, LF, and PF, had no interaction with interface systems. Moreover, as Chomsky (1986b) noted, since it is the central level in the T/Y-model, i.e. the only level that is the output of the DS-to-SS mapping, yet also the input to both the PF and LF components, it ought to be deducible from the demands imposed by the other three components it mediates between. This raised the question of whether the stipulated level-ordered architecture with its four levels of representation, to which the principles were assumed to apply, might all be eliminable and an entirely level-free theory of UG developed (see Epstein et al. 1998; Epstein 1999; Uriagereka 1999). (See Lasnik 2002 and the references cited there for discussion of these works in historical context, both their relation to earlier cyclic proposals in Standard Theory, notably Jackendoff 1972 on semantic cyclicity and Bresnan 1971 on phonological cyclicity, as well as the subsequent development of "minimized," hence level-free, current phase-based models.)

1.2.5   Language Variation and Parameters

It was not clear why GB researchers found the parameters they did, or why these parameters exhibited what might be a version of the formal diversity previously exhibited by specific rules. This diversity was not an impediment to learnability as long as the values of each parameter were determinable by (linguistic) experience (the nature of which is determined by UG). However, simplicity, elegance, and similar considerations led to the question of why we find parameterization of e.g. head-first versus head-last, +/−null subjects, and parameterization of bounding nodes for Subjacency. Why should *these* be the loci of parameterization?

Of course, if levels of representation are eliminated, there will then be no place at all for the (stipulated) filters on, or principles constraining, levels of representation to apply. Furthermore, parameters *in* the formulation of these constraints on levels of representation would be similarly undermined. If the principles and their parameterized instantiations in core grammars cannot be applied at levels of representation, we could incorporate the constraints back into the rules they had previously been factored out of, but this would only lead us back to the very questions that we began with and that rightly motivated GB, such as "Why do we find *these* specific rules and not others?" If Epstein (2003/2007) is on track, the Minimalist Program breaks this vicious circle by postulating that both the purely principle-based approach and the purely rule-based approach were, by virtue of their purported purity, on the wrong track. Rather, the minimalist hypothesis is that both approaches were in part on the right track in that there exist both rules and constraints on representation. The constraints on representation, however, are constraints on the independently motivated interface representations, the (arguably) ineliminable representations of sound (PF) and meaning (LF). Ideally, the constraints are entirely natural, not stipulative technicalia, but reducible to some form of Chomsky's (1986b) Full Interpretation, which requires that every element in an LF representation must be semantically interpretable and every element in a PF representation must be phonologically interpretable. For example, Case features, lacking semantic content, must be eliminated from the representation sent to LF but retained in the representation sent to (or spelled out at) PF. The rules are not devoid of empirical content (as was Move α or Affect α) but have a definite form, yet one which is reduced to a bare minimum. For example, Merge A and B forms C = {A, B}, which is arguably unifiable with Move (Kitahara 1995, 1997). This eliminates construction and language specificity from the rules and by Occam's Razor reduces rules to their minimal (binary) form. With recursive application of (bare minimum) rules postulated, the possibility arises in such a derivational system that natural, general, and perhaps not even specifically linguistic (see e.g. Chomsky 1965:59, 1998, 2005) constraints on computational efficiency might be invoked to explain modes of rule application (derivations) previously stipulated as either rule (ordering) constraints or formal technical conditions on syntax-internal levels of representation. Thus, ideally the minimal rules (or single rule Merge) apply in the most computationally efficient way (derivational economy) in order to satisfy the minimal (and natural) bare output conditions on interface representations (representational economy). Parameterization of principles (e.g. the Null Subject Parameter) must then be reduced to independently necessary, minimal, and constrained morpho-featural cross-linguistic variation in the lexicon (see Borer 1984; Fukui 1986).

2   THE 1990S: THE (RE-)EMERGENCE OF ECONOMY GUIDELINES

Since Chomsky (1981), the main concern in the field had been to determine what kind of linguistic principles are genetically determined and how (some of) those principles of UG are parameterized. Some of the postulated UG principles follow the spirit of "least effort" or economy in that they "legislate against 'superfluous elements' in representations and derivations" (Chomsky 1991:418). The principle of Full Interpretation (discussed in Chomsky 1986b), for example, requires representations at DS, PF, and LF to be minimized; i.e. they can contain no superfluous elements, while economy of derivation requires that derivations have as few steps as possible (see e.g. Chomsky 1991). This section is devoted specifically to addressing the concept of economy—how the most economical derivations and representations are generated.

2.1   Economy of Derivation: A Least Effort Condition

When there are multiple possible derivations all deriving the same representational output, economy conditions compel the grammar to perform the most economical one.[2] But how is economy to be quantified, characterized, or measured?

Let us consider verbal inflection formation as a case study, following Chomsky (1991).

(1)

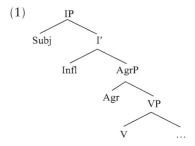

Given that verbal morphology on T and on Agr must be combined with V (Lasnik 1981) by SS in (1), there seem to be two logical solutions to meeting the SS demand: Either V moves to T/Agr, or T/Agr moves to V. The former involves V-raising to Agr, and then the V-Agr complex subsequently raises to T. The latter possibility involves T-lowering to Agr and then to V. Notice, however, that the lowering operation creates improper chains: The traces left behind by T and Agr are unbound. These representations then have to be "repaired" to create proper chains in the LF representation, to which the Chain Condition is assumed to apply. Chomsky (1991) suggests that by applying LF-raising of V, which is already combined with T and Agr by lowering, proper chains are formed. In both the lowering and the raising derivations, T and Agr can be amalgamated with V, and the resulting amalgam appears at T. Hence, the two derivations compete for most economical. Now the question is which derivation is more economical: the derivation with only raising or the derivation with both lowering and subsequent "repair" raising.

Chomsky (1991) suggests that in terms of least effort, the V-raising derivation is preferred over the T/Agr-lowering option in that the former (with only raising) involves fewer derivational steps than the latter (with both lowering and raising). The idea is that fewer transformational rule applications are more economical. As a concrete illustration of this, consider French and English V-movement data. According to Pollock (1989), French verbs obligatorily undergo overt movement in finite clauses, while English main verbs remain in situ in overt syntax:[3]

(2) a. John often kisses Mary
    b. *John kisses often Mary
(3) a. Jean   embrasse   souvent   Marie
        Jean   kiss   often   Marie
    b. *Jean souvent embrasse Marie

In English the verb must not precede the VP-adverb in (2), while in French (3) it must. In the English case, verbs never move across VP-adverbs in the mapping to SS/PF representation; i.e. there is no overt V-movement (of main verbs). If economy conditions are universal, how is this cross-linguistic variation to be captured? What is the formal difference between French and English? Pollock's hypothesis is that English main verbs cannot raise to Agr overtly since, as an irreducible lexical property, English "opaque" Agr prevents the verb raised to it from assigning its theta role at SS. However, inflectional elements must be attached/affixed by SS. Therefore, the only available derivation for the English case is that T undergoes lowering to Agr, and then [T-Agr] lowers to V. Subsequent LF-raising is then required to form a proper chain. Now a new question arises: Why is LF-raising allowed if SS raising to Agr was claimed to be a Theta Criterion violation? Chomsky's (1991) answer is that at LF, Agr, having no semantic interpretation, deletes, as required by economy of representation. Therefore, the LF-raised English V is not in fact attached to an Agr at LF, and, as a result, the theta role can be assigned. Thus, English lowers and then raises, yet this satisfies economy of derivation since it is the most economical derivation consistent with (i) the requirement that Infl/Agr affixes be attached at SS, (ii) the assumption that English Agr blocks theta role assignment by a verb attached to it, (iii) the application of the Theta Criterion throughout the derivation, and (iv) the hypothesis that well-formed chains cannot include unbound traces. In the French case, on the other hand, V can raise from post-adverbial position to pre-adverbial position by SS. In principle, it could do so only by raising or by overt lowering followed by subsequent overt raising. In the spirit of least effort, overt raising without prior overt lowering is the derivation that is chosen since it involves fewer derivational steps and satisfies all requirements. In summary, all languages obey economy of derivation, with apparent differences deriving from irreducible lexical properties of the language's functional categories, such as Agr. Thus, it appears that the fact that "raising is necessary if possible" (Chomsky 1991:426) follows from the economy condition. This is one of the case studies exemplifying the idea that fewer derivational steps ("least effort") are more economical.

Nevertheless, there are some cases where the "fewer-is-more-economical" hypothesis does not work straightforwardly, necessitating further elaboration of economy guidelines. Thus, consider the fact that the English *yes/no*-question in (4b) involves *do*-support.

(4) a. John kissed Mary
     b. Did John kiss Mary?

The derivation of (4b) should, like all derivations, observe the least effort requirement. In this case, however, inflectional morphemes are not amalgamated with V via V-raising but instead the inserted *do* "supports" these morphemes. Here it seems that only the raising operation is possible, much like in French: While the main verb, *kiss*, remains in situ, Agr raises to T, and then [T-Agr] raises to C, resulting in (4b). If the same analysis is applied to a past-tense declarative case, however, an unwanted output is obtained. Compare (5) with (4a):

(5) *John did kiss Mary   (*did* unstressed, non-contrastive)

If *do*-insertion renders T/Agr-lowering to V and subsequent LF-raising unnecessary as it does in (4b), there is no apparent reason why (5) should be ungrammatical. The derivation for (4a) contains many steps of movement made by lowering and LF-raising: two steps for lowering and two steps for LF-raising. Meanwhile, (5) requires only *do*-insertion and one step made by Agr-movement to T. If an economical derivation is determined only by the number of derivational steps, the derivation for (5) survives and blocks (4a). With respect to this puzzling problem, Chomsky (1991) suggests an additional economy condition: UG principles are less costly than language-specific rules (such as English *do*-support). Chomsky (1991:427) writes: "We may think of them [=UG principles], intuitively, as "wired-in" and distinguished from the acquired elements of language, which bear a greater cost." How is this relevant to least effort conditions? Chomsky states that UG principles can be applied whenever necessary, but language-specific rules are applied as "last resorts" to avoid violations that are not otherwise avoidable. In this analysis, applying only UG operations, which are allowed to apply wherever possible, requires less effort than applying language-specific rules.

Successive-cyclic *wh*-movement reveals another issue confronting economy of derivation, which we briefly mention here and develop further in Section 14.3. It has long been hypothesized that long-distance *wh*-movement is carried out by iterative application of (short) movement operations. However, such successive-cyclic movement includes many more derivational steps than would a single one-fell-swoop movement to the final landing site. Under the "fewer-is-more-economical" condition, long movement in a one-fell-swoop manner should be preferable to short movement by iterative application of the movement operation. Intermediate steps of *wh*-movement have been claimed to be "morphologically observable" in some languages (e.g. see McCloskey 1979, 2002 for Irish; Torrego 1984 for Spanish). In spite of involving many more derivational steps, it appears that successive short movement must somehow be a more economical option than long movement. This issue will be addressed in Section 14.3 (see also Zwart 1996).

2.2   Economy of Representation: Eliminating Superfluous Elements

As discussed in the last section, syntactic derivations are not allowed to contain any superfluous derivational steps. Chomsky (1991:437) suggests in addition that correspondingly "there can be no superfluous symbols in representations." Chomsky's (1986b, 1991) principle of Full Interpretation (FI) "holds that an element can appear in a representation only if it is properly 'licensed'" (Chomsky 1991:437). FI is a principle relating syntactic computation to the derived representations accessed by other/ external systems. The three levels interfacing with other systems, DS, PF, and LF, are naturally assumed to exhibit representations observing FI. DS representations that are assumed to interface with the lexicon satisfy FI by obeying X-bar Theory, so that elements selected from the lexicon have to project structure in accordance with the X^0-schema; otherwise, the lexicon cannot be linked to the computational system. Since PF is the interface to the external systems controlling pronunciation (or gesture for signed language) and perception, "each symbol is interpreted in terms of articulatory and perceptual mechanisms in a language-invariant manner" (p. 438). Similarly, for LF representations, "every element that appears at LF must have a language-invariant interpretation in terms of interactions with the systems of conceptual structure and language use" (p. 438). Thus, in the event that a syntactic representation contains a superfluous symbol, FI forces the symbol to disappear before reaching the interface levels. This is intended to underlie an explanatory account of the conditions under which certain deletion operations apply. That is, they apply "in order to" delete superfluous elements prohibited from an interface-level representation. (See Epstein 2003/2007 for relevant discussion of this mode of explanation.) Let us consider in more detail what a legitimate LF representation is.

Chomsky and Lasnik (1993) suggest that a chain is an LF-legitimate object only if the chain is uniform. There are three types of uniform chains. First, let us consider A-chains, in which all positions in the chain are A-positions.

(6)   John seems to like the car
        LF: [$_{TP}$ John [$_{vP}$ seems [$_{TP}$ t_2 to [$_{vP}$ t_1 [$_{vP}$ like the car]]]]]

John undergoes A-movement from the embedded [Spec, vP] to the matrix [Spec, TP] via the embedded [Spec, TP]. Since each position *John* occupies throughout the derivation is an A-position, the resulting chain (*John*, t_2, t_1) is uniform with respect to the A-property, so is LF-legitimate. The second type of chain is an A'-chain, in which all positions in the chain are A'-positions as in (7). In (7) the extracted element how is an adjunct, so that the launching site and all other landing sites are A'-positions. The resulting chain (*how*, t_3, t_2, t_1) is thus uniform with respect to A/A'-properties, and hence it is a LF-legitimate chain as it is.

(7)   How do you think that Sue fixed the car?
       LF: [$_{CP}$ how do [$_{IP}$ t_3 you think [$_{CP}$ t_2 that [$_{IP}$ Sue fixed the car t_1]]]]

The third type of chain is another kind of A'-chain, called an "operator-variable" chain, illustrated in (8).

(8)   What do you think that Anna bought?
       LF: [$_{CP}$ what do [$_{IP}$ t_3 you think [$_{CP}$ t_2 that [$_{IP}$ Anna bought t_1]]]]

In (8) the extracted *wh*-phrase *what* is an argument, so that the launching site is an A-position. However, the landing sites are all A'-positions, so that the chain formed (*what*, t_3, t_2, t_1) is not uniform with respect to A/A'-properties. If the LF representation retained this illegitimate object, the semantic interpretation of (8) could not be executed given FI, one aspect of which is assumed to be chain uniformity. Therefore, there is a need to apply a repair operation—a "last resort" operation that yields fully interpretable representations. To "save" the representation, Chomsky (1991) and Chomsky and Lasnik (1993) assume that the generalized operation Affect α (subsuming Move, Delete, Insert) discussed in Lasnik and Saito (1992) is applied only as a last resort operation to satisfy FI. In this case, the deletion operation is applicable to the intermediate traces in order to transform the illegitimate chain (*what*, t_3, t_2, t_1) into the legitimate chain (*what*, t_1), a two-member chain composed of a semantically interpretable operator and variable. This application of deletion is the only way to save the representation in this case. Again, the idea is to explain empirically motivated rule application as opposed to stipulating when it must and must not apply in order to yield correct predictions.

Worth mentioning here is a tension between economy of derivation and economy of representation inherent in this analysis. While Affect α is applied as a last resort in order to render a representation legitimate, its application increases the number of derivational steps. In other words, here the more economical representation (one satisfying FI) is derived by a more costly derivation: More work is needed to produce less representation. In order to allow such derivations, economy of derivation should be taken to apply the fewest operations necessary to yield representations satisfying FI. Perhaps this marks the beginning of the idea that the syntax operates in service to the interface conditions.

3 TOWARD THE MINIMALIST PROGRAM

Since the introduction of Chomsky's (1993) Minimalist Program, the ban on superfluous elements (in derivations and in representations) has also been applied to the entire architecture of UG. One of the characteristic manifestations is the elimination of SS (first alluded to in Chomsky 1986b) and of DS as well. The goal of minimalist architecture is to include within it only what is "conceptually necessary," namely the lexicon and the interfaces CI and SM; non-interface, entirely syntax-internal levels of representation such as SS and DS should be eliminated if possible. Chomsky (1993:3) argues that "each language will determine a set of pairs (π, λ) (π drawn from PF and λ drawn from LF) as its formal representations of sound and meaning, insofar as these are determined by the language itself." In other words, there are no representations that have nothing to do with the ineliminable aspects of sound and meaning, and the derivational system works only for the purpose of generating these fully interpretable representations. Those representational products produced by the computational system give fully interpretable instructions to the external systems. Also, these representations serve as inputs to the performance systems: PF representation for the articulatory-perceptual system and LF representation for the conceptual-intentional system. In this sense, PF/LF-legitimate objects can be defined as objects that can give appropriate instructions to the performance systems. Given this architecture, all the conditions (including FI) that have been applied to representations are now recaptured as interface conditions, imposed by the external systems needing instructions. If an LF representation includes something superfluous, the representation naturally receives a defective interpretation in the CI system.

Also, in order to execute a more economical derivation, not only are "fewer steps" and "shorter moves" postulated, but also the new concepts Procrastinate and Greed play important roles. The former states that LF movement is less costly than overt movement, so movement should be postponed to LF if possible. The latter, called "self-serving last resort," requires that the application of an operation to α is allowed only when morphological properties of α are not otherwise satisfied, enabling us to explain not only when operations do apply but also when operations do not apply.

The Minimalist Program provides us with clearer grounds regarding how/why linguistic representations are highly constrained under the spirit of least effort and also goes toward more restricted derivational procedures. By doing so, a higher level of explanation is attained in that the application and non-application of operations is not stipulated but rather is deduced from general economy conditions that are neither language-specific nor construction-specific and (following Chomsky 2005) are perhaps not uniquely syntactic or even linguistic by hypothesis but instead reflect general efficiency guidelines (least effort) and are formulated in service to interface interpretability (economy of representation).

3.1   The Advent of Checking Theory

Chomsky (1993) develops the first version of the "checking" theory of Case and agreement, and the analysis represents a milestone in minimalist theorizing: the deduction of GB's Case Filter from far more general interface conditions, and the unification of Case and agreement as specifier-head relations.

What motivates checking theory, and what are its central assumptions? One major development in Chomsky (1993) is the elimination of GB's most central and unifying relation, government. For Chomsky (1993:6), "[i]n a minimalist theory, the crucial properties and relations will be stated in the simple and elementary terms of X-bar theory." The structural relation of government played a central, unifying role in GB theory—for example, theta roles and Case were assigned under government. Thus, if the complex definition of government is dispensed with on minimalist grounds, all operations and principles that appeal to government "must be reformulated" (p. 6). How can this be accomplished?

A major concern of Chomsky (1993) was the reformulation of Case Theory. Within GB, Case assignment was configurationally diverse, hence non-unified, in that, say, Nom was assigned to Spec, TP, while Acc was assigned from a head to its complement, or, in the instance of Exceptional Case Marking (ECM), to the specifier of a head's complement. Alternatively, Chomsky (1995:173) takes a "narrower approach" whereby "all these modes of structural Case assignment [are] recast in unified X-bar-theoretic terms, presumably under the Spec-head relation." Adopting, and elaborating, the split-Infl analysis of Pollock (1989), Chomsky (1993) assumes the basic clausal structure of (9):

(9)

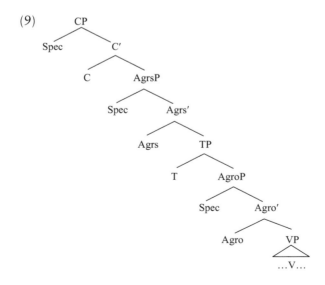

The Agr ("O" for Object and "S" for Subject were just mnemonic, not theoretical) heads bear the standard phi features, while T bears tense. Chomsky (1993) proposes that agreement and structural Case are "manifestations of the Spec-head relation" (p. 7). The elimination of government in favor of the "fundamental relations of X-bar theory" is a form of methodological Minimalism: To the extent that X-bar Theory is independently motivated, the relations available from it come for free and hence are to be preferred on conceptual grounds to (complex) relations such as government that are descriptively defined on phrase markers.

The traditional way to interpret agreement and structural case is as a form of feature assignment from one category to another. Some functional category lexically bears phi features, for example, and "gives them over" to a lexical head (to a verb, for instance) under the right structural licensing conditions; similarly for Case: a head such as finite T, or a transitive V, lexically "has" Case and "gives it over" to a local NP. The alternative developed in Chomsky (1993), and still assumed in modified form in more recent minimalist work (see below), is not one of feature assignment but rather of feature checking: A lexical head such as V and N enters the derivation not as a bare root but rather "with all of its morphological features, including Case and phi-features" (p. 29). Agreement features are assumed to be an "intrinsic property" of categories such as V (and, for example, Adj), while Case is intrinsic to N. Rather than being assigned inflectional features in the syntax, lexical categories such as V and N must now have their intrinsic inflectional features checked against a functional category with matching features. Checking can take place only in the restricted licensing configurations of the primitive X-bar relations. This, in turn, motivates a series of derivational operations, specifically head and phrasal movement. The intent is to try to deduce instances of obligatory movement of a category X from the requirement that X have its features checked, which requires X to get into the relevant checking relation.

Simplifying somewhat, let us consider subject agreement and nominative case checking, in, say, *He eats cheese*. The NP/DP *he* (specifically, its head) will have an intrinsic, lexically specified Case feature that it bears as it enters the derivation: *he*[nom]. Likewise, the head *eats* is fully inflected as *eats*[Agrs, Tns]. For convergence, the intrinsic inflectional features of these lexical categories must be checked. There are two checking relations available, head-head and spec-head. Since it is itself a head, the relevant checking relation for *eats*[Agrs, Tns] is head-head, and thus this verb will raise to Agrs in (9), where the relevant local configuration is represented in (10):

(10)

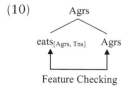

Here Agrs, which bears phi features, checks against the Agrs features of *eats*; if the phi features of the two heads are identical (i.e. if they "match"), then checking is successful and, as a result, Agrs (or each semantically uninterpretable feature within it) "disappears"—a prerequisite to semantic (LF) well-formedness. If the features of the two elements are not identical, then Agrs cannot delete, and the derivation fails to converge at LF. Next, the Agrs+*eats*[—, Tns] complex raises to T in order to check the Tns feature of *eats* against the matching Tns feature of T. Head-movement involves just this sort of checking, and it is motivated by the need for convergence at the interfaces. Under checking theory, and on the assumption that only the primitive relations of X-bar Theory constitute the available checking relations, head-movement is motivated by the need for convergence at the interfaces.

Chomsky (1993) assumes that the NP, *he* in our representative examples, includes "intrinsic" Case and phi features "and that these too must be checked in the appropriate position" (p. 29). Chomsky assumes that +tns T checks nominative case. Thus, the subject NP raises to Spec, TP for nominative Case checking. We will explore in the next section more recent developments related to which element "benefits" from checking: the mover or a category in a primitive relation to the landing site.

So far, we have sketched the basic ideas of checking theory as proposed in Chomsky (1993). A number of important developments within the minimalist theory emerged. One is a deduction of the Case Filter (with Case and agreement unified under the specifier-head relation). In Chomsky (1993) the motivation for NP-movement to Spec, T is essentially the need for feature checking: If the features are not checked by matching features in a primitive X-bar configuration, then the derivation fails to converge at the interfaces. The Case Filter then becomes "an interface condition" (p. 29). This leading idea develops in Chomsky (1995) into a generalized theory of the interface interpretability of features. The Case feature of an NP is not interpretable at the LF interface; this is assumed to be a fact about the structural Case feature—evidenced by there being no obvious semantic distinction between *he/him* in virtual minimal pairs such as *I believe he left* and *I believe him to have left*. Given economy of representation, which "we may take . . . to be nothing other than FI," it follows that "every symbol must receive an "external" interpretation by the language-independent rules" (p. 200). Since Case is not interpretable at LF, and since, crucially under checking theory, Case is an intrinsic feature of N (NP), it follows that the Case feature must be checked (assuming that checking is the only way to execute feature deletion). Here we see a milestone of Minimalism: the deduction of the Case Filter. Again, the central goal is to attempt to explain movement and eliminate purely syntax-internal (SS) filters.

But Chomsky (1993) also has other important consequences relevant to economy. Under checking theory "we need no longer adopt the Emonds-Pollock assumption that in English-type languages I lowers to V" (p. 195) as discussed in detail in Section 14.2. Rather, "V will have the inflectional features before Spell Out in any event, and the checking procedure may take place anywhere, in particular, after LF movement. French-type and English-type languages now look alike at LF" (p. 195). In both French and English, then, V will raise up to and through the functional projections (AgrO, AgrS, Tns) in order that V's intrinsic inflectional features be checked under the head-head relation. In French, such head-movement is overt, i.e. before Spell Out (yielding *Jean embrasse souvent Marie* "John kisses often Mary," (3a)); in English, it occurs after Spell Out, and it is covert (yielding *John often kisses Mary* (2a) at PF).[4] Chomsky (1993), adopting ideas of Pollock (1989) and of Chomsky (1991), postulates that this overt–covert distinction can be derived in terms of "feature strength." Agr is strong in French-type languages; Agr is weak in English-type languages. This notion of strength is an early form of interpretability of features at the interfaces (more fully developed in later minimalist work). The strong checking features of Agr are "visible" at PF. These strong features furthermore are *not* PF legitimate. In effect, then, strong features force overt movement. If Agr bearing strong features has not participated in checking, then its strong features are not deleted and hence make their way to PF, inducing a PF crash. If the features are checked, they "disappear" since "they have done their job." Thus, since Agr's checking features are strong, "overt" movement follows from the interface conditions. The Agr checking features in English are weak (in contrast to French), which means that they are not visible to PF and so do not cause a problem there.[5] An interesting question that now emerges is why overt raising is barred in English. Since Agr is weak in English, V need not raise, but this does not in and of itself entail that V cannot raise. Here is precisely where economy of derivation enters. According to Chomsky (1995), a natural economy condition is that LF movement is cheaper than overt movement. This principle is called "Procrastinate." Basically, the idea is that if an operation need not apply now, then it must not apply now; operations apply only when the time comes that they must, hence as late as possible, never prematurely. Hence, English overt V-raising is barred by this economy of derivation condition.

3.2 The Tension between Different Notions of Economy and a Possible Resolution

At this stage in the historical development of economy conditions, a tension between different notions of economy emerges. Chomsky (1993) notes two notions of derivational economy. Relative to the movement operation, one notion is that movements should be as short as possible. Thus, in minimality cases like Superiority, Superraising, the Head Movement Constraint, and *wh*-islands (cf. Rizzi 1990), the generalization seems to be that the shortest move is preferred. In (11), an example of Superiority, movement of *whom*[1] is shorter than movement of *whom*$_2$ (in terms of intervening categories or paths), and thus the shorter move (11a) is preferred via economy.

(11) a. Whom$_1$ did John persuade t_1 [to visit whom$_2$]?
  b. *Whom$_2$ did John persuade whom$_1$ [to visit t_2]?

"Looking at these phenomena in terms of economy considerations, it is clear that in all the 'bad' cases, some element has failed to make 'the shortest move'" (Chomsky 1993:14).

Another natural notion of economy, however, is 'fewest derivational steps,' as discussed in Section 14.2, where one derivation is compared to another based on the number of operations (or instances of an operation) that have applied: The derivation with the fewest operations (necessary for convergence) is preferred. Such a notion of economy is featured in Chomsky (1993) in an early minimalist analysis of word order variation between French and English, as detailed in Section 14.2 above.

Chomsky (1993) notes a tension between these two notions of economy: "[I]f a derivation keeps to shortest moves, it will have more steps; if it reduces the number of steps, it will have longer moves" (p. 15). In Chomsky this tension is resolved by taking "the basic transformational operation to be not Move alpha but *Form Chain*" (p. 15). Consider (12):

(12) seems [__ to be likely [John to win]]

Under standard successive-cyclic A-movement, construed in classic derivational terms, (12) would involve two instances of movement: First, *John* moves to Spec of intermediate T, yielding (13), and, second, *John* in intermediate position moves to matrix Spec, T, yielding (14).

(13) seems [John to be likely [*t* to win]]
(14) John seems [*t* to be likely [*t* to win]]

Each of these two movements is the shortest possible, but making such short moves entails that there are more derivational steps. The Form Chain approach, on the other hand, effectively eliminates derivation-internal steps. Form Chain takes (12) as input and directly gives (14) as output, all at once. Thus, in mapping (12) directly to (14), only one relevant operation has applied; i.e. there has been just one application of Form Chain. Form Chain is representational to the extent that there is no internal structure in the mapping of (12) to (14); the operation Form Chain takes (12) as input, the lights go out, and when they are back on again (14) is present. Form Chain then has one step. Shortest move is translated to keep links of a chain minimal, where the chain is formed all at once.

3.3   Global Economy versus Local Economy

Another important issue that arises in considerations of economy is whether economy is viewed as global, involving an entire derivation or comparisons between multiple derivations, or local, involving comparison of just some restricted set of operations internal to a single derivation at a single derivational point. As noted in Collins (1997), early economy principles were global. They involve comparison of alternative derivations with the same starting point (the same initial lexical array or numeration) and the same convergent endpoint. Consider, for example, Kitahara's (1995) formulation of "Fewest Steps" in a derivation:

(15) *Shortest Derivation Requirement*
Minimize the number of operations necessary for convergence.

Collins (1997) notes that (15) is global in the sense that the number of steps of alternative derivations (from the same numeration (Chomsky 1995) or to a single convergent interface representation) are compared. (15) is also global "in that it involves reference to the notion of convergence" (Collins 1997:5). Basically, we need to know where the derivation is going, and what its output will be (specifically, a convergent object at both interfaces), and then select the derivation among the available competitors that involves the fewest steps.
Collins argues for an alternative conception of economy: local economy. The basic idea is that economy is evaluated based on immediately available syntactic objects within a derivation, and not on the entire derivation. "During a derivation at any step the decision about whether to apply an operation (in an optimal derivation) is based on the syntactic objects to which the operation is applying" (Collins 1997:4). Last Resort is proposed as a principle of local economy. Last Resort states:

(16) An operation OP involving alpha may apply only if some property of alpha is satisfied.

Thus, head-movement can apply only if features of the head get checked as a result, and likewise for phrasal movement. Minimality is then stated in terms of operations that satisfy Last Resort:

(17) *Minimality:*

An operation OP (satisfying Last Resort) may apply only if there is no smaller operation OP^0 (satisfying Last Resort).

(Collins 1997:9)

Collins argues that the only economy conditions are local ones, like (16) and (17) above, and much subsequent literature in Minimalism adopted this locality approach.

4   FROM LOCAL ECONOMY TO EFFICIENT COMPUTATION

Since Collins (1997), the focus of minimalist inquiry has been shifted to the elimination of principles with "look-ahead properties" in favor of those that keep to local economy, and the attempt at such elimination has formed the basis for our understanding of the principles of efficient computation. In this section, we trace the development of the principles of local economy and of efficient computation.

4.1   Competitors under Local Economy

In Chomsky (2000) and his subsequent work, principles with "look-ahead properties" have been reformulated in terms of "local calculations," under which competitors are no longer entire derivations associated with the same lexical array LA; rather, competitors are alternative possible operations applied at a single point internal to a single derivation.[6] The decision as to which operation is the most efficient one can be made using only information available at that particular choice point in the derivation. Under this interpretation of local economy, Chomsky (2000:101) defined Move as the composite operation that combines Merge and Agree, and he demonstrated that preference for simpler operations over more complex ones captures the "last resort" character of Move. Consider (18):

(18) a. *there is likely [$_{TP}$ someone to be $t_{someone}$ in the room]
      b. there is likely [$_{TP}$ t_{there} to be someone in the room]

Each derivation involves the stage [T [*be someone in the room*]], where T requires that something occupy Spec, T.[7] At this point, Merge of expletive *there* in Spec, T and Move of *someone* to Spec, T are (in principle) available, but preference for simpler operations over more complex ones selects Merge of *there* in Spec, T over Move of *someone* to Spec, T, because "Move is more complex than its subcomponents Merge and Agree" (Chomsky 2000:101). Thus, the "last resort" character of Move (observed when constructing the embedded TP in (18b)) follows naturally from the local calculation.

This analysis, however, would make a wrong prediction. Consider (19):

(19) a. I expected [$_{TP}$ someone to be $t_{someone}$ in the room]
      b. *I expected [$_{TP}$ t_I to be someone in the room]

Here, too, each derivation involves the stage [T [*be someone in the room*]], and two options, Merge of I in Spec, T and Move of *someone* to Spec, T, are (by hypothesis) available to the narrow syntax (NS); but, if so, preference for simpler operations over more complex ones would select Merge of I in Spec, T over Move of *someone* to Spec, T, yielding the wrong result, namely (19b), along with the inability to generate (19a). Chomsky

(1995:313) took the contrast in (19) to indicate that an argument merged into a non-theta position becomes an illegitimate object, violating FI and thereby causing the derivation to crash. He suggested that at the stage in question, the crashing fate of Merge of I in Spec, T is calculated; hence, Move of *someone* to Spec, T—a more complex operation than Merge of I in Spec, T (which will crash the derivation later at the CI interface)—is allowed to take place. Chomsky (2000:103), however, presented an alternative analysis with no "look-ahead" calculation. He took the contrast in (19) to indicate that Merge of an argument in non-theta position is not available to the NS as a legitimate competitor operation at the corresponding stage. He proposed the following theta-theoretic condition (where pure Merge is Merge that is not a subpart of Move):

(20) Pure Merge in theta-position is required of (and restricted to) arguments.

(20), Merge of *I* in Spec, T in (19) is not an allowable or possible operation (by definition); hence, it is not a competitor. As desired, (19b) is simply underivable and is blocked without any reference to the "look-ahead" calculation, while (19a) is now derivable as desired. If operative complexity matters for minimalist design, this alternative analysis is arguably preferable to the one with the "look-ahead" calculation.[8]

Under (20), Merge of *there* in Spec, T in (18) is still permitted as a legitimate competitor operation (since *there* is not an argument), and this option is selected by preference of simpler operations over more complex ones. Note that this particular choice is logically possible only if *there* is an item present in the LA.

As shown above, the initial choice of LA plays a crucial role, but this cannot be the whole story. Consider (21):

(21) a. there is a possibility [$_{CP}$ that someone will be $t_{someone}$ in the room]
b. a possibility is [$_{CP}$ that there will be someone in the room]

(21a) is now seemingly paradoxical. The derivation of (21a) contains *there*, and, recall, inserting *there* is less complex than moving *someone*, yet in (21a) we see that Move of *someone* to Spec, T in the embedded CP is possible. It should not be, given that insertion of *there* is a simpler operation filling Spec, T. So somehow, when building the embedded CP, in particular Spec, (embedded)T, Move can be preferred over Merge—the exact opposite of what was motivated above, namely Merge over Move.

Chomsky (2000:106) presented a straightforward solution to this problem. The basic idea is that structures are built bottom-up, cyclically, in chunks called "phases," each associated with its own separate lexical subarray SA. So first we form SA = {*that, will, be, someone, in, the, room*}, needed to generate the embedded CP. Expletive *there* is absent from this SA.

Consequently, insertion of *there* is not an option, since *there* is absent from the SA (formed to build the embedded CP). Thus, movement of *someone*, in fact, satisfies Merge over Move, since we had nothing to merge in Spec, T, when movement to Spec, T took place.

Formally, Chomsky proposed that a subarray SA_i is extracted from LA and placed in the workspace of NS. As SA_i is exhausted, NS may proceed if possible, or a new SA_j may be extracted from LA and placed in the workspace, allowing NS to proceed as before. Under this proposal, NS accesses only part of the entire sentential LA at each stage of the derivation, thus contributing to the reduction of operative complexity.

In short, given the postulation of SA, (21a) and (21b) do not compete. In the derivation of (21a), the (embedded) CP is constructed from SA_i containing no expletive; hence, Move of *someone* to Spec, (embedded)T is the only option available to NS at the corresponding stage. In the derivation of (21b), the (embedded) CP is constructed from SA_j containing an expletive; hence, Merge of *there* in Spec, (embedded)T is selected over Move of *someone* to Spec, (embedded)T at the corresponding stage, because Merge (of *there* in Spec, (embedded)T) is simpler than Move (of *someone* to Spec, (embedded)T). Notice there is no optionality involved in the derivations of (21). Importantly, optionality has to be eliminated if we adopt the Strong Minimalist Thesis; i.e. NS is a computationally efficient satisfier of the interface conditions, though the option of having an expletive is available to the formation of lexical arrays and subarrays.

4.2   Phase-Based Cyclicity

The notion SA received more prominence when the cyclicity condition was reformulated. Chomsky (2000:106) assumed that SA should determine a natural syntactic object SO. Such an SO is taken to be "propositional"— either a verb phrase vP (in which all theta roles are assigned) or a full clause CP (including tense and illocutionary force). With this assumption, he proposed that (i) SA contains an occurrence of *v* or C, exactly one occurrence if it is restricted as narrowly as possible; and (ii) a SO derived in this way by choice of SA is a phase of a derivation; i.e. vP and CP are said to be phases. Given (i) and (ii), Chomsky (p. 108) formulated the Phase Impenetrability Condition (PIC) as a very strong cyclicity condition:

(22)   In phase α with head H, the domain of H is not accessible to operations outside α, only H and its edge are accessible to such operations.

Upon the completion of α, the PIC prohibits any head outside α from affecting lexical items inside the complement domain of H.[9] Furthermore, as discussed by Chomsky (2000:132), if H itself is no longer accessible after a new SA is extracted and a lexical item of this SA is merged with α, then the PIC ensures that, upon the completion of α, all lexical items inside the complement domain of H become "syntactically inert," undergoing no further syntactic operation.[10]

This phase-based analysis of cyclic derivation sheds light on the old problem posed by two apparently contradictory notions of economy: "[I]f a derivation keeps to shortest moves, it will have more steps; if it reduces the number of steps, it will have longer moves" (Chomsky 1993:15; see Zwart 1996 for relevant discussion). Given phase-based cyclic derivation, movement must always target the edge of the minimal phase containing the mover's departure site; hence one-fell-swoop movement crossing a phase is not a possible operation. Consequently, under this formalism there is no choice between fewest moves versus shortest move; the latter is required.

4.3   Uninterpretable Features and Syntactic Operations

Under the phase-based analysis of cyclic derivation, what happens inside a phase cycle has been at the center of investigation.

In the early stage of minimalist theorizing, the presence of semantically uninterpretable features (like structural Case or phi features on T) was recognized as a serious problem, and why they exist became one of the core questions. To answer this question, the Minimalist Program pursued the intuition that they are implemented for movement, where movement is, by hypothesis, required to satisfy FI; this pursuit substantiated the view that movement is carried out in the interest of deleting those (otherwise useless but by hypothesis offending) uninterpretable features.

Let us take a concrete case. Consider (23):

(23) [$_\alpha$ an unpopular candidate] T-was elected t_α

In Chomsky (2000, 2001), there are three kinds of uninterpretable features: the set of phi features on T (identifying T as a target of movement), the EPP feature of T (requiring that something be overtly merged with the projection headed by T), and the Case feature of an *unpopular candidate* (identifying α as a category for merger that satisfies EPP). The probe-goal system (itself constrained by Minimal Search, not illustrated here but hypothesized also to be optimal) is then proposed as a device to yield (23) by deleting all three kinds of uninterpretable features. In (23), for the phi-set of T, there is only one choice of matching features, namely the phi-set of *candidate*. Now, locating *candidate* as a goal, the phi-set of T, functioning as a probe, erases under phi-matching, and the Case feature of the goal erases as a reflection of such phi-matching. The operation Agree carries out such erasure of the uninterpretable features on probe and goal, and Merge (moving the goal of T's probe to Spec, T) satisfies the EPP feature of T. Thus, the combination of Agree and Merge dislocates α to Spec, T and eliminates all three kinds of uninterpretable features (listed above), and it does so inside the phase. Notice that in this phase, there is no competing operation that could carry out the same task; hence, NS has no option but to select the composite operation Move (combining Agree and Merge).

In Chomsky (2007, 2008), however, it is proposed that T does not inherently bear phi features; rather, it gets them in the course of the derivation, from the C that selects T, via feature-inheritance. This proposal entails that T bears phi features when selected by C. Under this proposal, the combination of Agree and Merge still dislocates α to Spec, T and eliminates all three kinds of uninterpretable features, but it does so necessarily after Merge of C with "spec-less" TP.[11]

Here, more detailed analysis of the deletion of uninterpretable features is needed. Prior to the deletion of uninterpretable features, they must receive some value; otherwise, their phonetic interpretation cannot be explained. We get *he* or *him* in English depending on the structural conditions for Case-valuation. Likewise, specifications of the phi features on English T (phonetically realized as -*s* or as Ø) are syntactically determined.

The assumption is then that structural Case and phi features on T "are unvalued in the lexicon, thus properly distinguished from interpretable features, and assigned their values in syntactic configurations, hence necessarily by probe-goal relations" (Chomsky 2007:18). Under this assumption, prior to Agree, such uninterpretable features are (by definition) offending features at the two interfaces; hence, they cannot be transferred. Once valued by Agree, they may yield a phonetic interpretation, but they will never yield a semantic interpretation.[12] Thus, even if they are valued by Agree, they still lack a semantic interpretation, and so they must be deleted, i.e. not transferred to the semantic component, where their appearance would violate FI. But such deletion cannot take place after they are valued by Agree, because "the uninterpretable features, and only these, enter the derivation without values, and are distinguished from interpretable features by virtue of this property" (Chomsky 2001:5); hence, in the eyes of Transfer, after valuation, they are indistinguishable from their interpretable counterparts, which are (by definition) undeletable. Thus, Chomsky (2007:19) concludes that they must be valued at the phase level where they are transferred, and such derivationally valued features are deleted when transferred to the semantic component, but they remain intact when transferred to the phonological component.[13]

4.4   Principles of Efficient Computation

In Chomsky (2007, 2008), the simple definition of Merge has been maintained, and the observed properties of Merge have been (largely) derived from local efficiency considerations, reformulated as principles of efficient computation.

Merge is defined as "an operation that takes n syntactic objects (SOs) already formed, and constructs from them a new SO" (Chomsky 2008:137), and "arguably restriction of computational resources limits n for Merge to two" (p. 138). The binary limitation, $n = 2$, yields Kayne's (1981) unambiguous paths—the binary-branching structures that Chomsky's (2000) Minimal Search and Kayne's (1994) Linear Correspondence Axiom (LCA)–based linearization operate on. Binarity is understood to be a property of Merge deducible from a general principle of efficient computation (not a specifically linguistic property stipulated in the definition of Merge).

Another principle of efficient computation is the No-Tampering Condition (NTC): "Merge of X and Y leaves the two SOs unchanged" (Chomsky 2008:138). Given NTC, Merge does not alter X or Y; rather, it places the two SOs in a set.[14] Furthermore, Merge of X and Y results in "syntactic extension," forming a new SO = {X, Y}, not "syntactic infixation" embedding X within Y, for example. One desirable consequence of NTC is that Merge invariably applies to the edge; hence, the empirical content of Chomsky's (1993) Extension Condition (largely) follows from NTC.

The inclusiveness condition is another natural principle of efficient computation: "[N]o new objects are added in the course of computation apart from rearrangements of lexical properties" (Chomsky 1995:228). Given the inclusiveness condition, Merge does not add bar levels, traces, indices, or any similar technicalia (invoked in GB theory) throughout a derivation.

Assuming Merge to be the sole structure building operation of NS, Chomsky (2005, 2007, 2008) argues that Move should reduce to an instance of Merge.[15] Suppose X is merged to Y (introducing the asymmetry only for expository purposes). There are (in principle) two possible positions where X originates: Either X originates external to Y (External Merge, EM) or X originates internal to Y (Internal Merge, IM). But they are simply two instances of the same operation Merge, and in both cases Merge yields a new SO = {X, Y}. Now, given NTC, IM necessarily yields two copies of X: one external to Y (in the landing-site position) and the other within Y (the departure site), as in [X [$_Y$ . . . X . . .]]. Thus, there is no need to stipulate a rule of formation of copies (or remerge), and Chomsky's (1993) copy theory of movement then follows from "just IM applying in the optimal way, satisfying NTC" (Chomsky 2007:10); it is a consequence of NTC-compliant execution of IM.

To generate a derivation, Merge must be able to find SOs, and how Merge gets access to SOs is also constrained by the principles of efficient computation. In the simplest case, only the label (i.e. head) of the full SO—either the root SO thus far constructed or the atomic SO not yet merged—can be accessed to drive further operations. Suppose X and Y are two separate full SOs. Then, their labels x and y can be accessed with "no search" (Chomsky 2000:132); they are "directly accessible" to NS. Suppose X is internal to Y (where Y is the root SO thus far constructed). Then, the accessed label y of Y, functioning as a probe, carries out the task of finding X as its goal. This probe-goal search, which reduces operative complexity by restricting the searchable domain of the probe to just its complement domain, is taken to be part of the generalized computationally efficient principle, Minimal Search (Chomsky 2007:9).[16]

Minimal Search is arguably the outgrowth or development and refinement of "derivational c-command" (Epstein et al. 1998; Epstein 1999; Epstein and Seely 2006), under which c-command is not stipulatively defined on output representations but is rather deduced from the bottom-up iterative application of binary Merge during the course of the derivation. Thus, it is natural, for example, that upon the merger of T with [*a man outside*], T minimally searches precisely the SO it was merged with, namely [*a man outside*], and this search by T finds (or matches) the phi features of *man* and values the unvalued phi features on T as 3rd person, masculine, singular, ultimately pronounced /iz/ as in *There is a man outside*. Interestingly, Epstein et al. (1998:Section 4.8) noted that c-command seems to be a necessary condition for a syntactic relation or phenomenon, but they also noted it is not sufficient—and wondered why. Specifically, c-command is an unbounded relation that can span multiple clauses, yet we see no syntactic relations spanning such distances. Under Chomsky's PIC-based analysis, coupled with Minimal Search, it is explained why "c-command within a phase" (a.k.a. Minimal Search) is derivationally deducible and c-command relations strictly bounded by the PIC.

As shown above, it is reasonable to maintain the simple definition of Merge and to derive the observed properties of Merge from principles of efficient computation such as the binary limitation, NTC, the inclusiveness condition, and Minimal Search.

5   SUMMARY AND CONCLUSION

In this chapter, we have reviewed the central notions of economy, including aspects of their history, motivation, modern form, and empirical content. There are two notions of economy: economy of representation and economy of derivation. As for the former, the goal is to minimize the theoretical constructs postulated, appealing only to those concerning irreducible lexical features (i.e. atoms), the products of their combination, and the "conceptually necessary" interface requirements (of sound and meaning) demanding interpretability of representations. As for economy of derivation, the goal is to deduce stipulated technical constraints on rules to independently motivated, ideally not linguistic-specific, principles of efficient computation. Indeed, the Strong Minimalist Thesis regarding syntax, phonology, and semantics might be encapsulated as computationally efficient satisfaction of natural interface conditions. Interestingly, the theory is neither rule-based (as was Standard Theory) nor filter-based (as was GB theory) but rather is mixed. There are simple, minimal rules (perhaps even just one, viz. Merge) the application of which is constrained by general principles of minimal computation; any effort must be motivated by the "functional" (see e.g. Epstein 2003/2007) goal of satisfying minimal, natural interpretability requirements of the interfaces. This program is consistent with Einstein's conception of "the grand aim of all science, which is to cover the greatest possible number of empirical facts by logical deduction from the smallest possible number of hypotheses," committed to the view that "our experience hitherto justifies us in believing that nature is the realization of the simplest conceivable mathematical ideas" (1954:274).

NOTES

1. For an excellent recent overview of GB theory, see Lasnik and Lohndal (2010); see also Chapters 2 and 4, and Chomsky and Lasnik (1993).
2. For the purposes of this section, we will assume that multiple derivations compete for most economical only if they result in identical output representations. See Section 14.4 for discussion of competitor sets.
3. As Pollock (1989) observes, verb movement in French is optional in infinitival clauses. In English, on the other hand, finite auxiliaries such as *be* and *have* behave like obligatory raising verbs in French. That is, the issue is not only French versus English. Following Lasnik (1981b), Chomsky (1991) makes a distinction between these languages in terms of the strength of Agr: Strong Agr, which French has, can accept any element, while weak Agr, which English chooses, can only accept 'light' elements, e.g. finite auxiliaries. This chapter does not go into detailed discussion of French infinitives and English auxiliaries but rather seeks to present the verb movement facts as an illustration of the properties of economy.
4. Note that the overt/covert distinction with V-raising is analogous to Huang's (1982) theory of overt versus covert *wh*-movement: Derivations are universal, but the specific point in the derivation at which PF interpretation applies is parameterized, with few options (before vs. after Spell Out). But for the Minimalist Program there is no SS, and hence no parameters can involve SS (hence no 'apply before/after SS'). For Chomsky, only properties of functional categories can be parameterized, leading to the notion of feature 'strength.'
5. As Chomsky (1995) notes, the weak versus strong distinction is stipulative. However, this stipulation involves features of functional categories and is thus consistent with the Borer (1984b) and Fukui (1986) hypothesis that such features, the atomic, i.e. irreducible, elements of the theory, are the loci of parametric variation.
6. Chomsky (1995:225) extended LAs to numerations, in order to distinguish independent selections of a single lexical item. A numeration is defined as a set of pairs (LI, i), where LI is an item of the lexicon and i is its index, understood to be the number of times that LI is selected. In his later work, however, Chomsky (2000:114) noted that this extension can be eliminated by leaving the removal of an item of LA when accessed in computation as an option. We leave this issue open and proceed with a simpler concept, namely LA. The choice between the two concepts, however, does not affect our discussion.
7. We ignore *to* here, since it is not relevant for our discussion.
8. Notice that here we see 'look-ahead' being avoided by recasting a representational constraint (on LF) as a constraint on rule application (see Section 14.1).
9. Suppose α is HP = [XP [H YP]]. Then, YP is the complement domain of H, and XP is the edge of H.
10. Chomsky (2001) slightly modified the formulation of the PIC. Under the modified version, the PIC applies to α as soon as α is embedded within a distinct phase. In his recent work, however, Chomsky (2007, 2008) adopts his (2000)

version of the PIC (given in (22)). We leave this issue open and proceed with a restrictive version, namely the PIC formulated as (22). The choice between the two versions, however, does not affect our discussion.

11. This 'feature-transmitting' property of C (allowing T to inherit features from C) is then assigned to phase heads generally: C and v. See Epstein et al. (to appear b) for precise presentation of step-by-step derivations in this theory. See also Epstein et al. (to appear a) for an attempt to explain on the basis of feature-inheritance (i) why it is that the phase-head complements, VP and TP, are what gets spelled out; and (ii) why these complements are spelled out when they are.

12. That is, while Case and agreement seem to be syntactically determined processes with phonetic reflexes, the claim is that there are no corresponding syntactically determined 'semantic feature valuation' operations, e.g. where an animacy feature is valued in proximity to some other animacy feature. See Epstein et al. (2010) for relevant discussion.

13. As concerns the timing of valuation and Transfer, see Epstein and Seely (2002a), Epstein et al. (2010), and Richards (2007).

14. Empirically, for example, Merging *the* and *dog* together to form a DP does not alter *the* or *dog*, though we can imagine and formulate combinatorial systems in which such Merger could change the meaning of *dog*, the meaning of *the*, their syntactic category membership, their lexical phonology, etc.

15. Note that in Chomsky (2005, 2007, 2008) Move is no longer the composite operation that combines Agree and Merge.

16. Given this interpretation of Minimal Search, the label cannot probe into its own specifier.

REFERENCES

Borer, H. 1984. The Projection Principle and Rules of Morphology. In Jones, C. and Sells, P. (eds.), *Proceedings of the XIV Annual Meeting of the North-Eastern Linguistic Society*, 16–33. Amherst: GLSA.

Bresnan, J. 1971. Sentence Stress and Syntactic Transformations. *Language* 47:257–281.

Chomsky, N. 1955. *The Logical Structure of Linguistic Theory*. Cambridge, MA: MIT Library. (Microfilmed 1961.)

Chomsky, N. 1964. Current Issues in Linguistic Theory. In Fodor, J. A. and Katz, J. (eds.), *The Structure of Language: Readings in the Philosophy of Language*, 50–118. Englewood Cliffs, NJ: Prentice Hall.

Chomsky, N. 1965. *Aspects of the Theory of Syntax*. Cambridge, MA: MIT Press.

Chomsky, N. 1973. Conditions on Transformations. In Anderson, S. and Kiparsky, P. (eds.), *A Festschrift for Morris Halle*. New York: Holt, Rinehart, and Winston.

Chomsky, N. 1975. *Reflections on Language*. New York: Pantheon Books.

Chomsky, N. 1980. On Binding. *Linguistic Inquiry* 11:1–46.

Chomsky, N. 1981. *Lectures on Government and Binding*. Dordrecht: Foris.

Chomsky, N. 1982. *Some Concepts and Consequences of the Theory of Government and Binding*. Cambridge, MA: MIT Press.

Chomsky, N. 1986a. *Barriers*. Cambridge, MA: MIT Press.

Chomsky, N. 1986b. *Knowledge of Language*. New York: Praeger.

Chomsky, N. 1991. Some Notes on Economy of Derivation and Representation. In Freidin, R. (ed.), *Principles and Parameters in Comparative Grammar*, 417–454. Cambridge, MA: MIT Press.

Chomsky, N. 1993. A Minimalist Program for Linguistic Theory. In Hale, K. and Keyser, S. J. (eds.), *The View from Building 20: Essays in Linguistics in Honor of*

Sylvain Bromberger, 1–52. Cambridge, MA: MIT Press. [Reprinted in *The Minimalist Program*, 167–217. Cambridge, MA: MIT Press, 1995.]

Chomsky, N. 1995. *The Minimalist Program*. Cambridge, MA: MIT Press.

Chomsky, N. 1998. Some Observations on Economy in Generative Grammar. In Barbosa, P., Fox, D., Hagstrom, P., McGinnis, M. and Pesetsky, D. (eds.), *Is The Best Good Enough?* 115–129. Cambridge, MA: MIT Press.

Chomsky, N. 2000. Minimalist Inquiries: The Framework. In Martin, R., Michaels, D. and Uriagereka, J. (eds.), *Step by Step: Essays on Minimalist Syntax in Honor of Howard Lasnik*, 89–155. Cambridge, MA: MIT Press.

Chomsky, N. 2001. Derivation by Phase. In Kenstowicz, M. (ed.), *Ken Hale: A Life in Language*, 1–52. Cambridge, MA: MIT Press.

Chomsky, N. 2005. Three Factors in Language Design. *Linguistic Inquiry* 36: 1–22.

Chomsky, N. 2007. Approaching UG from Below. In Sauerland, U. and Gärtner, H.-M. (eds.), *Interfaces + Recursion = Language?* 1–29. Berlin: Mouton de Gruyter.

Chomsky, N. 2008. On Phases. In Freidin, R., Otero, C. P. and Zubizarreta, M. L. (eds.), *Foundational Issues in Linguistic Theory: Essays in Honor of Jean-Roger Vergnaud*, 133–166. Cambridge, MA: MIT Press.

Chomsky, N. and Lasnik, H. 1977. Filters and Control. *Linguistic Inquiry* 8:425–504.

Chomsky, N. and Lasnik, H. 1993. The Theory of Principles and Parameters. In Jacobs, J., Von Stechow, A., Sternefeld, W. and Vennemann, T. (eds.), *Syntax: An International Handbook of Contemporary Research*, 1:506–569. Berlin: Walter de Gruyter. [Reprinted in *The Minimalist Program*, 13–127. Cambridge, MA: MIT Press, 1995.]

Collins, C. 1997. *Local Economy*. Cambridge, MA: MIT Press.

Einstein, A. 1954. *Ideas and Opinions*. New York. Bonanza Books.

Epstein, S. D. 1999. UN-principled Syntax: The Derivation of Syntactic Relations. In Epstein, S. D. and Hornstein, N. (eds.), *Working Minimalism*, 317–345. Cambridge, MA: MIT Press. [Reprinted in *Essays in Syntactic Theory*, 183–210. New York: Routledge, 2000.]

Epstein, S. D. 2007. On I(nternalist) Functional Explanation in Minimalism. *Linguistic Analysis* 33:20–53. (Originally written in 2003)

Epstein, S. D., Groat, E., Kawashima, R. and Kitahara, H. 1998. *A Derivational Approach to Syntactic Relations*. Oxford: Oxford University Press.

Epstein, S. D., Kitahara, H. and Seely, T. D. 2010. Uninterpretable Features: What Are They and What Do They Do? In Putnam, M. (ed.), *Exploring Crash-Proof Grammars*, 124–142. Language Faculty and Beyond series, Grohmann, K. and Pica, P. (series eds.). Amsterdam: John Benjamins.

Epstein, S. D., Kitahara, H. and Seely, T. D. To appear (a). Structure Building That Can't Be. In Valmala, V. and Uribe-Etxebarria, M. (eds.), *Ways of Structure Building*.

Epstein, S. D., Kitahara, H. and Seely, T. D. To appear (b). Derivations. In Boeckx, C. (ed.), *Handbook of Minimalism*. Oxford: Oxford University Press.

Epstein, S. D. and Seely, T. D. 2002. Introduction. In Epstein, S. D. and Seely, T. D. (eds.), *Derivation and Explanation in the Minimalist Program*, 1–18. Oxford: Blackwell.

Epstein, S. D. and Seely, T. D. 2006. *Derivations in Minimalism*. Cambridge: Cambridge University Press.

Fiengo, R. 1977. On Trace Theory. *Linguistic Inquiry* 8:35–62.

Freidin, R. and Lasnik, H. 1981. Disjoint Reference and WH-Trace. *Linguistic Inquiry* 12:39–53.

Fukui, N. 1986. A Theory of Category Projection and Its Applications. Doctoral dissertation, MIT, Cambridge, MA.

Huang, C.-T. J. 1982. Logical Relations in Chinese and the Theory of Grammar. Doctoral dissertation, MIT, Cambridge, MA.

Jackendoff, R. 1972. *Semantic Interpretation in Generative Grammar*. Cambridge, MA: MIT Press.

Jackendoff, R. 1977. *X-bar Syntax: A Study of Phrase Structure*. Cambridge, MA: MIT Press.

Kayne, R. 1981. Unambiguous Paths. In May, R. and Koster, J. (eds.), *Levels of Syntactic Representation*, 143–185. New York: Mouton de Gruyter.

Kayne, R. 1994. *The Antisymmetry of Syntax*. Cambridge, MA: MIT Press.

Kitahara, H. 1995. Target α: Deducing Strict Cyclicity from Derivational Economy. *Linguistic Inquiry* 26:47–77.

Kitahara, H. 1997. *Elementary Operation and Optimal Derivations*. Cambridge, MA: MIT Press.

Lasnik, H. 1981. Restricting the Theory of Transformations. In Hornstein, N. and Lightfoot, D. (eds.), *Explanation in Linguistics*, 152–173. London: Longmans.

Lasnik, H. 2002. The Minimalist Program in Syntax. *Trends in Cognitive Sciences* 6:432–437.

Lasnik, H. and Lohndal, T. 2010. Government-Binding/Principles & Parameters Theory. *Wiley Interdisciplinary Reviews: Cognitive Science* 1:40–50.

Lasnik, H. and Saito, M. 1984. On the Nature of Proper Government. *Linguistic Inquiry* 15:235–289.

Lasnik, H. and Saito, M. 1992. *Move α*. Cambridge, MA: MIT Press.

McCloskey, J. 1979. *Transformational Syntax and Model Theoretic Semantics: A Case-Study in Modern Irish*. Dordrecht: D. Reidel.

McCloskey, J. 2002. Resumption, Successive Cyclicity, and the Locality of Operations. In Epstein, S. D. and Seely, T. D. (eds.), *Derivation and Explanation*, 184–226. Oxford: Blackwell.

Pollock, J.-Y. 1989. Verb Movement, UG and the Structure of IP. *Linguistic Inquiry* 20:365–424.

Richards, M. 2007. On Feature Inheritance: An Argument from the Phase Impenetrability Condition. *Linguistic Inquiry* 38:563–572.

Rizzi, L. 1986. On Chain Formation. In Borer, H. (ed.), *The Grammar of Pronominal Clitics*, 65–95. Syntax and Semantics 19. New York: Academic Press.

Rizzi, L. 1990. *Relativized Minimality*. Cambridge, MA: MIT Press.

Ross, J. R. 1967. *Constraints on Variables in Syntax*. Doctoral dissertation, MIT, Cambridge, MA.

Sportiche, D. 1983. *Structural Invariance and Symmetry in Syntax*. Doctoral dissertation, MIT, Cambridge, MA.

Torrego, E. 1984. On Inversion in Spanish and Some of Its Effects. *Linguistic Inquiry* 15:103–129.

Uriagereka, J. 1999. Multiple Spell-Out. In Epstein, S. and Hornstein, N. (eds.), *Working Minimalism*, 317–345. Cambridge, MA: MIT Press.

Zwart, C. J.-W. 1996. "Shortest Move" versus "Fewest Steps." In Abraham, W., Epstein, S. D., Thráinsson, H. and Zwart, C. J.-W. (eds.), *Minimal Ideas*, 305–327. Amsterdam: John Benjamins.

3 Exploring Phase-Based Implications Regarding Clausal Architecture. A Case Study

Why Structural Case Cannot Precede Theta

Samuel D. Epstein, Hisatsugu Kitahara, and T. Daniel Seely

1 INTRODUCTION

There exists in contemporary theories of syntax a widely adopted hypothesis that syntactic representations of sentential phenomena exhibit a hierarchically organized clausal architecture. Essentially, there is the theta domain, above that the Case domain, and finally the scope domain. Why should this be true? Is it to be stipulated, or can aspects of clausal architecture be derived, within a level-free phase-based framework? More generally, might aspects of clausal architecture in mental representations be deduced from the architecture of Universal Grammar and 3rd factor principles? We suggest that (at least to some degree, and perhaps even more than we explore here) the answer is yes.

The history of the development of syntax has witnessed different approaches to basic clausal architecture. For example, within Government and Binding (GB) theory an argument DP could not be assigned structural Case *before* it was assigned a theta role. Why? This was a result of a conspiracy of the following "GB architectural axioms":

(1) The postulation of an "all at once" D-structure (DS) level of representation
(2) The application of the Theta Criterion at DS

An argument DP in a non-theta position at DS (the point of its "syntactic birth") violates the Theta Criterion at this level of representation (by definition), and the reception by DP of a theta role later on could have no effect (positive or otherwise) on this DS offense. At S-structure (SS) the argument DP might have both a theta role and structural Case,[1] but within GB, this is insufficient; it is simply "too late": Given the *stipulated* architecture of the GB system, the DP must get its theta role "first" at the initial level of DS and so could never possibly be assigned structural Case before receiving a theta role.

But within the more recent Minimalist Program (MP), where syntax-internal levels of representation including DS and SS are eliminated, such an axiomatic description of clausal architectural hierarchy is impossible; indeed, since there *is* no DS nor SS, the "conspiracy" indicated above, induced by ordering DS before SS and stipulating that certain filters (theta) do apply at DS while others apply at a subsequent level of representation (the Case Filter), can't even be formulated in the MP. For the MP, there are no non-interface levels such as DS and SS, and hence there is no ordering of them, and no syntactic filters apply internal to the narrow syntax. What then becomes of properties of clausal architecture for the MP? Must we adopt *stipulations*, such as that from Chomsky (2000) that an argument must be first merged into a theta position (which implies the existence of special properties of *first* Merger and of *argument* merger, as well)? How much, if any, of the attested clausal architecture, theta and then Case (and then scope), can be *explained* by being deduced from independently motivated components of the framework?

This paper explores this question, suggesting that at least some properties of clausal architecture may be deducible within the MP, specifically from the analysis of Chomsky (2008).[2] We explore the idea that Case before theta invariably results in crashing and/or interface gibberish (a violation of Full Interpretation (FI) at the conceptual-intentional (CI) interface) even within the level-less, optimality-seeking filter free minimalist system of Chomsky (2008). One central aspect of clausal architecture is shown to be deducible from Chomsky's current analysis, following strict minimalist tenets, positing nothing beyond irreducible lexical features, natural (and independently motivated) interface conditions, and 3rd factor considerations expressing optimality-seeking minimalist design. If on track, this provides another deep explanatory improvement over the level-ordered GB system, within which clausal architecture follows only from stipulated aspects of level ordering (DS precedes SS) and unexplained stipulations as to which filters apply at which levels and which do not (the Theta Criterion, but not the Case Filter, applies at DS).

2   UNDER THE PHASE-BASED FEATURE-INHERITANCE ANALYSIS STRUCTURAL CASE CANNOT PRECEDE THETA-MARKING

2.1   Phase Heads and Feature-Inheritance

Within Chomsky's (2008) analysis, the lexical entries for the phase heads (C and *v*) inherently contain unvalued phi features.[3] The valuation of a DP's structural Case feature is achieved via phi-feature agreement (under the probe-goal analysis) with a phase head.[4] But there is no *direct* agreement between the Probing phase head (C or *v*) and the DP goal that gets Case-valued. Rather, the phase head must first transmit its phi features to the head of its complement (see Chomsky 2007, 2008; Richards 2007).[5]

The head of the phase complement, in turn, agrees with the goal DP, valuing that DP's Case. Why does the phase head C transmit its phi features to its complement head T, as the phase head *v* does to its complement head V, thereby allowing T and V to induce Agree (i.e. feature valuation)?

Such feature-transmission is itself explicable, and need not be stipulated, since, on independent grounds, syntactically valued features (such as valued φ) appearing on a phase-edge will invariably induce crash at the CI interface, as insightfully explained by Chomsky (2008) and Richards (2007).[6] Simply put: phi-feature transmission must occur since, if it doesn't, convergence would be impossible. Chomsky (2001:5) proposed that "the uninterpretable features, and only these, enter the derivation without values, and are distinguished [in the narrow syntax, SDE, TDS, HK] from interpretable features by virtue of this property."[7] This proposal predicts that the distinction between unvalued and valued features is lost in the eyes of Transfer at the moment such unvalued features change from unvalued to valued. Once unvalued features get valued, they will be regarded just like inherently valued features, and thus Transfer cannot ("know" to) remove them since Transfer is a purely formal non-interpretive operation and hence knows nothing about interpretability at the (not-yet-reached) interface. However, even though non-interpretive and non-look-ahead, Transfer *can* see (purely formal) feature values and can make its decision regarding what to Transfer where based on these detectable formal feature values. The valuation analysis, however, confronts the so-called before-and-after problem—a problem regarding the exact timing of Transfer application. Transferring features before valuation is too early (i.e. unvalued features cause crash at the interface), and transferring features after they are valued is too late (i.e. after valuation, Transfer cannot remove valued features, also leading to crash). For example, Transfer cannot distinguish a valued phi feature on a DP from a valued phi feature on Tense—they are identically valued phi features in the eyes of Transfer, which, as a result, cannot discern that the valued phi features in T *will be* uninterpretable at CI, while the valued φ on DP *will be* interpretable at CI (see Epstein and Seely 2002 for detailed discussion and possible solutions). To solve this problem, Transfer must remove unvalued features at the point of their valuation. Thus, Chomsky (elegantly) seeks to explain cyclic phasal Transfer, not just stipulate it. As Chomsky (2008:19), echoing Chomsky (2001), states:

> If transferred to the interface unvalued, uninterpretable features will cause the derivation to crash. Hence both interface conditions require that they cannot be valued after Transfer. Once valued, uninterpretable features may or may not be assigned a phonetic interpretation (and in either case are eliminated before the SM [sensorimotor] interface), but they still have no semantic interpretation. Therefore they must be removed when transferred to the CI interface. Furthermore, this operation cannot take place after the phase level at which they are valued, because once valued, they are indistinguishable at the next phase level

from interpretable features, hence will not be deleted [by Transfer, SDE, HK, TDS] before reaching the CI interface. It follows that they must be valued at the phase level where they are transferred . . .

As illustration of this motivation for feature-inheritance whereby phi features must be moved from a phase head to the head of the phase head complement, consider (3).

(3) $[_{CP}$ Cφ $[_{TP}$ T $[_{vP}$ Sue $[v\ v^*$ $[_{VP}$ jumped$]]]]]$

The phase head C (inherently) bears phi features, while T does not. If C does not transmit its phi features to T, there could (in principle) be direct Agree (C, *Sue*) valuing φ of C and Case of *Sue*.[8] However, since C is a phase head, the TP complement of C will be transferred given the Phase Impenetrability Condition (PIC),[9] and only C (the phase-edge) remains. The problem, however, is that now the "derivational history" of the valuation of C's phi features (which happened via agreement with *Sue*) is representationally unrecoverable since the TP containing *Sue* has been transferred (under the PIC). Consequently, at the next phase level, Transfer will only "see" the now-valued phi features of C and will not have access to the information it needs—that these features were previously unvalued and became valued via Agree with a DP goal within TP (now gone). Consequently, Transfer cannot then "know" to remove these phi features from the CI-bound object; i.e. in the eyes of the non-interpretive operation Transfer, the valued φ on C (which need to be removed for CI convergence, since they are uninterpretable) are identical to the valued phi features on N, which are NOT to be removed. It follows, then, that C must transmit its phi features to T, allowing for Agree (T, *Sue*).[10] Internal to the TP (the phase head complement), Transfer can see that φ of T and Case of *Sue* went from unvalued to valued and thus must be removed from the CI-bound object, avoiding (correctly in this instance) CI crash.

To summarize, for Chomsky (2008) the phase heads C and *v* inherently bear phi features as a lexical property. Given the nature of valuation and the PIC, it follows that C/*v* must transmit these phi features to T/V, and T/V in turn must Agree with a minimally searchable nominal. Failure to transmit φ yields crash at the next phase. This analysis has a further, and unnoted, consequence; namely theta "assignment" must take place before structural Case-valuation, the details of which we reveal in the next section.

2.2   Feature-Transmission + Agree + PIC Entails: Structural Case Cannot Precede Theta-Marking

Minimalist analysis seeks to eliminate non-interface, syntax-internal levels of representation, such as GB theory's DS and SS, deriving their properties from (i) irreducible lexical features; (ii) interface conditions, the conditions that narrow syntax must satisfy to be "usable at all" by the systems with which it interacts (see Epstein 2007 for discussion of this Internalist Functionalism approach); and (iii) general properties, including those associated with optimal computation (3rd factor considerations; Chomsky 2005).

As noted, it has long been stipulated that structural Case assignment cannot precede theta role assignment; i.e. the clausal architecture is theta, then Case, then scope.[11] Interestingly, the same conclusion is (attractively) *deducible* from postulates of the minimalist analysis reviewed above, which has no syntax-internal levels, hence no level ordering, and no syntax-internal filters either. That structural Case cannot precede theta-marking is deducible from principles motivated on entirely independent grounds unrelated to Theta Theory. The short story is this: Any instance of a DP first merged into a non-theta, structural Case position by External Merge (EM), and then "moved into" a theta position by Internal Merge (IM), will necessarily result in that DP being problematic for the CI interface; i.e. a convergent, non-gibberish expression can be derived only if theta precedes Case.

Here we provide a reductio argument; i.e. we will provide the necessary properties of any derivation in which structural Case *is* assigned before theta and will show that it either crashes or else yields convergent gibberish at the CI interface. To illustrate, consider the DP in (4):[12]

(4) DP   where DP is an argument, and
    vl φ DP bears inherently valued phi features, and
    u Case   DP bears an unvalued Case feature

In order to value the Case of this DP, before assigning it a theta role, we must merge in a Case-valuing category and we must do so before any theta assigner is externally merged in such a way as to assign the DP a theta role. Suppose, for purposes of illustration, that the potential Case-valuer T is externally merged in:[13]

(5)[14] T > . . . > DP   where ". . ." may contain other categories but contains no theta assigner of DP, and therefore DP is not in a theta position

Now, for T to actually value Case on DP (prior to DP receiving theta) two prerequisite conditions must be met:

(6) In order for Agree (T, DP) to take place,
    a. there must be no phase head intervening between T and DP. This follows from the PIC: Such a phase head would induce Transfer and (given the PIC) DP would in effect be "gone," and hence unavailable for probe by T, and hence unavailable for Agree (T, DP), and
    b. T must inherit phi features from C.[15]

Thus, C must be externally merged with the T-projection so that C (lexically bearing unvalued phi features) can transmit φ to T.

Thus, the relevant configuration for structural Case-valuation before theta assignment would (have to) be of the following form:

(7) $C u\varphi + [_{TP} T > \ldots > DP v l \varphi / u Case]$
where "..." contains no phase head and no theta marker of DP, and therefore DP is *not* in a theta configuration

As discussed above, C must transmit its phi features to T; otherwise, the phi features would be stranded on the edge of C (causing crash at the next phase). Thus:

(8) Phi Feature Inheritance, from C to T:

$$C + [_{TP} T \quad \ldots \quad DP]$$

$$u\text{Phi} \quad v l \text{Phi} \quad u\text{Case}$$

where "..." contains no phase head and no theta marker of DP, and therefore DP is *not* in a theta configuration

Once T receives phi features from C, T can φ-probe DP and (since, by assumption, all relevant conditions are met) Agree (T, DP) can take place, valuing the phi features of T and nominative Case of DP:

(9) Result of Agree (T, DP):
$C + [_{TP} T v l \varphi > \ldots > DP v l \varphi / \text{Nom}]$
where "..." contains no phase head and no theta marker of DP, and therefore DP is *not* in a theta configuration

We have thus reached the first step in our reductio argument; i.e. we have performed a derivation in which valued structural Case on an argument DP is valued before assigning DP a theta role. But what happens next? By the PIC, Transfer of TP applies to (9).[16] Thus, the TP complement of the phase head C is transferred to the phonological component and transferred (minus CI-illegitimate features like structural Case) to the semantic component. What enters the semantic component, therefore, is

(10) $[T > \ldots > DP]$ where, crucially, DP is *not* in a theta configuration

That is, the DP has no theta role in the CI representation of the transferred TP. Thus, a "Theta Criterion" violation at CI results. But what exactly becomes of the "Theta Criterion," a GB postulate, within Minimalism? The relevant and more general CI interface condition in this instance is the arguably ineliminable principle of FI (Chomsky 1986); the DP itself can be interpreted, but it will have no computable semantic (i.e. theta) *relation* with anything else in the given local structure; no coherent compositional semantic relation *between* DP and the rest of the structure can be established. Thus, CI representations such as (10) will have essentially the same status as, say, *John seems that Sue sleeps* (which were called "Theta Criterion violations" in GB parlance) wherein *John* has its Case checked but has no semantic/theta relation to the rest of the sentence, yielding convergent gibberish at CI. The kind of strings receiving the analysis in (10) above include, for example

(11) [$_{CP}$ C = *that* [$_{TP}$ T = *is* . . . DP = *John*]
         for   to   John
         if   is   John
         "that/for/if . . . is/to . . . John"

Structural case (NOM) is valued, but no theta role is assigned, and the result is that the transferred TP is (correctly) predicted to be convergent gibberish at CI, the only level of representation at which it "makes sense" to apply interpretive conditions like the "Theta Criterion" (reconstrued as a facet of the far more general principle of FI). The prediction is obtained with no Theta Criterion stipulated to apply at a syntax-internal, all-at-once, derivation-initiating DS level of representation.

It thus seems to be a property of the system that if *any* gibberish (i.e. a single transferred gibberish phase head complement (henceforth, PHC)) reaches the CI interface, the entire subsequent derivation is semantically doomed to gibberish. That is, "gibberish of the part entails gibberish of the whole." Indeed, to say that PHCs are cyclically transferred *to the interface* is to say that they periodically do undergo interpretation at the interface. (Thus, semantic compositional recycling at LF, i.e. doing bottom-up compositional interpretation on an entire already built-up LF representation, as in GB, is avoided (Epstein et al. 1998). Given this, the appearance of any gibberish at the interface naturally entails a gibberish final complete sentential CI representation. Every PHC (each a syntactic object) is transferred to both PHON and SEM for interpretation. In SEM the object is converted into a semantic representation. If the object contains a "free" argument, unrelated semantically to the rest of the local representation, i.e. thematically unrelated to the rest of the transferred PHC, then that structure violates FI as gibberish. Crucially, once interpreted at SEM, the object is given over to CI, and now *no further semantic operations apply to its internal (gibberish) semantics*. It doesn't matter that the transferred PHCs will be combined at CI in assembling the complete, multiphasal sentential CI representation. The internal semantic interpretation of the PHC is done, and so no combination of the entire PHC with some other PHC(s) can salvage the PHC-internal gibberish. Thus, once a PHC is gibberish, it is impossible to continue the derivation and overcome this gibberish. To illustrate the immutability of a gibberish PHC, let's reconsider our core case where an argument DP begins in a non-theta position and has its Case checked; but now suppose it "escapes" the PHC and moves into a theta position,

(12) DP ... PH [$_{PHC}$ ... DP ...]

Although the argument DP has itself acquired a theta role (by assumption), the PHC now containing the copy of the argument DP (i.e. [$_{PHC}$ ... DP[–theta] ...] in (12)) will be transferred to PHON and SEM. In SEM this syntactic object will be converted into a semantic representation that will be gibberish in that the argument DP (copy) has no theta relation to the rest of the transferred PHC of which it is a part. This semantic representation is then given over to CI. Later, other PHCs of this syntactic derivation (and the root phase) will get transferred to SEM, and their internal semantics will be computed individually. Ultimately, these semantic representations will be connected together at CI, yielding the entire sentential CI representation (Root + PHC + PHC + PHC . . .). But the local *PHC-internal* gibberish could not be "corrected" or "repaired" by assembly of this *entire PHC* with another PHC or root. If this line of reasoning is on track, any gibberish within a transferred PHC entails gibberish in the final multiphasal complete sentential CI representation. If this logic is correct, the central argument of our paper is complete. Given general semantic considerations, phase-by-phase derivation with phase-by-phase semantic compositional interpretation at the interfaces yields the desired result: Structural Case-valuation before theta-"marking" cannot possibly yield convergent non-gibberish, and there need be no appeal to syntax-internal levels of representation, or constraints on external first Merge of arguments.

While we believe this argument to be very much on track, we could, of course, have it wrong. A counterargument might run as follows:

2.3   A Possible Counterargument against "Once Gibberish, Always Gibberish"

It might be argued that the PHC-internal gibberish *can* be repaired, so that even though a single transferred PHC has internal gibberish, subsequent derivation can nonetheless assemble a complete, multiphasal sentential CI representation in which there is no gibberish whatsoever. For example, an argument DP first merged in a non-theta position could move to a theta position, and in so doing it could "count" as having satisfied FI (since in the final multiphasal CI representation of the entire sentence, the argument has a theta role, i.e. appears in a theta configuration). To illustrate, consider again the situation where a transferred PHC is indeed gibberish. Suppose in the derivational continuation, the theta-less DP inside this PHC were to subsequently move to acquire a theta role (via the edge of the phase, as in (12)) or acquire a theta role phase-internally. In the final complete sentential CI representation reassembling all the cyclically transferred individual PHCs, the DP argument has a theta role, i.e. is in a theta position, and this "negates" or "cancels out" or "repairs" the prior gibberish internal to the individually transferred PHC. In the complete CI representation, although there is a copy of the argument DP in non-theta position, the argument has moved to a theta position, and so the chain in the complete CI representation *does* contain a theta position.[17]

The status of this counterargument to our above claim that "[i]f a PHC contains gibberish, then the entire CI representation containing this PHC will necessarily contain gibberish" is not entirely clear to us. And since we are unsure of this counterargument's status, let us tentatively assume it is right, thereby creating the "most trouble" for our proposal that we can. In the following sections, we explore just such derivations, ones in which the argument DP, first merged into a non-theta position, moves to get a theta role. There are two general types of cases: movement through the edge to get theta and within-phase movement to a theta position. Interestingly, we will argue that neither can possibly yield convergent non-gibberish. Thus, the overall logic is as follows: If "once gibberish, always gibberish" is right, and the counterargument is wrong, then we have explained what we set out to explain. If "once gibberish, always gibberish" is wrong, and the counterargument is right, we hope to show in the following sections that any attempt to repair gibberish by movement of an argument to a theta position is independently excluded. If "once gibberish always gibberish" is true of the system and in addition movement to overcome gibberish is indeed barred by the system, then we may be revealing in the following sections a redundancy in the system whereby BOTH first Merge of an argument in [−theta] condemns the complete derivation to immutable gibberish AND any movement of the argument to acquire theta is also excluded.

3   MOVEMENT TO ACQUIRE THETA

Suppose a DP has checked its Case but has no theta role: Could the DP *move into* a theta configuration,[18,19] thereby yielding Case before theta, with no gibberish in the final reassembled multiphasal CI representation? A number of independently motivated mechanisms within current theory mitigate against this possibility. Again, the situation we are considering is depicted in (13),

(13) . . . > PH > . . . > DP

   where DP has its Case checked by the phase head (PH) but that DP has no theta relation. Our question is: Can the DP move to the edge of the phase to be available for movement *into* a theta position, ultimately yielding convergent non-gibberish?

3.1   Theta Configurations

In Chomsky (1995) and his subsequent work (including Chomsky 2008), Hale and Keyser's (1993) configurational approach to theta relations is adopted. Under this approach, a "theta role" is "a relation between two syntactic objects, a configuration, and an expression selected by its head" (Chomsky 2000:103). Basically, an argument DP receives a theta role by being in a configuration with a theta assigner X only if DP is in a sister relation to X.[20]

3.1.1   *Theta Configurations and Chains*

But what counts as a syntactic object in a sister relation to X? More generally, just what counts as an argument? Chomsky (1995:313) states that only a trivial chain (i.e. a one-membered chain) can be in a sister relation. Thus, if an argument DP is externally merged (EM) with X, forming a one-membered chain CH (DP^1), then CH (DP^1) is in a sister relation to X; the DP would count as an argument in a theta configuration. However, for Chomsky, if Internal Merge (IM) subsequently merges DP with Y, forming a two-membered chain CH (DP^2, DP^1), then *neither* the entire chain CH (DP^2, DP^1) *nor* the head of the chain, DP^2, is in a sister relation to any configuration (including Y). In effect, it is only the tail of a movement chain that counts as an argument, i.e. as an object in a sister relation to X. Thus, the tail of CH (DP^2, DP^1) is (still) in a sister relation to X, thereby being capable of receiving a theta role from X. In short, it is a theorem of this approach that only EM (forming a one-membered chain) can form a configuration for thematic interpretation, thereby excluding movement (IM) of a theta-less argument DP *into* a theta relation; if the DP is to have a theta role, it must be EM'ed (i.e. first merged) into a theta relation.

The status of a chain-theoretic principle like the above is not clear; it is stipulative to the extent that it is stated rather than derived. Why, on a deeper level, should such a principle hold?

3.2   Theta Configurations and Movement to Complement Position

Interestingly, certain independently motivated aspects of Chomsky (2008) prohibit movement of a theta-less argument from its non-theta position into a theta-marked *complement* position. It is thus unnecessary to adopt/stipulate the chain-theoretic principle regarding argument positions reviewed above to exclude such cases. We will argue here that, in fact, there is no movement to a complement position, and hence there is no chance for a DP to move from a non-theta position to a theta position.

First, assume with Chomsky (2008) that each lexical array must contain a PH, v or C.[21] Let's also assume with Chomsky that all EM takes place before any IM, this too being motivated on efficiency grounds. Finally, assume Chomsky's Label Accessibility Condition (LAC), also independently motivated, which states that only the label of a syntactic object is accessible to the computational component (since only the label is available with minimal search).

With these three (arguably 3rd factor) independently motivated assumptions, we can derive that "there can be no movement to a complement theta position." How does this follow? Recall the configuration we're considering:

(14)   [. . . DP PH . . . [. . . DP . . .]]

where the argument DP is first merged into a position P in which its Case is valued but P is not a theta configuration; DP then moves to the edge of the phase to be accessible for further computation (given the PIC). Suppose we now externally merge in the theta assigner head, e.g. V (or N or Adj).

(15)   V + [DP [PH [. . . DP . . .]]]

At this point in the derivation, there is simply *no way* to create a structure where DP becomes the complement (sister/co-member) of V. By virtue of V externally merging to the object *containing* DP, V already has a sister, viz. the object containing the DP. No *new* sister relation involving just DP and V can now arise.[22] Thus, without stipulation, it follows from the independently motivated principles (i) each array contains a PH, (ii) EM before IM, and (iii) LAC *that the sister to a theta-marking head can never be created by IM*. One class of cases of an argument first merged into a (Case-valued) non-theta configuration but subsequently IM'ed to acquire theta is not possible, namely movement of an argument from a non-theta configuration into a complement theta position.

3.3   Movement to Spec of v'

What about movement of a theta-less Case-valued argument to a non-complement theta position, e.g. [Spec, v']? Consider first the spec of v' position, i.e. the "agentive subject position." Again, suppose an argument DP has its Case valued, that the DP has no theta role, and that the DP has moved to the edge of the phase and hence is available, in principle, for movement *to* a theta position:

(16)   DP + PH [. . . DP . . .] (= CP or vP)
       where DP had its Case checked and has moved to the edge of the phase to escape the PIC, but DP has no theta role.

Suppose we Transfer the PHC and then Merge in V,

(17) V + [DP PH]

and then Merge in the PH (e.g. v):

(18) v + [V [DP PH]

The PH v transmits its phi features to V, allowing V to now function as a φ-probe. V then tries to agree with DP, the only visible matching goal, given that the PHC has been transferred. But notice, if there is an activity condition, then since DP is already inactive (due to its Case feature being valued prior to its moving to the edge), the derivation crashes since v/V can't check phi features with a visible active goal; i.e. the previously Case-valued DP on the edge is the only visible goal in the current representation, but it is inactive.[23]

But what if there is no Activity Condition (as argued in Nevins 2005)? Without Activity, v/V could in principle φ-agree with the inactivated DP, thereby valuing V's unvalued φ (inherited from v), and the DP could then simultaneously raise (following Chomsky) to both [Spec, VP] and [Spec, vP], yielding the following DP movement configuration

(19) [$_{vP}$ DP v [$_{VP}$ DP V [$_{CP}$ DP (on edge) C [$_{TP}$ DP(EPP) T DP$_{NOM/-THETA}$

Now, at last, the (leftmost) DP would "get" a theta role from the v' (in Spec, vP position = external argument theta role position). Thus, although an earlier transferred PHC (TP) contained a theta-less argument, with this transferred PHC therefore violating FI at CI, why is this "still" an "offense" if, in the final completely reassembled multiphasal CI representation of the entire sentence, Case is valued and the DP argument is in a theta configuration—as in (19)? As we detailed above (section 2) it could well be that gibberish of the part in fact yields gibberish of the whole, this being a natural consequence of cyclic Transfer to the interfaces with cyclic interpretation. But note that even if local PHC gibberish could in principle be salvaged or corrected, such derivations can be independently excluded: The argument DP has moved "improperly" from A'-position (phase-edge = [Spec, CP]) and then to an A-position, namely Spec of V.

This is indeed A'-to-A-movement if we adopt

(20) Chomsky (2007:24): "A movement is IM (internal merge) contingent on probe by uninterpretable inflectional features, while A-bar movement is IM driven by EF."

By this definition, [Spec, VP] is an A-position (since V φ-probed DP, which then moved to [Spec, VP]) and [Spec, vP] is A', since this movement involved only the edge feature of v.

But why/how is improper movement excluded? Obata and Epstein (2007, 2011) argue that improper movement is an agreement phenomenon, hence parameterized. In their analysis this derivation crashes because the phi features of v-V find no matching goal in the DP occupying Spec-embedded CP. This is because the phi features of DP are moved to the A-position, Spec, TP under their "Feature Splitting Internal Merge" analysis, and hence DP at the edge lacks phi features. Thus, improper movement crashes, since DP at the edge has no φ, yet the theta marker introduced to assign DP theta in (19), namely v, inherently bears phi features, but they cannot be valued since DP at the edge of CP is φ-less (and, of course, the embedded TP is gone, so DP on the edge is the only visible/present goal). Thus, this kind of derivation in which the argument is first merged into a Case-valued theta-less position and then moves to a non-complement position to get theta crashes. Regardless, it has been assumed since 1973 that such derivations are in fact blocked (Chomsky 1973) or that the representation resulting from such movement is independently excluded (by Binding theory condition C; May 1979 or Fukui 1993). Thus, interphasal movement of an argument DP so as to acquire its first theta role, as in (19), is "improper" and by assumption excluded by independently motivated principles seemingly unrelated to "First merge of an argument must be into a theta position."

Thus, to summarize, perhaps gibberish of the part (a transferred PHC) entails gibberish of the whole. But, if not, we have now excluded central cases in which the theta-less DP copy is transferred to CI, yet the moved DP tries to get a theta role via IM; one case was movement to complement position, which is independently excluded; another is movement to non-complement position ([Spec, vP]), which as just shown is also excluded. Thus, even if gibberish of the part does not entail gibberish of the whole, a theta-less DP cannot "escape via the edge" in order to acquire its first theta role.

3.4   Exceptional Case Marking

But, now, what about intra-phasal movement of a DP, within a single phase, to acquire a theta role? In such cases, movement via an edge position would not be required, and, as a result, the movement would not be improper. Such cases are exemplified by ECM constructions, as in, for example:

(21) $[_{vP}$ John v [Vexpect $[_{TP}$ t_{John} to seem $[_{CP}$ that Bill left]]]]
      = *John expect to seem that Bill left

Interestingly, there seems to be nothing wrong with this string "as a vP"; i.e. if the derivation is now complete (and notice that *expect* has no agreement suffix since no φ-agreeing T appears above vP) and will not continue on, this vP converges. However, without the mood marker C, the object is still gibberish in that it will have no interpretation as "declarative," "imperative," etc.

Suppose we continue the derivation so that we generate a full CP representation of the string "John expects to seem that Bill left." This entails externally merging T and then C.

(22) C . . . T + (21)

But now, assuming the feature-splitting analysis of Obata and Epstein traced above, recall that *John* at the edge—in this case, the edge of vP in (18)—no longer bears phi features, since these features were split off and moved to the A-position, [Spec, VP]. Thus, the phi features on the matrix T, inherited from the matrix C, find no matching goal on the edge of v, and since VP and its contents are "gone" by the PIC, the derivation crashes with unvalued φ on the higher T.

4   CONCLUSION AND SPECULATION CONCERNING SCOPE POSITIONS IN CLAUSAL ARCHITECTURE

We argued that certain aspects of clausal architecture are deducible from independently motivated mechanisms of Chomsky's phase-based analysis. To summarize, if you first merge an argument DP in a non-theta position and are able to check that DP's Case, the transferred PHC containing the DP is gibberish. We argued that "once gibberish, always gibberish" follows from the architectural design whereby PHCs are periodically transferred to and interpreted by the interfaces; specifically, once a PHC is transferred to the interface, its internal interpretation is immutable and simply can't be "repaired" by assembly of the entire PHC with other PHCs. But we've also argued that even if gibberish can (somehow) be salvaged, independently motivated components of Chomsky's analysis still correctly disallow the relevant structures. Thus, theta before Case (and not Case before theta) is deduced within Chomsky's system with no appeal to syntax-internal ordered levels of representation.

If on track, this is just a case study of one aspect of clausal architecture that might be explicable by minimalist 3rd factor postulates (phasal, episodic Transfer, CI is the only level of representation undergoing semantic interpretation, including the Theta Criterion being reduced to FI), which were motivated on grounds having nothing to do with the phenomena examined here. A much larger project consists of systematically determining which aspects of articulated clausal architecture can and cannot be deduced (beyond Case can't precede theta). Toward this end, we note that Case and scope are both non-thematic, so why is scope above Case in the clausal architecture and not the other way around? One answer is that if scope is related to the phase head C (left periphery is headed by a PH), then if we did theta first, and then did scope (IM to edge CP), the next thing that happens is Transfer of TP by the PIC. But this crashes since DP has unvalued Case.

So if we have successive IM of a single DP as follows, with theta before Case (as argued above), but scope below Case,

(23) DP (CASE)   DP(scope) PH [$_{PHC}$ DP (theta) . . .
    3rd   2nd   1st

we would end up transferring the PHC, but the transferred DP within the PHC still has unvalued Case. If a crashed PHC that has been transferred to the interface cannot be salvaged (de-crashed) by subsequent derivation (since computational (local) efficiency dictates that crash ends the derivation; i.e. we don't continue the derivation ad infinitum to "see" if we can overcome the crash), then we have an explanation of why scope is above Case in the clausal architecture and not the other way around. If on track, then we have gone some distance toward explaining clausal architecture and operational ordering without appealing to descriptive rule ordering and without ordered levels of syntax-internal representation (DS < SS < LF), as in GB.

NOTES

We are also extremely grateful to Angel Gallego for his patience, his interest in our research, and all the work he did as creator and editor of the volume in which this paper originally appeared.

1. Thus, at SS the Case Filter would be satisfied.
2. Our focus is on the Case and theta domains although we do speculate about scope in section 3.
3. Chomsky (2008) argues that the apparent phase-head properties of T are in fact derivative from C: ". . . for T, φ-features and Tense appear to be derivative, not inherent: basic tense and also tense-like properties (e.g. irrealis) are determined by C (in which they are inherent . . .) . . ." (p. 143). Moreover, "[o]n optimal assumptions, transmission of the Agree feature should be a property of phase-heads in general, not just of C. Hence v^* should transmit its Agree feature to V . . ." (p. 148). And, finally, "C and v^* are the phase heads, and their Agree feature is inherited by the LI they select" (p. 148). Chomsky (2007, 2008) provides empirical and conceptual support for this proposal. See also the important discussion of Richards (2007).
4. It is important to note that we focus in this paper on structural Case, valued on DP under φ-feature agreement with a probe following Chomsky (2007, 2008) and provide no discussion or analysis of inherent Case. Furthermore, our central concern is Nom and Acc.
5. We leave aside whether tense is also transmitted from C to T. See Chomsky (2007:20) for discussion.
6. See Epstein and Seely (2002) and Epstein, Kitahara, and Seely (2010) for detailed discussion.
7. The same argument applies to valued Case on e.g. a *wh*-phrase moved to the edge; see Epstein, Kitahara, and Seely (2010); Obata and Epstein (2012); and Obata (2010).
8. Movement of *Sue* (to Spec-TP) triggered by Extended Projection Principle is ignored here, since it is not relevant for our discussion.

9. The PIC states that the complement of a phase head is transferred to the interfaces (as soon as the phase is completed), and this complement is "gone" thereafter in the derivation. Thus, Chomsky (2008:143) states: "For minimal computation, as soon as the information is transferred it will be forgotten, not accessed in subsequent stages of derivation: the computation will not have to look back at earlier phases as it proceeds, and cyclicity is preserved in a very strong sense."

10. And, similarly, v^* transfers its phi features to V. See Richards (2007).

11. GB architecture (assuming DS, SS and LF) in effect.

12. The symbol vl before a feature represents "valued feature," and u represents "unvalued feature."

13. Parallel reasoning holds for any other structural Case assigning head, for example, the potential Case-valuer V. We leave open what the structural Case-valuing heads are beyond T and V, e.g. P and possibly other heads.

14. One possibility is that T and the DP are externally Merged together. If we can show that this too yields "theta' gibberish" at the interface, then we have an argument that certain aspects of stipulated selectional properties (T selects vP, and hence T does NOT select e.g. DP) can be explained, without appeal to selection—which would be a significant simplification of the lexicon; see, for example, Boeckx (2008).

15. Strictly speaking, T could inherit φ-features just as well if it were selected by the phase head v. Similarly, V could inherit φ from a selecting C. That these selectional relations/clausal architectures do not occur seems to us at present to require lexical selectional requirements to account for such phenomena— i.e. this aspect of clausal architecture is not deducible from just inheritance, Agree, and Case-valuation, which by themselves allow any phase head to select any non-phase head. As Richards (2007) notes, a phase head must select a non-phase head, which can be the receptacle of the phase head's φ-features. But this alone fails to explain e.g. why T is the complement of C whereas V is not the complement of C, at least in standard clausal architecture.

16. Again, movement of DP (to [Spec, TP]) triggered by EPP is ignored here, since not relevant for our discussion.

17. One could of course respond as follows: "Yes, the gibberish is overcome/corrected, but the A-chain tail, not the head, must occupy the theta position in an A chain." But of course that is to stipulate that first Merge of an argument must be in a +theta position, yet this is one aspect of what we are trying to deduce.

18. Chomsky's (2000:103, note 6) theta-theoretic principle, "Pure Merge in theta-position is required of (and restricted to) arguments," was, in his words (Chomsky 2001:49, note 70), "a direct consequence of Hale and Keyser's (1993) conception of theta-theory," and it added only "that violation of the principle, which is detectable at once, causes crash." Under the phase-based system, to the extent we understand, the advantage of such an added assumption is slight, and we explore a possibility without it.

19. See O'Neil (1997) and Hornstein (1999) for proposals concerning movement to theta position.

20. Notice that X cannot be restricted to heads given external argument assignment by a non-head, i.e. v^*P. But the external argument may be the only exception (see Chomsky 2007, 2008). See also Narita (2009).

21. Recall that Chomsky motivates this assumption on grounds of efficient computation.

22. We assume here, contra e.g. Citko (2005) and other multidominance approaches, that a head cannot have two sisters in a multidominance "M"-structure. The

argument in text does not go through if the theory of transformations is expanded to allow derived multidominance M-structures, because this would allow DP to become a second sister of V in (15) , via IM of DP and V.

23. Note that if theta roles function as syntactic features, as in Bošković and Takahashi (1998), then the DP would still be active since its theta features are unchecked.

REFERENCES

Boeckx, C. 2008. *Bare Syntax*. Oxford: Oxford University Press.

Bošković, Ž. and Takahashi, D. 1998. Scrambling and Last Resort. *Linguistic Inquiry* 29:347–66.

Chomsky, N. 1973. Conditions on Transformations. In Anderson, S. and Kiparsky, P. (eds.), *A Festschrift for Morris Halle*, 232–286. New York: Holt, Reinhart and Winston.

Chomsky, N. 1986. *Knowledge of Language: Its Nature, Origin, and Use*. New York: Praeger.

Chomsky, N. 1995. *The Minimalist Program*. Cambridge, MA: MIT Press.

Chomsky, N. 2000. Minimalist Inquiries: The Framework. In Martin, R., Michaels, D. and Uriagereka, J. (eds.), *Step by Step: Essays on Minimalist Syntax in Honor of Howard Lasnik*, 89–155. Cambridge, MA: MIT Press.

Chomsky, N. 2001. Derivation by Phase. In Kenstowicz, M. (ed.), *Ken Hale: A Life in Language*, 1–50. Cambridge, MA: MIT Press.

Chomsky, N. 2005. Three Factors in Language Design. *Linguistic Inquiry* 36:1–22.

Chomsky, N. 2007. Approaching UG from Below. In Sauerland, U. and Gärtner, H.-M. (eds.), *Interfaces + Recursion = Language?*, 1–29. Berlin: Mouton de Gruyter.

Chomsky, N. 2008. On Phases. In Freidin, R., Otero, C.P. and M.L. Zubizarreta (eds.), *Foundational Issues in Linguistic Theory: Essays in Honor of Jean-Roger Vergnaud*, 133–166. Cambridge, MA: MIT Press.

Citko, B. 2005. On the Nature of Merge: External Merge, Internal Merge, and Parallel Merge. *Linguistic Inquiry* 36:476–497.

Epstein, S. D. 2007. On I(nternalist)-Functional Explanation in Minimalism. *Linguistic Analysis* 33:20–53.

Epstein, S. D., Groat, E., Kawashima, R., and Kitahara, H. 1998. *A Derivational Approach to Syntactic Relations*. Oxford: Oxford University Press.

Epstein, S. D., Kitahara, H. and Seely, T. D. 2010. Uninterpretable Features: What Are They and What Do They Do? In Putnam, M. (ed.), *Language Faculty and Beyond*, 125–142. Amsterdam: John Benjamins.

Epstein, S. D., and Seely, T. D. 2002. Rule Applications as Cycles in a Level-Free Syntax. In Epstein, S. D., and Seely, T. D. (eds.), *Derivation and Explanation in the Minimalist Program*, 65–89. Oxford: Blackwell.

Fukui, N. 1993. A Note on Improper Movement. *The Linguistic Review* 10:111–126.

Hale, K. and Keyser, S. J. 1993. On Argument Structure and the Lexical Expression of Syntactic Relations. In Hale, K. and Keyser, S.J. (eds.), *The View from Building 20: Essays in Linguistics in Honor of Sylvain Bromberger*, 111–176. Cambridge, MA: MIT Press.

Hornstein, N. 1999. Movement and Control. *Linguistic Inquiry* 30:69–96.

May, R. 1979. Must COMP-to-COMP Movement Be Stipulated? *Linguistic Inquiry* 10:719–725.

Narita, H. 2009. Full Interpretation of Optimal Labeling. *Biolinguistics* 3:213–254.

Nevins, A. 2005. Derivations without the Activity Condition. In McGinnis, M. and Richards, N. (eds.), *Perpectives on Phases*, 283–306. (*MIT Working Papers in Linguistics* 49). Cambridge, MA: MIT Press.

Obata, M. 2010. Root, Successive-Cyclic and Feature-Splitting Internal Merge: Implications for Feature-Inheritance and Transfer. Ph.D. dissertation, University of Michigan, Ann Arbor.

Obata, M. and Epstein, S. D. 2007. Deducing Improper Movement from Phase Based C-to-T Phi Transfer: Feature-Splitting Internal Merge. Manuscript, Ann Arbor: University of Michigan.

Obata, M. and Epstein, S. D. 2011. Feature-Splitting Internal Merge: Improper Movement, Intervention, and the A/A' Distinction. *Syntax* 14:122–147.

Obata, M. and Epstein, S. 2012. Feature-Splitting Internal Merge: The Case of *Tough*-Constructions. In Valmala, V. and Etxebarria, M. (eds.), 366-384. Oxford: Oxford University Press.

O'Neil, J. 1997. Means of Control: Deriving the Properties of PRO in the Minimalist Program. Doctoral dissertation, Harvard University, Cambridge, MA.

Richards, M. D. 2007. On Feature Inheritance: An Argument from the Phase Impenetrability Condition. *Linguistic Inquiry* 38:563–572.

4   On I(nternalist)-Functional Explanation in Minimalism

Samuel D. Epstein

1   INTRODUCTION: EXPLAINING PRINCIPLES

I believe that Minimalism, a generative, derivational theory, and the concomitant departure from the Government and Binding (GB) filter-based approach, reflects a commitment to the idea that while filters *might* cover the data, *generating* representations of the data is another matter, a task that appears more difficult, and arguably more deeply explanatory (if feasible), than formulating a filter-based description. This perspective regarding generative explanation is not restricted to linguistics. As J. M. Epstein (1999) notes, describing something as an equilibrium is not the same as generating such an equilibrium and thus showing one way it might have emerged. The former merely classifies or describes ("x = an equilibrium"), while the latter, if successfully implementable at all, models one way the equilibrium might have come to be. The GB Case Filter, while undeniably an extremely important breakthrough, states a regularity, whereas the minimalist approach seeks to explain it at a deeper level by asking, "Why would this particular requirement be imposed?"

This type of deeper explanation is sought by what I think can be accurately characterized as generative "I-functional explanation." There is no stipulated axiomatic, purely syntactic Case Filter. Rather, independently motivated and arguably natural interpretive demands imposed by the interface require elimination of the uninterpretable Case feature, and the narrow syntax provides mechanisms whereby this interface "need" can be met. This is arguably the, or one, *function* of the narrow syntax and so, by hypothesis, functionally *explains* previously stipulated syntactic properties (e.g. the GB Case Filter). As will be discussed below, there are no minimalist syntactic filters mapping an unstarred representation to a starred representation. Rather, there are, by hypothesis, ineliminable lexical features, each having "sound-meaning" properties, i.e. interpretive properties at the acoustic-phonetic (AP) and conceptual-intentional (CI) interfaces.

Minimalist theorizing thus represents yet another Chomskyan inroad toward the establishment of a scientific explanation-seeking mode of linguistic inquiry.

2   GENERATIVE LINGUISTIC EXPLANATION: RULES VERSUS PRINCIPLES[1]

If the theory includes a system of rules (i.e. Standard Theory) the explanatory question will be "Why do we have *these* rules and not others? How can we explain the rules?" Within GB theory, the (revolutionary) answer runs as follows: We have *these* rules because there are general filters that the application of these rules satisfies. This general approach actually began earlier, with the search for general conditions on transformational rules; see e.g. Ross (1967) and Chomsky (1973). The leading idea, as elegantly implemented in e.g. Lasnik (1981), is this: What the different individual rules are "really doing" is enforcing an overarching representational output requirement (e.g. that affixes have to be attached in S-structure representation). The hypothesis is that this purported generalization, the overarching representational output requirement, is not truly captured if it is "unwittingly" enforced by an "accidental conspiracy" opaquely encoded within "scattered" parts of different rules. Under current minimalist theorizing, all rules operate purposefully, in order to satisfy e.g. the Case Filter (or what has come to be called the "Inverse Case Filter"; see e.g. Bošković 1997). This strategy seeks to *explain rules by appeal to filters*.

But if there are such filters, an interest in explanation will prompt the following question, analogous to the one posed above: "Why do we have *these* filters and not others? How can we explain the filters?"

One possible answer would be, "We have *these* filters (conditions on representations), because the rules are such that they produce representations satisfying these filters. In other words, the rules conspire to yield representations with a certain property, P." However, notice that such a strategy seeks to *explain filters by appeal to rules*.

A question that arises then is, "Can we in fact do *both* (explain rules by appeal to filters and explain filters by appeal to rules), or is this methodology circular?" In other words, can we try to explain everything?

The minimalist answer to this question is, "Yes, if filters are in fact *not* entities internal to the syntax but are actually external, outside of the syntax proper." Because the bare output conditions are, in fact, assumed to be outside of the syntax proper, we can now pursue (what I will call) "I-functional Explanation."

3   I-FUNCTIONAL EXPLANATION

A central aspect of the shift from GB to the Minimalist Program is the hypothesis that by exiting the syntax proper and focusing on other modules with which the syntax interacts (i.e. the systems that "impose" natural bare output conditions), we may be able to explain why the syntax is as it is. Perhaps, as Chomsky conjectures, the narrow syntax (NS) is "an optimal solution" to the demands imposed by the interfaces: for example, structural Case on DP is arguably uninterpretable, and hence it naturally must be absent from Logical Form (LF) representations. This is precisely what the Agree operation within the syntax does (or can do; more on this below): The application of Agree results in the deletion (or valuation) of an uninterpretable Case feature. This is an example of I-functional explanation: Legibility conditions explain why we have the rules we have. The rules we have are the way they are, and apply the way they do, because their sole purpose is to produce objects that satisfy the legibility conditions.[2] How, then, do we explain these legibility conditions? We can by hypothesis appeal to natural assumptions here: LF requires objects that are LF-legible (prohibiting Phonetic Form [PF] features), and PF requires objects that are PF-legible (prohibiting LF features).

However, there are still many (perhaps an infinite number of) ways that a computational system/syntax might operate to satisfy the same legibility conditions. What should we at least initially (though tentatively) hypothesize regarding what goes on inside the syntactic black box—the NS—that produces output representations that satisfy the legibility conditions? One proposal, which appeals to computational efficiency, is that the syntax "provides no machinery beyond what is needed to satisfy minimal requirements of legibility *and* . . . functions in as simple a way as possible" (Chomsky 2000a:112–113). Thus, Chomsky proposes a two-part explanation of the syntax: First, it operates (I-functionally) *in order to* satisfy interface conditions, not to satisfy syntactic filters. "[Language's] design must satisfy an 'interface condition' IC: the information in the expressions generated by L must be accessible to other systems including SM (sensorimotor) and CI systems" (Chomsky 2001b:2). Second, the syntax satisfies the interface conditions in one of the computationally simplest ways possible.

Language (L) generates expressions containing information that (naturally enough) must be legible at the interfaces. This is the hypothesis that summarizes the minimalist method, which seeks to explain aspects of the syntax in this way: Neither the interface conditions, nor the principles of computational efficiency, are themselves syntactic, yet properties of the syntax are, by hypothesis, functionally explicable, as follows: "Insofar as properties of L can be accounted for in terms of IC and . . . computational efficiency, they have a principled explanation" (Chomsky 2001b:2).

In other words, the Minimalist Program seeks to explain properties of the syntax by postulating that efficient satisfaction of the demands imposed by the interfaces will explain both the existing machinery internal to the syntactic component (e.g. why we find an Agree operation in the syntax) as well as its mode of application (why, in this particular derivation, does Agree apply as it does?) internal to a particular derivation.

Notice that this first question—the question of why the Agree operation is part of the syntax at all—concerns the very existence of an abstract (variabilized) formulation of e.g. Agree within the I-language/knowledge state. That is, this question seeks to explore why Agree constitutes part of the knowledge state in the same way as e.g. Merge constitutes a part of the knowledge state. On the other hand, the second question concerns the application of Agree in a particular derivation, with the values of the variables appearing in the statement of Agree instantiated by particular syntactic categories. For example, in a given (e.g. English existential) derivation, Agree applies to the probe T and the goal *man* in a particular representation within this derivation, thereby valuing the phi features of this particular occurrence of T and the Case feature of this particular occurrence of *man*. I think that these two questions concern different issues—the first tries to explain the existence of certain abstract rules internal to the I-language, while the second tries to explain why this particular rule applies within this particular derivation, with values of the variables in the rule assigned by particular syntactic categories. However, these two explanatory questions, which I have just argued to be distinct, frequently seem not to be systematically distinguished. We will return to this issue below.

Now, if computational efficiency matters, i.e. if the syntax is to be explained as a computationally efficient satisfier of the ICs, derivations (i.e. computation) must be explicitly formulated, so that efficiency can be characterized operationally. But what is a derivation? Chomsky (1998:126) writes:

> By a derivational approach, I mean one that takes the recursive procedure literally, assuming that one (abstract) property of the language faculty is that it forms expressions step-by-step by applying its operations to the pool of features: on the assumptions just outlined, it assembles features into lexical items, then forms syntactic objects from these items by recursive operations to yield an LF representation L, at some point applying Spell Out and the operations of PHON to form the PF representation P. By a "representational approach" I mean one that takes the recursive procedure to be nothing more than a convention for enumerating a set of expressions, replaceable without loss, by an explicit definition in a standard way.

Concerning the relationship between derivations, computational efficiency and the ICs, Chomsky (2001b:3) writes:

> The language L generates a set of derivations. *The last line* [my emphasis] of each derivation D is a pair <phon, sem> where PHON is accessed by Sensorimotor SM and SEM by CI. D converges if PHON and SEM each satisfy IC; otherwise it crashes at one or the other interface.

Recall that the question under discussion is "What is a derivation?" Phases (cyclic computation) have been postulated largely for reasons of computational efficiency.[3] It is not just the "last line" of a derivation that undergoes interpretation at the interface; rather, interpretation takes place upon the completion of each phase. Within the phasal system, in direct contrast to GB, we do not wait until all transformations have applied to perform interface interpretation; instead, interpretation occurs at certain points during the derivation. Thus, the quote above from "Beyond Explanatory Adequacy" entails that the last line of derivation #1 can be the first line of derivation #2: Note that this is also in direct contrast to GB. Namely, within the phasal system, unlike in GB, interface interpretation can be followed by further transformational application.

4   DEPARTING FROM THE Y-MODEL FOR EFFICIENT CYCLIC COMPUTATION

As described above, current minimalist architecture departs from the standard GB Y-model in postulating that derivation occurs by phase.[4] Instead of interpretation being postponed until after all transformations have been applied (as in the GB Y-model and certain predecessors), interpretation applies piece by piece. Chomsky (2001b:4) writes:

> In this conception there is no LF; rather, the computation maps LA (lexical array) to <PHON, SEM> piece by piece, cyclically. There are therefore no LF properties and no interpretation of LF strictly speaking, though the phonological component and the semantic component interpret units that are part of something like LF in a non-cyclic conception.

Chomsky (2001b:5) posits phasal cyclic computation on grounds of computational efficiency:

> [The] Phase Impenetrability Condition (PIC) sharply restricts search and memory for the phonological component, and thus plausibly falls within the range of principled explanation. . . . It could be that PIC extends to Narrow Syntax as well, restricting search in computation to the next lower phase.

Furthermore (Chomsky 2001b:4),

> The phonological component is greatly simplified if it can "forget about" what has been transferred to it at earlier phases; otherwise the advantages of cyclic computation are lost.

Of course, extensive empirical arguments, which I will not review here, are presented in support of this architecture as well as the aforementioned arguments of computational efficiency (see Epstein and Seely 2006 for one such investigation). Thus, the overarching hypothesis is that properties of the syntax can be functionally explained by appeal to the idea that operations apply so as to satisfy interface conditions. Moreover, these operations apply efficiently in satisfying these conditions. In summary, the syntax is to be explained in terms of efficient satisfaction of the interface conditions.

5   WHAT'S A PHASE? CONVERGENCE OR COHERENCE?

If phasal, cyclic computation is proposed, we immediately confront the entirely empirical question: "What is a cycle or phase?" Chomsky (2001b:22) writes:

> Ideally, phases should have a natural characterization in terms of IC; they should be semantically and phonologically coherent and independent. At SEM, vP and CP (but not TP) are propositional constructions; vP has full argument structure, CP is the minimal construction that includes Tense and event structure . . . and (at the matrix at least) force.

To clarify the above, we may say that phases are naturally characterized in terms of IC. In other words, the proposed phases, vP and CP, are, by hypothesis, distinguishable from other projections/categories by virtue of being naturally IC-characterizable as in (1) (an itemization of the properties just mentioned in the above excerpt):

(1) i. Semantically coherent
     ii. Phonologically coherent
     iii. Semantically independent
     iv. Phonologically independent
     v. Propositional at SEM
     vi. Bearing full argument structure
     vii. Constituting minimal structure containing Tense and event structure and (at the matrix) force

This set of properties is claimed to provide a "natural characterization [of phases] in terms of IC." But notice that these properties (which are in some respects undefined, I think) actually do NOT represent what the ICs specify. Recall that a derivation "converges if PHON and SEM each satisfy IC" (Chomsky 2001b:3). Thus, it is satisfying the ICs, which yields convergence; that is, the ICs demand convergence, and only convergence. In other words, *the ICs demand only that no uninterpretable formal feature appears at the interface.*

Therefore, convergence is not a property concerning propositionality, full argument structure, coherence, or independence. These properties concern not convergence but compositional and perhaps truth functional semantics. On the "sound side," there are corresponding compositional (e.g. prosodic) properties. By contrast, convergence is instead defined in terms of *uninterpretable single features and their categorial hosts,* such as phi features on T or Case features on N. There is good reason to assume that the two notions, convergence versus propositionality (or phonological independence or full argument structure or any of the other properties listed in (1)), are distinct. In fact, Chomsky (2000a:107) explicitly argues that phases are not and cannot be properly defined as convergent objects, but can and should be defined as propositional entities. (See below for detailed discussion of this claim.) This presumes that propositionality is not a criterion for convergence.

5.1 Two Interpretations of *Interpretation*

If I am on track, there are two very different meanings of the term *interpretable.* The first interpretation of the term is what we might call "semantic (and phonological) compositional interpretability," as in: A syntactic object X is considered interpretable if it has full argument structure and/or if it is propositional. The second interpretation of *interpretable* is: A syntactic object X is (LF) interpretable if and only if no uninterpretable phi or Case feature appears at the LF interface within X. This second interpretation concerns the formal definition of the term *convergence,* not (quasi-)semantic notions, for example of bearing a truth value, or coherence, or independence.

Notice that the first interpretation of *interpretable* is a compositional notion, while the second, by contrast, concerns individual features. Consider (2).

(2) $[[_T \text{is}] [_{DP} \text{(a) man}]]$

This contains no uninterpretable features, since the phi features on T and the Case feature on *man* are valued by application of Agree. On the other hand, the syntactic object in (2) is arguably not propositional, semantically coherent or semantically independent, and perhaps not phonologically independent or coherent either. Conversely, the syntactic object shown in (3)

(3) I desire Bob to sleep.
    (cf. I want Bob to sleep.)

fails to converge (because the DP *Bob* retains unvalued Case) but is nonetheless propositional (by hypothesis, this syntactic object is assigned propositional content).

To sum up this section, the phases vP and CP are claimed to have a natural characterization in terms of interface conditions; however, the specific characterizing properties given seem NOT to concern convergence but rather semantic and phonological compositional interpretability. But the ICs concern only convergence, and the two interpretations of *interpretable,* as outlined above, seem to reflect quite different notions—an issue to which we will return. First, however, I'd like to briefly discuss some additional possible problems confronting the notion "phase."[5]

5.2   Why vP and CP?

As I argued in the previous section, the characterization of phases as independent, coherent, propositional, and bearing full argument structure at the interface arguably needs to be more clearly defined. However, regardless of the "level of formalization," this characterization problematically seems to concern compositional interpretation instead of featural legitimacy.

A second issue concerning the above characterization of phases is this: How can Spell Out know that a given CP will be relatively independent (whatever the precise meaning of "relatively independent" is) or propositional *at the interface*, if Spell Out applies before the interface is reached, and without access to interface properties? It is a potential architectural paradox to hypothesize that vP and CP are spelled out *cyclically, internal to the NS,* by virtue of them having the property of being, "later," independent *at the interface*. We are not yet at the interface when Spell Out needs to apply, yet Spell Out needs to "know" that vP and CP will be independent at the interface after they are spelled out. One way to overcome this possible architectural paradox is to allow Spell Out to apply at any point. This, by hypothesis, induces crashing if the wrong categories (that is, categories other than vP or CP, within Chomsky's framework) are spelled out. Allowing for Spell Out at every point importantly constitutes a generate-and-test, or generate-and-crash, approach.

More precisely, it cannot be determined pre-syntactically that each lexical array *will be* either a CP or a vP when its contents are later inserted into the derivation of a syntactic object. For example (in perhaps the simplest case) nothing appears to pre-syntactically rule out the selection of two separate arrays as shown in (4).

(4) a. ARRAY #1 {to, be, a, man, outside}
     b. ARRAY #2 {there, be, likely}

However, these arrays would incorrectly allow the overgeneration of the (convergent) syntactic object in (5).

(5) There is likely a man to be outside.[6]

A third issue can be raised, this time with respect to the specification of a phase as having "full argument structure." This specification cannot mean that all relevant theta roles are in fact discharged, because this would have the unintended result that raising TPs, passive, and unaccusative vPs are phases; all theta roles associated with the head are, in fact, discharged in e.g. passives. Consequently, I think that "full argument

structure" must be a *translexical* notion. That is, in executing the derivation of a passive verb form, the syntax looks up the lexical entry of the
active form and notices that the passive form has morphologically reduced
theta assigning properties (contra Baker, Johnson and Roberts 1986) as
compared to the active form. With this information "in mind," the syntax then returns to the (passive) derivation, categorizes it as not bearing
full argument structure and then (somehow) assigns to the derivation the
following disclaimer: "No separate array is to be used for this not-yet-
constructed construction."

Still other possible problems confronting the timing of Spell Out are
discussed in detail in Epstein and Seely (2002). As they argue, within the
Derivation by Phase (DBP) (= Chomsky 2001a) system, spelling out before
feature valuation is too early, and spelling out after feature valuation is too
late. One solution they suggest is that Spell Out applies inside each transformational rule application, so that in effect all phrasal categories are phases;
i.e. each transformational application (not just those yielding vP and CP)
is a phase and undergoes Spell Out, so that no categories are stipulated as
special phases.

5.3   What Actually Gets Spelled Out? Phases Themselves, or Phase-Head Complements?

Even if vP and CP turn out to be naturally characterizable in terms of interface conditions and the possible problems noted in the previous section are
not in fact problematic, there remains an unclarity as to whether *phases are
the entities spelled out*, or whether phases instead define the point in the
derivational process at which the *complement of the phase head is spelled
out*. The latter interpretation, under which phase-head complements—not
phases themselves—get spelled out is suggested by the following passage
(Chomsky 2001b:21).

> We understand PIC as before; the sister of the head [v or C] is spelled
> out obligatorily; the fate of the edge—the head and its SPECS—is not
> determined until later.[7]

Within this conception, the system cyclically spells out big VP (the complement of the phase head v) and TP (the complement of the phase head C), and
not the actual phases vP and CP themselves. Under this analysis, although
vP and CP define when Spell Out occurs (that is, any time that a vP or a CP
has been built), vP and CP are *not* what is spelled out. What is spelled out is
instead VP and TP, the phase-head complements.

However, VP and TP are claimed to have NONE of the interface properties in (1) above that are alleged to make vP and CP natural candidates for
phasehood. Thus, the objects that actually get cyclically spelled out, VP and
TP, are not (by implicit assumption) naturally characterizable in terms of

semantic interpretability. Recall that the idea was to claim that the phases needn't be stipulated as vP and CP, because the objects sent to the interface are interpretable there—i.e. by virtue of being propositional, having full argument structure, being coherent, it is natural that these objects, and not others, get cyclically spelled out. But now we see that the objects actually sent to the interfaces cyclically are VP and TP, which, by hypothesis, lack all these interface properties.

Thus, according to the assumptions of the DBP/BEA (Chomsky 2001a, 2001b) system, the following table can be constructed, the columns of which are of most direct concern here.

	CP	TP	vP	VP
Phase/Has separate lexical array	yes	no	yes	no
Propositional/Full argument structure/Coherent	yes	no	yes	no
Cyclically spelled out	no	yes	no	yes

To sum up: What gets cyclically spelled out and what has its own lexical array are not the same, and what gets cyclically spelled out to the interfaces is perhaps *not* naturally characterizable in terms of interface conditions.[8] A fourth row that should and will be added to this table is labeled "Always convergent." We return to this momentarily.

Now that we have discussed the leading important idea of efficient satisfaction of the interface conditions, and the role of phasal Spell Out in implementing efficiency, we turn to the critical question of what happens *at* the interface, when the phase-head complements are (efficiently) sent there. What will be of central importance to the discussion is that the analysis proposed assumes that *there is crashing at the interfaces*.

6 TWO KINDS OF CRASHING

6.1 The Fatal Kind

BEA (Chomsky 2001b) assumes that the operation Merge is unconstrained. This assumption is crucial, since in this respect the BEA system is similar to GB theory in the sense that although the application of the operation is unconstrained, the results of it will undergo "filtration." (But in contrast to the filters invoked in the GB system, the filtration in the BEA system will be achieved by natural, independently motivated demands imposed by the interpretive modules, the bare output conditions [BOCs].) Given unconstrained Merge, the system generates what has been called "fatal crashing" (as opposed to nonfatal, salvageable crashing, which will be discussed in the following subsection). Example (3) above is a sentence the derivation of which fatally crashes.

Another, different kind of crashing, the nonfatal kind, is discussed in the following section.

6.2   Nonfatal Crashing: Inter-phasal *Wh*-Movement

Chomsky (2000a:107) provides an explicit argument that phases are not convergent entities but instead are propositional entities. Chomsky's argument is based on successive cyclic (inter-phasal) *wh*-movement, as in the following example, originally presented by Chomsky.

(6) [CP1 Which article is [IP there some hope [CP2 ~~which article~~ that [TP John will [vP ~~John~~ v [VP read ~~which article~~]]]]]]
   "Which article is there some hope that John will read?"

Chomsky's argument proceeds as follows. The right result is that *John* raises from [Spec, vP] to [Spec, TP] within the embedded clause. However, the Merge-over-Move Principle prohibits this movement, if *there* is available (as a Mergeable member of the numeration) at the time when *John* needs to raise. Consequently, it must be the case that *there* is not available in the numeration to be merged at the time *John*-raising needs to apply. One solution to this problem is that CP₂ constitutes a separate phase, hence possessing its own unique lexical array, which, importantly, does not contain *there*. As a result, *there* is not part of the lexical array/numeration at the time when *John* is ready to raise, and the Merge-over-Move Principle permits movement of *John* to [Spec, TP], the correct result.

However, this solution seems to create a new problem. If CP₂ is a separate phase, and the DP [which article] bears an uninterpretable *wh*-feature, the following situation arises: As just described, CP₂ is a phase, with its own lexical array lacking *there*. However, CP₂ (as well as the phase-head complement TP), by itself, is not a convergent object, since CP₂ contains a *wh*-copy *still bearing* an uninterpretable *wh*-feature, which won't be valued/deleted until *which article* reaches its final resting place in the matrix [Spec, CP] (note this *wh*-movement could be unbounded).

In summary, then, phases (like CP₂) are defined by Chomsky not as convergent entities but rather as propositional entities.

At this point, we have the information we need to add the fourth ("Always convergent") row to our table and to fill in two of the cells in this row; the TP and VP cells will remain empty for the time being.

	CP	TP	vP	VP
Phase/Has separate lexical array	Yes	no	yes	no
Propositional/Full argument structure/Coherent	Yes	no	yes	no
Cyclically spelled out	No	yes	no	yes
Always convergent	no		no	

To summarize, although vP and CP are phases, they are not convergent objects, because they contain uninterpretable features. Assuming the analysis in BEA, the phases vP and CP are *not* actually spelled out to the interface; instead, the phase-head complements are, namely VP and TP respectively. While VP and TP are not phases, they are the objects that actually get spelled out cyclically to the interfaces. Do VP and TP always converge there? Apparently not: For example, in the *wh*-movement derivation outlined above, at the CP$_2$ phase when the TP complement is cyclically spelled out, it contains an identical copy of the DP *which article*, which at this stage in the derivation still has an unvalued *wh*-feature. In fact, in successive cyclic *wh*-movement generally, the phase-head complements: VP, TP, VP, TP, . . . are repeatedly spelled out, each containing uninterpretable (as yet unvalued) *wh*-features on the *wh*-copies, even though the moved *wh*-element is itself escaping Spell Out by moving to the edge of the phase before the phasal complement is spelled out.

Thus, the last two remaining cells of the table can be completed as follows:

	CP	TP	vP	VP
Phase/Has separate lexical array	yes	no	yes	no
Propositional/Full argument structure/coherent	yes	no	yes	no
Cyclically spelled out	no	yes	no	yes
Always convergent	no	no	no	no

This means that, within the phasal system, there is nonfatal crashing at the interface. In other words, in the case of long distance successive cyclic *wh*-movement there are subderivations that crash (e.g. each TP crashes as it is spelled out), but these nonfatally crashing subderivations are extended to other "bigger" derivations that *do* converge. This view is not particular to Chomsky (2000a) but is maintained throughout Chomsky (2001b:13: fn 51), where he notes that "the *wh*-feature of a trace is not valued until a higher phase . . . all A-movement properties are handled within a phase, but not A′ movement properties."

Therefore, *wh*-movement necessarily involves inter-phasal valuation, since under PIC *wh*-copies bearing an unvalued *wh*-feature appear at the interface.

Recall (Chomsky 2001b:4):

> More controversially, for each derivation D, L makes a one-time selection of elements of LEX that will be accessed in D; a LEXICAL ARRAY LA (a numeration if elements of LEX are accessed more than once).

Thus, the construction of each phase is a derivation in its own right, by virtue of having its own unique lexical array/numeration. Hence, in the BEA system (unlike the GB system), a derivation can be "continued," that is, mapped to another derivation (see Epstein and Seely 2006 for a detailed discussion). Also unlike the GB system, the BEA system allows crashing at the interface of any subderivation within a bigger (more inclusive) derivation without the bigger derivation itself necessarily crashing. That is, there is nonfatal crashing, which can be "salvaged" by embedding the crashed derivation within a more inclusive derivation that converges.[9,10]

This proposed nonfatal crashing is similar to the hypothesis advanced in Epstein and Seely (1999, 2002), in which transformational rule application creates an object having an interface semantic interpretation, e.g. [$_{DP}$ the dog]. This DP is a linguistic object that, by hypothesis, has a meaning and sound known by me; however, it crashes at the interface. This (crashing) derivation can then be incorporated into a new derivation, which builds upon the earlier one and ultimately creates a new, convergent syntactic object with different interface properties than the object generated within the subderivation. This capacity to "continue the derivation into another derivation" might account for human knowledge of the sound-meaning (presumably interface) properties of even crashed representations like [$_{DP}$ the dog], which, according to the Epstein and Seely analysis, does get sent to the interfaces where it crashes. It may also illuminate the properties of certain nonsentential elliptical constructions, as insightfully investigated in Fortin (2007).

To sum up, BEA has both pervasive fatal crashing and pervasive nonfatal (i.e. salvageable) crashing at the interface.[11] But now what becomes of the Strong Minimalist Thesis? In particular, the hypothesis that the NS can be (I-functionally) explained in terms of efficiently *meeting* the needs of the interfaces?

7   CRASHING AND I-FUNCTIONAL EXPLANATION

As just discussed, within the analyses proposed in DBP/BEA (and previous analyses as well), *uninterpretable features do appear at the interface; i.e. the NS delivers representations containing such features to the interfaces, where these features are uninterpretable.* In this way, the NS generates (an infinite number of) crashes. But if this is so, a possible inconsistency arises between this formal implementation, which postulates a crashing NS, and the expression of what is arguably the leading idea of the Minimalist Program. Recall (Chomsky 2001b:2):

> If language is to be usable at all, its design must satisfy an interface condition IC; the information in *the* [my emphasis] expressions generated by L, must be accessible to other systems including the SM (sensorimotor) and CI systems. . . . Insofar as properties of L can be accounted for in terms of IC and general properties of computational efficiency . . . they have a principled explanation.

In a similar vein, consider (Chomsky 2001a:1):

> . . . to what extent is the human faculty of language FL an optimal solution to minimal design specifications, conditions that language must satisfy to be usable at all? We may think of these specifications as legibility conditions for each language L (a state of FL), *the* [my emphasis] expressions generated by L must be legible to systems that access these objects at the interface between FL and external systems—external to FL, internal to the person. The strongest Minimalist thesis SMT would hold that language is an optimal solution to such conditions.

And finally (Chomsky 2002:88):

> The components of expressions—their features, in standard terminology—must be interpretable by the systems that access them; *the* [my emphasis] representations at the interface with sensorimotor and thought systems consist of interpretable features.

This is a central premise of I-functional explanation.[12] But, given unconstrained Merge (as discussed in Section 6.1) and inter-phasal *wh*-movement (considered in Section 6.2), the NS necessarily generates crashing. Thus, it is not the case that *the* (as in "all the") representations at the interface consist purely of interpretable features. Consequently, there arises an inconsistency between the formal implementation (that is, with crashing) and the leading idea of the Minimalist Program regarding usability (that is, for language to be usable at all, the expressions must be legible at the interface), which implicitly assumes that there is no crashing.

For the faculty of language to be usable *at all*, i.e. to be usable *in the least bit*, it is required only that at least one expression be interpretable.[13] Interestingly, exactly this (different) view is expressed by Chomsky (2000c:17): "To be usable, the expressions of the language faculty (*at least some of them*) [my emphasis] have to be legible by the outside systems."

But the passage immediately continues:

> So the sensorimotor system and the Conceptual-Intentional system have to be able to access, to "read" *the* [my emphasis] expressions; otherwise the systems wouldn't even know it's there.[14]

This point is crucial. Recall that the central explanatory idea is that properties of NS are to be functionally explained by the demands imposed by the interface and computationally efficient satisfaction of these legibility conditions. That is, properties of NS have a principled I-functional *explanation*. But in the analyses proposed, a syntactic system that generates infinite crashing is postulated. Interestingly, in the case of *wh*-movement (involving inter-phasal valuation) the crashing is induced precisely because of the phasal system itself, which has been motivated on grounds of computational efficiency (a form of optimality) with the goal of eliminating or reducing globality, look-back, look-ahead and search in the course of the (derivational) process of satisfying the interface conditions. Furthermore, if unconstrained Merge is also computationally efficient (an optimal form of Merge), then this same kind of crashing is also a result of the goal of implementing computational efficiency in the operation Merge. That unconstrained Merge is a plausible candidate for a computationally efficient form of Merge is indirectly expressed by the following (Chomsky 1998:121–122):

> One plausible element of optimal design is that there are no constraints on application of operations. Accordingly, Spell Out can apply anywhere.

This perspective would seem to embrace unconstrained transformational rules (in addition to unconstrained Merge), as did GB (e.g. Move α), with resultant crashing at the interface.[15] Thus, the GB "freely generate and filter" approach is substantively reformulated within the BEA system as a "freely generate and try to interpret" approach; once again, the goal is to explain filters by appeal to independently motivated lexical features and ineliminable (sound-meaning) interface interpretation of them.

In the phase-based system, considerations of computational efficiency motivate phasal design, which generates crashing. But if there's crashing, then it cannot be maintained that if language is to be usable at all, *the* expressions must be interpretable at the interface. Instead, language is by hypothesis usable (at all, i.e. to some extent) although within the analyses proposed *the* expressions are not interpretable at the interface; only *some* expressions are, while others are delivered by the syntax to the interface, where they crash. This is, however, entirely consistent; in order for language to be usable, only some expression(s) must converge; it isn't necessary that *the* expressions, i.e. all of them, converge.

But if there is crashing, *a given syntactic rule application* cannot be explained by demands imposed by the interface. The interface does not *impose* properties on the derivation. As long as there is crashing, it is clear that the interfaces are incapable of imposing invariably convergent generation upon the syntax. Uninterpretable features are not in fact "barred" at the interface; rather, they appear there, and induce crash. In other words, such features are uninterpretable and appear at the interface. Consider a concrete case. Suppose we ask the deep explanation-seeking question, "Why does Agree apply in the following derivation?"

(7) There [$_T$ is] a [$_N$ man] outside.

Why does Agree apply in this derivation, valuing the Case feature of *man* and the phi features of T? The question of why an operation applies has been and remains central. Arguably, the Principles and Parameters (P&P) (generate-and-test) framework was itself developed to rid Universal Grammar (UG) of non-explanatory, obligatory transformational rule application, and sought to explain obligatoriness (i.e. to explain why certain rules must apply) in terms of filter violations resulting from the failure to apply optional operations/rules. That is, within the P&P system, the rules are in fact optional. Their apparent obligatoriness is explained by appeal to filters; that is, non-application of the formally optional rule violates the filter. The standard view is that the minimalist framework provides an answer to the question, "Why does this rule apply?"—in fact, a deeper answer than the P&P framework is able to provide—that is rooted in interpretive interface demands. The minimalist answer to this question is, "Agree applies because its structural description is met, and because uninterpretable features, namely Case on N and phi on T, are barred at the interface and rule application (of Agree) eliminates these uninterpretable features." But we see now that this answer is unmaintainable, since under the analyses proposed, uninterpretable features are not barred at the interface; rather, uninterpretable Case, phi and *wh*-features are delivered by the syntax to the interface, where they are uninterpretable/uninterpreted. In this way, an infinite number of crashing derivations is generated by the NS within the DBP/BEA system. But, unlike a filter-based approach, there is no star-marking within this system; instead, features appear at the interface and are uninterpretable there. (Therefore, we cannot say that a vP (or VP) that contains an uninterpretable *wh*-feature is starred at the interface. An absolutely central explanatory assumption within this system is that there are no purely syntactic filters, nor star-marking mechanisms.[16] This assumption is central since we are trying to *explain* syntactic filters by appeal to independently motivated bare output conditions, i.e. interpretive conditions applying at the interface.)

Thus, if we postulate a NS that generates derivations that crash, questions like "Why does Agree apply in this derivation?" cannot be satisfactorily answered by asserting that "for language to be usable at all, *the* expressions must be interpretable at the interface," nor by asserting that uninterpretable features are *barred* at the interface, nor by saying that such rule application is *imposed* by systems external to the NS. If the NS is assumed to deliver uninterpretable features to the interface, i.e. if it is hypothesized to generate crashing derivations, then none of these responses is maintainable. If I am on track, this standard mode of minimalist explanation for derivation-internal particular rule applications is simply not maintainable.

Before turning to possible solutions, it is important to note that the issue presented here complements a different issue raised and addressed in BEA. As noted by Chomsky (2001b:4), the requirement that *the* expressions be legible at the interface is, in a sense, too weak; it allows, in principle, what are presumed to be unavailable I-languages, such as I-languages that (while meeting the requirement of infinite legibility) generate only indefinite reiteration of a legible element bearing no uninterpretable features, e.g. "no, no, no . . ." Consequently, Chomsky notes that the requirement that *the* expressions be legible at the interface is in actuality too *permissive*, because it incorrectly allows unattested (and by hypothesis prohibited) indefinite-legible-reiteration I-languages. But a principle being "too permissive on its own" does not make it necessarily wrong. That which is wrongly permitted may turn out to be correctly excluded by a different principle (for example, compositional semantic coherence, and propositionality; see Section 5.1) than the too permissive one (featural interpretability) that fails to exclude the case (i.e. the class of indefinite-legible-reiteration I-languages) under consideration.

What I have argued here, however, is actually the complementary point to Chomsky's claim; that is, I have argued that the requirement that *the* expressions be interpretable at the interface is too *restrictive*. My central point is that this requirement is so restrictive that an internal inconsistency arises between (i) the assumption/leading idea that (inter-modular) usability demands that *the* expressions converge (which entails that there is no crashing) and (ii) the postulation that I-languages, which are assumed to formally implement this leading idea, each generate (an infinite number of) crashes precisely as a result of phase-based computational *efficiency* in conjunction with the assumption that unconstrained rule application (unconstrained Merge) is the optimal formulation of a rule.

If all this is on track, then what class of I-languages is permitted by UG? I don't have an answer to this question but hope to have revealed in this discussion one possibly interesting problem confronting one extremely compelling, intriguing and characteristically pioneering search for an explanatory answer. The remaining section explores some (of many) possible solutions.

8 TWO POSSIBLE "SOLUTIONS"

8.1 *The* Expressions *Are* Interpretable (i.e. All I-Languages Are Crash-Proof)

One way to eliminate this inconsistency is to maintain the strongest version of the minimalist leading idea that in order for languages to be usable at all, *the* expressions must be interpretable. One could then formally implement exactly this idea, by postulating only grammars that generate no crashing at all. Just such a theory of grammars is proposed by Frampton and Gutmann (2002). They hypothesize that each grammar generates only convergent derivations. They achieve this result by postulating that all features of a head must be satisfied before the interfaces interpret. Thus, there are multiple operations that are applied before the interfaces see a (complex) representation; additionally, in the representations seen by the interfaces, all features of the head are already satisfied. They call this type of grammar "crash-proof syntax." Under this approach, the question "Why does Agree apply in this derivation?" is answered with the following: "Because the theory of I-languages asserts that each I-language is crash-proof, since uninterpretable features are indeed barred at the interface."

There are, however, some *possible* problems confronting this approach. First, it is (on its own) too weak, allowing indefinite reiteration grammars (a point that will be discussed momentarily). Second, the fundamental operation is "Satisfy (all) features of head," not binary Merge. As a result, the interfaces never see the non-convergent intermediate steps of a derivation, since each step consists of satisfying all the features of the head. But if "Satisfy all features of head" is indeed the fundamental operation, and the interfaces cannot see smaller non-convergent substeps, we are forced to confront questions such as: Why is there binary branching/set-membership, if binary Merge is not the fundamental operation? Similarly, it may be problematic that derivational accounts of syntactic relations, based on step-by-step binary concatenation, are unmaintainable within this approach.

In addition, if C_{HL} (human language) generates only convergent derivations, then it is arguably the case that a native speaker's grammar/knowledge of English supplies no direct characterization of "ungrammaticality." By contrast, within the GB system, we can clearly identify the problem with examples such as (8).

(8) It is likely Bob to go.

This string violates the Case Filter at S-structure, and native speakers of English know it to be anomalous, while a Hindi monolingual lacks this specific knowledge regarding this string. Knowledge of the Case Filter and lexical properties (and of restricted (e.g. government) relations, among other things), by hypothesis, underlies the native English speaker's perception of this string as anomalous. On the other hand, within a rule-based approach, it isn't clear to me that grammatical theory can provide an account for knowledge of degrees and types of ungrammaticality, if the grammar generates all and only convergent derivations.

In response to the criticism I just raised, one might argue that trying to characterize types and degrees of ungrammaticality represents a premature commitment to formalization, before there is sufficient understanding to make that formalization enlightening. That too may be true. But if so, it is noteworthy that within the GB framework, and its predecessors, concern with types and degrees of ungrammaticality always played what I believe to be a fairly central role. (Perhaps, within that theory, it was methodologically sound to do so, while perhaps it isn't given the developing state of minimalist theory. I don't know.) I suspect the issue remains an important and investigable one as we evaluate rule systems versus filter-based systems versus bare output conditions, and the "balance" between them. A particular balance struck in the work under investigation assumes that some cases are ungenerable, while others are generated and crash.[17] Striking this balance seems to be a central issue, especially if we are trying to explain filters and properties of the partly, but not entirely, constrained ("efficient") rule system, the NS, in terms of the interpretive demands "imposed" by the interfaces.

8.2 Only Some Expressions Converge

Another way to eliminate the inconsistency between the assumption that *the* expressions are convergent, yet there is crashing, is to maintain that there is crashing and eliminate the assertion that *the* expressions converge. Rather, only some do: In other words, usability presupposes only that some expressions converge. As Noam Chomsky (personal communication) points out, this requirement (in conjunction with the infinite legibility requirement) is too weak (on its own), since it allows the indefinite reiteration type of "no, no, no . . ." grammars, which are arguably not possible I-languages (see Chomsky 2001b:3). However, I believe that this issue concerns the clarification of the two distinct notions of "interpretable," as discussed in Section 5.1. More precisely, the "no, no, no . . ." expressions each converge by hypothesis,[18] but what they mean is unclear, unless they are taken to be convergent elliptical expressions such as "No <I don't like cake>." Assuming such expressions are instead non-elliptical, perhaps these expressions converge but are (in Chomsky's terms) "gibberish." That is, they are

(i) *Interpretable*, in the sense that they converge at the interface containing no uninterpretable features.

But they are also

(ii) *Uninterpretable*, in the sense that they do not receive a fully propositional, coherent (compositional) semantic interpretation, even though each feature is individually legitimate at the interfaces.

If this reasoning is on the right track (i.e. these kinds of expressions are convergent gibberish), then it may be that the requirement that some expressions converge is not too weak, pace Chomsky. Instead, it's the right requirement from the point of view of the syntax, but there are other requirements (compositional semantic ones, for example) that must also be satisfied for "grammaticality" to be attained; specifically, non-elliptical "no" indeed converges but isn't (propositionally) interpretable. It is interpretable in the sense that its meaning is understood as "no," and not as, for example, "cat." But either in isolation is not *propositionally* interpretable. Thus, if indefinite reiteration grammars are, in fact, not possible I-languages, this does not necessarily constitute evidence that the requirement that some expressions converge is too weak; it might instead indicate that this requirement does exist but is not the only requirement operative.

Recall that within the Minimalist Program we can't productively ask directly, "What is grammatical?" but rather must ask more circumscribed questions like, "What satisfies theta theory?" Similarly, if this whole line of argument is on track, we cannot productively ask the direct question, "What grammars are allowed by UG?" but must ask more circumscribed questions: "What universal interface-interpretability conditions are there on *features*? And what universal compositional "coherence" conditions are there on *structures*?"

One might argue, then, that for a grammar to be usable, some expressions must converge; that is what usable in fact means (leaving aside note 12 above). Crucially, usability, in the central minimalist sense, is not concerned with communicative function or compositional semantics or coherence. If some uninterpretable feature appears at the interface, then perhaps compositional interpretation fails, since one of the elements entering into such composite interpretation is illegitimate. Conversely, we can indeed have convergence without coherence, as convergence simply demands that each feature be legitimate (as in e.g. "no" or [Tense + a man]) while demanding nothing regarding compositional semantic coherence. The requirement that some expressions converge is then possibly not too weak but instead is supplemented by other principles, e.g. those governing compositional semantic interpretability. This to a certain degree separates the "syntax" from the "compositional semantics." But, crucially, such a separation does not exclude us from explaining aspects of "grammaticality" in terms of convergence conditions, supplanting less explanatory syntactic filters.

If it is the case that usability by the interfaces requires only that some expressions generated by the NS converge, then we are unable to answer the question "Why does Agree apply in this derivation?" If only some derivations generated by NS converge, then we cannot answer as follows: "Agree applies in this derivation because uninterpretable features are barred at the interface; the features at the interface must be interpretable." This is not a possible answer because we are now explicitly assuming crashing at the interface. Given this assumption, it is not true that *the* expressions at the interface (universally) satisfy interface conditions; only some of them do, and it follows that some do not (the "last lines" of crashing derivations).

Although this question ("Why does Agree apply in this derivation?") may remain unanswered, Daniel Seely (personal communication) points out that a different question can be posed: "Why does the NS contain the operation Agree?" This question is, I believe, distinct from the question "Why does Agree apply in this derivation?" However, the two questions appear to be conflated in the following citation, which equates grammar-usability with crash-proof generation.

. . . to what extent is the human faculty of language FL an optimal solution to minimal design specifications, conditions that language must satisfy to be usable at all? We may think of these specifications as legibility conditions for each language L (a state of FL), *the* [my emphasis] expressions generated by L must be legible to systems that access these objects at the interface between FL and external systems—external to FL, internal to the person. The strongest Minimalist thesis SMT would hold that language is an optimal solution to such conditions.

(Chomsky 2001a:1)

One possible direction to pursue in answering the question "Why does the NS contain the operation Agree?" which seeks to explain the properties of the NS in terms of I-functional convergence demands is as follows:

(9) Seely's Conjecture:
   Perhaps it is the case that all the operations we find in the syntax are motivated in terms of achieving the goal of getting some (i.e. at least one) expressions to converge. (See also Chomsky 2000a:112–113, as cited in Section 3.)

In other words, in order for language to be usable at all, some derivations must converge. More specifically, the claim "Operation X (e.g. unconstrained Merge) is ceteris paribus needed to get one derivation to converge" does *not* entail that in each and *every* derivation generated, Operation X (e.g. unconstrained Merge) applies in a manner that contributes to that particular derivation's convergence. (The distinction might be reflected in the difference between the algebraic rule as it appears in the grammar/ knowledge state, vs. its application, with values assigned to variables, in a particular derivation.) Unconstrained Merge might indeed be employed in some derivations to get convergence but might at the same time also apply (in other derivations) in a non-convergent manner, by virtue of its being unconstrained.

Along these lines, then, we can generate the hypothesis that in order for the faculty of language to be usable, it is necessary only that some expressions converge. In order to get some (even just one) expressions to converge, the grammar needs (or it is not surprising that the grammar contains) *all* the relevant apparatus (e.g. Merge, Agree, etc.) that exists within the NS. If this argumentation is on the right track, then we *do* have an I-functional explanation of the properties of the mechanisms found in the NS, but we do not have an explanation of why unconstrained Merge applies in a particular derivation. That is, we cannot answer the question "Why does Agree apply in this derivation?" with "Because uninterpretable features are barred at the interface." This purported answer isn't maintainable, given that unconstrained Merge can, in fact, apply in a crash-inducing manner as well.

As Fred Mailhot (personal communication) points out, if it is true that in order to get even one expression to converge, the grammar needs (or it is not surprising that the grammar contains) all the apparatus found in the NS, then removing any one part of the apparatus results in no convergence, entailing "Mailhot's Generalization" that *the derivation of each expression must involve every operation*. Surprisingly, that isn't as unlikely as it might at first seem. With construction-specific rules, it was out of the question, since the generation of e.g. passives did not necessarily involve the application of e.g. relative clause formation. However, given contemporary theory, it may well be that the derivation of each expression does involve the application of all the operations within the NS (namely Merge and Agree). In any given derivation, operational application is optional; if an operation doesn't apply, the result might be an object with uninterpretable features. If the operation does apply, then the result will be a different object, perhaps a legitimate one (see Epstein and Seely 1999, 2002, 2006).

To summarize, the possible solution discussed in this section runs as follows:

Q: Why do we find the operations we find internal to the NS?
A: To be usable at all, some expressions must be interpretable. Each operation found within the NS is motivated by this requirement; i.e. each operation has the property that its application *can* be used (but isn't always used, as in the case of unconstrained Merge) to attain (or contribute to the attainment of) convergence. Holding all else constant, the removal of this operation would render the grammar incapable of generating even one convergent derivation.

The following question is not answered under this approach, in which the NS generates crashing:

Q: In this derivation, why does Agree apply?

Given the postulation of crashing, we cannot answer, "Agree applies in this derivation because uninterpretable features are barred at the interface." Uninterpretable features are actually not barred but rather appear there as generated by the NS, which is postulated to generate crashing derivations.

9   SUMMARY

I began by arguing that Minimalism, as a research program, constitutes normal science; that is, Minimalism seeks explanation, not just data "coverage." I then noted that both of the following strategies have been employed in syntactic explanation: trying to explain rules by appeal to filters and trying to explain filters by appeal to rules. This potential circularity is possibly overcome with I-functional explanation, whereby the syntax-external interface requirements are met efficiently. For this reason, the DBP/BEA framework abandons the Y-model and derives by phase. But what's a phase? I noted some potential unclarities regarding the distinction between non-convergent structures (which result from an uninterpretable feature at the interface) and compositionally uninterpretable structures. Under the phasal system, there is crashing at the interface—Spell Out isn't postponed until a convergent representation has been derived, which entails that non-convergent representations are sent to the interfaces. Specifically, there are two distinct kinds of crashing: Fatal crashing is the result of unconstrained Merge, and nonfatal crashing occurs in the case of successive cyclic *wh*-"movement" (spelled-out *wh*-copies appear at—and are uninterpretable at—the interface).[19]

After discussing these two types of crashing, I noted an arguably central assumption, the Strong Minimalist Thesis that "if language is to be usable at all, its design must satisfy an interface condition IC; the information in *the* expressions generated by L must be accessible to other systems including the SM and CI systems." But within the DBP/BEA systems themselves, this thesis is not maintainable; rather, there is crashing at the interface (an infinite number of expressions are generated by the NS that crash at the interface because Merge is unconstrained and *wh*-movement is unbounded). Therefore, it is not the case that "*the* expressions are interpretable at the interface." But if they are not *all* interpretable, then by the central assumption of the Strong Minimalist Thesis, language is not usable at all.

I then suggested two approaches to resolving the inconsistency and distinguished between two different questions: "Why does Agree apply in this derivation?" versus "Why does Agree exist within the NS?" The first approach conjectures that the expressions *are* interpretable, as in Frampton and Gutmann's (2002) crash proof syntax. But I noted some possible problems confronting this approach. The second approach hypothesizes that for language to be usable at all, *some* expressions must be interpretable at the interface, as is the case in DBP/BEA. If this hypothesis is right, one cannot say, "Agree applies in this derivation since uninterpretable features are barred at the interface," because in fact they are not barred; that is, the system, as proposed, delivers uninterpretable features to the interface.

On the other hand, as discussed, maybe we can say with Chomsky (2000a:112–113) and Seely that the NS provides only machinery needed to satisfy requirements of legibility and functions as simply as possible. In fact, the (or one) simplest way possible of satisfying the interface conditions—by hypothesis unconstrained Merge and derivation by phase—is precisely what induces an infinite number of *failures* to satisfy these minimal requirements of legibility at the interface. From this counter-intuitive, but I think perfectly sound, perspective, optimal efficiency in the system induces "infinite failure" in its output.

NOTES

1. This section would not have been possible were it not for discussions with Daniel Seely.
2. For more detailed discussion of the "physiological function" of the narrow syntax, see Epstein (2007).

3. As a reviewer rightly notes, phase-based computation is not the only way to implement computational efficiency. See Boeckx and Grohmann (2007) for very insightful theory comparison regarding this issue. Cyclic application of rules, in all its many formal implementations, seems equally characterizable as a form of "efficiency." The present paper seeks to clarify the notion "efficiency" and its relation to phase-based computation. Of course, the formal properties of possible human I-languages is an entirely empirical matter.

4. For some other proposed departures from the Y-model, see Epstein et al. (1998); Epstein and Seely (1999, 2002, 2006); and Uriagereka (1999).

5. Some of this section is adapted from Epstein and Seely (2002).

6. Noam Chomsky (personal communication) argues that there is no architectural paradox, nor look-ahead, involved in the NS sending vP and CP to the interfaces. Rather, it is a hard-wired "reflex" property of the NS that whenever a vP or CP is constructed, the syntax automatically sends the phase to the interfaces. This could be regarded as "good design" without the NS being "cognizant" of the (alleged) interpretive naturalness of these two categories at the "later" reached interfaces.

7. Note, by the way, that the edge (SPECS) + HEAD is not a term/constituent given bare phrase structure; i.e. the underlined is not a single term. The following is then a possible question: How can the edge remain accessible to the syntax, if the syntax operates ONLY upon terms?

   [*SPEC (SPEC*)* [X′ X [YP]]]

   Similarly, consider successive phasal Spell Out:

   [CP [TP [vP [VP]]]]

   Upon constructing vP, we Spell Out the complement of v, namely VP. Then, upon constructing CP, we Spell Out the complement of C, namely TP—but notice that the VP within this TP has already been Spelled Out (when we built vP). Thus, what actually gets Spelled Out when we reach CP is

   [TP [T′ T [vP v′ v

   This too is not a term.

8. A reviewer also notes that there is a problem concerning how to ever Spell Out the edge of the matrix CP, which is not a term of the phase-head-complement.

9. By contrast, GB offers no such salvation—any violation at any point predicts ungrammaticality.

10. If "forgetting about" previous phases is the central argument for (all) efficient phase-based computation, it isn't clear to me how Spelled-Out unvalued *wh*-copies can be forgotten, if later operations are assumed to value them, i.e. augment the feature values of these categories.

11. As Charles Reiss (personal communication) notes, the theory distinguishes between ungenerable representations (e.g. representations that cannot be generated given e.g. the Merge-over-Move Principle) and representations that are generated by the NS but crash at the interface. The empirical content, if any, of this seemingly important "mixture" between generate and exclude-by-output conditions, vs. fail to generate at all, is unclear to me, but I think merits further investigation concerning its empirical content or an explanation of why it is a non-empirical theoretical distinction. Notice there's nothing inherently wrong (and perhaps a lot inherently right) about such "mixed theories" if, as appears to be the case, there is both a generative system and systems of interpretation. The question, under this theory, seems entirely empirical, e.g. "What is it about Jones' knowledge state (his NS or his interpretive procedures) that

underlies his perception of this stimulus as anomalous in exactly this way?" Of course, to say the question is empirical is not to say that this is an opportune time in the development of the theory to delve deeper into this particular question. That's an issue regarding the timeliness and projected benefit of exploring formalization of particular aspects of an emerging theory. Arguably, the time is not always right for doing this. On the issue at hand, I don't know. For an extremely interesting and insightful discussion of this kind of issue in linguistics and adjacent fields, see Ludlow (1992). I am indebted to Noam Chomsky for bringing this article to my attention.

12. See also e.g. Chomsky (1995:221), Chomsky (2000b:9), Chomsky (2000c:17), and Chomsky (2005:9).

13. More strictly, the system might be "usable at all" if even one part—say one feature—of one expression is usable. As Chomsky (1998:119:fn 3) notes, it is apparently not the case that uninterpretable features can simply be ignored by the interfaces, but rather induce interpretive "anomaly": "[A] weaker condition would suffice in principle (presumably not in fact). A non-convergent derivation may form an object that is usable and interpretable at the interfaces—for example by ignoring its illegible parts." Why it is that uninterpretable features cannot simply be ignored remains a fundamental topic for future inquiry.

14. I believe there is a potential unclarity here regarding the faculty being usable, as opposed to a given expression (or features thereof) being usable.

15. A reviewer rightly notes that this seems at odds with constrained rule application, i.e. Greed and the like. This raises the fundamental question of whether optimal rules are by definition unconstrained or not, and, if not, to what degree and in what way they might be (I-functionally) restricted in their application.

16. Regarding the elimination of star-marking, see Kitahara (1999) for extremely interesting discussion concerning the ECP, as formulated by Chomsky and Lasnik (1993).

17. Thanks to Charles Reiss (personal communication), who brought to my attention the potentially predictive content of this distinction.

18. Strictly speaking, such grammars may not satisfy the infinite legibility requirement. None of these strings converges within the DBP/BEA system if universally only vP/CP or TP/VP get sent to the interface. Depending on the categorial status of "no" and of "no, no, no . . .," these expressions may not ever reach the interface, in which case none of the expressions in fact converge; i.e. none of them are interpreted at the interface, although all of them would be interpretable were they to appear there. This perhaps demonstrates that even grammars that generate only expressions bearing interpretable features could in principle be entirely unusable, since the "interface-linker" never sees any of the infinite number of legible expressions. This is because the phasal system sends expressions to the interface only if they have a certain categorial status (e.g. vP or CP), which none of the expressions ("no," "no, no, no") has. Herein may also lie an argument for "big" phases (contra Epstein and Seely 1999, 2002, 2006). Building something big enough to be a phase is necessary to get convergence at the interface, since only phases undergo interface interpretation. And to get just one phase (and they are "big"—that is, bigger than "no") to converge, the structure building apparatus within NS is necessary (or unsurprising). On the possible relevance of phasal generation to explaining so-called nonsentential speech, see Fortin (2007).

19. Of course, another approach to one half of the crashing problem, namely the half created by inter-phasal, nonfatal crashing *wh*-movement (see Section 6.2), is to change the hypothesis regarding the uninterpretability of *wh*-features. If *wh* is instead [+interpretable], such successive cyclic movement would not induce crashing. (Unconstrained Merge would still generate fatalities.) If *wh* is

interpretable, what motivates *wh*-movement? One standard answer is "edge" or Extended Projection Principle (EPP) features on the attracting phase head, but this seems descriptive at best. (See e.g. Epstein, Pires and Seely 2005 and Epstein and Seely 2006 for extensive discussion.)

REFERENCES

Baker, M., Johnson, K. and Roberts, I. 1986. Passive Arguments Raised. *Linguistic Inquiry* 20:219–251.

Boeckx, C. and Grohmann, K. (2007). Putting Phases into Perspective. *Syntax* 10:204–222.

Bošković, Z. 1997. *The Syntax of Nonfinite Complementation: An Economy Approach*. Cambridge, MA: MIT Press.

Chomsky, N. 1973. Conditions on Transformations. In Anderson, S. and Kiparsky, P. (eds.), *A Festschrift for Morris Halle*, 232–286. New York: Holt, Rinehart, and Winston.

Chomsky, N. 1995. *The Minimalist Program*. Cambridge, MA: MIT Press.

Chomsky, N. 1998. Some Observations on Economy in Generative Grammar. In Barbosa, P., Fox, D., Hagstrom, P., McGinnis, M. and Pesetsky, D. (eds.), *Is the Best Good Enough?*, 115–127. Cambridge, MA: MIT Press.

Chomsky, N. 2000a. Minimalist Inquiries: The Framework. In Martin, R., Michaels, D. and Uriagereka, J. (eds.), *Step by Step: Essays on Minimalist Syntax in Honor of Howard Lasnik*, 89–155. Cambridge, MA: MIT Press.

Chomsky, N. 2000b. *Noam Chomsky: New Horizons in the Study of Language and Mind*. Cambridge: Cambridge University Press.

Chomsky, N. 2000c. *Noam Chomsky: The Architecture of Language*. Mukherji, N., Patnaik, B. N. and Agnihotri, R. K. (eds.). Oxford: Oxford University Press.

Chomsky, N. 2001a. Derivation by Phase. In Kenstowicz, M. (ed.), *Ken Hale: A Life in Language*, 1–52. Cambridge, MA: MIT Press.

Chomsky, N. 2001b. Beyond Explanatory Adequacy. Ms., Massachusetts Institute of Technology, Cambridge, MA.

Chomsky, N. 2002. Language and the Brain. In Belletti, A. and Rizzi, L. (eds.), *Noam Chomsky: On Nature and Language*, 61–91. Cambridge: Cambridge University Press.

Chomsky, N. 2005. Three Factors in Language Design. *Linguistic Inquiry* 36:1–22.

Chomsky, N. and Lasnik, H. 1993. The Theory of Principles and Parameters. In Jacobs, J. et al. (eds.), *Syntax: An International Handbook of Contemporary Research, Vol. 1*, 506–569. Berlin: Walter de Gruyter. [Reprinted in *The Minimalist Program*, 13–127. Cambridge, MA: MIT Press, 1995.]

Epstein, J. M. 1999. Agent-Based Computational Models and Generative Social Science. *Complexity* 4:41–60.

Epstein, S. D. (2007). Physiological Linguistics, and Some Implications Regarding Disciplinary Autonomy and Unification. *Mind and Language* 22:44–67.

Epstein, S. D., Groat, E., Kawashima, R. and Kitahara, H. 1998. *A Derivational Approach to Syntactic Relations*. Oxford: Oxford University Press.

Epstein, S. D., Pires, A. and Seely, T. D. 2005. EPP in T: More Controversial Subjects. *Syntax* 8:65–80.

Epstein, S. D. and Seely, T. D. 1999. SPEC-ifying the GF "Subject": Eliminating A-Chains and the EPP within a Derivational Model. Manuscript, University of Michigan, Ann Arbor, and Eastern Michigan University, Ypsilanti [Presented at the Linguistic Society of America Summer Institute (1999).]

Epstein, S.D. and Seely, T.D. (eds.) 2002. *Derivation and Explanation in the Minimalist Program*. Oxford: Blackwell.

Epstein, S.D. and Seely, T.D. 2006. *Derivations in Minimalism*. Cambridge: Cambridge University Press.

Fortin, C. (2007). Some (Not All) Nonsententials Are Only a Phase. *Lingua* 117:67–94.

Frampton, J. and Gutmann, S. 2002. Crash-Proof Syntax. In Epstein, S.D. and Seely, T.D. (eds.), *Derivation and Explanation in the Minimalist Program*, 90–105. Oxford: Blackwell.

Kitahara, H. 1999. Eliminating * as a Feature (of Traces). In Epstein, S.D. and Hornstein, N. (eds.), *Working Minimalism*, 77–93. Cambridge, MA: MIT Press.

Lasnik, H. 1981. Restricting the Theory of Transformations: A Case Study. In Hornstein, N. and Lightfoot, D. (eds.), *Explanation in Linguistics*, 152–173. London: Longman.

Ludlow, P. 1992. Formal Rigor and Linguistic Theory. *Natural Language and Linguistic Theory* 10:335–344.

Ross, J.R. 1967. Constraints on Variables in Syntax. Doctoral dissertation, MIT, Cambridge, MA.

Uriagereka, J. 1999. Multiple Spell-Out. In Epstein, S.D. and Hornstein, N. (eds.), *Working Minimalism*, 251–282. Cambridge, MA: MIT Press.

5 Uninterpretable Features
What Are They and What Do They Do?

Samuel D. Epstein, Hisatsugu Kitahara, and T. Daniel Seely

This paper consists of four sections. Section 1 identifies an important unclarity regarding the central concept "crash" and suggests a way to rectify it. Section 2 reveals a pervasive empirical problem confronting Chomsky's (2007, 2008) attractively deductive valuation-transfer analysis. Section 3 offers a possible solution to this problem, reanalyzing the relation between uninterpretable features and Transfer. Section 4 presents a possible modification of a crash-proof aspect of the proposed model and briefly discusses a remaining question.

1 UNCLARITIES REGARDING THE DISTINCTION BETWEEN CRASH VERSUS CONVERGENT GIBBERISH

The basic intent of the concept "crash" and its complement "converge" and their central explanatory role in the Minimalist Program are intuitively clear: A derivation D converges at an interface level if and only if (iff) the interface can actually interpret each and every feature appearing in the expression generated by D. Expressions must be "usable," and they are usable (by hypothesis) if they contain only legible features in certain arrangements. Derivations failing to generate such expressions crash. Thus, Chomsky (2000:95) writes: "[A] computation of an expression Exp converges at an interface level IL if Exp is legible at IL, consisting solely of elements that provide instructions to the external systems at IL and arranged so that these systems can make use of them; otherwise, it crashes at IL. The computation converges if it converges at all interfaces." Simply put: if an object is not entirely readable by an interface, then that object is not usable to that interface (see Epstein 2007 for further discussion of optimal usability and its possible incompatibility with the existence of crashing derivations).

The more formal characterization of "crash," however, is, we believe, not entirely clear. For example, there are two distinct but often implicitly conflated notions of "crash." One (familiar) kind of crashing is induced by the presence of a single interface-illegitimate feature. For example, if a structural Case feature appeared at the conceptual-intentional (CI) interface, then this single feature would induce CI crashing. Structural Case is taken to be visible to but not interpretable by the CI interface. Chomsky (1995:278) called structural Case "the formal feature par excellence." But there is another kind of CI crashing, which might be called "feature-composition crashing," involving, for example, the valued phi features on T. Just like single-feature inspection at the interface, each individual feature is assessed for its interface legitimacy. But, in addition, the composition of individually legitimate features is also computed, and the result induces interface uninterpretability. Crucially, notice that each valued phi feature on T is a legitimate feature at CI, as is Tense. Thus, phi-valued T contains no single feature that is CI-illegitimate; each feature is a legitimate feature at CI. However, when valued phi and Tense co-occur within T, CI crashing is nonetheless routinely claimed to ensue.

Two questions immediately emerge regarding such compositional crash. First, just what exactly is this compositional crash due to? Second, does explanatory adequacy require appeal to a compositional feature-interpretability algorithm, in addition to a non-compositional one? More specifically, is the more powerful (and in fact not entirely formalized) compositional feature-interpretability algorithm required, as seems to be the case in the transfer-valuation analysis of agreement and Case (Chomsky 2000, 2001, 2007, 2008), or could the simpler non-compositional feature-interpretability algorithm inspecting each feature for interface legitimacy, one by one, suffice?

Regarding the first question, although valued phi and Tense are each CI-legitimate features, it could be that the combination of phi and Tense is semantically anomalous at CI. Thus, 3rd person "in" a certain time period (e.g. PAST) might not make (compositional semantic) sense. In support of this conception of (phi-valued T inducing) compositional crash, we find such statements as: "[I]f π contains a stressed consonant or a [+high, +low] vowel, then D crashes . . . " (Chomsky 1995:194), even though each feature appearing in such statements is a legitimate feature and so is in fact readable by the sensorimotor (SM) interface.

But we believe there is unclarity here concerning possible distinctions between crashing versus mutually exclusive feature specification vs. gibberish. Suppose that the combination of valued phi and Tense is semantically anomalous. But it seems that cases like "a stressed consonant" and "a [+high, +low] vowel" exhibit a different kind of anomaly; i.e. they are ruled out as a combination of mutually exclusive phonological features. If [+consonant] entails [−stress], then a stressed consonant consists of mutually exclusive phonological features. Similarly, if [+low] entails [−high], then a [+high, +low] vowel consists of mutually exclusive phonological features. But it is not obvious whether such an entailment exists in cases like phi-valued T. If not, this mutual exclusivity analysis does not extend to the cases in question. Also note, even if the combination of phi and Tense is semantically anomalous, whether such semantic anomaly induces CI crashing is a different question. Given that each phi feature and the Tense feature are each

CI-interpretable features, under inspection by a non-compositional feature-interpretability algorithm, this category (namely phi-valued T) is legitimate; i.e. it does not induce crash at the CI interface. If each feature is indeed interface-legitimate, then the representation containing only such legitimate features is also interface-legitimate. As a derivation yields such a legitimate representation, it converges; otherwise, it crashes. Now, the combination of interface-legitimate features could nonetheless still be argued to yield a gibberish interpretation. For example, phi-valued T could be interpreted as an X^0 analog of a "syntactically well-formed but semantically anomalous" sentence, e.g. "Colorless green ideas sleep furiously." If so, phi-valued T would be a case of convergent gibberish, where each feature is a CI-legitimate feature, but the compositional X^0-internal semantics is anomalous (hence, gibberish). Important here, however, is that, unlike its sentential counterpart "Colorless green ideas sleep furiously," there is no data exhibiting such an X^0 analog of compositional-feature anomaly; i.e. we cannot provide data, e.g. a lexical item, that exhibits phi-valued Tense. This suggests that valued phi on T can never make its way to the CI interface, as if this system were designed to remove "automatically" such derivationally valued features from a CI-bound object, or else such features are "simply" invisible to the CI interface. We will return to these two possibilities in sections 3 and 4, respectively. In section 3, we develop a model by assigning the standard feature-removal function to Transfer. In section 4, we modify such a model by assuming uninterpretable features to be entirely invisible to the CI interface.

Regarding the second question ("Must we appeal to a compositional feature-interpretability algorithm?"), there is an argument suggesting that the non-compositional feature-interpretability algorithm suffices (at least in all cases with no expletive). That is, any derivation that yields a CI representation containing valued phi on T would crash even under inspection by the simpler non-compositional feature-interpretability algorithm, because it would invariably result in single-feature crash due to the appearance of a valued Case feature. Recall that the valuation of phi features entails the valuation of Case; the latter is hypothesized to be a "reflex" of the former (Chomsky 2000:122). Yet valued Case appearing at CI is sufficient to induce crash. So, for example, probing from T successfully values phi on T (probe) and Case on N (goal), and such a nominal goal (bearing valued Case) moves to Spec, T, satisfying an edge feature (EF) on T. Now, if Transfer fails to remove valued phi on T, then it will also fail to remove valued Case on the nominal goal occupying Spec, T (since T and Spec, T are both within the potential TP target of Transfer). More specifically, let's take [$_{CP}$ C [$_{TP}$ NP [$_{T'}$ T vP]]]. If, as is widely assumed, Transfer can target only a single full category (i.e. discontinuous transfer is prohibited), then the only way for T to remain for the next phase cycle is to let Transfer target vP or lower at this phase level. But, then, both valued phi on T and valued Case on NP (occupying Spec, T) remain un-transferred, and the latter feature, namely valued Case, alone would suffice to induce CI crashing. Thus, the more complex compositional feature-interpretability algorithm would not be necessary to induce crash.

To summarize this section, we argued that (i) semantic anomaly caused by the combination of CI-legitimate features (e.g. phi-valued T) does not itself induce CI crashing, and (ii) the non-compositional feature-interpretability algorithm indeed suffices to exclude CI representations with phi-valued T by appealing to the presence of valued Case. To the extent that these arguments hold, the best way to rectify the unclarity regarding the concept "crash" is to develop a model incorporating solely the simpler and sufficient non-compositional feature-interpretability algorithm. Later in this paper, we develop such a model that turns out to be a crash-proof system at least for the CI interface, and possibly for the SM interface as well. But before turning to our proposal, let us examine a problem of massive undergeneration confronting Chomsky's (2007, 2008) valuation-transfer analysis (which incorporates the compositional feature-interpretability algorithm, whereby phi-valued T is assumed to induce CI crash).

2   A PERVASIVE EMPIRICAL PROBLEM FOR THE VALUATION-TRANSFER ANALYSIS

Chomsky (2001:5) proposed: "[T]he uninterpretable features, and only these, enter the derivation without values, and are distinguished from interpretable features by virtue of this property." As he notes, this proposal predicts that the crucial distinction between unvalued and valued features is lost at the moment such unvalued features go from unvalued to valued. One vitally important aspect of this valuation analysis is that it entails (without stipulation) that there must exist a phase-based cyclic application of Transfer. That is, since unvalued features, once valued, are regarded by Transfer like any other valued (hence, CI-legitimate) features, they cannot be removed by Transfer. Chomsky (2001, 2007, 2008) thus argued that transferring features before valuation is "too early"—i.e. unvalued features cause crash—and after, "too late"—i.e. after valuation, Transfer cannot remove valued features (e.g. phi on T), also leading to crash, detected by the (assumed) compositional feature-interpretability algorithm (see Epstein and Seely 2002 for detailed discussion). The solution to this apparent paradox is that, inside each phase, Transfer must remove unvalued features at the point of their valuation, assuming all phase-internal operations can apply, to cite Chomsky (2008:151), "in either order, or simultaneously, with only certain choices converging." Thus, Chomsky (2007:18–19) writes:

> If transferred to the interface unvalued, uninterpretable features will cause the derivation to crash. Hence both interface conditions require that they cannot be valued after Transfer. Once valued, uninterpretable

features may or may not be assigned a phonetic interpretation (and in either case are eliminated before the SM interface), but they still have no semantic interpretation. Therefore they must be removed when transferred to the CI interface. Furthermore, this operation cannot take place after the phase level at which they are valued, because once valued, they are indistinguishable at the next phase level from interpretable features, hence will not be deleted before reaching the CI interface. It follows that they must be valued at the phase level where they are transferred, that is, at the point where all operations within the phase take place and the Transfer operation therefore "knows" that the feature that has just been valued is uninterpretable and has to be erased at (or before) CI. Since all operations take place at the phase level, there is no memory or search problem. [fn.24 deleted, EKS]

Given that Transfer applies to the phase-complement (PC) at each phase level, Chomsky (2007), following Richards (2007), concludes that every occurrence of a derivationally valued feature (e.g. phi on T, Case on N) must remain inside PC, so that Transfer can remove it for convergence. Equivalently, a derivationally valued feature can never appear at the edge outside PC. If it appears at the edge, then (at the next phase cycle, and all subsequent ones) it will be "too late" for Transfer to recognize that this now-valued feature—in contrast to inherently valued features—was previously unvalued (at an earlier phase level), assuming the phase-impenetrability condition (PIC). Since Transfer fails to remove such derivationally valued features, they will invariably induce CI crash: the wrong result for virtually every derivation.

The central argument of this valuation-transfer analysis (from which cyclic Transfer follows) is very clear. Suppose a category X with an unvalued feature –f moves to the edge out of PC, after –f gets valued. Then, PC (containing the departure site of X) will get transferred, given that PIC ensures the inaccessibility of PC from this point on. In effect, the now-valued feature +f on the mover X will be un-removable forever. Since its derivational history is lost through earlier-phase Transfer, there will be no way for later-phase Transfer to know that the feature f went from unvalued to valued, and hence no way for Transfer to recognize +f as a CI-offending feature that must be removed from a CI-bound object. This feature will appear at CI, and CI crash would result.

Let us highlight the main points of this argument below. Consider the following illustration (where PH is a phase head, PC is a phase complement, –f is an unvalued feature, and X is an element bearing –f):

(1) [PH [$_{PC}$ . . . X . . .]]
                   –f

Suppose (i) Agree values the unvalued feature $-f$ on X and (ii) Internal Merge (IM) moves X bearing the now-valued $+f$ to Spec, PH. Then, X bearing the valued $+f$ now occupies Spec, PH (i.e. an edge position) outside PC and remains there (for the next phase cycle), while Transfer sends PC (containing the departure site of X) to the interface, as illustrated in (2) (where the transferred materials are in gray):

(2) [X [PH [$_{PC}$ . . . X . . .]]]
      $+f$

As a consequence, at the next phase level, a serious problem emerges: $+f$ is valued, and given PIC there is no indication that it was previously unvalued. If Transfer removes only those features that it "sees" go from unvalued to valued, then Transfer will not be able to remove $+f$ because all Transfer can see is valued $+f$. In short, it is now "too late" since a derivationally valued feature is now indistinguishable from its inherently valued counterpart; hence, it appears at CI and by hypothesis induces CI crash.

It is important to note that the basic form of the argument that derivationally valued features cannot appear at the edge is explicitly appealed to by Chomsky (2007) and Richards (2007), to importantly derive (not stipulate) CP (not TP) and vP (not VP) as phases, and also to derive (not stipulate) feature-transmission from C to T and from v to V (for detailed and important analysis of both variation and unification concerning phi-feature-transfer, see Ouali 2006a, 2006b, 2008). Adopting observations of Richards (2007), Chomsky (2007:19) states: "[I]t follows that the PIC entails that TP cannot be a phase, with operations of valuation and A-movement driven by properties of T. Suppose TP were a phase. Then its interior will be transferred by PIC, but the head T will retain its valued uninterpretable features. The derivation will therefore crash at the next phase"—precisely because derivationally valued features appear at the edge, which by hypothesis invariably induces CI crash. As for feature-inheritance, following Richards (2007), Chomsky (2007:19) argues: "[T]he uninterpretable features of C must be "inherited" by T. If they remain at C, the derivation will crash at the next phase"—again because derivationally valued features appear at the edge. Thus, feature-inheritance, like cyclic phasal Transfer itself, is deduced from the assumption that derivationally valued features on the edge will cause CI crash; if they appear outside PC, then it will be "too late" for Transfer to remove them from a CI-bound object (at the next or any subsequent phase level). Thus, the argument that derivationally valued features cannot appear at the edge plays a central explanatory role in the valuation-transfer analysis.

By this very same logic, however, the valuation-transfer analysis faces a serious problem: Empirically desirable instances of movement out of PC are blocked. For example, "simple" data such as the declarative "They like him" and the *wh*-interrogative "Whom do they like?" pose a problem of massive undergeneration. Consider the following vP phases for the relevant derivations:

(3) the vP phase for "they like him"
   [$_{vP}$ they [$_{v'}$ v+like(valued phi) [$_{VP}$ him(valued Case) [$_{V'}$ t_V t_{him}]]]]
(4) the vP phase for "whom do they like?"
   [$_{vP}$ whom(valued Case) [$_{v'}$ they [$_{v'}$ [$_{v'}$ v+like(valued phi) [$_{VP}$ t_{whom} [$_{V'}$ t_V t_{whom}]]]]]]

In (3), V(like) adjoins to v (a step required to restore the original VO order); hence, the valued phi on V(like) appears outside PC (=VP). Recall that feature-inheritance is taken to be a property of PHs in general, not just of C but also v (Chomsky 2007, 2008). Thus, upon V(like)'s inheritance of phi from v, probing from V(like) values phi on V(like) and Case on NP(him), and NP(him) and V(like) move to Spec, V and to v, respectively. In extending this analysis to so-called Exceptional Case Marking (ECM) constructions (e.g. in "They believe him to be intelligent"), Chomsky (2007:21) argues that V(believe) adjoins to the matrix v (restoring the original VO order).

In (4), in addition to the valued phi on V(like) (adjoined to v), NP(whom) moves to Spec, v (a step required to form an operator-variable construction at CI); hence, the valued Case on NP(whom) appears outside PC (=VP). Chomsky (2007:18) notes data like (4) and suggests that "[v]aluation of uninterpretable features clearly feeds A̅-movement (e.g., in "whom did you see?"). Hence valuation is "abstract," functioning prior to transfer to the SM interface, as are the uninterpretable features themselves." However, it is not clear to us how such "abstract" valuation would operate here. Note that Chomsky (2005:13), following Nissenbaum (2000), assumes that "[i]f internal Merge precedes transfer, movement is overt; otherwise, it is covert." This assumption makes the following prediction. Suppose Transfer removes both phonological features and derivationally valued features from a CI-bound object. Then, if Transfer applied to VP after valuation of Case on NP(whom) but before movement of NP(whom) to Spec, v, it could remove the valued Case feature on NP(whom) at the "in situ" point of valuation, but in doing so, it would also necessarily transfer those phonological features of NP(whom) to the phonological component, forcing NP(whom) to be pronounced inside VP, contrary to fact.

As already noted, within the valuation-transfer analysis, later-phase Transfer after valuation induces CI crash. Thus, for all data like (3) and (4), there are in fact no convergent derivations. For the valuation-transfer analysis, if X bears a feature that could be derivationally valued, overt movement of any such X out of PC is predicted to result in CI crash.

In the preceding sections, we discussed a certain unclarity regarding the concept "crash." Particularly, we pointed out an implicit but important distinction between single-feature crash and feature-compositional gibberish, and we suggested a model incorporating solely the non-compositional feature-interpretability algorithm. Also, we reviewed the central assumptions of Chomsky's (2007, 2008) (explanatory) valuation-transfer system and revealed a pervasive empirical problem existing in this system. As noted, the problem stems from a foundational aspect of the Chomsky–Richards analysis, from which (i) the limitation of PHs to C and v and (ii) the transmission of features from PH to the head that PH selects are both explained.

3   DESIGNING A PERFECT SYSTEM "PRIMARILY" FOR CI AND "SECONDARILY" FOR SM

In this section, we consider a solution to the problem raised above. As we have seen in the abstract illustration (2), the derivationally valued $+f$ feature appearing outside PC is the main "culprit." Transfer does not have the derivational history it needs to remove this CI-offending feature from the CI-bound object—it is now "too late" since its history is inaccessible, given the PIC—and thus it makes its way to the CI interface where it by hypothesis induces crash. There is massive undergeneration by such a system. Now, there are (at least) two possible approaches to this problem.

One approach is to block the derivationally valued $+f$ on X from ever appearing outside PC. This is essentially the approach of Obata and Epstein (2008). The leading idea is that although X (or a subpart of X) moves to the edge outside PC, the CI-offending $+f$ feature does not; rather, it remains inside PC. This is what Obata and Epstein call "feature-splitting." The derivationally valued $+f$ feature will not induce crashing, since, by hypothesis, the derivationally valued $+f$ feature does not move out of PC, although some other features of X do. The derivationally valued $+f$ feature remains inside PC, and it is successfully transferred to the phonological component (along with all other materials inside PC).

Another possible approach is to allow the derivationally valued $+f$ on X to appear outside PC, but assume, contra Chomsky (2007, 2008) and Richards (2007), that this $+f$ feature is such that Transfer can recognize it as a CI-offending feature and will remove it from a CI-bound object; in fact, it is not "too late" after all. This is essentially the approach we explore below. Our main proposal is that although the derivationally valued $+f$ feature is present on X appearing outside PC, it is nonetheless still (and quite naturally) recognized by Transfer as a CI-offending feature that must be removed from a CI-bound object. But before turning to our detailed proposal, let us examine some underlying assumptions, especially those distinguishing our proposal from Chomsky's (2007, 2008) valuation-transfer analysis.

Recall that Chomsky (2000:119) had earlier proposed the strongest sustainable inclusiveness/interpretability condition: "Inclusiveness holds of narrow syntax, and each feature is interpreted at the level LF or associated with phonetic features by the phonological component." Now, under Chomsky's (2001:5) proposal, unvalued features are formal features lacking semantic values; i.e. they are not interpreted at CI. But if so, such features are then expected to be "associated with phonetic features by the phonological component." This implies that in the lexicon, unvalued features are formal features lacking semantic values, but they are then, by the strongest sustainable inclusiveness/interpretability condition, "associated with phonetic features by the phonological component." That is, by hypothesis, the lexical status of unvalued features is formal but not semantic, and, later in the derivation, phonological.

Interestingly, this interpretation of unvalued features fits well into a recent "minimalist scenario" concerning the logical minimum regarding evolution of a narrow syntax (NS). Chomsky (2007:14) notes: "At the minimum, some rewiring of the brain, presumably a small mutation or a by-product of some other change, provided Merge and undeleted EF (unbounded Merge), yielding an infinite range of expressions constituted of lexical items (LIs) (perhaps already available in part at least as conceptual atoms of CI systems), and permitting explosive power of the capacities of thought." In essence, this suggests that NS evolved originally as a system feeding only one interface, namely CI; it was a mode of expression of thought, or, as a leading biologist put it, it bore a crucial relation to "development of abstract or productive thinking" (Luria 1974:195, cited in Chomsky 2005:3–4). But then something happened. Chomsky (2007:14) continues: "At some stage modes of externalization were contrived. Insofar as third factor conditions operate, UG would be optimized relative to the CI interface, and the mappings to the SM interface would be the "best possible" way of satisfying the externalization conditions." So, at some point, a completely different interface, namely SM, "demanded" a link to NS, already evolved as a "perfect solution" to the CI conditions; and a best possible link between NS and SM was established with what was available then.

We take this hypothesized primacy of the CI interface seriously and raise the following two questions. First, what would be a perfect NS feeding CI? Second, what would be the best possible link between NS and SM, given a previously established perfect NS-CI function?

Regarding the first question, let us ask what type of features would be minimally required for NS to be a perfect solution to the CI-legibility conditions. Consider the following two types of features:

(5) a. features that are themselves interpreted at CI; call this type [+Int]
   b. features that are not themselves interpreted at CI (e.g. EF, unvalued features); call this type [−Int]

The type [+Int] is rather straightforward, but what about the type [−Int]? Why do [−Int] features such as EF and unvalued features (such as phi on

T and Case on N) enter this model in the first place? Chomsky (2000:96) formulated the Strong Minimalist Thesis (SMT): "Language is an optimal solution to legibility conditions," and under SMT, it has been assumed that such [–Int] features are implemented for some optimal function in service to creating CI representations. First consider EF. As demonstrated in Chomsky (2007, 2008), EF is necessary to generate any hierarchical structures, including "generalized argument structures (theta roles, the "cartographic" hierarchies, and similar properties)" and "discourse-related properties such as old information and specificity, along with scopal effects" (Chomsky 2008:140). The CI interface imposes certain interpretations (e.g. interpretation of quantification), and NS generates expressions subject to such interpretations. Now what about unvalued features (such as phi on T and Case on N)? Chomsky (2007:24) suggested that "they compel phases to be as small as possible consistent with IM and (possibly) assignment of argument structure, CP and v*P, and they impose cyclicity of Transfer (strict cyclicity, given PIC), thus reducing memory load in computation. Hence, they contribute to SMT." Also, assuming each instance of IM is triggered by EF, Chomsky (2007:24) distinguishes A-movement from Á-movement as follows: "A-movement is IM contingent on probe by uninterpretable inflectional features, while Á-movement is IM driven by EF of [a phase head] P." Following Chomsky (2007, 2008), we assume that [–Int] features include (at least) EF and unvalued features (such as phi on T and Case on N), and their existence is justifiable under SMT; they exist as part of an optimal solution to the CI-legibility conditions. The lexicon for NS thus contains LIs consisting of these two types of features—[+Int] and [–Int]—but crucially no phonological features, given no link to SM yet.

As discussed above, [–Int] features are not themselves interpreted at CI but are implemented for some optimal function in service of creating CI representations; hence, for a derivation to converge, either they must get deleted before reaching the CI interface, or they must be invisible (hence not offensive) to the CI interface. Now suppose, as is widely assumed, that the condition of inclusiveness, or, more generally, the law of the conservation of features—our conception of the synthesis of inclusiveness and Recoverability—holds of NS (cf. Martin and Uriagereka 2000):

(6) The Law of the Conservation of Features
    In NS, features cannot be created or destroyed throughout a derivation.

Then, regardless of whether a [–Int] feature is valued or not, its lexical status being [–Int] cannot be altered in NS, and so it remains [–Int] throughout a derivation. Thus, for CI convergence, there must be some special operation to remove all [–Int] features from a syntactic object SO (constructed by NS), or alternatively [–Int] features are by definition invisible to the CI interface. We will return to the latter possibility in section 4. Here we proceed with the former possibility, namely the [–Int] removal function, and suggest, as is standard, that Transfer performs this function.

(7) Transfer (version 1)
Transfer deletes all [–Int] features from SO (constructed by NS), forming SO<+Int> (bearing only [+Int] features); and it sends SO<+Int> to the semantic component.

Crucially, this formulation of Transfer can remove features such as phi on T and Case on N at any derivational point, since they are unproblematically recognized by Transfer as [–Int] throughout the derivation. That is, contra Chomsky (2007, 2008) and Richards (2007), after valuation is not "too late" for [–Int] removal by Transfer.

Here notice, by definition, that neither single-feature crash nor feature-compositional gibberish (caused by phi-valued T) can occur at CI. This model of NS (incorporating Transfer formulated as such) is a crash-proof system (at least) for the CI interface (cf. Frampton and Gutmann 2002). Recall that in section 1 we first suggested that phi-valued T, if appearing at CI, would be a case of convergent gibberish—each feature is a CI-legitimate feature, yet the compositional semantics is anomalous (hence, gibberish)— but we then noted that, unlike its sentential counterpart "Colorless green ideas sleep furiously," there is no data exhibiting such an X^0 analog of compositional-feature anomaly. Under the current assumptions, it follows that, regardless of whether [–Int] features are valued or not, [–Int] features such as phi on T and Case on N never make their way to CI, because Transfer can recognize such [–Int] features and will always remove them throughout the course of a derivation. After Transfer, the semantic component carries out the following task:

(8) The semantic component converts SO<+Int> to a CI representation.

Under inspection by the non-compositional feature-interpretability algorithm, such a CI representation always meets the CI-legibility conditions; hence, by definition, there is no CI crashing derivation; the concept "crash" as well as its counterpart "convergence" is dispensable at CI under this model. A crash-proof computation to CI is arguably an optimal solution to the CI-legibility conditions, and comports with the most fundamental formulation of SMT, which asks: "[T]o what extent is the human faculty of language FL an optimal solution to minimal design specifications, conditions that must be satisfied for language to be usable at all? We may think of these specifications as "legibility conditions": for each language L (a state of FL), the expressions generated by L must be "legible" to systems that access these objects at the interface between FL and external systems—external to FL, internal to the person" (Chomsky 2001:1).

Let us now turn to the second question: What would be the best possible link between NS and SM, given this pre-established optimal (crash-proof) NS-CI function? Assuming such a link to be a phonological component (being neutral about options in modality, e.g. sign language vs. spoken language), we first propose the following minimum revision to Transfer:

(9) Transfer (version 2)
Transfer deletes all [–Int] features from SO (constructed by NS), forming SO<+Int> (bearing only [+Int] features); and it sends SO<+Int> to the semantic component, while it sends SO to the phonological component.

Given this revision, Transfer sends (the entire) SO (constructed by NS) to the phonological component. But recall that this SO contains LIs bearing both [+Int] and [–Int] features but (by hypothesis) no phonological features. If so, how can each LI of SO be associated with phonetic features? Here, as is standard practice, we assume that phonetic features appear in the phonological component:

(10) The phonological component assigns phonetic features to SO, forming SO<pf> (bearing phonetic features), and converts SO<pf> to an SM representation.

The next question is, of course, How exactly does the phonological component assign phonetic features to SO? To answer this question, we would like to adopt Chomsky's (1995) idea of phonological coding in the lexicon (cf. Halle and Marantz 1993). He (1995:230) proposed that "the phonological matrix of a lexical item is essentially *atomic*, as far as overt operations are concerned. It is the form in which the instructions for certain rules of the phonological component are "coded" in the lexical item. For N → λ computation, nothing would change if the phonological properties of *book* were coded in the lexicon as *23*, with a rule of the phonological component interpreting *23* as the phonological matrix for *book*." With this phonological coding analysis, we propose the following revision to the lexicon:

(11) Each LI is phonologically coded in the lexicon.

Assuming such a phonological code is part of an optimal function in service to creating SM representations, let us extend the type [–Int] to include also those phonological codes.

(12) a. features that are themselves interpreted at CI; call this type [+Int]
b. features that are not themselves interpreted at CI (e.g. EF, unvalued features, phonological codes); call this type [–Int]

With this extension, Transfer removes [–Int] features (including phonological codes) from a CI-bound object but lets SO (bearing both [+Int] and [–Int] features) enter the phonological component. The phonological component then interprets each phonological code as its phonological matrix and assigns the relevant phonetic features to it.

Under this proposal, it follows that the phonological component interprets the phonological code of each LI and assigns the relevant phonetic features to it (perhaps vacuously in some cases, i.e. no phonetic features). Such code-based assignment of phonetic features can be implemented in various ways. Chomsky (1998:122:n. 5) notes that it can be implemented "by rules assigning phonetic features to a bundle of formal features, or rules deleting formal features only in combination with appropriate phonetic features, so that otherwise the derivation will crash at PF." Putting aside the exact implementation, it is important to note that the assignment of phonetic features is crucially contingent on what happens in NS, in particular, the valuation of unvalued features such as phi and Case. So, for example, if a pronoun bears a phonological code *12* and other features such as phi features (3rd person, singular, masculine) and a Case feature (Nominative), then this complex of features (code 12, 3rd person, singular, masculine, Nominative) will be interpreted as the phonological matrix for *he* and assigned the relevant phonetic features by the phonological component.

Let us review the central aspects of the model of NS designed "primarily" for CI and "secondarily" for SM. The lexicon contains LIs consisting of [+Int] and [–Int] features. [+Int] features are interpreted at CI, whereas [–Int] features are not themselves interpreted at CI. The latter type includes EF (required to generate hierarchical structures) and unvalued features such as phi on T and Case on N (part of an optimal function in service to creating CI representations) and phonological codes (part of an optimal function in service to creating SM representations). NS executes Merge and Agree to construct structures and establish relations. Every time NS reaches a phase level, Transfer targeting SO deletes all and only the [–Int] features from SO, forming SO<+Int>; and it sends SO<+Int> to the semantic component, while it sends (the entire) SO to the phonological component. The semantic component then converts SO<+Int> to an invariably convergent CI representation, while the phonological component interprets phonological codes of SO (interacting with some formal features such as phi and Case) and assigns phonetic features to SO, forming SO<pf> (bearing phonetic features), and then converts SO<pf> to an SM representation. This is the model of an NS that first emerged for perfect interactions with the CI interface and was later retro-fitted as the best possible link to the SM interface. Note that the two types of features (12a–b) reflect the primacy of the CI interface in that CI interpretability determines whether a feature *f* is [+Int] or [–Int] in the lexicon, and this model introduces phonetic features later in the phonological component.

Finally, let us examine how this model of NS deals with the pervasive undergeneration discussed in section 2. Recall the relevant examples (3) and (4), repeated in (13) and (14):

(13) the vP phase for "they like him"
    [$_{vP}$ they [$_{v'}$ v+like(valued phi) [$_{VP}$ him(valued Case) [$_{V'}$ t_V t_{him}]]]]
(14) the vP phase for "whom do they like?"
    [$_{vP}$ whom(valued Case) [$_{v'}$ they [$_{v'}$ [$_{v'}$ v+like(valued phi) [$_{VP}$ t_{whom}
    [$_{V'}$ t_V t_{whom}]]]]]]

In (13), V(like) adjoins to v (a step required to restore the original VO order); hence, the valued phi on V(like) appears outside PC (=VP). In (14), in addition to the valued phi on V(like) (adjoined to v), NP(whom) moves to Spec, v (a step required to form an operator-variable construction at CI); hence, the valued Case on NP(whom) appears outside PC (=VP). Under the analysis proposed here, such valued [−Int] features (e.g. phi on V(like), Case on NP(whom)) will be recognized by Transfer as CI-offending features that must be removed from the CI-bound object. Recall that the lexical status of each feature—either [+Int] or [−Int]—remains unaltered throughout a derivation, given the law of the conservation of features (6). Thus, regardless of whether valued or not, [−Int] features (e.g. EF, phi on T, Case on N, and phonological codes) are recognized as CI-offending features and are removed from CI-bound objects by Transfer. Contra Chomsky (2007, 2008) and Richards (2007), it will never be "too late" for Transfer to do so, and we correctly allow derivationally valued features on the edge as in (13) and (14), overcoming the undergeneration of such examples.

If Transfer applies before valuation, however, [−Int] features lacking values (e.g. unvalued phi on T) will enter the phonological component and will induce crash at SM (or terminate a derivation in the phonological component), due to the underspecification of a feature value. If so, Transfer before valuation is for us, just like Chomsky (2007, 2008), "too early" for the SM interface. This analysis receives some empirical support over the valuation-transfer analysis (appealing to CI crash). Consider deviant cases like (15):

(15) *It is likely Bob to go.

Under our analysis, the derivation of (15) converges at CI but crashes at SM (or terminates in the phonological component), due to the underspecification of a Case-value; whereas under Chomsky's (2007, 2008) valuation-transfer analysis, it crashes at both interfaces. If a native speaker's perception of (15) is one of phonological but not semantic anomaly, then data like (15) may be understood as support for our analysis. Given this SM crashing (or terminating) effect of underspecified values, the before (too early), after (too late) paradox discussed in section 2 is dissolved (along with its beautiful entailments regarding cyclicity and inheritance).

4   A CRASH-PROOF SYSTEM AND A REMAINING QUESTION

As noted above, our analysis has positive empirical consequences; it avoids the problem of massive undergeneration that we revealed for Chomsky's (2007, 2008) valuation-transfer analysis. Furthermore, the present system is CI crash-proof in that Transfer deletes [–Int] features (e.g. EF, unvalued features such as phi on T and Case on N, and phonological codes) before SO reaches the CI interface. Any SO must "pass through" Transfer before heading to CI, and since Transfer deletes all [–Int], no such features ever arrive at CI; hence, there is no CI crashing (nor convergent gibberish induced by phi-valued T). As for the SM interface, if [–Int] features lacking values terminate a derivation in the phonological component as suggested in the preceding discussion (see also Chomsky 1995 for the notion "terminate/cancel"), here too there is no SM crashing. In this final section, we present a possible modification of this crash-proof aspect of the proposed model and briefly discuss a remaining question.

In the preceding three sections, following Chomsky (2007, 2008), we have adopted the assumption that the CI interface recognizes every feature appearing at CI; hence, the [–Int] removal function was motivated and assigned to Transfer. But under the present assumptions, there is no need to stipulate that the CI interface is designed to recognize (and be crash-offended by) features that it cannot use. Instead, we simply assume that the CI interface is designed to recognize all and only [+Int] features, which are precisely the ones it can use. The potentially infinite number of entities that are not [+Int] are not recognized; rather, they are simply invisible. Let us explore this possibility. Consider the following assumption:

(16) [–Int] features (e.g. EF, unvalued features such as phi on T and Case on N, phonological codes) are invisible to CI.

With this assumption, the CI interface, by definition, cannot recognize [–Int] features; hence, the [–Int] removal function is empirically unmotivated and (therefore) unnecessary. The internal mechanism of Transfer is thus simplified:

(17) Transfer (version 3)
Transfer sends SO (constructed by NS) to the semantic component and to the phonological component, respectively.

As stated in (17), Transfer no longer converts SO to SO<+Int>. Rather, Transfer is simply the name for the "split" where the semantic component and the phonological component each receive (the entire) SO (constructed by NS).

With this modification, let us briefly go over all three cases discussed in this paper, repeated in (18), (19), and (20):

(18) the vP phase for "they like him"
[$_{vP}$ they [$_{v'}$ v+like(valued phi) [$_{VP}$ him(valued Case) [$_{V'}$ t_V t_{him}]]]]

(19) the vP phase for "whom do they like?"

[$_{vP}$ whom(valued Case) [$_{v'}$ they [$_{v'}$ [$_{v'}$ v+like(valued phi) [$_{VP}$ t_{whom} [$_{V'}$ t_V t_{whom}]]]]]]

(20) *It is likely Bob to go.

In (18), V(like) adjoins to v (a step required to restore the original VO order); hence, the valued phi on V(like) appears outside PC (=VP). In (19), in addition to the valued phi on V(like) (adjoined to v), NP(whom) moves to Spec, v (a step required to form an operator-variable construction at CI); hence, the valued Case on NP(whom) appears outside PC (=VP). Now, notice, Transfer has no deletion function; hence, such valued [–Int] features (e.g. phi on V(like), Case on NP(whom)) will make their way to CI, but they are invisible to CI; hence, there is no effect of their undetected presence at CI. As for the SM interface, such valued [–Int] (unlike its unvalued counterpart) won't terminate a derivation in the phonological component; hence, it yields an SM representation. In (20), on the other hand, Case on NP(Bob) remains unvalued. Such unvalued Case does not induce any effect at CI since it is [–Int], hence invisible to CI, but it does terminate a derivation in the phonological component, due to the underspecification of a Case-value. This may be a source for a native speaker's perception of (20) as one of phonological, rather than semantic, anomaly.

The crash-proof model of NS presented above, however, leaves one important question: What now motivates feature-inheritance and cyclic Transfer (if they are real)? Since, for us, there is no need to transfer newly valued features at the exact point of their valuation, feature-inheritance and cyclic Transfer no longer follow. We have argued that neither Richards' (2007) deduction of feature-inheritance nor Chomsky's (2007, 2008) explanation of cyclic Transfer is tenable on empirical grounds since both (incorrectly) prohibit derivationally valued features to appear on the edge. So, how do we seek to ensure or, better yet, deduce feature-inheritance and cyclic Transfer within the proposed model? There are (at least) two possibilities. We could keep and develop Chomsky's (2000) version of Transfer, based on what Chomsky (2005) called the 3rd factor, in particular, the concept "computational efficiency." Or we could attempt to deduce feature-inheritance and cyclic Transfer from independently motivated mechanisms, presented as part of an optimal system. We think the latter possibility is indeed tenable and more interesting. We will return to this issue (and other related ones) in separate works (Epstein, Kitahara, and Seely 2008, 2012), where we argue that (i) feature-inheritance is motivated on Case-theoretic grounds and (ii) cyclic Transfer is an optimal result of eliminating anomalous (derivationally defined) syntactic relations (Epstein et al. 1998; Epstein and Seely 2006) that we reveal are in fact generated by Chomsky's (2007, 2008) "counter-cyclic" application of IM taking place at a phase level.

REFERENCES

Chomsky, N. 1995. *The Minimalist Program*. Cambridge, MA: MIT Press.
Chomsky, N. 1998. Some Observations on Economy in Generative Grammar. In Barbosa, P., Fox, D., Hagstrom, P., McGinnis, M. and Pesetsky, D. (eds.), *Is the Best Good Enough?*, 115–127. Cambridge, MA: MIT Press.
Chomsky, N. 2000. Minimalist Inquiries: The Framework. In Martin, R., Michaels, D. and Uriagereka, J. (eds.), *Step by Step: Essays on Minimalist Syntax in Honor of Howard Lasnik*, 89–155. Cambridge, MA: MIT Press.
Chomsky, N. 2001. Derivation by Phase. In Kenstowicz, M. (ed.), *Ken Hale: A Life in Language*, 1–52. Cambridge, MA: MIT Press.
Chomsky, N. 2005. Three Factors in Language Design. *Linguistic Inquiry* 36:1–22.
Chomsky, N. 2007. Approaching UG from Below. In Sauerland, U. and Gärtner, H.-M. (eds.), *Interfaces + Recursion = Language?*, 1–29. Berlin: Mouton de Gruyter.
Chomsky, N. 2008. On Phases. In Freidin, R., Otero, C. P. and Zubizarreta, M. L. (eds.), *Foundational Issues in Linguistic Theory: Essays in Honor of Jean-Roger Vergnaud*, 133–166. Cambridge, MA: MIT Press.
Epstein, S. D. 2007. On I(nternalist)-Functional Explanation in Minimalism. *Linguistic Analysis* 33:20–53.
Epstein, S. D. and Seely, T. D. 2002. Rule Applications as Cycles in a Level-Free Syntax. In Epstein, S. D. and Seely, T. D. (eds.), *Derivation and Explanation in the Minimalist Program*, 65–89. Oxford: Blackwell.
Epstein, S. D. and Seely, T. D. 2006. *Derivations in Minimalism*. Cambridge: Cambridge University Press.
Epstein, S. D., Groat, E., Kawashima, R. and Kitahara, H. 1998. *A Derivational Approach to Syntactic Relations*. Oxford: Oxford University Press.
Epstein, S. D., Kitahara, H. and Seely, T. D. 2008. The "Value" of Phonological Underspecification in the Narrow Syntax. Manuscript, University of Michigan, Ann Arbor, Keio University, Tokyo, and Eastern Michigan University, Ypsilanti [Presented at Carson-Newman College (Exploring Crash-Proof Grammars, February 29, 2008) and at Michigan State University (Linguistics Department Colloquium Series, February 7, 2008).]
Epstein, S. D., Kitahara, H. and Seely, T. D. 2012. Structure Building That Can't Be! In Valmala, V. and Etxebarria, M. (eds.), *Ways of Structure Building*, 253–270. Oxford: Oxford University Press.
Frampton, J. and Gutmann, S. 2002. Crash-Proof Syntax. In Epstein, S. D. and Seely, T. D. (eds.), *Derivation and Explanation in the Minimalist Program*, 90–105. Oxford: Blackwell.
Halle, M, and Marantz, A. 1993. Distributed Morphology and the Pieces of Inflection. In Hale, K. and Keyser, S. J. (eds.), *The View from Building 20: Essays in Linguistics in Honor of Sylvain Bromberger*, 111–176. Cambridge, MA: MIT Press.
Luria, S. 1974. Transcript of remarks at "A Debate on Bio-linguistics," a conference organized by the Centre Royaumont pour une Science de L'homme, Paris, held at Endicott House, Dedham, MA, May 20–21.
Martin, R. and Uriagereka, J. 2000. Some Possible Foundations of the Minimalist Program. In Martin, R., Michaels, D. and Uriagereka, J. (eds.), *Step by Step: Essays on Minimalist Syntax in Honor of Howard Lasnik*, 1–29. Cambridge, MA: MIT Press.
Nissenbaum, J. 2000. *Investigations of Covert Phrase Movement*. Doctoral dissertation, MIT, Cambridge, MA.

Obata, M. and Epstein, S. D. 2008. Deducing Improper Movement from Phase Based C-to-T Phi Transfer: Feature-Splitting Internal Merge. Manuscript, University of Michigan. [Presented at Carson-Newman College (Exploring Crash-Proof Grammars, February 29–March 1, 2008), at Newcastle University (The 31st GLOW, March 26–28, 2008), and at University of California, Los Angeles (The 27th WCCFL, May 16–18, 2008)].

Ouali, H. 2006a. Agreement Suppression Effects and Unification via Agree. In Baumer, D., Montero, D. and Scanlon, M. (eds.), *Proceedings of the 25th West Coast Conference on Formal Linguistics*, 320–327. Somerville, MA: Casccadilla Proceedings Project.

Ouali, H. 2006b. Unifying Agreement Relations: A Minimalist Analysis of Berber. Doctoral dissertation, University of Michigan, Ann Arbor.

Ouali, H. 2008. On C-to-T Phi-Feature Transfer: The Nature of Agreement and Anti-agreement in Berber. In D'Alessandro, R., Hrafnbjargarson, G. H. and Fisher, S. (eds.), *Agreement Restrictions*, 159–180. Berlin: Mouton de Gruyter.

Richards, M. 2007. On Feature Inheritance: An Argument from the Phase Impenetrability Condition. *Linguistic Inquiry* 38:563–572.

6 Merge, Derivational C-Command, and Subcategorization in a Label-Free Syntax

T. Daniel Seely

1 INTRODUCTION

This paper argues for a modification of Merge and explores the consequences of the modification for the derivational definition of c-command (developed by Epstein in a series of important recent papers in 1994 and 1999). Following Collins (2000, 2002), I'll attempt to defend the proposal that (1), the characterization of Merge given in Chomsky's (1995) "Bare Phrase Structure" (henceforth BPS), be replaced with (2):

(1) "Merge A and B" produces {A, {A, B}}, where A is the label of the derived category.

(2) "Merge A and B" produces {A, B}.

I'll argue that (2) represents a simplification of Merge that is motivated on minimalist grounds and does not lose empirical coverage.

It will be argued further that the proposed simplification of Merge has as its consequence the elimination of labels and, more generally, the elimination of projection. If Merge is defined as in (2), then there are no labels nor projection (as labels and projection are characterized in BPS). Within the generative tradition,[1] Collins's (2000, 2002) "Eliminating Labels" (hereafter EL) is the first to suggest that labels (and projection) can (and should) be eliminated. EL suggests that constituents be represented as in (3), not as in (4):

(3) {A, B}

(4) {A, {A, B}}

The present work attempts to advance this central insight of EL. I'll argue that the source of the elimination of labels (and projection) is to be found in the modification of Merge (i.e. (2)). Viewing the matter derivationally, I ask the question: If representations are indeed label free (as proposed by Collins), why do they have this property; in other words, can labellessness be explained?

EL presents a set of important insights that motivate the present work. EL argues that (3) replace (4), and EL suggests that label-free syntax is tenable in that principles and operations of the syntax that appeal to labels (specifically, X'-theory, Selection, the Minimal Link Condition, and the Phonetic Form [PF] interface) can operate in an empirically adequate manner without labels. EL argues that the effects of labels can be deduced from independently motivated principles of the syntax. However, EL does not consider the consequences of the elimination of labels for the definition of Merge nor for the definition of c-command. But an examination of the consequences of label-free syntax for Merge and c-command is important since labels and projection figure crucially in the BPS statement of Merge; indeed, Merge produces labels and projections, and labels figure prominently in the definition of c-command as well.

In section 2, I'll argue that we can deduce that labels are syntactically "inert," that labels cannot participate in syntactic relations. Label "inertness" follows from BPS, along with the hypothesis that derivational c-command is a necessary condition for the application of syntactic operations. I'll attempt to show that in effect labels are "already" eliminated in the syntax.

I'll argue in section 3 that the "actual" elimination of labels and projection follows directly from a revised version of Merge, that version given informally in (2), and that this simplification is well motivated on minimalist grounds. In section 2, I argue that labels are "inert." But although they are inert, labels (and projection) are still present in the representation of BPS constituent structure; i.e. a label is a member of the set that constitutes a constituent. In section 3, I'll argue that labels and projections should be eliminated: that they are not merely inert but rather non-existent.

As for c-command, I'll argue in section 4 that it must be defined derivationally, that a representational definition of this crucial syntactic relation is not compatible with a label-free syntax. However, I will argue that the definition of derivational c-command, and more specifically the definition of "term" adopted from BPS in Epstein (1999), must be modified in order to carry out the label-free syntax program established by EL.

Finally, in sections 6 and 7 I'll present a series of potential problems with the EL theory of subcategorization, and certain other problems for the label-free program, and will sketch potential solutions.

2 DEDUCING THE ELIMINATION OF LABELS FROM BARE PHRASE STRUCTURE, DERIVATIONAL C-COMMAND, AND THE DERIVATIONAL THEORY OF SYNTACTIC RELATIONS

EL considers four major areas where labels have traditionally been used:

(5) a. X'-theory
    b. Selection (subcategorization)

    c. Minimal Link Condition
    d. PF interface

EL argues that in each of these areas, labels need not be appealed to; relevant syntactic generalizations in these domains can ". . . be derived from the interaction of economy conditions, the properties of individual lexical items . . . and interface conditions" (EL:44).[2] Rather than review the details of EL's interesting treatment of (5), I'd like to start my discussion with another area where labels have figured prominently, specifically, in the definition of the relation of c-command. The standard representational definition of c-command appeals to the notion "first branching node." But if a "first branching node" is a phrasal label, the elimination of labels will clearly impact the representational definition of c-command—similarly, as we'll see in detail below, for derivational c-command.[3] C-command, moreover, plays a central role in EL's theory of Selection and in EL's recasting of the Minimal Link Condition. But the matter of how c-command is defined in a theory without labels is not addressed in EL. Since c-command is (crucially) exploited in the EL program, the definition of c-command in a label-free syntax becomes important. Indeed, within EL's own program, c-command is arguably the single most important elementary syntactic relation.

In this section, I will argue that the "elimination" of labels is, in fact, deducible from independently motivated mechanisms of the grammar. Specifically, I will show that the claim in (6)

(6) Labels cannot be involved in syntactic operations; labels are syntactically inert and are, in effect, "already" eliminated (i.e. for all intents and purposes, absent) from the syntax.

is deducible from the derivational definition of c-command proposed in Epstein (1999) combined with the proposal that derivational c-command between X and Y is a necessary condition for a syntactic operation to involve X and Y (like, for example, feature "checking" between X and Y). EL essentially asserts that the labels of phrasal categories can be eliminated. What is argued here is that elimination of the labels of phrasal categories can, in fact, be deduced from a certain set of (natural) definitions and principles. I present the deduction itself, with rather little commentary, in this section, which lends support to the central claim of EL that labels can, and should, be eliminated. But our paths to that conclusion, and certain key details of the resulting label-free syntax, are different.

2.1   The Definition of Merge in BPS

Consider (7), the characterization of Merge from BPS.

(7) The algorithm for the Merge of A and B, where A projects:
    i. create the set {A, B}
    ii. make a copy of A

iii. create the two-membered set consisting of the copied A and the set {A, B}; thus create {A, {A, B}} (see BPS:395–400)

Merge "puts" two elements A and B into a set (i.e. Merge creates a set containing A and B), thus {A, B}. But Merge also renders the set {A, B} that it creates a member of another set, a set containing the initial set {A, B} and what is called the label of the second set. Thus, Merge creates the set {*A*, {A, B}}, which consists of *A* (called the label, and italicized merely for ease of exposition) and the set {A, B}. What is called the label, namely *A*, is nothing more than a copy of A. In BPS, the label *A* of the set {*A*, {A, B}} is identified with A.[4] BPS states that relative to the set {*A*, {A, B}}, where this set is formed by Merge of A and B: "*A* is either A or B" (BPS:397; my emphasis). Consequently, in the set {*A*, {A, B}}, the label *A* is the category A (*A* and A are instances of the same thing).[5] Let me point out further that the copy-and-build-second-set sub-operation of Merge is basically what projection is in the BPS system; i.e. projection is steps ii and iii of (7) above. We see, then, that Merge in BPS is a three-step operation; it involves the creation of two sets (steps i and iii), and it involves the copying of the head of one of the "mergees" (step ii).

2.2 The Derivational Definition of C-Command, the Notion "Term," and the Centrality of C-Command in Syntactic Operations

Consider next the derivational definition of c-command given in Epstein (1999:329):

(8) Derivational Definition of C-Command:
X c-commands all and only the terms of the category Y with which X was paired (by Merge or by Move) in the course of the derivation.

This definition appeals directly to the notion "term." The definition of "term" adopted by Epstein is as follows. Note that this definition of term, from Chomsky (1995), is entirely (set-) representational, i.e. defined on the output representations created by Merge, as characterized in (7):

(9) Definition of "term": for any structure K,
   i. K is a term of K
   ii. if L is a term of K, then the members of the members of L are terms of K

(Chomsky 1995:399)

It was pointed out above that EL does not present an explicit definition of c-command, even though c-command figures crucially in the EL theory of subcategorization and in the EL reformulation of the Minimal

Link Condition. Since there is no definition of "c-command" given in EL, it is not clear that EL would accept (8)/(9). However, I'll argue later that the standardly assumed "first branching node" definition of c-command, which is purely representational, is not compatible with a label-free syntax. In fact, I'll suggest that a derivational definition of c-command is required. Moreover, I adopt the view of Epstein (1994, 1999) that the derivational definition of c-command is superior to the representational definition (I presuppose Epstein's argumentation here). And I adopt Epstein's specific formulation as given in (8) and (9) to keep the present discussion as concrete as possible.

Finally, consider (10), proposed by Epstein (1999):

(10) X may enter into a syntactic relation with Y iff X derivationally c-commands Y.

From (10), it follows that c-command between X and Y is a necessary (but not always sufficient) condition for a syntactic operation to involve X and Y.

So far, we have put into place the BPS characterization of Merge, as well as Epstein's derivational definition of c-command, which make crucial use of BPS's notion of "term"; and we've reviewed the natural assumption that derivational c-command is a necessary condition for syntactic operations. I will now argue that it follows from Merge, derivational c-command, and (10) that labels cannot participate in syntactic operations, that the "elimination" of labels is, in fact, deducible.

2.3   Labels Are Never Derivationally C-Commanded by Any Category

There is an interesting (and, as far as I know, unnoticed) consequence of derivational c-command, a consequence that arises given the definition of "term" that derivational c-command assumes; the consequence is this:

(11) The label of a category X is never derivationally c-commanded (by any category Y).

The label of a category X is never derivationally c-commanded because the label of the category X is by definition never a term of X (and recall that A c-commands all and only the terms of the category with which A is concatenated). To illustrate the point, consider (12), the output of the Merge of *the* and *picture*, under the definition of Merge given in BPS:

(12) {*the*, {the, picture}}

The entire object {*the*, {the, picture}} is a term by (9i)—repeated below for ease of reference:

(9) Definition of "term": for any structure K,
  i. K is a term of K
  ii. if L is a term of K, then the members of the members of L are terms of K

(Chomsky 1995:399)

First, the set {*the*, {the, picture}} = K, so by (9i) this is a term. Next, the set {*the*, {the, picture}} in (12) has two members: *the* (called the label) and the set {the, picture}. The first member of the set {*the*, {the, picture}}, namely *the*, is not a member of a member, and therefore *the* is not a term of {*the*, {the, picture}}. The second member of the set {*the*, {the, picture}}, namely the set {the, picture} DOES itself have two members, *the* and *picture*. Therefore, both *the* and *picture* are each terms of {*the*, {the, picture}} (by (9ii)). Overall, then, the set {*the*, {the, picture}} has three terms: (i) {*the*, {the, picture}}, (ii) *the*, and (iii) *picture*. But the label *the* is not a term of {*the*, {the, picture}}.

Let us now merge the object in (12) with *see*. This Merge of *see* and {*the*, {the, picture}} produces (13), assuming that *see* projects:

(13) {*see*, {see, {*the*, {the, picture}}}}

In (13), the lexical category *see* does not derivationally c-command the label, *the*, of the category {*the*, {the, picture}} that *see* is merged with. Recall, the label *the* is not a term of {*the*, {the, picture}}, and *see* by definition derivationally c-commands all and only the terms of what *see* is merged with. Thus, (13) illustrates (14).

(14) The label of a category X is not derivationally c-commanded by the category Y with which X is concatenated (by Merge or Move).

Informally put, the label of X is never locally derivationally c-commanded by Y (where by "locally" we mean "by the category with which X itself is concatenated") since the label of X is not a term of X (the label is never a member of a member of X).

But in fact the stronger claim of (11), i.e. that a label is never derivationally c-commanded, locally or non-locally, also follows. The label of X is not derivationally c-commanded by the category Y with which X is concatenated, nor is the label of X derivationally c-commanded by any "higher" category Z that is merged with Y. To illustrate, suppose we merge the object in (13) with *Bill*, and suppose that the verb projects. This merge produces (15):

(15) {*see*, {Bill, {*see*, {see, {*the*, {the, picture}}}}}}

Bill derivationally c-commands all and only the terms of the category with which *Bill* is merged. *Bill* was merged with the category in (15a):

(15) a. {*see*, {see, {*the*, {the, picture}}}}

This entire object is a term ("for any structure K, K is a term of K"). Thus, *Bill* c-commands the entire object. The set {*see*, {see, {*the*, {the, picture}}}} with which *Bill* was merged has two members ("if L is a term of K, then the members of the members of L are terms of K"):

(15) b. The members of {*see*, {see, {*the*, {the, picture}}}} are
Member 1: *see*
Member 2: {see, {*the*, {the, picture}}}

Since it is not a member of a member, *see* is not a term of {*see*, {see, {*the*, {the, picture}}}}; thus, *Bill* does not c-command *see*. Member 2, i.e. {see, {*the*, {the, picture}}}, does have members, namely *see* and the set {*the*, {the, picture}}. Thus, *see* and {*the*, {the, picture}} are members of the members (of L where L is a term of K), and so are terms. As a consequence of this, *Bill* derivationally c-commands *see* and {*the*, {the, picture}}. Notice that *Bill* derivationally c-commands the lexical item *see*, and *Bill* c-commands the SET {*the*, {the, picture}}.

So far so good. But notice that *Bill* does not derivationally c-command the label of {*the*, {the, picture}}. As we just saw, the set {*the*, {the, picture}} is a member of a member of the set {*see*, {see, {*the*, {the, picture}}}}. The set {*the*, {the, picture}} thus counts as a term of the larger set. Since {*the*, {the, picture}} is a term of the larger set, then we now appeal to the second part of the definition of term in (9), repeated here again for ease of reference:

(9) Definition of "term": for any structure K,
i. K is a term of K
ii. if L is a term of K, then the members of the members of L are terms of K

So in the present case, the set {*the*, {the, picture}} counts as L of (9ii). And the members of the members of L = {*the*, {the, picture}} will count as terms; but note that although *the* is a member of L = {*the*, {the, picture}}, *the* is not a member of a member of this set. Therefore, the label *the* is NOT a term. Overall, then, *Bill* does not c-command the label *the*, and nothing "higher" than *Bill* will c-command the label either.

Labels are never derivationally c-commanded since labels are never terms. A label is never a structure K, and hence a label can't be a term under clause (9i). A label is produced by the structure building operations Merge and Move, but the label itself is not the output of the structure building operations. The output of the Merge of A and B is the set {A, {A, B}}; the label of that set is produced by Merge, but the label itself is not a "structure." Moreover, a label is never a member of a member of a term of K. We see, then, that (11) follows.

2.4 Labels Never Derivationally C-Command (Any Category)

Not only are labels never c-commanded, but, moreover, labels do not derivationally c-command other categories. This follows straightforwardly since labels are never themselves merged with any category (and, more generally, labels themselves are never concatenated, by Merge or Move, with any category). A label is "created" by Merge, but the label itself is not the final output of Merge. Rather, a label is always contained within the set that is the final output of Merge. The final output of the merge of A and B is not the label *A* but rather the set {A, {A, B}}, which contains the label. And within this set, the label *A* is inaccessible to Merge.

2.5 Labels Are Syntactically Inert; They Are, in Effect, "Already" Eliminated

Notice, then, that in effect labels are already "eliminated." This is deducible from (i) the definition of Merge in BPS, (ii) the definition of derivational c-command, and (iii) the hypothesis that derivational c-command is a necessary condition for the application of a syntactic operation. We have argued that it follows from the above three premises that labels are not c-commanded and do not themselves c-command any category. Therefore, labels cannot participate in syntactic operations; they are syntactically inert. Labels are, in effect, "already" eliminated.

Two questions (at least) immediately arise from the above deduction of the syntactic inertness of labels:

(16) a. Why are labels proposed in BPS in the first place?
b. Does the elimination (i.e. the syntactic inertness) of labels result in the loss of important information?

2.6 Why Are Labels Proposed in the First Place? Are Labels Necessary for Interface Interpretation?

Question (16a) is considered in more detail in section 4. But note that even without derivational c-command, BPS does, at least implicitly, realize that labels play no role in the syntax; labels are not terms, and only terms are "functioning elements" of the syntax—thus, labels are not functioning elements. Consider (17), which is an "informal," graph-theoretic transposition of BPS's set-theoretic phrasal construct:

(17)

ZP names the actual set $\{z, \{z, w\}\}$; X′ names the set $\{x, \{x, y\}\}$; and XP represents $\{x, \{\{z, \{z, w\}\}, \{x, \{x, y\}\}\}\}$. Regarding (17), BPS states that "[t]he functioning elements in [(17)] are at most the nodes of the informal representation: that is, the lexical terminals z, w, x, y; the intermediate element X′ and its sister ZP; and the "root element" ZP standing for the full structure formed." BPS then states: "These [elements] alone can be functioning elements; call them the *terms* of XP . . ." and, finally (and crucially for the present discussion), "Terms correspond to nodes of the informal representations, where each node is understood to stand for the sub-tree of which it is the root" (BPS:398–399, my emphasis). It is clear from the last quote that the node X′ in (17) does NOT represent the label of the set $\{x, \{x\ y\}\}$, but rather X′ represents the entire set $\{x, \{x, y\}\}$; i.e. it represents "the sub-tree of which it is the root." The entire set $\{x, \{x, y\}\}$ is a functioning element (it is a term), but the label of this set, namely x, is NOT a term and is NOT a functioning element. There is something of a mismatch between the graph-theoretic and the set-theoretic representations of BPS phrases. Compare (18a) and (18b) for example:

(18) a. X′   b. $\{x, \{x, y\}\}$
     /\
    x y

We might be tempted to think of the node X′ as the label of the set in (18b). But the node X′ does NOT equal the label x of $\{x, \{x, y\}\}$. Rather, X′ is just the name of the entire set $\{x, \{x, y\}\}$.

To summarize, we have deduced that labels (understood in the sense of BPS) are syntactically "inert." They CANNOT play any role in the syntax, and this seems to be recognized even in BPS itself. This immediately gives rise to the question in (16a), that is, why are labels proposed in BPS in the first place? It can't be because the label is required by the syntax; indeed, the syntax can't "use" the label at all: The label is not a "functioning element." Rather, according to BPS, labels are required AFTER the syntax (by the interfaces). BPS (396) states:

(19) Applied to two objects α and β, Merge forms the new object γ. What is γ? γ must be constituted somehow from the two items α and β. . . .

The simplest object constructed from α and β is the set {α, β}, so we take γ to be at least this set, where α and β are the *constituents* of γ. Does that suffice? *Output conditions dictate otherwise; thus verbal and nominal elements are interpreted differently at LF and behave differently in the phonological component.* γ must therefore at least (and we assume at most) be of the form {δ, {α, β}}, where δ identifies the relevant properties of γ; call δ the *label* of γ.

The idea here seems to be that the LF and PF interfaces must be able to distinguish what are traditionally referred to as NPs versus VPs. Thus, LF must recognize that the set {A, B} is verbal or nominal. And the implication is that the interfaces can distinguish a verbal from a nominal element only with labels. Looking at the matter in a graph-theoretic way, we might say that the interfaces must distinguish [destroyed it] from [destruction of it] and that the interfaces can make the distinction only by "seeing" the nodes V′ and N′. Thus:

(20)

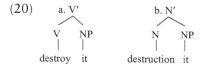

The traditional idea is that the two elements *destroy* and *it* COMBINED are/ is a verbal object, whereas the elements *destruction* and *it* COMBINED are/is a nominal object. But recall from our discuss above that the nodes V′ in (20a) and N′ in (20b) do NOT represent the labels of the corresponding set-theoretic object of BPS. In more precise BPS terms, the object *destroy it* is represented as

(21) a. {*destroy*, {destroy, it}}

and the object *destruction of it* is represented as in

(21) b. {*destruction*, {destruction, it}}

The entire set (21a) is what V′ stands for in (20a). But the interfaces can't inspect just this set {*destroy*, {destroy, it}} and determine that it is "verbal" or "nominal." Rather, the interface must look inside the set; the interface must (apparently) "look" at the label of the set, which is a MEMBER of the set. It is not clear, however, how the label facilities this. If the interfaces must in fact look inside the set to see the label, then why couldn't the interfaces look inside what BPS claims is the "simplest" set, namely {destroy, it} and "see" the verbal element *destroy*? We have to stipulate that the label is what the interface looks at to determine how to interpret a set, to interpret that set as verbal or nominal. So it is not clear that labels are required even in this sense.

2.7   Does the Inclusion of Labels Create Trouble?

As for question (16b), namely "Does the elimination of labels result in the loss of information?," note that although a category X does not derivationally c-command the label of the category Y with which X is concatenated; X DOES derivationally c-command the category with which the label is identified. To illustrate, consider (22), which was discussed in a different context above.

(22) {*see*, {see, {*the*, {the, picture}}}}

As shown, *see* does not derivationally c-command the label *the*. However, *see* does derivationally c-command the lexical category *the*. The label *the* is not a term of {*the*, {the, picture}} since the label *the* is not a member of a member of {*the*, {the, picture}}. However, the lexical category *the* IS a term of {*the*, {the, picture}} since it is a member of a member of {*the*, {the, picture}}. We pointed out earlier that the label *the* is identified with (i.e. the label is an instance of) *the*. The label *the* and the lexical category *the* are occurrences of precisely the same thing. Overall, then, there is nothing lost relative to the specific information contained in the label itself. Specifically, *see* can have a relation with *the*. *The* is identical with the label *the*. Thus, in effect, *see* does not "lose sight of" the information contained in *the* (even though *see* does not c-command *the*).

So, again, an important question arises: Are labels necessary? Or, to put the matter historically, why were/are labels postulated to begin with? The hypothesis, which I share with EL, is that labels are not necessary, But the question of why labels are postulated within BPS remains, and will be taken up in more detail a bit later.

In this section we presented a deduction of the "elimination" of labels. The argument is summarized as follows:

Premise 1:   "Phrases" and labels are defined as in BPS; i.e. assume Merge as in BPS.

Premise 2:   Derivational c-command is defined as in Epstein (1999).

Premise 3:   Derivational c-command is a necessary condition for syntactic relations.

THEREFORE: Labels do not participate in syntactic relations.

Since labels, as defined in BPS, are not terms, and since derivational c-command crucially appeals to terms (X derivationally c-commands all and only the terms of Y with which X is merged), it follows that labels never c-command nor are c-commanded by any other category. Since c-command is required for a syntactic relation, then labels can't participate in syntactic relations.

Having completed the deduction, let us turn to other issues in Collins' label-free syntax program.

3 "SIMPLIFYING" MERGE RESULTS IN THE ELIMINATION OF LABELS AND PROJECTION

In section 2 above, it was argued that although labels are indeed postulated in BPS representations (i.e. the label *A* is a member of the set {A, {A, B}}), labels themselves are syntactically inert. In this section I argue that the actual elimination of labels (and projection) results from a modification (which arguably represents a simplification[6]) of the operation Merge, as Merge is defined in BPS. I argue that the simplification of Merge is desirable on minimalist grounds. Like EL, I argue that the labels of phrasal categories can (and, in fact, should) be eliminated; that is, that the label, as defined in BPS, is NOT part of constituent structure representation. However, I consider a set of arguments for this conclusion, and I explore consequences of it, that EL does not.

Both BPS and EL note that the "simplest" statement of Merge is:

(23) "Simplest" algorithm for Merge of A, B:
      Create the set {A, B}

What Merge does here is (merely) establish a relationship between A and B, by putting A and B into a set. That's it.

What BPS actually adopts, however, is the more complex mechanism with three sub-operations, the details of which were considered above in section 2.1:

(24) "Actual" BPS algorithm for the Merge of A and B is:
      i.   create the set {A, B}
      ii. "make" a copy of A (more generally: make a copy of whichever element, A or B, "projects")[7]
      iii. create the set consisting of the copied A and the set {A, B}; thus, create {A, {A, B}}

Below, we argue that the "simplified" Merge, as in (23), is motivated on minimalist grounds. And, crucially, this simplification of Merge has two immediate consequences:

(25) a. There are no labels, as labels are characterized in BPS.
      b. There is no projection, as projection is characterized in BPS.

Recall that in BPS, the label, A, of the set {A, {A, B}} is identical with (since it is a copy of) A. Since simplified Merge (23) eliminates step ii of (24), where step ii is the label-creating sub-operation, then labels, as characterized in BPS, are eliminated. Furthermore, since steps ii and iii of (24) are eliminated in simplified Merge, then to the extent that steps ii and iii represent projection, it follows that projection as characterized in BPS is eliminated, too.

As noted, EL proposes that representations as in (26), which contain a label, be replaced with representations as in (27), where the label is eliminated.

(26) {A, {A, B}}
(27) {A, B}

But it is more than just the label, A, that is eliminated in (27). If only the label itself were eliminated from (26), the result would not be (27) but rather {{A, B}}. Also eliminated from (26) is the set that contains the label. This set, i.e. the set {A, {A, B}}, represents, at least in part, the projection of A. Thus, it is not just the label that is eliminated; projection is eliminated as well.

It is important to stress that, viewed derivationally, it is not labels and projection that are eliminated in and of themselves; rather, what is actually eliminated are two sub-operations of the "complex" operation Merge. It is a consequence of adopting the "simplest" version of Merge, namely (23), that there are no phrasal labels nor projections; i.e. it is a consequence of the simplification of Merge that phrases are represented as in (27), and not as in (26). I'll argue that this simplification of Merge is motivated on minimalist grounds. The absence of labels is an immediate consequence of a well-motivated simplification of a fundamental, and arguably necessary, structure building (derivational) operation, namely Merge as in (23). In short, the question I am asking is: If indeed (27) is the "right" type of representation, what is the nature of the generative procedure from which the relevant properties of these representations could be deduced? I will then focus on the implications of this (arguably necessary) modification of Merge for the statement of (derivational) c-command. I'll argue that the modification of Merge forces a modification of the definition of (derivational) c-command, and more specifically a (rather simple) modification of the definition of "term." The consequences of this modified version of c-command for EL's theory of subcategorization will then be considered. Ultimately, it will be argued that we must render explicit the definition of c-command since, on the standardly assumed definitions of c-command (both representational and derivational definitions), certain problems with EL's label-free framework arise, particularly with EL's theory of subcategorization.

3.1 Three Arguments for Merge as a One-Step Operation

In this subsection, I present three arguments for the simplification of Merge in (23). I'll argue (i) that the simplified version of Merge is motivated by the inclusiveness condition to the extent that the simplified Merge requires fewer elements beyond the features of lexical items, fewer elements, that is, than Merge as defined in BPS; (ii) that Merge, simplified as in (23), eliminates an undesirable redundancy between labels and categories; and (iii) that the simplified Merge dissolves problems with the notion of "label" in BPS.

3.1.1 *Is Simplified Merge Motivated by Inclusiveness?*

Chomsky (1995) in "Categories and Transformations" (hereafter CT) formulates the inclusiveness condition in this way:

(28) Another natural condition is that outputs consist of nothing beyond properties of items of the lexicon (lexical features)—in other words, that the interface levels consist of nothing more than arrangements of lexical features.

(CT:225)

It follows from the inclusiveness condition, which is arguably the fundamental formal characterization of the minimalist approach, that we should posit in the syntax as little as possible beyond the features of lexical items; thus, the syntax, to as great an extent as possible, should not appeal to indices, bar levels, relations, etc.

As characterized in BPS, Merge takes as input the elements A and B, and Merge gives as output the set {A, {A, B}}. Note that Merge creates an identity relation between the label A and the category A. This identity relation is not itself a lexical feature, nor is it a combination of features. The relation itself does not occur in the lexicon, and therefore it violates the inclusiveness condition. Simplified Merge, (23), does not involve the identity relation, and in fact it cannot, since no label is created. Thus, the simplified version of Merge does not violate inclusiveness relative to the identity relation.

3.1.2 *Simplified Merge Avoids Possible Redundancy*

As noted, simplified Merge, (23) (Merge A, B = {A, B}), results in the elimination of phrasal labels and projection. I argue here that this is a desirable result since phrasal category labels, as defined in BPS, are redundant with independently motivated elements of the grammar; specifically, the information that labels themselves encode (and this is particularly true in the case of the merger of lexical categories) is independently available and independently necessary. Therefore, phrasal labels should be eliminated.

Recall that in BPS, the label of a phrasal category is identified with (certain) other categories. The idea in BPS is that the operation Merge takes, say, *see* and *Mary* as input and gives as output the set {*see*, {see, Mary}}. The label (i.e. *see*) of this set is identified with the lexical item *see*. (Recall that BPS states that relative to the set {A, {A, B}}, where this set is formed by merger of A and B, "A is either A or B"; BPS:397.) If what is called the label of the derived set is identified with the lexical item *see*, in the specific case under consideration here, then the label is the lexical item *see*. That is, the label of the set {*see*, {see, Mary}} is identified with (i.e. it is) the lexical item *see*. So the label, in this case, is entirely redundant with the lexical category with which the label is identified. The label *see* is precisely the lexical category *see*. Thus, there is no information contained in the label itself that is not already present in the derived set that contains the label and the lexical category. Lexical categories are necessary; this is a fundamental assumption of all syntax.[8] As we will argue in some detail in section 4, the label A is made available at a different point in the derivation than the lexical category A. But the information contained in the label itself is already present in the derivation; eliminating the label does not result in the loss of this information. Since the label is redundant with a lexical category, then the label "should" be eliminated.

3.1.3   *What* Is *a Label?*

The labels of phrases are problematic; since eliminating phrasal labels eliminates the problems with these labels, it follows that the labels of phrases should be eliminated.

In Chomsky (2001b), the label of the set {*see*, {see, Mary}} is identified with the verb *see*. This identification raises certain questions. For example, the verb *see* has a complement (in this case *Mary*). Does it follow from the identity relation that the label *see* also has this same complement? Does the label have all the selectional and featural properties of the item *see*? Since the lexical category can move (under head-movement), does this mean that the label can also move (under the same circumstances)?

The point here is that questions involving the status of the label in BPS are eliminated with the elimination of the label: Quite simply, if there is no label, then there is no question about what a label is—and it is not clear what a phrasal label is exactly. Eliminating labels eliminates these questions.

In this section I have attempted to motivate a simplification of Merge. This simplification of Merge automatically results in the elimination of labels and projections, as labels and projection are characterized in BPS. The main claim is simple: If there is no copy and no set created from that copy (i.e. if we remove from (24) steps ii and iii), then there are no phrasal labels nor projection. The simplest, and arguably necessary, generative procedure produces no labels nor projections.

So far, then, I have attempted to give added support to the central assertion of EL. And, like EL, I must consider how principles of the syntax that make explicit reference to labels and projection are to be stated without labels and projections. To that end, I will consider the implications of simplified Merge (23) for the definition of derivational c-command.

4   SOME CONSEQUENCES OF THE SIMPLIFICATION OF MERGE FOR DERIVATIONAL C-COMMAND

In this section I consider some consequences of the proposed simplification of Merge (and more generally of the proposed elimination of labels and projection) for the derivational definition of c-command. This is important since it will be argued that a label-free syntax is not compatible with a representational definition of c-command. We argue that once we adopt Merge as in (23), we must assume derivational c-command. And, as noted above, c-command plays an important role in EL's theory of subcategorization. To fully evaluate that theory of subcategorization, it is crucial to have a precise definition of (derivational) c-command in place.

The section is organized as follows. First, we argue that the traditional "first branching nodes" definition of representational c-command is not compatible with a label-free syntax; a derivational definition, on the other hand, is compatible. Second, we argue that the definition of derivational c-command (of Epstein 1999), and specifically the notion "term," must be modified to accommodate the elimination of labels and projections. Finally, we point out certain problems with the EL theory of subcategorization, which relies crucially on c-command, and suggest tentative solutions to these problems.

The problems with the EL theory of subcategorization that are raised in this section also help to answer a question left open in section 2.5 and 2.6. We deduced that labels are syntactically inert, and this gives rise to the question: Why are labels posited in the first place (if they play no role in syntactic operations)? We pointed out that a label is a copy of (i.e. the label is identified with) a lexical category. Consequently, the information contained in a label is redundant with the lexical category with which the label is identified. So, again, why are there labels, and why is there projection? The answer, in part, is this: Although the information encoded in a label L is exactly the information contained in the lexical category that L is identified with, the point at which this information is available is different. On one view, projection is a device for making the same information available at different points in the derivation. For example, the lexical information of the lexical category *see* is available at the point when *see* is merged with, say, *Bill* to produce the object {see, Bill}. What projection does is allow this same lexical information to be available again at the point when the object {see, Bill} is merged with, say, *Sue* to produce {Sue, {see, Bill}}. Projection allows *see* to behave as though *it* is being merged directly with *Sue*.

Note, furthermore, that a label is a representational construct. A label encodes the information that was available at an earlier stage of the derivation; given Merge as defined in BPS, a label L basically tells us that the lexical category that L is identified with was merged with some other category, and that merger was at an earlier point in the derivation. Given that labels are representational constructs (as are phrase markers more generally), the elimination of labels seems to move the syntax one step closer to a purely derivational system.

4.1   A Note on Representational C-Command without Labels

Before turning to the implications of the elimination of labels (more specifically, the proposed simplification of Merge, which results in the absence of labels/projection) for the derivational definition of c-command, let me make a brief point regarding label-free syntax and representational c-command.

Consider the representational view of c-command (under the traditional "first branching node" definition). It is not entirely clear how a traditional graph-theoretic structure like (29)

(29)   VP
       ⌒
      V NP

would be represented without labels. If there is no VP label, does (29) become (30), for example?

(30)   ⋀
      V NP

In other words, is there still a "node" (and a branching node) above V and NP, but this node has no label? If there is no node, then we must abandon the standard representational definition of c-command (since that definition crucially relies on the notion "branching node," and if there is no node at all above V and NP in (30), then there is no branching node). If there is a node, but no actual label for that node, we could presumably maintain the representational definition of c-command; thus, V would c-command NP since the first branching node dominating V (the "empty" node) would (presumably) dominate NP. But the status of such an "empty" node is unclear. Would it be interpretable? Presumably not, since it has no features. And if it is not interpretable, how could it survive at the LF interface?

What is clear is that once we adopt the BPS characterization of phrases, we must modify the traditional representational definition of c-command. Thus, in a set-theoretic model, we'd have to use some notion of "containment" rather than "dominance." Consider, for instance, {read, {Jim, {read, {read, {*the*, {the, man}}}}}}, which is the BPS object representing "Jim read the book." There are no "branching nodes" in the traditional sense. We'd need a definition like "X c-commands Y iff X and Y are members of the set *S*; or X c-commands Y if Y is a member of a member of the same set as X."

But there is a much deeper point. As soon as we accept Merge, as in (23) or (24), then, given the argumentation of Epstein (1999), we should assume a *derivational* definition of c-command. The representational view is not explanatory (see Epstein 1999 for detailed discussion).

Let us turn, then, to the derivational account of c-command.

4.2   Some Consequences of the Elimination of Labels for Derivational C-command as It Relates to EL's Theory of Subcategorization

Suppose Merge is defined as in (23), repeated here as (31):

(31) Algorithm for Merge of A, B: Create the set {A, B}

And suppose that we adopt, verbatim, Epstein's definition of derivational c-command, repeated below:

(32) Derivational Definition of C-Command (from Epstein 1999:329):
      X c-commands all and only the terms of the category Y with which X was paired (by Merge or by Move) in the course of the derivation.

(33) For any structure K,
      i. K is a term of K
      ii. if L is a term of K, then the members of the members of L are terms of K

(Chomsky 1995:399)

Taken just this far, we confront an immediate problem for the EL theory of subcategorization, and we confront a related problem for the derivational theory of syntactic relations. To illustrate the subcategorization problem, suppose we Merge *the* and *picture*, producing (by (31)) the object in (34).

(34) {the, picture}

Suppose next that we Merge (via (31)) *see* with the object in (34) to produce (35):

(35) {see, {the, picture}}

Here, *see* derivationally c-commands the object {the, picture}; *see* is merged with {the, picture}, and {the, picture} is a term (by (33i)). But notice that *see* does NOT c-command *the*, and *see* does not c-command *picture*. This is because neither *the* nor *picture* is a term of {the, picture} (and *see* derivationally c-commands all and only the terms of the category with which *see* is merged). The object {the, picture} has two members: *the* and *picture*. But the members *the* and *picture* are not members of a member, and therefore neither is a term of {the, picture}. Since *see* derivationally c-commands all and only the terms of the category with which *see* is concatenated (concatenated in this case by our modified version of Merge), and since *the* and *picture* are NOT terms of the category with which *see* is concatenated, then *see* does not c-command *the* nor *picture*.[9]

This result poses a problem for EL's theory of subcategorization. Informally stated, the problem is this: With respect to (35), *see* does not c-command *the*; however, EL's theory of subcategorization crucially assumes that *see* DOES c-command *the*. Without this c-command relation, the subcategorization requirements of *see* cannot be satisfied under EL's assumptions. Notice, moreover, that this represents a much more general problem. Basically, if we merge (by Merge in its proposed simplified form) the lexical items A and B to produce {A, B}, and then we merge C with {A, B} to produce {C, {A, B}}, C will derivationally c-command the whole object {A, B}, but C will not c-command the lexical items A and B. However, there is evidence that C does participate in syntactic relations with A and B. Thus, a subject (=C) can bind a direct object (=B). But if there is no derivational c-command relation, then, under the assumption that c-command is a necessary condition for syntactic phenomena such as binding, even the simplest binding relations would be incorrectly disallowed.

Before moving to the more formal statement of this problem relative to the EL theory of subcategorization, let me make clear that I am not, at this point, challenging any specific proposal in EL. I am not arguing that the problem I am now developing exists internal to the specific workings of EL. It is true, however, that EL's theory of subcategorization appeals to c-command. It is also true that EL does not render explicit the definition of c-command that it assumes (whether derivational or representational). What I seek to do here is consider a precise definition of c-command, a definition that is consistent with a label-free syntax (indeed, I have argued that derivational c-command is required by a label-free syntax), and try to determine if that definition works within the EL theory of subcategorization. It is unclear that the EL theory of subcategorization can be adequately evaluated otherwise, since without a precise definition of c-command, it is not clear what predictions that theory actually makes.

4.3   A Problem for the EL Theory of Subcategorization

Let's assume that *see* has a subcategorization feature (let's assume that feature is +D). EL assumes further that the subcategorization feature of a head must be checked, where feature checking is accomplished through EL's modified version of the more general feature checking system proposed by Chomsky (2000, 2001b), i.e. the probe-goal analysis. Basically, features are checked through the syntactic operation Agree. Now, in a theory with labels, the checking of the subcategorization feature of *see* can be done as follows (to state the matter informally, which suffices for present purposes): The subcategorization feature of *see* is satisfied (i.e. checked) if *see* is merged with a DP. But in a theory without labels (like "DP"), feature checking must be handled differently.

EL's theory of selection/subcategorization assumes that

(36) a. the subcategorization feature of a lexical head X must be satis-
          fied (i.e. "checked/deleted")
      b. feature "checking" between X and Y takes place under the rela-
          tion Match (as Match is stated in Chomsky (2000, 2001b); i.e.
          X and Y must Match for the feature(s) F (X and Y must be iden-
          tical for the feature F but not necessarily for the value of F).

The EL theory of subcategorization also assumes, crucially, that

(37) a. For Y to "check" the features of X, X must c-command Y.
      b. Feature checking obeys minimality.

Minimality for EL is as follows:

(38) If X selects Y (where Y is a lexical category), then *X Z Y, where Z
      intervenes between X and Y, and Z is any lexical category.

Finally, EL defines "intervention" as follows:

(39) Z intervenes between X and Y if X c-commands Z, and Z
      c-commands Y.

Notice that c-command figures directly in the central (37a) and in (39), but c-command is undefined in EL.

Assuming the definition of Merge in (31)—Merge A and B gives {A, B}— and assuming the explicit definition of derivational c-command given in (32) and (33), and assuming the EL theory of subcategorization traced above, let us return to (35), repeated below:

(35) {see, {the, picture}}

The lexical item *see* must have its subcategorization feature (+D) checked (by (36a)). The potential checker is *the*, since *the* matches *see* for the feature D. For *the* to check *see*'s feature, *see* must (locally) c-command *the* (by (37)– (38)). However, as we argued above, *see* does not derivationally c-command *the* (nor is it clear how representational c-command could be successfully applied in the label- (node-) free EL system). Thus, feature checking cannot take place, and (35) is incorrectly disallowed as a subcategorization (i.e. feature checking) violation. In fact, it is unclear that subcategorization can ever be satisfied.

4.4   Eliminating Just Labels ≠ Eliminating Labels and Projection

As a brief side note, recall that it was pointed out above that EL eliminates more than just labels. Consider the BPS construct {A, {A, B}}, which results from the merge (as defined in BPS) of A and B. If we eliminated from {A, {A, B}} just the label *A*, the result would be {{A, B}}. In order to produce {{A, B}}, Merge would have to put A and B into the set {A, B}, and then render that set the sole member of another unit set, one without a label. However, following Collins, I propose that {A, {A, B}} be replaced with {A, B}. It is interesting to note that if we eliminated just the label of {A, {A, B}}, if we propose that a residue of "projection" remained, i.e. if we replace {A, {A, B}} with {{A, B}}, the specific problem posed above for the EL theory of subcategorization does not arise. (35) would be represented as in (40):

(40)   {{see, {{the, picture}}}}

Here *see* would derivationally c-command *the* and *picture* (given Epstein's definition) since *the* and *picture* are both terms of {{the, picture}}. *The* and *picture* are terms since each is indeed a member of a member of {{the, picture}}. The set {{the, picture}} has the member {the, picture}, and *the* and *picture* are members of this member. So we see that there is an empirical difference between eliminating just the label of a BPS object like {A, {A, B}} and eliminating the label along with what has been referred to here as "projection."

However, I will not pursue this option since (i) the added complexity of having (a form of) projection without labels is undesirable on conceptual grounds and (ii) the further problems we address next are not solved under this type of analysis.

4.5   A Solution to the EL Subcategorization Problem?

Assuming that Merge creates from the input A and B the output set {A, B}, note that there is a simple modification of derivational c-command, and more specifically of the definition of "term," that appears to solve the problem traced in section 4.3 above.

Let us maintain Epstein's definition of derivational c-command, repeated below:

(41)   Derivational Definition of C-Command (from Epstein 1999:329):
       X c-commands all and only the terms of the category Y with which
       X was paired (by Merge or by Move) in the course of the derivation.

But let us modify the definition of "term" as follows:

(42) For any structure K,
     i. K is a term of K
     ii. the members of K are terms of K
     iii. the members of the members of K are terms of K

We can now account for (35), {see, {the, picture}}. Here, *see* does derivation-ally c-command *the* (and *picture*). *The* is a term of {the, picture} since *the* is a member of {the, picture} (by case (42ii)). Thus, feature checking can take place between *see* and *the*, and the subcategorization requirements of *see* are (correctly) satisfied.

4.6 Another Problem for the EL Theory of Subcategorization

But, interestingly, there is another problem with (35). We noted above that in (35), *see* derivationally c-commands *picture* (under revisions (41)/(42)). Notice, moreover, that *picture* derivationally c-commands *the* (by virtue of the fact that *the* and *picture* are merged). What this leads to, however, is a violation of EL's version of minimality, repeated below:

(43) If X selects Y (where Y is a lexical category), then *X Z Y, where Z intervenes between X and Y, and Z is any lexical category.
(44) Z intervenes between X and Y if X c-commands Z, and Z c-commands Y.

Relative to (35), {see, {the, picture}}, *see* (=X) selects *the* (=Y), but there is a Z (=*picture*) that intervenes between *see* and *the*. *See* c-commands *picture* and *picture* c-commands *the*, and *picture* is "any lexical category." Thus, minimality is violated, and (35) is incorrectly excluded, along with the desir-ably excluded *John saw [[of Fred] [the picture]]*.

Note that our reasoning for (35) is exactly parallel to EL's reasoning (minus our explicit definition of c-command) for (45), modeled on EL's example (21c), p. 52):

(45) *the destroy cities

The selects a N (i.e. the subcategorization feature of *the* is satisfied by a category hosting the +N feature). However, *cities* in (48) can't satisfied the subcategorization feature of *the* since *destroy* intervenes: *The* c-commands *destroy*, and *destroy* c-commands *cities*. This is the correct result.

(45) illustrates two things. First, we need, under EL's label-free the-ory of selection, the "intervention" clause (44). Minimality constrains

subcategorization feature checking. Second, (45) illustrates that we want a general form of intervention for minimality as minimality relates to subcategorization; i.e. even though in (45) *destroy* does not match (for the feature D) *the* and *cities*, *destroy* still counts as an intervener between *the* and *cities*—thus, we apparently want (44) to be stated in terms of "any lexical category" (and not "a Matching feature"). As we will see in more detail below, this raises the added problem that there are really two kinds of "minimality": one for subcategorization and one for Agree.

Note that EL explicitly considers an example like (46) (see Collins 2002:52, example (21c)).

(46) *the destroy a city

The argumentation here is the same as for (45): *Destroy* intervenes between *the* and *city*. Looking at (46), we might propose a solution to the problem raised by (35), a solution along the following lines. Basically, we want *destroy* to intervene between *the* and *city* in (46), but we do not want *picture* to intervene between *see* and *the* in (35), {see, {the, picture}}. One way to get the distinction is to modify the definition of "intervene" in this way:

(47) If X selects Y (where Y is a lexical category), then *X Z Y, where Z intervenes between X and Y, and Z is any lexical category.
(48) Z intervenes between X and Y if X ASYMMETRICALLY c-commands Z, and Z ASYMMETRICALLY c-commands Y.

The distinction between (46) and (35) now follows. Given our definition of Merge, (46) is represented as:

(49) *{the, {destroy, {a, city}}}

Here, *the* asymmetrically (derivationally) c-commands *destroy*, and *destroy* asymmetrically c-commands *city*. Thus, subcategorization feature checking between *the* and *city* is blocked by *destroy* since *destroy* is an intervener between *the* and *city*. That is the correct result. Next, consider, yet again, (35) {see, {the, picture}}. In this case, *see* asymmetrically c-commands *the*, but *picture* does NOT asymmetrically c-command *the* (*the* and *picture* c-command each other). Thus, subcategorization feature checking between *see* and *the* is not blocked by *picture*. That is the correct result.

So far so good. But we still can't get the distinction between (35) and (45), repeated here:

(45) *{the, {destroy, cities}}

In this case, *the* asymmetrically c-commands *destroy*, but *destroy* does NOT asymmetrically c-command *cities*; *destroy* and *cities* c-command each other.

Thus, *destroy* would NOT intervene between *the* and *cities*, and subcategorization feature checking between *the* and *cities* would (incorrectly) occur.

Notice that a related problem arises for the EL treatment of *tell on*. EL argues that the subcategorization feature of *tell* is +*on* (thus, *tell* selects for a specific lexical category). In a structure like (50)

(50) {tell {on Bill}}

EL argues that "[t]his feature [i.e. the subcategorization feature of *tell*] is satisfied by the lexical item *on*, which is contained in the sister of *tell*." EL then claims that "[s]ince no lexical category intervenes between *tell* and *on*, Minimality is satisfied" (EL:50). But I don't see how this last claim can be true. In fact, in (50), *Bill* IS a lexical category that intervenes between *tell* and *on*. *Tell* c-commands *Bill*, and *Bill* c-commands *on*. Thus, *Bill* intervenes between *tell* and *on*, and the satisfaction of the subcategorization between *tell* and *on* is consequently (and incorrectly) blocked.

4.7 A More General Statement of the Problem with Label-Free Subcategorization

4.7.1 A Note on Subcategorization-as-Feature-Checking with Labels

EL attempts to subsume subcategorization under the more general feature checking system of Chomsky (2000, 2001b). Subcategorization essentially becomes for EL an instance of the syntactic operation Agree, which, under the right conditions, deletes ("checks" in traditional terminology) certain features. The goal of EL is to subsume subcategorization under Agree, without appealing to labels or projection.

It was pointed out in the beginning of section 4 that labels make information that was introduced into the derivation at one point available again at a later point in the derivation. If we use graph-theoretic representations, we seem to see this (at least at first glance) in a pretty direct way. Assume, for the moment, Merge as defined in BPS (thus, Merge A and B produces {A, {A, B}}). Consider (51):

(51)   see
        ╱╲
     see *the*
        ╱╲
     the picture

The structure in (51) is an "informal representation" of the set {*see*, {*see*, {*the*, {*the*, picture}}}}. Given traditional interpretations of phrase markers, it might be tempting to think that in (51), the label *the* is the sister of *see*. It's tempting to think, then, that *the* (more specifically, the feature +D that *the* contains) can check the subcategorization feature of *see* since *see* and *the* are "close enough" to each other; i.e. they are sisters. On this (erroneous) view, it seems as though the information contained in the lexical item *the* (its D feature) is made available twice: The first time is when *the* is merged with *picture*, and then it is made available later in the derivation, namely at the point in the derivation where {*the*, {the, picture}} is merged with *see*.

In fact, however, we are being misled by the representation. The label *the* is not a sister to anything in (51). The sister of *see* is the entire set {*the*, {the, picture}}. What we actually have, in set-theoretic terms, is:

(52)   {*see*, {see, {*the*, {the, picture}}}}

And with this, more accurate, set-theoretic representation, we find that the label *the* is clearly contained in the sister of *see*; i.e. it is contained within the category with which *see* is merged, that category being {*the*, {the, picture}}. Still, in (52) the label *the* does seem to be closer to *see* than the lexical category *the* is to *see*. A concrete definition of "closeness," for example, could be stated as follows:

(53)   A category X can have its subcategorization feature F checked by a Matching category Y iff Y is a member of the (set which constitutes the) sister of X. (Note also that X can have its feature F checked by Y if X and Y are sisters—and X, Y Match.)

By (53), *see* in (52) can have its subcategorization feature checked by *the*; *see* and *the* match for the feature (D in this case), and *the* (the host of the checking feature) is a member of the category with which *see* is merged (whereas the lexical item *the* is not a member of the set that is the sister of *see*; thus, the label *the* is closer to *see* than the lexical category *the* is to *see*).

But there is a fundamental problem with this type of analysis of subcategorization-as-feature-checking with labels. The problem is that the label is not a term, and therefore it can't participate in syntactic operations since the label will not derivationally c-command nor be c-commanded by any category (we will explore this point in a somewhat different form in just a moment). My point is that even with labels, the attempt to subsume subcategorization under the more general feature checking operation seems problematic. With labels, we would have to abandon the idea that derivational c-command is a necessary condition for syntactic operations. Or else we'd have to redefine "term" such that labels are terms. But each of these moves is problematic (see below for further elaboration); furthermore, the proposed analysis uses labels, which we seek to eliminate.

As a final comment, note that BPS seems to assume that subcategorization can be done more or less in the traditional way. Thus, we say that *see* subcategorizes for a DP. However, the notion "DP" in BPS has content only by the convention that a set whose label is a D qualifies as a DP. It is in this sense that the information of the label is made available later in the derivation. Thus, in { . . . see, {*the*, {the, picture}}} we say that {*the*, {the, picture}} is a DP by the stipulation that a set whose label is a D counts as a DP. We take up this matter again in section 4.8 below.

4.7.2   *Subcategorization-as-Feature-Checking without Labels*

Without labels, we basically want a selector (i.e. the subcategorization feature of) X to "look inside" the set that X is merged with to probe for a Matching feature (that can check the subcategorization feature of X). We don't want X to look too deeply into the set that is its sister. But characterizing "how deep to look," which is essentially what EL's minimality condition does, is difficult. The general problem is illustrated with (54) versus (55):

(54) see {the, picture}
(55) *the {destroy, it}

We want *see* to look into its sister and match (and "check") with *the* in (54). But in (55) we don't want *the* to be able to look into its sister and match (and "check") with *it*. Since sets abstract away from linear order, the problem is that the relation between *see* and *the* in (54) is exactly parallel to the relation between *the* and *it* in (55). It is not obvious how any definition of the intervention clause of the minimality condition can do this, at least not in a natural way, i.e. in a way consistent with our basic assumptions here. What is clear is that the minimality condition proposed in EL does not yield the required distinction between (54) and (55).

4.8   More on the Nature of Labels

The above problem with subcategorization-as-feature-checking without labels does help to reveal the potential empirical value (at least in principle) of constituent structure representation with labels. It may help answer the question: If labels are not "functioning elements," then why are they proposed in BPS in the first place? Or, in other words, why are there labels, and why is there projection?

With labels, (54) and (55) would be represented as (54′) and (55′) respectively:

(54′) see {*the*, {the, picture}}
(55′) *the {*destroy*, {destroy, it}}

Suppose that the subcategorization feature of X can be checked only by a Y which is the sister of X, or by a Y[10] which is the label of the sister of X. The idea here is that the subcategorization feature of X can probe only as far as its sister or the label of its sister to find a Matching "checker." If it doesn't find a Matching checker in that (very) limited domain, then all bets are off;

feature checking between X and Y fails. In addition, if, following Chomsky (2000), we assume that if A selects B, and A and B are merged, then A projects; then we can account for (54') vs. (55'). In (54') *see* can have its subcategorization feature checked by (the Matching features of) *the*, since *the* is the label of the sister of *see*. In (55') *the* as a "probe" seeks to have its subcategorization feature checked. It can look to its sister for a Matching element, but its sister is the SET {*destroy*, {destroy, it}}, and this set itself does not have Matching features (although the members of this set do have features). So *the* looks to the label of its sister, the only other option available to it. But the label (i.e. *destroy*) does not (or at least could be argued not to) have Matching features (the label *destroy* does not have the Matching +N feature).[11] There is no other option for the feature checking of *the* (the "checker" of the subcategorization feature of X must be found in the sister of X or in the label of the sister of X—after that all bets are off). Thus, (55)' represents a subcategorization violation since the subcategorization feature of *the* can't be checked (neither the sister of *the* nor the label of the sister has a Matching feature). Notice what the label is doing on this view of subcategorization as feature checking. In the structure { . . . X, {A, {A, B}}}, the label is basically indicating which of the members of the set that is the sister of X can count as the potential checker of X. (And this serves the function of the minimality condition in the system without labels.)

But although the system sketched above accounts for the distinction between (54) and (55), a distinction that is problematic for the system of subcategorization-as-feature-checking without labels, we run into the problem that labels are not terms and hence can't participate in syntactic relations in the first place. For BPS labels are not terms, and all and only terms are "functioning elements." We could propose that labels are fully functional elements. But this proposal would face a number of difficult questions. If the label is a fully functioning element, then why is it never pronounced? Why does the label itself not move? But even if such questions could be satisfactorily answered, we'd still have the problems with labels raised in section 3.1; specifically, labels are redundant with lexical categories, and labels seem to violate inclusiveness.

Is there a way of doing the work of labels in the above cases without explicit appeal to labels? According to Chomsky (2000), when A and B are merged, the "projector" is the selector. Thus, A projects (and its copy becomes the label) if A selects B.[12] Note that it is this property (i.e. this stipulation) of the theory of projection that (ultimately) allows us to distinguish (54') and (55'). In (55'), *the* is required by the theory to look only at the label of its sister for a possible checker; thus, *destroy* is the only potential checker, but it turns out not to be an actual checker (since it doesn't have the right feature). It is crucial in (55') that *destroy* projects and not *it* (since if *it* projected, then the label *it* could check the subcategorization feature of *the*). But *destroy* projects only because of the stipulation that if A and B merge, it is the selector that projects. We can get the same results without labels in the following way. Suppose A and B merge to produce the simple set

{A, B}. Suppose A is the selector of B. Suppose that C is merged with {A, B} to produce {C, {A, B}}. Assume next that C can subcategorization-feature-check with the member of its sister whose selector was itself checked. Thus, we can merge *the* and *picture* to produce {the, picture}, and note that *the* selects *picture*. Now we Merge *see* with {the, picture} to produce {see, {the, picture}}. *See* can "check" with *the* (by hypothesis) since *the*'s selectors were checked at the point when *the* was merged with *picture*. This gets the effect of labels. But note that we are appealing to an earlier point in the derivation. We have, in essence, a "look-back" mechanism which gives us the crucial information about what happened earlier. That is, at the point in the derivation where *see* is merged with {the, picture}, we need the information that at the earlier point in the derivation where *the* was merged with *picture*, it was *the* that selected *picture*, and not the other way around. Here again, we see that labels serve the function of making information that was "used" at one point in the derivation available at a later point in the derivation. Labels are a "look-back" mechanism.

Note, finally, that on this view, there is an interesting parallel between labels-as-copies and a moved element and its copy (i.e. trace). Consider the movement of a category X from position P1 to position P2 (under copy theory). In the case of movement, certain information contained in X (e.g. its semantic information) is available at its original Merge site (a *wh*-word checking a theta feature, for example), and other information of X (e.g. its phonetic information) is available (i.e. overtly expressed) at its movement (landing) site. Information is made available at different points in the derivation. A label is similar to a moved element in this sense. The subcategorization feature of *the*, for example, is available at the point when *the* is merged with *picture*. After the label *the* is created to produce {*the*, {the, picture}} (and note that the label is a copy just as a moved element is a copy), the label *the* makes the feature +D of *the* available later in the derivation, at the point, for example, where *see* is merged with {*the*, {the, picture}}. Thus, *the* has its subcategorization feature checked by *picture*. And then *the* checks the subcategorization feature of *see*.

5   A SUMMARY SO FAR

To summarize, in section 2 it was deduced that labels are syntactically inert. The inertness of labels follows from (i) the BPS definition of Merge, (ii) derivational c-command, and (iii) the derivational theory of syntactic relations, specifically the idea that derivational c-command is a necessary condition for the application of syntactic operations. Labels are not terms. Therefore, labels do not derivationally c-command any other category, nor are labels c-commanded by any other category. Labels are consequently inert.

Although labels are syntactically inert on the above set of (well-motivated) hypotheses, labels still "exist," in that a label is a member of the set which constitutes a phrase in BPS. In section 3, however, it was argued that the "existence" of labels and projection is undesirable. The conclusion that labels can and should be eliminated from phrasal representations, I share with EL. However, the argumentation given in section 3 for this conclusion is rather different than EL. I argued in section 3 that a simplification of Merge (Merge A and B produces just {A, B}, not {A, {A, B}}) is motivated on minimalist grounds. And it was demonstrated that this simplification of Merge results in the elimination of labels and projection, as labels and projection are defined in BPS. EL does not consider the implications of the elimination of labels for Merge. EL argues that labels should be eliminated from the representation of phrases, but EL does not address in any detail the derivational operation, namely Merge, that produces these representations. I "start" with this derivational operation and argue that in its simplest form, Merge of A and B creates a relation between A and B, and nothing more. The absence of labels and projections immediately follows. The proposed simplification of Merge, and the consequent elimination of labels and projection, has implications for various syntactic operations and principles. Although the argumentation is quite different, EL and this paper share the conclusion that there are no labels (nor projection), and we must address the issue of how syntactic principles and operations that traditionally appeal to labels are to be stated without labels.

Section 4 focused on the implications of the elimination of labels for the relation "c-command." C-command plays a fundamental role in the label-free syntax program initiated by EL. However, EL does not present an explicit definition of c-command, nor are the implications of label-lessness for c-command considered. I argued in section 4 that a label-free syntax is not (obviously) compatible with the standard representational definition of c-command. However, it is compatible with Epstein's (1999) derivational definition of c-command. Equipped with this derivational definition, section 4 considered EL's theory of subcategorization, and it was found that certain modifications of the derivational definition of c-command, more specifically in the definition of "term," are apparently required. Certain further problems for the resulting theory of subcategorization were then presented, and possible solutions were sketched.

6   SUBCATEGORIZATION-AS-FEATURE-CHECKING AND THE LOCUS PRINCIPLE

6.1   On the Locus Principle

In deriving certain properties of X'-theory in a label-free syntax, EL makes crucial use of a version of a condition on lexical access (from Chomsky 2000), a condition that EL calls "the Locus Principle":

(59) Let X be a lexical item that has one or more probe/selectors. Suppose X is chosen from the lexical array and introduced into the

derivation. Then the probe/selectors of X must be satisfied before any new unsaturated lexical items are chosen from the lexical array. Let us call X the locus of the derivation.

(EL:46)

One property of X'-theory that EL derives with the Locus Principle is this:

(60) Complements and specifiers are maximal projections.

That the complement Y of a head X must be maximal follows in that if Y is not maximal, i.e. if Y is a head or an X', then the Locus Principle will be violated; similarly for specifiers. To illustrate this in more detail, note that it is a property of X'-theory that, for example, [$_{CP}$ Comp Infl'] is illicit. EL derives this from (60) as follows: Suppose we build up, through a sequence of Merges, the object

(61) [will [John sleep]]

i.e. we first merge *John* and *sleep* (which satisfies the subcategorization feature and the theta role feature of *sleep*); we then merge [John sleep] with INFL (which is *will*) to produce (61). Note that the merge of *will* and [John sleep] results in the satisfaction (i.e. the checking) of the subcategorization feature of *will*. Suppose that we now (try to) choose the COMP *that* from the lexical array to produce [$_{CP}$ Comp Infl'], i.e. to produce:

(62) [that [will [John sleep]]]

The problem is that in (62), although the subcategorization feature of *will* is satisfied, the EPP of *will* (= INFL) is not satisfied. *Will* (= INFL) is the Locus as *will* is still unsaturated (i.e. it has unchecked probes/selectors) at this point. *That* is a lexical item which is unsaturated in that its subcategorization feature is as yet unchecked. Thus, at point (61) the Locus Principle prohibits choosing *that* from the lexical array. (62) is consequently disallowed.

What I'd like to point out here is that the Locus Principle seems to provide a ready solution to the specific empirical problems with the EL theory of subcategorization that we raised in section 4.

6.2 Solving Problems with EL Subcategorization with the Locus Principle

In section 4 a simplified version of Merge was considered, and the definition of derivational c-command was adopted; relevant definitions are repeated below:

(63) Algorithm for Merge of A, B: Create the set {A, B}

(64) Derivational Definition of C-Command (from Epstein 1999):
X c-commands all and only the terms of the category Y with which
X was paired (by Merge or by Move) in the course of the derivation.

(65) For any structure K,
i. K is a term of K
ii. if L is a term of K, then the members of the members of L are
terms of K

Chomsky (1995:247)

It was argued that (63) was motivated on minimalist grounds, and (63)
results in the elimination of labels and projection. Furthermore, it was
argued that a derivational definition of c-command is (arguably) required
in a label-free syntax.

However, in sections 4.3 and 4.6, we pointed out problems for the EL
theory of subcategorization, problems that involve c-command and minimality. EL's theory of subcategorization crucially appeals to c-command,
but c-command is not explicitly defined in EL. (64) represents an explicit
definition of c-command that is compatible with the label-free program.
But we were not able to account for certain instances of subcategorization
phenomena. Problematic examples are repeated below:

(66) {see, {the, picture}}
(67) *{the, {destroy, cities}}
(68) *{the, {destroy, {a, city}}}

Recall that we want *see* and *the* to participate in subcategorization feature
checking in (66), but we don't want *the* and *city/cities* to participate in feature
checking in (67) and (68). The problem, however, is that if we account for (67)
and (68) by claiming that *destroy* intervenes between *the* and *cities/city*, it is
not clear how we "stop" *picture* from intervening between *see* and *the* in (66).

What I'd like to point out here is that these examples seem to be accounted
for by the Locus Principle, without any explicit appeal to minimality.

Consider (67), under the following derivation.

(69) a. Choose *destroy* from the lexical array.
b. Choose *cities* from the lexical array.
c. Merge *destroy* and *cities* to produce {destroy, cities}, satisfying
the subcategorization feature of *destroy*.
d. (Try to) choose *the* from the lexical array.

Step d violates the Locus Principle in that the Locus *destroy* in step c is
not saturated, and it is not saturated by virtue of the fact that it still has an
undischarged theta role (its "external" theta role, to use standard terminology). We assume that the merger of *destroy* and *cities* results in the checking
of the subcategorization feature of *destroy*, and this merger results in the

checking of the internal theta role of *destroy*; assume that both the subcategorization and the internal theta role features of *destroy* are checked by *cities* under sisterhood. But the lexical item *the* is also unsaturated since it has an unchecked subcategorization feature. Thus, by the Locus Principle, step d in (69) is illicit. We can't choose a new unsaturated lexical item from the lexical array (i.e. we can't choose *the*) since the locus of the derivation up to that point, namely *destroy*, is still unsaturated. Similar reasoning holds for (68).

Consider next (66). Here we merge *the* and *picture* to give {the, picture} and thereby satisfy the subcategorization feature of *the*. Note that {the, picture} is saturated—it contains no unsatisfied probes/selectors.[13] We are thus free to choose *see* from the lexical array and merge *see* with {the, picture} and thereby satisfy the subcategorization feature of *see*. Note then that for these cases the locality condition on minimality (i.e. the intervention condition) appears to be derived from the Locus Principle.

In order to account for certain instances of the Dutch partitive construction, the details of which I will not review here, EL (tentatively) proposes the following revision of minimality:

(70) If X selects Y (where Y is a lexical category), then *X Z Y
    a. where Z intervenes between X and Y, and
    b. where Z is any lexical category, and
    c. where Z contains a probe/selector.

Note that (70) could be modified to deal with the English cases above, i.e. (66), (67), and (68). But it should be noted that (70c) is really a restatement of the Locus Principle. If Z, which contains a probe/selector, is present in the derivation, then, because it has a probe/selector, it will be unsaturated. Thus, the Locus Principle prohibits choosing X from the lexical array, since X has a selector and hence is also unsaturated. In light of this overlap with the Locus Principle, (70c) would be a curious addition to the grammar. Moreover, (70c) does not deal with the case to which we now turn.

6.3 A Problem with EL Subcategorization and the Locus Principle

Unfortunately, not all subcategorization phenomena can be reduced to the Locus Principle. A locality condition on subcategorization-as-feature-checking is still apparently required. Consider (71):

(71) *{the[1], {the[2], picture}} (superscripts used only for ease of exposition)

In this case, we merge *the[2]* and *picture*, producing the saturated constituent {the[2], picture}; the constituent {the[2], picture} is saturated assuming that *picture* checks the subcategorization feature of *the[2]* (checks it under sisterhood). At this point, the Locus Principle itself does not prohibit Merging *the*[1] with {the[2], picture}, yielding (71). {the[2], picture} is saturated, and thus I'm free to choose *the*[1] from the lexical array. The question is: Can *picture* in (71) now check the subcategorization feature of *the*[1]? If there were no minimality condition on feature checking, then (71) would apparently be (incorrectly) allowed.

To summarize, the theory we are dealing with directly above includes:

(72) a. Merge A and B produces {A, B}. There are no labels nor projection.
   b. Derivational c-command is a necessary condition for the application of syntactic operations.
   c. Subcategorization is (a type of) feature checking.
   d. Y can "check" the subcategorization feature F of X iff X and Y match for F, and
      i. X and Y are sisters (i.e. X is merged with Y), or
      ii. Y is a member of the sister of X (Y is a member of the set with which X is merged).
   e. The Locus Principle. The probes/selectors of X must be satisfied before any new unsaturated lexical item is introduced into the derivation.

We explored the hypothesis that the Locus Principle, (72e), can take over the work of minimality with respect to subcategorization-as-feature-checking. We have seen that relative to certain troublesome examples, namely

(66) {see, {the, picture}}
(67) *{the, {destroy, cities}}
(68) *{the, {destroy, {a, city}}}

the Locus Principle, more specifically, the theory outlined in (72), gives the right results. But the theory outlined in (72) does not account for examples like (71).

To put the matter in more abstract terms, note that when X and Y are merged to produce {X, Y}, it follows from the theory in (72) that Y can "check" the subcategorization feature of X, assuming that X and Y match. (Thus, *picture* can check the subcategorization feature of *see* in {see, pictures}.)

In the configuration {X, {Y, Z}}, Y can "check" the subcategorization feature of X, since Y is a member of the sister of X, again assuming that Y and X match (note that Z can check X as well). On the other hand, in {X, {Z, {Y, W}}}, Y cannot "check" the subcategorization feature of X, since Y is not a member of the sister of X (rather, Y is a member of a member of sister of X).

To say that Y can check the feature of X only if Y is a sister of X or if Y is a member of the sister of X gets us a local relation between X and Y. So the key examples to consider will have this form:

(73) {X, {Y, Z}}

Now, if {Y, Z} is unsaturated, then the Locus Principle will rule out the merger of {Y, Z} with X since X, by virtue of its unchecked subcategorization feature, will be unsaturated as well. This disallows (66) and the like. But if {Y, Z} is saturated, then the merger of X and {Y, Z} does not run afoul of the Locus Principle itself. This (correctly) allows (66). But it also (incorrectly) allows (71). (66) and (71) are repeated here:

(66) {see, {the, picture}}
(71) *{the^1, {the^2, picture}}

If we bring back in minimality to rule out (71), then we would also incorrectly rule out (66). That is, if *the*^{2} intervenes between *the*^{1} and *picture* in (71), then *picture* should intervene between *see* and *the* in (66).

One technical solution to (71) would be to assume this "freezing principle": If the feature(s) F of Y "check" the subcategorization features of X, then F is/are not available for further feature checking. Since the N feature of *picture* "checks" the subcategorization feature of *the*^{2} at the point in the derivation where *the*^{2} and *picture* are merged, then these same features of *picture* are not available for checking *the*^{1}. Since it is the features of *the* (and not *picture*) that check the features of *see* in (66), the "freezing principle" does not block the feature checking relation between *the* and *see* in (66). Note that the "freezing principle" is similar to a constraint in Chomsky (2000) according to which the Case features of an N, once checked, can't check a probe; in essence, once the Case features of an N are checked, the NP is "inactive."

7   FURTHER NOTES ON THE LOCUS PRINCIPLE

In this section, a number of further issues with EL's Locus Principle are considered.

7.1   Can There Be More Than One Locus in a Derivation?

EL observes that there are similarities between a label and a Locus. EL states:

(74) For example, if a word X with a probe/selector is merged with a constituent Y to form [X Y], then X is the label in a theory with labels and X is the locus in a theory without labels.

(EL:48)

In BPS, as we pointed out above, there is the stipulation that if A has a selector (for example, a subcategorization feature) and A and B are merged, then A projects; i.e. A is copied, and the copy of A becomes the label of the derived constituent, {A, {A, B}}. This is similar to the Locus in that if A has a selector (and A and B are merged), then A is the Locus. In both cases, elements that have unchecked probes/selectors play a "special" role.

EL then claims that

(75) The major difference between a label and a locus is that there is only one locus in a derivation, while there are many labels; each constituent has a different label.

(EL:48)

It is not clear that (75) is true. Rather, it arguable that there are as many Loci in a derivation as there are lexical categories with unchecked probes/selectors. To illustrate, consider again the EL statement of the Locus Principle:

(76) Let X be a lexical item that has one or more probe/selectors. Suppose X is chosen from the lexical array and introduced into the derivation. Then the probe/selectors of X must be satisfied before any new unsaturated lexical items are chosen from the lexical array. Let us call X the locus of the derivation.

(EL:46)

Suppose *the* is chosen from the lexical array. Then, since *the* has a selector (its subcategorization feature), then *the* is a Locus; by the Locus Principle, we must satisfy the subcategorization feature of *the* before any new unsaturated lexical item is chosen from the lexical array (thus, immediately after *the* is chosen from the lexical array, we can't choose, say, *saw*). So suppose we choose *picture* from the lexical array. Assuming that the (unchecked) Case feature of *picture* does not count as a probe/selector, the choice of *picture* does not violate the Locus Principle. Thus, we can merge *the* and *picture* and thereby satisfy the subcategorization feature of *the*. Up to this point in the derivation, *the* is the Locus. Suppose next that we choose *saw* from the lexical array. This choice of *saw* does not violate the Locus Principle, since {the, picture} is saturated; i.e. there are no elements in the "workspace" that are unsaturated. Once we choose *saw*, then since *saw* has unchecked probes/selectors, *saw* is the (new) Locus. We must, consequently, satisfy all the probes/selectors of *saw* before choosing any new unsaturated elements from the lexical array, which means that we first must merge *saw* with {the, picture}. We can proceed in this way until a final saturated constituent (namely a sentence) is generated. On this view, there will be as many Loci in the (whole) derivation as there are points in the derivation where we are allowed, by the Locus Principle, to choose a new unsaturated lexical item.

In fact, it is not clear that there could be only one Locus in a derivation. Suppose, for example, that we merge *likes* and *it* to produce:

(77) {likes, it}

We want *likes* to be a Locus here since we want the Locus Principle to pro-hibit choosing, say, *will* from the lexical array to produce *{will, {likes, it}}. The Locus Principle forces the next move with (77) to be to merge (77) with an N (or NP). Suppose we merge (77), for example, with *Bill* to produce:

(78) {Bill, {likes, it}}

(78) is a saturated constituent since it contains no unchecked probes/selectors (there are unchecked Case features, but Case features, as we'll argue in some detail below, do not count as probes/selectors for EL). As we've just seen, the Locus in producing (78) is the verb *likes*. After (78) is generated, then the probes/selectors of *likes* are checked and *likes* no longer counts as a Locus. Suppose that we now choose *will* from the lexical array to produce:

(79) {will, {Bill, {likes, it}}}

Here, *will* is the new Locus. And *will* must be a Locus since we want to be sure not to merge the object in (79) with, say, *that*. That *will* is a Locus is crucial for EL's argument that it is possible to derive from the Locus Prin-ciple the fact the complements and specifiers are maximal projections. (See section 6 for further detail.) Overall, then, on EL's own reasoning, a deriva-tion must include more than one Locus.

7.2   Case Features Are Exempt from the Locus Principle

The Locus Principle (LP), (76) above, is sensitive to probes and selectors in that a lexical item with "unchecked" probes or selectors is subject to the LP. What are the probes and selectors? The list would seem to include:

(80) a. theta roles (e.g. an "unsatisfied" theta role of a V renders the V unsaturated)
   b. phi features of Infl
   c. Case feature of Infl
   d. EPP feature of Infl
   e. subcategorization feature of any category

If an element X contains any one of the features in (80), and if the feature is unsatisfied ("unchecked," "unassigned"), then X is unsaturated. And if X is unsaturated, then the LP comes directly into play. Thus, if a verb like *see* is introduced into the derivation, then, since *see* is unsaturated by virtue of its unsatisfied theta role(s), according to the LP the unsatisfied feature of *see* must be satisfied before any new unsaturated element is introduced into the derivation.

As far as I can tell, a theta feature (a theta role) and a subcategorization fea-ture are considered "selectors" while the other features in (80) are "probes."

Another way that EL seems to state the distinction (see EL:48) is that selectors require Merge, while probes require Agree for their satisfaction. But this distinction between selector and probe is not meaningful in the sense that the LP itself doesn't care about the distinction. What the LP cares about is whether an element is unsaturated. The LP doesn't care that an element X is unsaturated because it contains an unsatisfied theta role (a selector) or an unsatisfied EPP feature (a probe); it only cares that there is some feature that makes X unsaturated. It is in this sense that we could subsume the names "probe" and "selector" under the single label, like "unsaturators." So for the LP, probes and selectors are equivalent (both are related to unsaturation).

But note that the (unchecked) Case feature on N is (crucially) NOT an unsaturator for N (the Case feature of N does not count as a probe or selector). Thus, suppose I choose *see* from the lexical array. Since *see* has unchecked probes/selectors, it is subject to the LP. To satisfy the subcategorization and theta features of *see*, something must (ultimately) be chosen from the lexical array, but what is chosen better not have probes/selectors since if did have probes/selectors, the LP would be violated. In fact, after *see* is chosen from the lexical array, I can choose, say, *it* from the lexical array to produce {see, it}. So even though *it*, and nominals generally, have an unchecked Case feature, a feature which triggers Agree, *it* still counts as saturated for the LP. It is clear that Case must be exempt from the LP; if Case were not exempt from the LP, virtually nothing could be generated without violating the LP.

NOTES

Earlier versions of this paper were circulated beginning in 2000. For extensive written commentary and discussion, including very helpful clarifications and many suggestions for improvement, I'd like to thank Andrew Carnie and Samuel David Epstein (very special thanks to Sam for his insightful discussion of many of the arguments of this paper). I'm particularly grateful to Chris Collins for the example of his work and for his generous and very helpful comments and suggestions. Many thanks to Cedric Boeckx for his interest in and support of this work. Of course, all faults are mine.

1. A type of label-free syntax is proposed by Dependency Theory; see Chametzky (2000) and Hudson (1990).
2. All page references are to Collins (2002). See also Boeckx (2004) for extensive discussion of label-free syntax, and Chomsky (2005).
3. As Chris Collins (personal communication) points out, there is a difference between eliminating labels and eliminating constituent structure. One can eliminate labels but still define "first branching" node if there are still constituents. We'll return to this matter below.
4. For the set {A, {A, B}}, the label A is identified with A where A is a lexical item. If A is itself a phrase, then the label A is identified with the head of A; thus, the label A is always identified with a lexical item.
5. Chomsky (1995, 2000, 2001b) also uses copies for movement. Thus, in [who^1 did you see who^2], where *who* has moved from the position of who^2 to the

position of who[1], who[1] and who[2] are "occurrences" of the same category. See Epstein and Seely (1999, 2006) and references therein for extensive discussion.

6. I am not proposing an explicit complexity metric with respect to which the claimed "simplicity" of the modified version of Merge can be measured. Thus, I use the phrase "simplification of Merge" with some caution.

7. The "copy" operation can be stated in various ways. But some notion of "copy" is needed. We can't say: Create the set {A, B}; then remove A from this set, giving {B}; and then create a new set consisting of A and {B}—that would give {A, {B}}; it would not give {A, {A, B}}. A copy is thus required.

8. This seems an obvious point that does not require further justification, and EL itself claims that the labels of heads are not eliminated: "Note that I am not arguing against category labels like N, V, P, Adj for lexical categories" (EL:43).

9. Note that *the* and *picture* are terms of the object {see, {the, picture}, but this is irrelevant in the present context: *See* is not merged with {see, {the, picture}}; rather, *see* is merged with just {the, picture}.

10. Y here is to be understood as the host of the features that Match and potentially check the subcategorization feature of X. Technically speaking, it is the features of lexical categories that participate in feature checking.

11. The probe-goal analysis of Chomsky (2000, 2001b) characterizes the relation Match between X and Y as having the same feature but not necessarily the same feature value. Thus, the phi features of INFL have "minus" value, and the phi features of an N have "plus" value, but INFL and N still match. In (55'), we are assuming that the subcategorization feature of *the* is +N. The label of the sister of *the*, i.e. *destroy*, by virtue of bearing the feature –N, would Match according to Chomsky. Thus, we would have to require that subcategorization feature checking requires identity not just same feature but same value for the feature.

12. See Berwick and Epstein (1995) for comparison with Montague grammar.

13. Notice that {the, picture} (specifically *picture*) does have an unchecked Case feature. But the Case feature does not count as a probe/selector. Even though {the, picture} has an unchecked Case feature, it still counts as saturated. EL does not explicitly address this issue, but the logic of the matter seems pretty clear—see section 6 for further comment.

REFERENCES

Berwick, R. and Epstein, S.D. 1995. On the Convergence of 'Minimalist' Syntax and Categorial Grammar. In Nijholt, A., Scollo, G., and Steetkamp, R. (eds.), *Algebraic Methods in Language Processing 1995*, 143–148. Enschede: University of Twente.

Boeckx, C. 2004. Bare Syntax. Manuscript, Harvard University, Cambridge, MA.

Chametzky, R. 2000. *Phrase Structure: From GB to Minimalism*. Malden, MA: Blackwell.

Chomsky, N. 1995. *The Minimalist Program*. Cambridge, MA: MIT Press.

Chomsky, N. 2000. Minimalist Inquiries: The Framework. In Martin, R., Michaels, D. and Uriagereka, J. (eds.), *Step by Step: Essays on Minimalist Syntax in Honor of Howard Lasnik*, 89–155. Cambridge, MA: MIT Press.

Chomsky, N. 2001a. Beyond Explanatory Adequacy. Manuscript, MIT, Cambridge, MA. [Revised version appeared in Belletti, A. (ed.), *Structures and Beyond*, 104–131. Oxford: Oxford University Press, 2004.]

154 T. Daniel Seely

Chomsky, N. 2001b. Derivation by Phase. In Kenstowicz, M. (ed.), *Ken Hale: A Life in Language*, 1–52. Cambridge, MA: MIT Press.Chomsky, N. 2005. Three Factors in Language Design. *Linguistic Inquiry* 36:1–22.

Collins, C. 2000. *Eliminating Labels*. Manuscript, Cornell University, Ithaca, NY.

Collins, C. 2002. Eliminating Labels. In Epstein, S.D. and Seely, T.D. (eds.), *Derivation and Explanation in the Minimalist Program*, 42–64. Oxford: Blackwell.

Epstein, S.D. 1994. The Derivation of Syntactic Relations. Manuscript, Harvard University, Cambridge, MA.

Epstein, S.D. 1999. Un-principled Syntax: The Derivation of Syntactic Relations. In Epstein, S.D. and Hornstein, N. (eds.), *Working Minimalism*, 317–345. Cambridge, MA: MIT Press. [Reprinted in *Essays in Syntactic Theory*, 183–210. New York: Routledge, 2000.]

Epstein, S.D. and Seely, T.D. 1999. SPEC-ifying the GF "Subject": Eliminating A-chains and the EPP within a Derivational Model. Manuscript, University of Michigan, Ann Arbor, and Eastern Michigan University, Ypsilanti.

Epstein, S.D. and Seely, T.D. 2006. *Derivations in Minimalism*. Cambridge: Cambridge University Press.

Hudson, R. 1990. *English Word Grammar*. Oxford: Blackwell.

7 Structure Building That Can't Be!

Samuel D. Epstein, Hisatsugu Kitahara, and T. Daniel Seely

1 INTRODUCTION

This paper proposes and explores the form and empirical consequences of a deduction of cyclic Transfer. The basic idea is this: First, we adopt Chomsky's (2007, 2008) feature-inheritance analysis whereby the phase heads C and v (inherently) bear phi features and transmit these features to the heads of their complement, T and V, respectively. Second, T and V, once they bear such inherited phi features, then raise, via their edge feature (EF), a local DP to their Spec. This raising, e.g. raising to Spec, T after C is merged and after T inherits phi features from C, is, informally speaking, "counter-cyclic" Internal Merge (IM); i.e. it is non-extending Merge that fails to apply to the "root" node, namely the C-projection. Chomsky (2000) formulates the No-Tampering Condition (NTC) so as to allow such "counter-cyclic" operations. Unlike Chomsky, however, we argue that such "counter-cyclic" IM cannot actually "infix" Spec, T inside the C-rooted object but rather yields a structure with (again, informally) "two peaks"—a tree with no single root (to merge to)—causing the derivation to (deducibly) halt.[1] For the derivation to continue, one peak (the phase-head complement—for reasons that we will return to) must be removed by Transfer from the workspace. In this way, we seek to deduce the timing of Transfer: always and only when a phase head is externally merged and phi features are inherited by the head of the phase-head complement. And we seek to deduce the syntactic object targeted by Transfer, namely the phase-head complement—transforming the two-peaked object into a single-peaked object to which Merge can once again apply.

Our analysis is based on a number of fundamental assumptions. One is that (following Chomsky 2008:137) Merge "comes free": Some structure building operation is required of any system, and Merge $(X, Y) \rightarrow \{X, Y\}$ is the simplest such operation. By the Strong Minimalist Thesis (SMT), then, we seek to maximize the explanatory effects of Merge: The only relations available to the narrow syntax (NS) are those that directly follow from the simple, single, necessary structure building operation Merge $(X, Y) \rightarrow \{X, Y\}$. In effect, this is the derivational approach to syntactic relations of Epstein et al. (1998), Epstein (1999), and Epstein and Seely (2002, 2006).

Another key assumption of our analysis is what we call the Label Accessibility Condition (LAC) (adapted from Chomsky 2000:132):

(1) The Label Accessibility Condition (LAC)
     Only the label of an entire syntactic object, the root, is accessible to NS.[2]

Any system must access something, and given 3rd factor considerations, access is made with least effort; hence, LAC is itself deducible if the label of the root is available to NS that has accessed the root.

We argue that our system has both conceptual and empirical advantages compared to that of Chomsky (2007, 2008). For example, Chomsky argues that "counter-cyclic" IM is an instance of Merge. However, we show that in fact his analysis incorporates an additional "replacement" process (see Freidin 1999 for compelling arguments in favor of a ban on replacement operations in an earlier framework). Replacement poses a problem for the SMT, a problem that does not arise with the analysis proposed here. Our system also derives the "invisibility" of Spec, T to C. Given the derivational approach to syntactic relations, C is not in a relation to Spec, T since at the point in the derivation when C was merged to T, the Spec, T position was not yet created. This allows us to deduce a series of empirical effects noted but unexplained in Chomsky (2007, 2008). We argue that there are further empirical differences between the "traditional" Phase-Impenetrability Condition (PIC) and our two-peak-effect Transfer, and the latter gives apparently correct results for object agreement in Icelandic that are problematic for the timing of Transfer as formulated in the Chomsky (2007, 2008) system.

To illustrate our approach in more detail, consider a typical instance of what is referred to informally as "counter-cyclic" IM at the CP phase for a simple sentence like:

(2) Bill ate rice.

Under Chomsky's analysis, once the phase head C is externally merged (EM) in

(3) $[_{CP} [C [_{TP} [T [_{\nu P} Bill [\nu [_{VP} ate rice]]]]]]]$

C transmits its lexically inherent phi features to T. T now acts as a probe, locates the external argument *Bill*, and raises it to Spec of T, resulting in:

(4) $[_{CP} [C [_{TP} Bill [T [_{\nu P} Bill [\nu [_{VP} ate rice]]]]]]]$

The claim in Chomsky (2007, 2008) is that "counter-cyclic" IM as in (4) (along with IM at the root, e.g. *wh*-movement) is an instance of Merge. Recall there is one and only one structure building operation, namely Merge $(X, Y) \rightarrow \{X, Y\}$.[3] But notice that, in fact, a form of "replacement" is required to get the (desired) result illustrated in (4). Informally speaking, to derive (4) from (3), the TP complement of C must be "disconnected" from this C; then IM merges *Bill* to this "existing" (spec-less) TP, creating a "new" (specful) TP; and then this "new" TP is "reconnected" to C, creating a "new" CP, one with a different TP (i.e. a TP containing Spec) now appearing as sister to C, and the previous (spec-less) TP sister to C is no longer C's sister. In set-theoretic terms, IM of *Bill* to the "existing" TP takes (5) as input

(5) $\{C, T^1\}$ (where $T^1 = [T$ $[_{vP}$ Bill $[v$ $[_{VP}$ ate rice]]]])

and produces a new syntactic object T^2 as in (6):

(6) $T^2 = [$Bill $[T$ $[_{vP}$ Bill $[v$ $[_{VP}$ ate rice]]]]]$

T^2 (with *Bill* as Spec, T) then replaces T^1 in (5): Such replacement removes T^1 from (5) and merges T^2 with C. Note furthermore that a "new" CP now results, namely:

(7) $\{C, T^2\}$

It is this "new" CP in (7), and not the "old" one in (5), that enters into further derivational processes.

What we suggest is that given SMT, there is Merge, but Merge alone cannot replace existing terms; i.e. it cannot map (5) to (7). Accepting this, one might then argue that the application of two operations, namely Delete (= "disconnect") and Merge (= "reconnect") might be capable of mapping (5) to (7). However, we will argue that this possibility is banned by a Law of Conservation of Relations (LCR), which we propose as a generalization of the extension condition (EC) (which subsumes NTC):

(8) The Law of Conservation of Relations (LCR)
    In NS, syntactic relations (among existing terms) cannot be altered throughout a derivation.

This is by hypothesis an "economy" condition, whereby it is arguably computationally natural that no relations are created only to be destroyed. LCR in effect forces NS to preserve all existing relations.[4],[5] Thus, "counter-cyclic" IM, e.g. subject raising in (4), will necessarily result in (9), presented in informal graph-theoretic terms:

(9)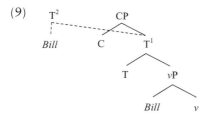

In effect, a "two-peaked" object is created. More formally, "counter-cyclic" IM, generating (9), will produce *two* distinct but intersecting set-theoretic syntactic objects (SOs), which happen to share a term, namely $T^1 = \{T, vP\}$. That is, as a result of this "counter-cyclic" IM, NS yields two intersecting sets: $\{Bill, T^1\}$ and $\{C, T^1\}$. We argue that these intersecting set-theoretic SOs do not have a single root; there is no single category that (reflexively) contains all terms. Since there is no root, then given LAC, NS cannot access either of these sets' labels. These intersecting SOs thus cannot undergo Merge after the series of phase-level operations that generated them; i.e. the derivation halts.[6] We propose further that in order to continue the derivation, one "peak" (i.e. one of the two intersecting sets) must be eliminated, precisely the job of Transfer. Thus, cyclic Transfer is deduced, and the positive empirical consequences that we consider then follow.

2   VALUATION-INDUCED TRANSFER: A PROBLEM

In this section, we consider the valuation-induced deduction of cyclic Transfer of Chomsky (2007, 2008) and Richards (2007). This is important since it might be asked: If a deduction of cyclic Transfer already exists, why propose an alternative? Our answer is that a viable deduction does not exist since, in fact, valuation-induced Transfer leads to massive undergeneration. Reviewing Epstein, Kitahara, and Seely (EKS) (2010), this section details the empirical problem with the valuation-induced approach, thus setting the stage for our alternative deduction of cyclic Transfer, as outlined above.

According to Chomsky (2000, 2001), syntactically determined features, like phi features of C/T and Case of N, are lexically unvalued,[7] becoming valued in the course of a derivation if the appropriate conditions for the application of Agree (i.e. valuation) are met. Such syntactically valued features must be removed by Transfer from an object bound for the conceptual-intentional (CI) interface, since they are uninterpretable at CI and would induce CI crash.

A central question for Chomsky (2007, 2008) is: When does Transfer (more specifically, its Spell Out function) remove such CI-offending features? *Before* valuation is *too early*. Unvalued features won't be "implementable" at the sensorimotor (SM) interface; in effect, they would induce SM crash. But *after* valuation is *too late*. Once valued, the distinction between valued and unvalued is lost; thus, Transfer won't "know" to spell out, say, the valued phi features of C/T, since after valuation they are identical to the (inherently) valued phi features of N; thus, these CI-offending features would not be removed from the CI-bound object, and CI crash would result. As detailed in Epstein and Seely (2002), Transfer must, in effect, operate *during* *v*aluation; i.e. Transfer must take place internal to a valuation operation, or else internal to the ("all-at-once"-created) phase (see Chomsky 2004, 2007, 2008). A crucial consideration for present concerns is that valuation-induced Transfer requires at least some derivational history, minimized as much as possible; it must "see" what goes from unvalued to valued in order to "know" to spell out (or remove) from the CI-bound object just those features whose values it witnessed changing from unvalued to valued.[8]

The logic of valuation (attractively) induces cyclic Transfer in Chomsky's analyses. The logic is also explicitly appealed to in Chomsky (2007, 2008) to derive CP, and not TP, as a phase, and to derive feature-inheritance (from C to T, and v to V). Adopting Richards (2007), Chomsky (2007:13) states:

> . . . it follows that the PIC entails that TP cannot be a phase, with operations of valuation and A-movement driven by properties of T. . . . Suppose TP were a phase. Then its interior will be transferred by PIC, but the head T will retain its valued uninterpretable features. The derivation will therefore crash at the next phase.

The logic of valuation-induced Transfer is clear: Syntactically valued features at the phase-edge induce CI crash (thus, Richards (2007) deduces that phi features must not remain on the phase head and be valued there, by direct agreement between the phase-head (functioning as a) probe and a goal; this would yield valued features at the edge, causing CI crash at the next phase). But, as revealed in EKS (2010), this very same logic leads to a pervasive empirical problem with the valuation-induced cyclic Transfer system: *All* instances of movement across a phase boundary are disallowed, and this leads to massive undergeneration. If T cannot be a phase head because syntactically valued features at the edge of T will induce crash at the next phase cycle, then C and v cannot be either since syntactically valued features do in fact occur at the edge of C and v.

Consider a specific example of this problem for a simple sentence like *Whom did they like?* The relevant vP is:

(10) $[_{v\text{P}}$ they $[_{v'}\ v\ [_{\text{VP}}$ like whom$]]]$

The phase-head v transmits its phi features to V. V probes and agrees with *whom* (valuing Case). To escape the phase-head complement, VP, *whom* is raised (by the EF of v) to Spec, v, and *like* adjoins to v.[9] As a result, NS yields:[10]

(11) $[_{v\text{P}}$ whom $[_{v'}$ they $[_{v'}\ [_{v'}\ v+\text{like}\ [_{\text{VP}}$ like whom$]]]]]$
　　　　+Acc　　　　　　　　+Phi

By the PIC, the phase-head complement VP is transferred and hence inaccessible. But note that both *whom*, bearing syntactically valued Case, and *like*, bearing syntactically valued phi features, appear at the edge of the phase-head v (i.e. v and its specifiers). Indeed, all syntactically valued features are at the phase-edge in (11).[11] The derivational history of the valuation of these features is then "lost" by the PIC, and Transfer has no way to "know" to remove these features at the next higher phase from the CI-bound object. In effect, these features are stranded at the phase-edge and will induce CI crash. Thus, under the valuation-induced Transfer system, there is massive undergeneration.

If EKS (2010) are on the right track, then it would seem that valuation-induced Transfer (along with valuation-induced feature-inheritance) "does not work" since valued features must be allowed to (i.e. do) occur at phase-edges in convergent derivations. Thus, the (elegant) valuation-based attempt to deduce cyclic Spell Out apparently confronts serious empirical problems. It is thus important that we consider alternative approaches attempting to explain the timing and nature of cyclic Transfer.

3   RESOLVING THE *BEFORE/AFTER* PROBLEM

EKS (2010) provide a potential solution to the empirical problem of the valuation-induced Transfer system reviewed above. The short story is that syntactically valued features are [−CI] features; this is not stipulative but rather follows from a natural and attractively restrictive view of the nature of features as either interpretable to CI (= +CI) or not (= −CI). By definition, [−CI] features are those that are uninterpretable at CI (which include all phonological features). EKS propose that all and only [−CI] features are removed from the CI-bound object, and this is done by Transfer. Thus, *after* valuation is not "too late." Since syntactically valued features are [−CI], their derivational history is no longer required for Transfer to operate effectively.

On what basis can EKS claim that syntactically valued features are [−CI]? EKS first assume, under SMT (with the primacy of CI), that features are either [+CI] or [−CI]. EKS then assume what can be referred to as a law of conservation of features, a generalization of the inclusiveness condition:

(12)   The Law of Conservation of Features (LCF)
        In NS, features cannot be created or destroyed throughout a derivation.

According to LCF, the nature of a feature cannot be changed during the course of a derivation. Given these two assumptions, in effect, [−CI] features are always [−CI] features; likewise for [+CI] features. It thus follows that since lexically unvalued features are [−CI], they *remain* [−CI] features regardless of whether they are valued in the course of a derivation. Thus, syntactically valued features are [−CI] features.

LCF thus expresses the generalization that syntactic feature valuation never creates semantically interpretable features anew. Inclusiveness fails to express this since valuation satisfies inclusiveness (no new feature is added), yet we need to express the (apparent) fact that valuation of a given feature never creates anew a semantic interpretation of that same feature.

With this much in place, the pervasive empirical problem revealed above is eliminated. Consider again (11), the structure troublesome for Chomsky (2007, 2008). The syntactically valued features—Case of *whom* and phi features of *like*—are at the phase-edge. However, Transfer still knows to remove them from the CI-bound object under the proposed framework, since they are [–CI] features, and Transfer removes all such features (including both syntactically valued phi features and phonological features) from the CI-bound object in the next phase cycle.[12] Transfer *before* valuation is still too early, since unvalued features will not be "implementable" at SM. However, *after* valuation is no longer too late, and the massive undergeneration problem is therefore resolved.

So far, we argued that valuation-induced Transfer "doesn't work," since it is internally inconsistent with the concurrently adopted assumption that syntactically valued features *do* in fact appear at phase-edges. Guided by SMT, we then reviewed a solution to one aspect of this problem: After valuation is not "too late," under a natural, and attractively restrictive, appeal to the nature of features (as either [+CI] or [–CI]), independently needed for Transfer to remove phonological features destined for the CI interface. But, interestingly, we now must return to the questions we started with: When, and to which SO, does Transfer apply, and why? The valuation-induced Transfer system, we suggest, ultimately fails to answer these questions. Must we then stipulate the timing of Transfer, or can it be deduced? If after valuation is not too late to Transfer, then when, after valuation, does Transfer apply? As mentioned at the outset, we argue that the timing and the target of Transfer can be deduced; it follows from the simplest characterization of structure building, and from key 3rd factor considerations.

4 DEDUCING CYCLIC TRANSFER

Recall our basic idea of Transfer outlined in section 1: Applying "counter-cyclic" IM, but without appeal to replacement, produces a "two-peaked" object, or, more formally, two intersecting set-theoretic SOs:

(13)

Since there is no single root that (reflexively) contains all terms, LAC prevents these "two-peaked" intersecting SOs from undergoing Merge (after the series of phase-level operations that generated them). For the derivation to continue, one peak (i.e. one of the two intersecting SOs) must be removed, and this task can be carried out, we suggest, by Transfer. Thus, "counter-cyclic" IM creates intersecting SOs that are not accessible to further Merge (effectively halting the derivation), and this "forces" Transfer to apply—see also notes 1 and 6 above. Let us now consider the details of this approach, motivating and articulating our central assumptions.

4.1   How Merge Applies

A number of key assumptions enter into our approach. First, we assume SMT, according to which

> language is an *optimal solution* to interface conditions that FL [the Faculty of Language] must satisfy; that is, language is an optimal way to link sound and meaning. . . . If SMT [the Strong Minimalist Thesis] held fully, UG would be restricted to properties imposed by interface conditions. A primary task of the MP [Minimalist Program] is to clarify the notions that enter into SMT and to determine how closely the ideal can be approached.
>
> Chomsky (2008:2)

The "goal" of NS is to optimally build SOs that are legible, and hence usable to, the interfaces SM and CI. This has been a standard assumption of the minimalist program since its inception.

We assume further that 3rd factor considerations play an important role in what counts as "optimal." 3rd factor involves "[p]rinciples not specific to the language faculty," in particular, ". . . principles of structural architecture and developmental constraints . . . including principles of efficient computation, which would be . . . of particular significance for [all] computational systems. . . ." (Chomsky 2005:6).

One such 3rd factor efficiency consideration is LAC: Only the label of an entire syntactic object, the root, is accessible to NS. But what is the root? We assume the following definition, under which not-yet-merged lexical items and non-intersecting set-theoretic SOs form a natural class:

(14) K is the root iff:
      for any Z, Z a term of K, every object that Z is a term of is a term of K.

As for "term," we adopt a simplified definition, adapted from Chomsky (1995):

(15) For any structure K,
      (i) K is a term of K, and
      (ii) if L is a term of K, then the members of L are terms of K.

The central (standard) idea is that the root is the term that reflexively contains all relevant terms (as defined above).

Any system must access something, namely the units out of which other units are constructed. Given 3rd factor considerations, access is optimal if made with least effort. By accessing only the label of the root, search is minimized, and therefore efficient. Thus, we assume with Chomsky (1995), EM applies at the root only.

Merge is an indispensable part of the human faculty of language. It comes, as Chomsky suggests, "for free." But how Merge operates is constrained by 3rd factor considerations. We thus take seriously the idea of minimal search. The basic intuition is that NS executes Merge with minimal search, so that computational complexity is greatly reduced. Thus far, minimal search has been invoked to constrain only IM. Here we would like to extend the 3rd factor notion of "minimal search" to EM (as we must if there is indeed only Merge). In principle, there are two ways of finding SOs: direct finding and finding through search. Regardless of whether SO is a lexical item or not, NS finds it directly if it is the root. If an SO is an internal term of the root, however, NS must search into the root to find that SO. Thus, regardless of whether the root is a lexical item or a set-theoretic object, merger of two roots (i.e. EM) is always preferable to merger of one root and its subpart (i.e. IM), because finding roots involves no search. Thus, it follows from this general 3rd factor consideration that all applications of EM necessarily precede any application of IM within the construction of each phase (this is reminiscent of "Merge over Move" of Chomsky 1995, 2000). And if the label of the root is available to NS that has accessed the root, then LAC, which states that only the label of the root is available to NS, also follows. NS can find the root and its label directly, but it must search into the root to find any internal terms.

We would like to point out one important consequence of this efficiency-based analysis, which involves EM. By LAC, NS has access to only the highest label of the root. Thus, only EM of two roots is possible. NS cannot "reach" inside the root and "pull out" its term for EM. Thus, in (16),

(16)

only the entire object Z can participate in EM; X and W, contained within Z, are inaccessible to EM. Take a simple case. Suppose EM merges V^1 and NP, forming $\{V^1, NP\}$. Then, it follows from 3rd factor considerations that EM cannot merge V^2 and NP (the latter a term of $\{V^1, NP\}$). Such merger of V^2 and NP has been (in essence) adopted by the sideward movement analysis of Hornstein (2001) and Nunes (2001) and the multidominance analysis of Citko (2005). But if the analysis proposed here is on the right track, then such merger of V^2 and NP is prohibited on 3rd factor grounds (see also Chomsky 2007:8; Kitahara 2007). Of course, more research into the phenomena in question is required, and we note here only the conditional and formal entailment regarding incompatibility of theories.

However, after NS exhausts EM (meaning all lexical items from a sub-array are now terms of the single root), search into the root is permitted. And in accord with minimal search, operations other than EM can be initiated. Such operations include feature-inheritance, Agree, and IM. With Chomsky (2007, 2008), we assume that the phase heads C and v inherently bear phi features (and EF). Thus, once C and v are accessed, feature-inheritance from C to T and from v to V may take place. Agree values phi features and Case, which takes place under the (restrictive) probe-goal mechanism. An accessed phase head itself has access only to "PIC visible" SOs within its derivational c-command domain (= terms of the category merged with the phase head), and such SOs can undergo IM to the edge of the accessed head.[13]

Recall that Merge "comes free." Given SMT reviewed above, we thus seek to maximize the explanatory effects of Merge. Thus, the only relations available to NS are those that directly follow from the simple, single, necessary structure building operation Merge.

With this much in place, "replacement" cannot be postulated as a new operation, and, of course, Merge alone cannot replace existing terms. But might the application of two distinct non-replacement operations, namely Delete (= "disconnect") and Merge (= "reconnect") carry out this task? We argue that this possibility is banned by LCR, which in effect forces NS to preserve all existing relations. Thus, "counter-cyclic" IM (e.g. subject raising) will necessarily result in (17):

(17)

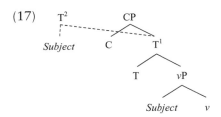

Recall that (17) is an informal representation of the two intersecting SOs: {C, T^1} and {Subj, T^1}, which happen to share the term T^1. Crucially, these "two-peaked" SOs have no root, given the definition of "root" above. Neither T^2 nor CP is a term that contains all other terms: T^2 fails since one of its terms, say, T, is a term of CP, yet CP is not a term of T^2. CP fails since one of its terms, say, T, is a term of T^2, yet T^2 is not a term of CP. Since there is no root, LAC prevents both T^2 and CP (and all other terms in (17)) from undergoing Merge after the series of phase-level operations that formed the two intersecting SOs in (17).

Given these assumptions, the derivation halts,[14] but to see just where and how Transfer comes into play, we must first explore other central mechanisms of the system, beginning with feature-inheritance.

4.2 Feature-Inheritance

With Chomsky (2007, 2008), we assume that the phase-heads C and v inherently bear phi features. Recall that Chomsky/Richards deduce feature-inheritance from C/v to T/V, given the "before and after" problem noted above. For Chomsky/Richards, C/v cannot keep their phi features, since if they did, these features would be valued at the phase-edge. But then, given PIC, their former unvalued status would be "lost." The syntactically valued features on the edge are then, in the eyes of Transfer, indistinguishable from inherently valued features and so are un-transferred, ultimately causing CI crash.

Recall that for us, since syntactically valued features are [–CI], there is no "after" problem for Transfer; after valuation is not too late, since Transfer "knows" to spell out [–CI] features, and syntactically valued features are [–CI]. How, then, do we induce feature-inheritance?

We propose that phi features must in fact be a necessary but not sufficient condition for Case-valuation. Case-valuation is achieved not by phi features alone—which would fail to distinguish the Case valued by V (Acc) from the Case valued by T (Nom)—but by the combination of phi features plus the "transitive property" (of transitive active voice verbs) or phi features plus the tense element, borne by T (see Chomsky 1995, 2000, 2001). Case-valuation is thus done through the feature complexes: (i) phi + tense $\rightarrow$ Nominative and (ii) phi + transitive $\rightarrow$ Accusative. So we resurrect and maintain the standard (and we suggest ineliminable) Case-theoretic assumption: (i) finite T "assigns" Nom, and (ii) transitive V "assigns" Acc.

Thus, phi feature-transmission from C/v to T/V is motivated when Case-valuation is required (and possible). Presumably, in languages like West Flemish, C exhibits phi-agreement but not Tense. Chomsky (2007:20) continues:

> If that is basically accurate, then there are two possibilities. One is that Tense is a property of C, and is inherited by T. The other is that Tense is a property of T, but receives only some residual interpretation unless selected by C (or in other configurations, e.g., in English-like modal constructions).

Note that the first option (i.e. C bears tense, and T inherits it from C) is adopted by Richards (2007) (without discussion). Here notice that if the second option (i.e. T inherently bears tense) is adopted, then feature-inheritance is for us necessary for Case-valuation (hence, a prerequisite for convergence). Keeping this in mind, consider the following passage continued from the above quote:

> One advantage of the latter option [the second option above] is that T will then have at least some feature in the lexicon, and it is not clear

what would be the status of an LI [lexical item] with no features (one of the problems with postulating AGR or other null elements). Another advantage would be an explanation for why C never manifests tense in the manner of phi features (if that is correct).

With these advantages, we adopt the second option, which forces feature-inheritance to take place for Case-valuation.

4.3   Extended Projection Principle = "Double" EF

The next question is: What motivates IM? Chomsky (2007, 2008) proposes that for a lexical item LI to permit Merge (regardless of whether EM or IM), it must have some "mergeability" property. This property is called "the EF" of LI. We suggest that EF is in fact a higher order property of features; similarly, the property "strength" is a higher order property of features in Chomsky (1995).[15] All linguistic features, and specifically for present concerns the phi features of C/v, have the higher order property of "mergeability." There is transmission of phi features from the phase head to the head that it selects. What this means is that C will transmit unvalued phi features to T, as will v to V. After feature-inheritance, T and v will bear "double" EF: one inherent on T/V (by virtue of the features that make up T and V) and one from inheritance of features from C/v. We propose that this "double" EF *requires* merger to its bearer T/V (while "single" EF only permits merger). In effect, this "double" EF is (our version of) Extended Projection Principle (EPP) (a property requiring merger to its bearer). But, for us, the EPP is a derived property, emerging only with feature-inheritance. We have not deduced the EPP; we have no more to add about *why* "double EF" requires a Spec than anyone else does about why the EPP requires a Spec. But our derived EPP (emerging in the course of a derivation), combined with our overall approach, does have positive empirical consequences.

5   CONSEQUENCES

The analysis considered above provides a deduction of cyclic Transfer. It also has other empirical consequences.

5.1 Deriving the "Invisibility" of Spec, T to C

Chomsky (2008) suggests that the ban on the extraction of the PP complement from within Spec, T, as in (18),

(18)   *[$_{CP}$ [$_{PP}$ of which car] did [$_{TP}$ [the driver t_{PP}] cause a scandal]]?

follows in part from the stipulation that Spec, T is invisible (as a goal) to (the probe) C. Specifically, he proposes that Spec, T becomes invisible to further computation once its Case is valued, generalizing the inactivity condition of earlier work (cf. Nevins 2005; Obata and Epstein 2008). By contrast, however, Spec, C (unlike Spec, T) continues to be visible after the valuation of its Case, as is required to allow successive cyclic *wh*-movement (e.g. *who do you think saw her?*). Exempting the construction of A'-chains from such a generalized inactivity condition is a stipulation, and this asymmetry remains to be explained. The alleged invisibility of Spec, T poses another problem as well. Take the indirect question (e.g. *I wonder who saw her*). Under Chomsky's (2008) phase-based model, Spec, C and Spec, T (each occupied by *who*) must be created simultaneously, and Spec, T becomes invisible upon the valuation of its Case. But, then, how can Spec, T, being invisible, count as a position lower than Spec, C?

Chomsky's (2008) analysis thus confronts (at least) the following two questions: (Q1) How does Spec, T become invisible, while Spec, C continues to be visible? and (Q2) How can the relative height of Spec, T be calculated when Spec, T itself is invisible? In this section, we seek to provide a principled answer to each of these questions, and argue that this can be done by deducing the invisible status of Spec, T as a property of the independently motivated derivational model (Epstein et al. 1998; Epstein 1999; Epstein and Seely 2002, 2006).

Under the derivational approach, NS establishes syntactic relations derivationally through the application of the indispensable structure building operation Merge, and no syntactic relation can be arbitrarily defined on output representations (contra Government and Binding theory). Specifically, c-command is the relation that Merge establishes between α and terms of β at the exact point of merging α with β. One unique property of this approach is the following: Suppose α is merged counter-cyclically with an embedded category γ, where γ is not the root but is a distinct term of β (i.e. γ is embedded within β). Representationally, all the terms of β that appear above γ would either c-command or dominate α. But, derivationally, these higher terms of β will neither c-command nor dominate α. Why? Because when these higher terms of β underwent their birth-merger, they were not merged with a category containing α now residing in the counter-cyclically merged position. Thus, these higher terms of β bear no derivational relation to such a counter-cyclically merged α. (See Kawashima and Kitahara 1996 and Epstein et al. 1998.) Under the current assumptions, this conclusion is strengthened. That is, it follows (without stipulation) that neither C nor Spec, C c-commands (counter-cyclically created) Spec, T derivationally; notice also that in the two-peaked representation, (13), C does not representationally c-command Spec, T either.

To see why this is, recall the indirect *wh*-question (e.g. *I wonder who saw her*) and consider the following tree (indices are introduced only for expository purposes, and the linear order is irrelevant):

(19)

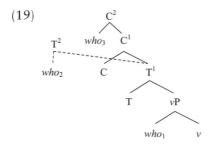

The question is: Does *who*$_3$ (= Spec, C) or C c-command *who*$_2$ (= Spec, T)? Within Chomsky's (2008) feature-inheritance analysis reviewed above (see also Richards 2007), EM merging C with T^1 precedes the necessarily simultaneous applications of IM, which create Spec, T and Spec, C by merging *who* with T^1 (forming T^2) and *who* with C^1 (forming C^2), respectively. With this execution of merger operations, it naturally follows that *who*$_2$ (= Spec, T) c-commands every term of its merged sister T^1, but neither C nor *who*$_3$ (= Spec, C) c-commands *who*$_2$ (= Spec, T), as represented in (19). This is the case because C was merged with T^1 (of which Spec, T was not at the time a term), *who*$_3$ (= Spec, C) was merged with C^1 (of which Spec, T was not at the time a term), and c-command relations are established derivationally, at the exact point of merger. The present analysis thus deduces the invisible status of Spec, T to both C and Spec, C as a property of the derivational model, while allowing Spec, C to continue to be visible to any "higher" category merged to a category of which Spec, C is a term—thereby allowing successive cyclic *wh*-movement, as desired.

Relative to such "counter-cyclic" IM, Chomsky (2008:150) notes:

> EF of C cannot extract the PP complement from within SPEC-T: if it could, the subject-condition effects would be obviated. It must be, then, that the SPEC-T position is impenetrable to EF, and a far more natural principle would be that it is simply invisible to EF.

No analysis of this optimal result is offered in Chomsky (2007, 2008). But the present analysis explains the "invisible" status of the Spec, T position.

As for calculating the height of invisible Spec, T from its visible occurrence, consider again (19) above. Chomsky (2008) suggests that the simultaneous applications of IM form a relation between *who*$_2$ and *who*$_1$, and a relation between *who*$_3$ and *who*$_1$, but not a relation between *who*$_3$ and *who*$_2$. Why is there no such relation? Presumably because there is no application of

IM involving the positions of who_3 and who_2, and if there is no such Merge application, there will be no relation between them (assuming a derivational theory of relations). We argue that the "invisible" status of Spec, T to both C and Spec, C is deducible from how Merge has applied in accord with the 3rd factor principle. If this deduction is on the right track, then the height of Spec, T is not calculated by the position of Spec, T itself. Instead, we propose that the height of Spec, T should be calculated by the position of its occurrence. Chomsky (1995) defines an occurrence of K as the category to which K is merged. An occurrence of Spec, T is then its merger-sister T^1. Under this occurrence-based calculation, the position of a category is uniquely determinable by reference to its merger-sister. Thus, Spec, T counts as a position lower than Spec, C, because T^1 (= the occurrence of Spec, T) is a distinct term of C^1 (= the occurrence of Spec, C), and this crucial "term-of" relation between T^1 and C^1 was established derivationally.

5.2   Icelandic Object Agreement Revisited

Chomsky (2000) postulates that the complement domain of the phase-head v is not accessible to operations outside of the phase vP. Thus, as desired in the following case, T cannot agree with NP_{OBJ} inside the phase-head complement VP:

(20) a. *John   like   these socks
         John.Nom   like.PL   these socks.PL.Acc
     b. * . . . T.PL . . . [$_{vP}$ v [$_{VP}$ V NP.PL.Acc]]

This follows from the stipulation that Transfer removes the phase-head complement VP from the workspace of NS at the completion of the phase vP. So when T is introduced, the VP (containing NP_{OBJ}) is "gone."

However, it has been widely discussed that in languages like Icelandic, T can agree with NP_{OBJ}, as illustrated in (21) (an example discussed in Jónsson 1996, also cited in Bobaljik 2008):[16]

(21) a. Jóni   líkuðu   þessir   sokkar
         Jon.DAT   like.PL   these   socks.PL.Nom
     b. . . . T.PL . . . [$_{vP}$ v [$_{VP}$ V NP.PL.Nom]]

To allow this, Chomsky (2001, 2004) delays Transfer application (removing the VP) until the merger of the next "higher" phase head (= C). T—inherently bearing lexical phi features of its own in Chomsky (2001, 2004)—thus can agree with NP_{OBJ}, exactly when T is merged, and hence before the subsequent merger of C, which triggers Transfer of VP.

Crucially, however, recall that Chomsky (2007, 2008) proposes that T does not inherently bear phi features of its own but instead inherits phi features from C. But this feature-inheritance analysis creates a new problem:

Before the merger of C to TP, T (lacking phi features of its own) cannot possibly phi-agree with NP_{OBJ}, but *after* the merger of C to TP, T (now bearing phi features inherited from C) cannot find the NP_{OBJ}, because the phase-head complement VP (containing the NP_{OBJ}) has been removed by Transfer.

Under the current assumptions, in particular, the new deduction of cyclic Transfer developed in the preceding sections, such T-NP_{OBJ} agreement receives a principled account without recourse to an independent agreement parameter.

Recall that Transfer removes the phase-head complement if and only if the phase head transmits its phi features to the head of the phase-head complement, which in turn values Case (ultimately creating the two-peaked effect). Consequently, in (20), Transfer removes the phase-head complement VP, whose head V values Case, thereby correctly blocking T-NP_{OBJ} agreement. By contrast, in (21), Transfer does not remove the phase-head complement VP, whose head V does not value Case, thereby allowing T-NP_{OBJ} agreement. Thus, (20) vs. (21) follows, and the English-Icelandic "parameter" is reduced to independent morpho-lexical Case-variant properties of heads.

This analysis also explains why T-NP_{OBJ} agreement occurs with passive/raising verbs, as illustrated in (22) (an example discussed in Zanen, Maling, and Thráinsson 1985, also cited in Bobaljik 2008):

(22) a. Um   venturinn voru   konunginum gefnar ambáttir
          In   the winter were.PL the king.DAT given   slaves.PL.NOM
          "In the winter, the king was given (female) slaves."
      b. . . . T.PL . . . [$_{vP}$ v [$_{VP}$ V$_{passive}$ NP.PL.NOM]]

Legate (2002) argues that a verbal phrase with a passive/raising verb is phasal. Chomsky (2001) stipulates that these are "weak" phases, which, unlike his original "strong" phases, escape from Transfer application. We eliminate this *ad hoc* distinction, reducing it to independently motivated Case properties.

Finally, let us address, once again, why Transfer removes the phase-head complement if and only if the head of the phase-head complement values Case.[17] Under the feature-inheritance analysis, in order for V/T to value Case, they must first inherit unvalued phi features from later-merged v/C respectively. This merger of v/C in turn projects vP and CP. But then "EPP/double-EF" satisfaction (i.e. creation of Spec, V and Spec, T) is necessarily "counter-cyclic"; i.e. it is merger but not at the root. As argued above, such "counter-cyclic" merger necessarily yields a "two-peaked" object—formally two intersecting SOs with no single root (to merge to)—causing the derivation to (deducibly) halt. To continue, one peak (the phase-head complement) must be removed from the workspace of NS by Transfer.

NOTES

Versions of this material were presented at the "Ways of Structure Building" conference held in November 2008 at the University of the Basque Country. We are grateful to Vidal Valmala Elguea and Myriam Uribe-Etxebarria for their hospitality and for their continued interest in our work. Aspects of this research were also presented at a colloquium talk at the Michigan State University Department of Linguistics. For valuable feedback we are grateful to Kyle Grove, John Hale, and Alan Munn. This research was also presented at a University of Maryland Department of Linguistics colloquium in April 2011. We thank especially Norbert Hornstein, Terje Londahl, and Dave Kush for very helpful feedback. We are also indebted to students in our "triply co-taught" 2009 syntax seminar for very valuable contributions, including Miki Obata, David Medeiros, Tim Chou, and Dan Parker. Finally, but by no means least, we thank Noam Chomsky for his interest in and immeasurable contributions to our research.

1. Below, we consider two analyses regarding the offensiveness of the "two-peaked" phenomenon: One is that there is no single root, causing the derivation to halt until Transfer can apply, removing one of the peaks. The other is that the two-peaked structure will never result in a single semantic value at the CI interface; consequently, one of the peaks must be removed by Transfer in the syntax; i.e. each of the syntactic objects in the two-peaked structure is given over to CI individually.

2. As we will see in a moment, this formulation does not prohibit IM; however, IM takes place only after all EM (given some lexical array) has been exhausted. Notice also that under the simplified representation generated by Merge (i.e. one lacking "labels" in the sense of Chomsky 1995), an element of $\{X, Y\}$ is still designated as "the label."

3. For expository convenience we continue to use the terms "External Merge" and "Internal Merge," but there is, in fact, just a single operation, Merge $(X, Y) = \{X, Y\}$.

4. LCR is more general (hence more restrictive); so, if LCR derives the empirically desirable aspects of EC and NTC, then LCR is preferable.

5. Note that if Chomsky's (2004) theory of adjunction is extended to head-movement, head-adjunction does not alter existing "head-complement" relations. Whether head-movement exists in NS is an open question, but it is not clear whether LCR eliminates "syntactic" head-movement.

6. Alternatively, under the law of semantic composition, these intersecting set-theoretic SOs will not yield a single semantic value. Thus, there must be a way to overcome the intersecting situation in NS. One possible remedy is to send them to the semantic component separately, and we propose that Transfer dissolves this intersecting situation by removing one intersecting set from the workspace of NS. Informally speaking, one "peak" (i.e. one of the two intersecting sets) must be sent to the semantic component by Transfer. *Which* of the peaks is Transferred will be considered below, as we attempt to explain why it is the phase-head-complement that is transferred (which is currently stipulated, though empirically motivated).

7. Crucially (as argued in Epstein et al. 1998 and Epstein and Seely 2002), Transfer cannot "know" which features will be interpretable at the not-yet-reached interfaces, since this requires look-ahead and Transfer being sensitive to Interpretability at the interface. This is precisely why feature valuation was incorporated into the theory. All Transfer can possibly be sensitive to is whether a feature is valued vs. unvalued, and so it then follows that once a feature is

valued it is too late to Transfer it since it is indistinguishable from an inherently valued (+interpretable) feature.

8. Note that Transfer also removes phonological features, which do not undergo valuation. In section 3, we present an analysis under which syntactically valued features and phonological features form a natural class.

9. Note that the motivation for the adjunction of V to v is not entirely clear, but it is a step required to restore the original VO order.

10. We leave aside the raising of *whom* also to Spec-V, since it is not relevant here.

11. Chomsky (2007:20) noted the relevance of examples such as (11) in which valued features seem to appear at the edge—which induces crash under the Chomsky–Richards analysis. But Chomsky regards such examples as unproblematic, writing "[v]aluation of uninterpretable features clearly feeds A'-movement (e.g., in *whom did you see?*). Hence valuation is 'abstract,' functioning prior to transfer to the SM interface. . . ." It is not clear to us, however, how his "abstract valuation" would circumvent the appearance of syntactically valued features at the phase-edge in (11). Note that this problem is very general, both in English (e.g. *Him, I like*) and cross-linguistically.

12. Under the current assumptions, Chomsky's (1998) definition of Transfer will suffice. It essentially states: Transfer deletes all [–CI] features from SO (constructed by NS), forming SO<+CI> (bearing only [+CI] features), and it sends SO<+CI> to the semantic component, while it sends SO to the phonological component. Note, given this formulation of Transfer, there is no way for [–CI] features to get to the CI interface; i.e. CI is "crash-proof" with respect to CI features.

13. The PIC (Chomsky 2000) states, in effect, that the complement of a phase head is inaccessible to the syntax at the next phase level.

14. An alternative analysis is that the two-peaked object would not yield a single semantic interpretation, and thus in the syntax one peak would be removed and sent to the CI interface alone.

15. This view sheds light on the otherwise curious characteristics of EF as formulated in Chomsky; namely (i) EF is a property of LI (Chomsky 2008:139), (ii) EF is undeletable from LI (Chomsky 2007:11), (iii) EF (unlike phi features) does not involve feature-matching (Chomsky 2008:161:fn 49), and (iv) EF can be inherited from the phase-head along with the phi features (Chomsky 2008:157). (i) follows from the natural assumption that if a LI is made up of features that have the property "mergeability," then the LI itself will have that property (likewise in Chomsky 1995 a category had the property "strong" by virtue of one of its features having this property). (ii) follows from Recoverability: There is no edge *feature* but rather only lexical features with the property "mergeability"; since a feature cannot be deleted under Recoverability, then neither can the edge property. (iii) Since "mergeability" is a (higher order) property of a feature and not a feature itself, then there is no feature-matching associated with EF. Finally, (iv) follows since phi features can be inherited, and "mergeability" is a property of these phi features.

16. We leave aside how Nominative Case (NOM) gets realized on NP_{OBJ} in (21), since Nom can appear on NP_{OBJ} even when an intervening NP clearly blocks agreement between T and NP_{OBJ}, as in (i) (an example discussed in Schütze 1997, also cited in Bobaljik 2008):

    (i) Mér   virðist   [Jóni   vera   taldir t   líka hestarnir]
        Me.DAT seemed.SG Jon.DAT be   believed.PL like horses.PL.NOM
        "I perceive Jon to be believed to like horses"

17. At the time this paper was going to press, we learned that Takahashi (2010), on entirely independently grounds and based on extensive empirical evidence, argues that Case determines phasehood. We have attempted to deduce this conclusion.

REFERENCES

Bobaljik, J.D. 2008. Where's Phi? Agreement as a Postsyntactic Operation. In Harbour, D., Adger, D. and Béjar, S. (eds.), *Phi Theory: Phi-Features across Modules and Interfaces*, 295–328. Oxford: Oxford University Press.

Chomsky, N. 1995. *The Minimalist Program*. Cambridge, MA: MIT Press.

Chomsky, N. 1998. Some Observations on Economy in Generative Grammar. In Barbosa, P., Fox, D., Hagstrom, P., McGinnis, M. and Pesetsky, D. (eds.), *Is the Best Good Enough?*, 115–127. Cambridge, MA: MIT Press.

Chomsky, N. 2000. Minimalist Inquiries: The Framework. In Martin, R., Michaels, D. and Uriagereka, J. (eds.), *Step by Step: Essays on Minimalist Syntax in Honor of Howard Lasnik*, 89–155. Cambridge, MA: MIT Press.

Chomsky, N. 2001. Derivation by Phase. In Kenstowicz, M. (ed.), *Ken Hale: A Life in Language*, 1–52. Cambridge, MA: MIT Press.

Chomsky, N. 2004. Beyond Explanatory Adequacy. In Belletti, A. (ed.), *Structures and Beyond*, 104–131. Oxford: Oxford University Press.

Chomsky, N. 2005. Three Factors in Language Design. *Linguistic Inquiry* 36:1–22.

Chomsky, N. 2007. Approaching UG from Below. In Sauerland, U. and Gärtner, H.-M. (eds.), *Interfaces + Recursion = Language?*, 1–29. Berlin: Mouton de Gruyter.

Chomsky, N. 2008. On Phases. In Freidin, R., Otero, C.P. and Zubizarreta, M.L. (eds.), *Foundational Issues in Linguistic Theory: Essays in Honor of Jean-Roger Vergnaud*, 133–166. Cambridge, MA: MIT Press.

Citko, B. 2005. On the Nature of Merge: External Merge, Internal Merge, and Parallel Merge. *Linguistic Inquiry* 36:475–496.

Epstein, S.D. 1999. Un-principled Syntax: The Derivation of Syntactic Relations. In Epstein, S.D. and Hornstein, N. (eds.), *Working Minimalism*, 317–345. Cambridge, MA: MIT Press. [Reprinted in *Essays in Syntactic Theory*, 183–210. New York: Routledge, 2000.]

Epstein, S.D. and Seely, T.D. 2002. Rule Applications as Cycles in a Level-Free Syntax. In Epstein, S.D. and Seely, T.D. (eds.), *Derivation and Explanation in the Minimalist Program*, 65–89. Oxford: Blackwell.

Epstein, S.D. and Seely, T.D. 2006. *Derivations in Minimalism*. Cambridge: Cambridge University Press.

Epstein, S.D., Groat, E., Kawashima, R. and Kitahara, H. 1998. *A Derivational Approach to Syntactic Relations*. Oxford: Oxford University Press.

Epstein, S.D., Kitahara, H. and Seely, T.D. 2010. Uninterpretable Features: What Are They and What Do They Do? In Putnam, M. (ed.), *Exploring Crash Proof Grammars*, 125–142. Philadelphia: John Benjamins.

Freidin, R. 1999. Cyclicity and Minimalism. In Epstein, S.D. and Hornstein, N. (eds.), *Working Minimalism*, 95–126. Cambridge, MA: MIT Press.

Hornstein, N. 2001. *Move! A Minimalist Theory of Construal*. Oxford: Blackwell.

Jónsson, J.G. 1996. Clausal Architecture and Case in Icelandic. Doctoral dissertation, University of Massachusetts, Amherst.

Kawashima, R. and Kitahara, H. 1996. Strict Cyclicity, Linear Ordering, and Derivational C-Command. In Camacho, J., Choueiri, L. and Watanabe, M. (eds.), *Proceedings of the West Coast Conference on Formal Linguistics* 14:255–269. Cambridge: Cambridge University Press.

Kitahara, H. 2007. Subjecting Sideward Movement to a Minimalist Critique. Manuscript, University of Michigan, Ann Arbor. [Presented at Eastern Michigan University (The 37th MLS, November 10, 2007).]

Legate, J.A. 2002. Some Interface Properties of the Phase. *Linguistic Inquiry* 34:506–516.

Nevins, A. 2005. Derivations without the Activity Condition. In McGinnis, M. and Richards, N. (eds.), *Perspectives on Phases (MIT Working Papers in Linguistics 49)*, 283–306. Cambridge, MA: MIT Press.

Nunes, J. 2001. Sideward Movement. *Linguistic Inquiry* 32:303–344.

Obata, M. and Epstein, S. D. 2008. Deducing Improper Movement from Phase Based C-to-T Phi Transfer: Feature-Splitting Internal Merge. Manuscript, University of Michigan, Ann Arbor. [Presented at Carson-Newman College (Exploring Crash-Proof Grammars, February 29–March 1, 2008), at Newcastle University (The 31st GLOW, March 26–28, 2008), and at University of California, Los Angeles (The 27th WCCFL, May 16–18, 2008).]

Richards, M. 2007. On Feature Inheritance: An Argument from the Phase Impenetrability Condition. *Linguistic Inquiry* 38:563–572.

Schütze, C. T. 1997. INFL in Child and Adult Language: Agreement, Case, and Licensing. Doctoral dissertation, MIT, Cambridge, MA.

Takahashi, M. 2010. Case, Phases, and Nominative/Accusative Conversion in Japanese. *Journal of East Asian Linguistics* 19:319–355.

Zanen, A., Maling, J. and Thráinsson, H. 1985. Case and Grammatical Functions: The Icelandic Passive. *Natural Language and Linguistic Theory* 3:441–483.

8   Simplest Merge Generates Set Intersection

Implications for Complementizer-Trace Explanation

Samuel D. Epstein, Hisatsugu Kitahara, and T. Daniel Seely

1   INTRODUCTION

A unique aspect of the analysis presented in this paper is that even though we propose Merge in its simplest, strictly binary form, it is nonetheless the case that a category can have more than one sister (i.e. more than one element that it was merged with). The multiple sisters of a given category arise at different derivational points, generating a "two-peaked" structure, or, more formally, intersecting sets, neither of which is a term of the other, in the set-theoretic notation of bare phrase structure (Chomsky 1995a). We assume an analysis with a very general, independently motivated deletion algorithm, which retains only the highest copy of multiple copies of an internally merged element, for sensorimotor (SM) systems. This is presumably an application of the independently necessary overarching principle of Minimal Computation (categories or features must be retained in an optimal fashion), entailing that copies cannot have additional phonological features above and beyond the single set of lexical features of the mover. Conversely, we also assume the principle of recoverability of deletion (categories or features must not be deleted in a random fashion). We then argue that our proposed simplest formulation of Merge (generating set intersection when applied "counter-cyclically") coupled with the very general laws of Minimal Computation (informally forcing features to be interpreted at most once) and Recoverability (informally forcing features to be interpreted at least once) allows us to deduce the core complementizer-trace phenomena with no further mechanisms required. Complementizer-trace effects turn out to be an immediate consequence of these arguably quite natural and general principles, having no *ad hoc* language-specific, construction-specific or operation-specific motivation regarding complementizer-trace phenomena. We then address the cross-linguistic variation of complementizer-trace effects and the apparent problem of undergeneration that our analysis faces given that it deduces complementizer-trace effects from deep, i.e. unparameterizable, principles.

2   SIMPLEST MERGE AND ITS INEVITABLE CONSEQUENCE FOR THE DERIVATION OF "COUNTER-CYCLIC" MOVEMENT

In this subsection, we provide a brief overview of the development of the simplest conception of Merge from X'-theory through bare phrase structure in the sense of Chomsky (1995a). The goal is to factor out of the Merge operation any property that can itself be deduced from deeper principles, leaving the optimal structure building operation, what we refer to below as *simplest Merge*.

2.1   Brief Overview of X'-Theory in Early Minimalism

X'-theory sought to eliminate phrase structure rules, leaving only the general X' format as part of Universal Grammar (UG). Determining that format, and avoiding construction-specific and language-specific phrase structure rules, was the central research goal of subsequent work. In early Minimalism, X'-theory was still given, with specific stipulated properties. The outputs of the applications of structure building operations—binary and singulary Generalized Transformation (GT)—were then assumed to be constrained by X'-theory, by definition (see Chomsky 1993):

(1) a. binary GT
    (i) takes K and K', where K' is not a phrase marker within K
    (ii) adds Δ external to K
    (iii) substitutes K' for Δ, forming K*, which must satisfy X'-theory
  b. singulary GT
    (i) takes K and K', where K' is a phrase marker within K
    (ii) adds Δ external to K
    (iii) substitutes K' for Δ, forming K*, which must satisfy X'-theory

Basically, binary GT takes two separate syntactic objects and combines them into a single object, which as we'll see in a moment is the "ancestor" of *External Merge* (EM). Singulary GT is the precursor of the more recent *Internal Merge* (IM), where one of the objects being joined together is contained within the other. In effect, X'-theory, together with its stipulated (or axiomatic) properties (endocentricity, head-to-complement, and spec-head relation), was taken to be a UG filter on transformational output representations.

2.2   Subjecting X'-Theory to a Minimalist Critique

Under the strong minimalist thesis, however, X'-theory was not exempt from explanatory scrutiny; it was asked why X'-theory seems to hold, as opposed to an infinite number of formally definable alternative phrase structure systems. By adherence to minimalist method, this question prompts the following question: How "should" phrase structures be generated under minimalist (ideal, simplest) assumptions? Chomsky's (1995a:396) answer was:

> Given the numeration N, C_{HL} may select an item from N (reducing its index) or perform some permitted operation on the structure it has already formed. One such operation is necessary on conceptual grounds alone: an operation that forms larger units out of those already constructed, call it Merge. Applied to two objects α and β, Merge forms the new object γ. What is γ? γ must be constituted somehow from the two items α and β; . . . The simplest object constructed from α and β is the set $\{\alpha, \beta\}$, so we take γ to be at least this set, where α and β are constituents of γ. Does that suffice? Output conditions dictate otherwise; thus verbal and nominal elements are interpreted differently at LF and behave differently in the phonological component . . . γ must therefore at least (and we assume at most) be of the form $\{\delta, \{\alpha, \beta\}\}$, where δ identifies the relevant properties of γ, call δ the label of γ.

Merge was introduced as an operation (the central structure building operation of the narrow syntax (NS)), necessary on conceptual grounds alone, and the simplest object γ constructed from α and β by Merge was taken to be the set $\{\alpha, \beta\}$. Chomsky (1995a) assumed the set $\{\alpha, \beta\}$ was too simple; it was assumed that empirical adequacy demanded some departure from the simplest assumption (the standard scientific tension between explanation and "empirical coverage"); that is, the set must be labeled as in e.g. $\{\delta, \{\alpha, \beta\}\}$, where δ identifies the relevant properties of γ.[1]

Given that an output of Merge is a labeled set $\gamma = \{\delta, \{\alpha, \beta\}\}$, Chomsky (1995a:397–398) asked what exactly the label of γ is:

> If constituents α, β of γ have been formed in the course of computation, one of the two must project, say α. At the LF interface, γ (if maximal) is interpreted as a phrase of the type α (e.g. a nominal phrase if its head κ is nominal), and it behaves in the same manner in the course of computation. It is natural, then, to take the label of γ to be not α itself but rather κ, the head of the constituent that projects, a decision that also leads to technical simplification. Assuming so, we take $\gamma = \{\kappa, \{\alpha, \beta\}\}$, where κ is the head of α and its label as well.

Under this definition, the label of γ is the head of one of its constituents. If α projects, then the object γ constructed from α and β by Merge is $\{H(\alpha), \{\alpha, \beta\}\}$, where $H(\alpha)$ is the head of α (see also Chomsky 1995b). Additionally, the notion "term" is defined as follows: (i) K is a term of K, and (ii) if L is a term of K, then the members of the members of L are terms of K (Chomsky 1995a:399).

Chomsky (1995a, 1995b) did not discuss exactly how Merge operates to form such labeled sets, but one way is to formulate Merge as an operation consisting of the following two steps:[2]

(2) a. Applied to α and β, where neither α nor β is a term of the other, Merge
    (i) takes α and β, forming {α, β}, and
    (ii) takes H(α) and {α, β}, forming {H(α), {α, β}}.
  b. Applied to α and β, where α is a term of β, Merge
    (i) takes α and β, forming {α, β}, and
    (ii) takes H(β) and {α, β}, forming {H(β), {α, β}}.

In (2a,b), the second step in effect labels the simplest object {α, β} constructed by the first step. A question is whether we can eliminate or derive the empirically desirable aspects of this second step—i.e. whether we can predict or explain by general principles what the label of any α, β pair will be (see Chomsky 2000:133). If the answer is positive, Merge can be formulated in the simplest form: Merge (α, β) → {α, β}, with the label eliminated from the representational notation and instead simply identified as H(α) or H(β), as in Chomsky (2013).

2.3   On the Complexity of "Counter-cyclic" Covert Movement

In addition to the labeling algorithm, Chomsky (1995b:254) noted an additional complexity, one concerning covert movement:

> The computational system CHL is based on two operations, Merge and Move. We have assumed further that Merge always applies in the simplest possible form: at the root. What about Move? The simplest case again is application at the root: if the derivation has reached the stage Σ, then Move selects α and target Σ, forming {γ, {α, Σ}}. But covert movement typically embeds α and therefore takes a more complex form: given Σ, select K within Σ and raise α to target K, forming {γ, {α, K}}, which substitutes for K in Σ.

We can formally represent this additional complexity by adding a third step to the formulation of Merge:[3]

(3) Applied to α and β within Σ, where α is a term of β, Merge
    (i) takes α and β, forming {α, β}, and
    (ii) takes H(β) and {α, β}, forming {H(β), {α, β}}, and
    (iii) replaces β in Σ by {H(β), {α, β}}.

Again, a question is whether we can eliminate this third step (counter-cyclic IM replacement, or "substitution" to use Chomsky's (1995b:254) terminology), along with the second step (labeling), and thereby derive an empirically adequate, simplest formulation of Merge. If the answer is positive, Merge can be formulated in the simplest form: Merge (α, β) → {α, β}.[4]

2.4 An Inevitable Consequence of Simplest Merge

In a series of recent papers, Epstein, Kitahara, and Seely (hereafter EKS) have proposed precisely this form of simplest Merge. Unlike Chomsky's Merge, which allows "counter-cyclic" replacement as in (3iii), simplest Merge cannot perform replacement. EKS have explored its effects (see EKS 2012; Kitahara 2011) including the inevitable consequences of simplest Merge. Let's review. Consider the following sentence:

(4) Bill ate rice.

At some point in the derivation of (4), Merge takes the phase-head C and merges it with TP, yielding (5):

(5) {C, {T, {Bill, {v, {ate, rice}}}}}

At this point, C transmits unvalued phi to T. T, then, functioning as a phi-probe, locates the goal *Bill* (bearing lexically valued phi and unvalued Case), and Agree between T and *Bill* applies, valuing phi on T and Case on *Bill*. The standard assumption (see Chomsky 2007, 2008) is that as these features get valued, *Bill* is raised to the so-called Spec(ifier) of T (such raising required by some residue of the Extended Projection Principle [EPP]), yielding (6) (where we use the notion "Spec(ifier)" only for expository purposes):

(6) {C, {Bill, {T, {Bill, {v, {ate, rice}}}}}}

This "counter-cyclic" application of Merge (which, recall, is not simplest Merge), mapping (5) to (6), executes a form of replacement (= (3iii)) since Merge, not applying at the root, "infixes" *Bill* into Spec, TP. In set-theoretic terms, "counter-cyclic" Merge of *Bill* to the then specless T_1 = {T, {Bill, {v, {ate, rice}}}} yields a new specful syntactic object, namely T_2 = {Bill, {T, {Bill, {v, {ate, rice}}}}}. But recall, this creation of Spec, TP is not at the root, since C was necessarily already externally merged with the spec-less TP = T_1 (as in (5)).[5] Therefore, T_2 (with *Bill* as "newly appointed" Spec, TP) *replaces* spec-less T_1 in {C, T_1}, removing T_1 from {C, T_1} (destroying a relation/set) and merging T_2 as the newly appointed "sister" to C. Such replacement—T_2 replaces T_1, and T_1 "vanishes"—yields a new CP (= {C, T_2}). It is important to note that it is this "new" CP (= {C, T_2}), and not the "old" CP (= {C, T_1}), that enters into further derivational processes; i.e. the spec-less TP = T_1 has disappeared from the continuing derivation.

EKS (2012) argue that, given the strong minimalist thesis, NS should contain only the simplest structure building operation, namely Merge $(X, Y) \rightarrow \{X, Y\}$. EKS then point out that Merge, defined in this simplest form (= (3i) only), cannot replace existing categories (see Freidin 1999 for important earlier discussion of replacement as a non-primitive operation). Thus, it must be the case that NS equipped only with simplest Merge cannot map (5) (= $\{C, T_1\}$) to (6) (= $\{C, T_2\}$) in the manner just discussed above. But, then, what kind of object does "counter-cyclic" application of Merge (e.g. raising to Spec, TP) create?

It is important to note that EKS adopt the idea of Chomsky (2007, 2008) that given a lexical array (which itself must contain a phase head C or v), all instances of EM must take place before any instance of IM. This is motivated on grounds of efficiency; specifically: EM involves no search (there is immediate access to lexical items within an array), while IM (and other operations of the NS such as Agree) involve search (into an already-existing syntactic object). Thus, it follows that EM must be exhausted before any other operation can apply. In (5), then, the NS builds up to CP via EM, and only then can IM take place, creating (6)—if replacement were allowed. Thus, the nature of "counter-cyclic" IM is crucial in that it is in effect "forced" under efficiency. Since, by hypothesis, C is merged to TP before raising of the external argument to Spec, TP, it follows that when such raising does take place, it is "counter-cyclic" in the sense specified above.

EKS suggest that the "counter-cyclic" application of Merge cannot execute the complex operation "replacement" but rather necessarily results—speaking informally now—in a "two-peaked" or "doubly rooted" representation, informally represented in (7) (where indices appear only for expository purposes, and linear order is irrelevant):

(7)

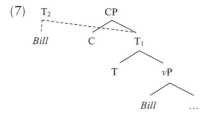

In set-theoretic terms, first we created the set CP = $\{C, T_1\}$ since C was merged with spec-less T_1. Then, the "counter-cyclic" application of simplest Merge (incapable of replacement, by our assumptions) merges *Bill* to T_1, forming another set, namely $T_2 = \{Bill, T_1\}$. This results in two distinct but intersecting set-theoretic syntactic objects (SOs), which happen to have T_1 (= $\{T, vP\}$) as their "shared" element. That is, as a result of this "counter-cyclic" Merge (of *Bill* to T_1), the single "workspace" of NS contains two intersecting set-theoretic SOs, CP = $\{C, T_1\}$ and $T_2 = \{Bill, T_1\}$, as shown in (8a,b), where neither is a term of the other.[6]

(8) a. {C, {T, {Bill, {v, {ate, rice}}}}}
    b. {Bill, {T, {Bill, {v, {ate, rice}}}}}

Interestingly, notice that although Merge is the simplest possible operation, crucially binary and incapable of replacement, thus creating only two-membered sets, it is nonetheless the case that T_1 (= {T, {Bill, {v, {ate, rice}}}}) has two different sisters. That is, simplest Merge generates intersecting sets: Both C and ("later") *Bill* were merged with T_1 (= {T, {Bill, {v, {ate, rice}}}}) at different derivational points; hence, C and *Bill* are sisters of T_1.

Given this result, EKS (2012) further argue that, under the law of semantic composition, these two intersecting set-theoretic SOs, each functioning as a root, would not yield a single semantic value if they were sent to the semantic component together, "as one." Thus, there must be some way to decompose this "two-peaked" or "doubly rooted" representation in the "workspace" of NS, prior to the semantic component. One possible way out of this situation, outlined by EKS (2012), is to send the two intersecting SOs to the semantic component separately. Specifically, EKS propose that Transfer dissolves this intersecting situation by removing one intersecting set from the "workspace" of NS. In effect, one "peak" (i.e. one of the two intersecting sets) must be sent to the semantic component by Transfer at this point of the derivation. Under this proposal, cyclic Transfer of TP once CP is built is *deduced* (given that the phase-edge must be left for the derivation to continue). Suppose that (i) the "workspace" contains (8a) (= {C, T_1}) and (8b) (= {Bill, T_1}), and (ii) cyclic Transfer removes (8b) (= {Bill, T_1}). Then, the phase-edge, namely {C, —}, where "—" is transferred material, in effect is left for subsequent operations. Note, if vP, in addition to CP, is a phase, then cyclic Transfer of VP at vP also follows.

Summarizing, the "counter-cyclic" application of Merge (raising Subject to Spec, TP after the merger of C and spec-less TP) cannot map {C, {T, vP}} to {C, {Subject, {T, vP}}}. Instead, it necessarily forms {Subject, {T, vP}}, which intersects with {C, {T, vP}}, and neither {Subject, {T, vP}} nor {C, {T, vP}} is a term of the other. This "two-peaked tree" (or these intersecting sets) thus arises as an inevitable consequence of simplest Merge when applied "counter-cyclically." In effect, Merge can create (but not destroy) syntactic relations. It naturally guarantees that all established syntactic relations (among existing categories) remain unaltered in NS.

3 SIMPLIFICATION BY DELETION

In NS, all syntactic relations, each established by Merge, remain unaltered, but when transferred to SM, a set-theoretic SO will be simplified by deletion. Although an SO that enters the phonological component will contain all relevant lexical features and all relevant syntactic structures (created in the course of its derivation), by SM what will remain of this SO is just a "pure" phonological representation; all but the phonological features will be deleted from it. What is particularly relevant for present concerns is the case of movement, i.e. cases where there are multiple copies of a mover. Here, too, there will be simplification by deletion; specifically, only one copy of a moved element is present at SM, and all other copies are deleted. In this section, we review the relevant assumptions concerning deletion in the phonological component, setting the stage for our analysis of *that*-trace effects.

One of the underlying and enduring assumptions in generative grammar is the principle of recoverability of deletion (Recoverability). This principle states that each SM- or conceptual-intentional (CI)-interpretable feature borne by a lexical item must be present at the relevant interface. Thus, no CI- or SM-interpretable feature of a lexical item can simply vanish in the course of a derivation. Thus, the lexical item *cot* with its phonological features (associated with /kat/) cannot be realized in SM as just /ka/ with no sign of /t/. Likewise, if the overt complementizer C*that* enters into a derivation, then its phonological features, represented (informally) as /that/, must be present in the phonological representation; these phonological features can't be lost or vanish in the course of the derivation. So Recoverability guarantees the presence (at an interface) of relevant CI- and SM-interpretable features. But, while by hypothesis empirically necessary (given Recoverability), mere presence at the interface is not empirically sufficient.

Another basic assumption, assigned more prominence in recent minimalist literature, is the principle of minimal computation (Minimal Computation). This principle states that an interface-interpretable lexical feature, which must be present (at least once) at the interface given Recoverability, cannot be present *more than once*. Chomsky (2013:41) notes that "universally in language, only the structurally prominent copy is pronounced," which, he suggests "follows from another application of the third factor principle of Minimal Computation: Pronounce as little as possible." So, for example, if a category bearing phonological features, e.g. *Bill*, undergoes movement, then there will be two copies of *Bill* in the output, but only the structurally prominent (universally the highest) copy of *Bill* will be phonologically realized as /Bill/. Consider (9):

(8) {Bill, {T, {Bill, {v, left}}}}

In (9), assuming that *Bill* moves just from Spec, vP to Spec, TP, there would be two copies of *Bill*, only the highest of which is "pronounced"; hence, at SM it's /Bill left/ and not /Bill Bill left/. The relative height of such copies is calculated by the positions of their occurrences, where, following Chomsky (1995b), an occurrence of X is defined as a category to which X is merged, i.e. its derivational sister. Thus, in (9) there is one *Bill* (i.e. just one category, *Bill*, entered the derivation via a lexical array) with two occurrences determined by *Bill*'s sisters, namely the two occurrences {v, left} and {T, {Bill, {v, left}}}. The latter occurrence is higher than the former occurrence since the latter occurrence contains the former occurrence as its term; hence, *Bill* in Spec, TP is the (only) copy that is phonologically realized. Under this occurrence-based calculation, the position of each copy of X is uniquely determinable by reference to its merged sister, namely its occurrence. As the derivation proceeds, the merged sisters of the lower occurrences of X are all deleted, and only the highest copy of X will remain for SM.

To summarize, Recoverability requires that each CI- and SM-interpretable feature of a lexical item is present (hence present at least once) in the relevant interface representation. Minimal Computation requires that interpretable features are present at most once. Finally, the very general and completely independently necessary Full Interpretation guarantees that interface interpretation actually takes place. That is, the features that are (guaranteed to be) present in an interface representation can't simply be ignored but must be implemented by the interface. Putting this all together, independently of anything having to do with *that*-trace, the system determines that although the representation underlying, say, *Bill was arrested* involves [Bill was arrested Bill], the object *Bill* is phonologically realized once, but only once.

4   COMPLEMENTIZER-TRACE EFFECTS: A NEW ANALYSIS

Adopting simplest Merge, along with its inevitable consequence of set-intersected representation ("doubly rooted" tree), we argue that complementizer-trace effects, or at least the core cases discussed in the context of *that*-trace (see Abe 2011; Browning 1996; Chomsky 1981, 1986; Chomsky and Lasnik 1977; Ishii 2004; Lasnik and Saito 1984, 1992; Perlmutter 1971; Rizzi and Shlonsky 2007; Sobin 1987, 2002; among many others), are deducibly excluded, based on simplest Merge (as detailed above) and very general, deep principles, specifically: Recoverability and Minimal Computation. It is important to stress again that we are not adding any new principles or "technical" mechanisms of any sort; rather, we are appealing to operations (simplest Merge) and deep principles (Recoverability and Minimal Computation) that are independently necessary and well supported empirically. Our goal is to reveal that core complementizer-trace effects fall out as a natural consequence of components of the system that are "virtually conceptually necessary" or (seemingly) simplest—e.g. Merge as defined in (3i) is by hypothesis simpler than Merge defined as (3i, ii, and iii).

4.1   Core Cases

Consider the following well-known contrast between (10) and (11):

(10) Who do you think left?
(11) *Who do you think that left?

Let's consider the derivation of (10), key parts of the derivation of which are represented informally as in (12), with C_2 the embedded CP:

(12)

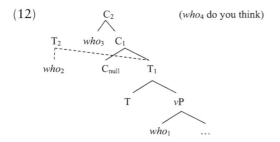

(who_4 do you think)

This tree representation informally depicts the "embedded" clause, which, of course, at the "time" of its generation has not yet become embedded. Recall that there is exactly one lexical item *who* associated with this derivation (*who* is selected exactly once from the lexicon), and this *who* has (at least) three copies in the embedded CP, the copies represented as who_3, who_2, and who_1 (where the indices are used just for expository convenience). The lexical item *who* originated in Spec, vP, and it was "cyclically" merged with C_1, yielding C_2, and then it was "counter-cyclically" merged with T_1, yielding T_2. The creation of T_2 is precisely the "two-peaked" situation we detailed above. In the course of this derivation, $T_1 = \{T, vP\}$ ends up having two different sisters, namely, C_{null}, which T_1 was cyclically merged with, and who_2, which T_1 was "counter-cyclically" merged with. Now, we know that the string of copies of *who* are not all pronounced (the final SM implementation of the derivation is certainly not /who do you think who who who left/). Thus, the merged sisters of the lower occurrences of *who* are all deleted in accord with Minimal Computation.

To illustrate in more technical detail, the (relevant part of the) derivation "starts" with the lower CP phase:

(13) $\{C, \{T, \{who_1, \{v, \{\text{l̶e̶f̶t̶}\}\}\}\}\}$

Since the option of applying EM is now exhausted, phi feature (C to T) transmission and (then) valuation (of phi of T and Case of *who*) are carried out. And, crucially for present concerns, there is IM of *who* to TP (to create Spec, TP), and there is also IM of *who* to CP (to create Spec, CP). These simultaneous applications of IM map (13) to both (14) and (15), (where (14) and (15) are informally represented in (12)):

(14) $\{who_2, \{T, \{who_1, \{v, \{\text{l̶e̶f̶t̶}\}\}\}\}\}$
(15) $\{who_3, \{C, \{T, \{who_1, \{v, \{\text{l̶e̶f̶t̶}\}\}\}\}\}\}$

At this point, there are three occurrences (i.e. derivational sisters) of *who*:

(16) a. {v, {~~left~~}}
   who was merged to {v, {~~left~~}},
   yielding {who$_1$, {v, {~~left~~}}}

  b. {T, {who$_1$, {v, {~~left~~}}}}
   who was merged to {T, {who$_1$, {v, {~~left~~}}}},
   yielding {who$_2$ {T, {who$_1${v, {~~left~~}}}}}

  c. {C, {T, {who$_1$, {v, {~~left~~}}}}}
   who was merged to {C, {T, {who$_1$, {v, {~~left~~}}}}},
   yielding {who$_3$, {C {T, {who$_1$, {v, {~~left~~}}}}}}

Notice that at each derivational step in (16), in fact throughout any derivation, only simple, binary Merge is employed, and sisterhood is characterized derivationally in the simplest way, as "merged with"; i.e. X and Y are sisters if and only if Merge (X, Y) applied (see Epstein et al. 1998). But, interestingly, the object {T, {who, {v, {~~left~~}}}}, an occurrence of *who*, has two (derivational) sisters: namely the category C (see (15)) and (what is now a copy of) *who* (see (14)). Given Minimal Computation, the single lexical item *who*, bearing one and only one set of phonological features that entered the derivation, must be pronounced once and only once, at the highest copy position. But at this point we must consider with some care just how Minimal Computation is to be stated.

The intuitive idea, as we've seen, is that only one (the highest) copy of a moved element is realized in the phonological component (only the highest is phonologically implemented). And what this entails is that all other copies determined by the lower occurrences of the moved element must be deleted, and such deletion takes place phase by phase. Now we know that in the mapping from NS to SM, there is massive deletion of all but the purely phonological (i.e. SM-interpretable) features; given the strong minimalist thesis, all and only SM-interpretable features are present in the representation that exits the phonological component. Thus, all syntactic structures, all semantic features, and all but the highest copy of a moved element must be deleted (i.e. removed) from the SO that undergoes this mapping.

With this in mind, consider again (14) and (15). Assuming that every copy of *who* represented in (14) and (15) is determined to be the sister of a lower occurrence of *who*, it must be deleted. Recall, occurrences of X are the (derivational) sisters of X. So the general deletion algorithm looks at {T, {who$_1$, {v, {~~left~~}}}} and {v, {~~left~~}} (since they are lower occurrences of *who*) and says: "Delete all their sisters; i.e. delete the *who* copies which are the sisters of {T, {who$_1$, {v, {~~left~~}}}} and of {v, {~~left~~}}." Thus, the operation deletes all the lower copies of *who* from (14) and (15). But that's not the end of the story.

As we pointed out above, for the EKS analysis, even though Merge is itself simple(st) and binary, with "counter-cyclic" IM creating Spec, TP, the object $\{T, \{who_1, \{v, \{left\}\}\}\}$ can have two derivational sisters. In short, sister is not uniquely defined in that sister of X is not always just one object. It now follows that our PF deletion operation (Minimal Computation) cannot be stated as: Delete *a* sister of each lower occurrence (of some mover). This statement will not do, since in our target case, it would allow us to delete C rather than *who*, since each counts equally as a sister of $\{T, \{who_1, \{v, \{left\}\}\}\}$. That is, referring back to our informal representation (12), it won't do to say: Delete *a* sister of T_1 (= $\{T, \{who_1, \{v, \{left\}\}\}\}$) since one could then delete just C_{null} since in fact it is *a* sister of T_1 (= $\{T, \{who_1, \{v, \{left\}\}\}\}$).

But this would (incorrectly) leave *who₂*, thereby overgenerating **who do you think who left*. To properly select the highest copy of a mover, the general deletion algorithm must be stated as: Delete *all* sisters of lower occurrences of a mover. And what this means is that the required deletion of who_2 in (14) entails the deletion of C in (15); i.e. the system compels us to delete the local complementizer whenever there is an unpronounced "trace" in Spec, TP (which there will be only in the case of subject extraction). And this is required precisely because the Spec, TP copy of *who* must be deleted (i.e. **Who do you think who left*), but under the simplest deletion algorithm (deleting sisters), the C, in cases of subject extraction, is in the same position as the *who*-copy in Spec, TP; i.e. both are sisters of $\{T, vP\}$. So, given simplest Merge, and simplest deletion, whenever the general deletion algorithm deletes a copy of a subject *wh* (a subject "trace"), it necessarily also deletes the local (and only the local) C—since the two are in the exact same position, i.e. sister to $\{T, vP\}$. Overall, *that*-trace effects with subject (not object or adjunct) extraction follow; i.e. we can't "say" *who do you think that left* for the same reason that we can't say *Bill was arrested Bill*: In both cases we have "pronounced" too much, in violation of Minimal Computation.

Returning to the *that*-trace contrast, exhibited between (10) and (11), it now follows immediately. Recall that in the "doubly rooted" tree or the corresponding intersecting set representation (12), C_{null} counts as a merged sister of $\{T, vP\}$. Now, if the two lower copies of *who* get deleted, the phonological features of *who* are in principle recoverable, because the highest copy of *who* (in the edge of the lower CP phase at this point of the derivation) still remains. And since C_{null} bears no phonological features, deleting the phonological features of C_{null} is vacuous, with no problem resulting from this. Thus, the deletion of the two copies of *who* and C_{null} does not violate Recoverability in the case of (10). Similarly, in the derivation of (11), the merged sisters of the lower occurrences of *who* are all deleted in accord with Minimal Computation. However, consider the corresponding "doubly rooted" tree of (11), in which the complementizer bears phonological features, e.g. /that/, as given in (17):

(17)

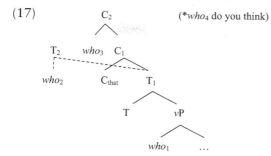

(*who_4 do you think)

There are (at least) two lower occurrences of *who* in the embedded CP: {T, vP} and {v, VP}. The merged sisters of these occurrences include two copies of *who* and C_{that}. Now, if the two copies of *who* get deleted, the phonological features of *who* are in principle recoverable, because the highest copy of *who* (in the edge of the lower CP phase at this point of the derivation) still remains. So the deletion of the two copies of *who* does not violate Recoverability. But what about the deletion of C_{that}? Recall again that, under the "two-peaked" or intersecting situation, represented in (17), C_{that} counts as a merged sister of {T, vP}, and if the deletion rule must (indiscriminately) apply to all the merged sisters of the lower occurrences of *who* (understood to be the simplest application of this deletion algorithm), then C_{that} must undergo deletion, together with who_2 (= Spec, TP) and who_1 (= Spec, vP). In other words, the deletion of C_{that} is an inevitable consequence of the demand imposed by Recoverability ("not too little") and Minimal Computation ("not too much"). But C_{that} does bear phonological features (and it is the sole copy), so the deletion of C_{that} violates Recoverability. That is, *that* with a single set of phonological features never underwent SM interpretation of those phonological features. Thus, the only derivation that survives when performing subject extraction is the one in which C_{null} is (randomly) chosen (and this is without look-ahead, of course).

Notice, if we analyze *if* as C_{if}, then the contrast between (18) and (19) follows in the same way:

(18) ?how many cars did he wonder [t_{wh} C_{if} [the mechanics fixed t_{wh}]]
(19) *how many mechanics did he wonder [t_{wh} C_{if} [t_{wh} fixed the cars]]

Observing this contrast, Chomsky (2013:41) notes that what (19) expresses is "a fine thought, but it has to be expressed by some circumlocution." He speculates that there is something about language design which poses a barrier to communication. We suggest that Recoverability and Minimal Computation constitute just such barriers.

4.2   Related Cases

As we have seen in the derivation of (11), if C_{that} is chosen, the derivation is in trouble because the deletion rule (applying to Spec, TP) will "unrecoverably" delete *that* occupying the same position as Spec, TP, which itself undergoes deletion. So, if the deletion rule does not apply to Spec, TP, e.g. if Spec, TP is phonologically realized, then C_{that} will not be in trouble, and it will be phonologically realized as /that/. This prediction is confirmed. Consider (20), in which Spec, TP is phonologically realized as /John/, and (21), in which Spec, TP is phonologically realized as /there/ (Safir 1985; Chomsky 1991, 1995b:158):

(20)   Who do you think $[_{CP} t_{wh} C_{that} [_{TP} John likes t_{wh}]]$

(21)   How many men did John say $[_{CP} t_{how} C_{that} [_{TP}$ there were t_{how} in the room]]

In each derivation, a *wh*-element moves directly to (embedded) Spec, CP (i.e. there is no movement of *wh*-element to Spec, TP), so the deletion rule does not apply to Spec, TP; therefore, as shown above, it does not apply to the local C. Instead, Spec, TP is phonologically realized, and C_{that} is phonologically realized as /that/. There is no obligatory deletion of C in such cases, and Recoverability is thereby satisfied. Similarly, this analysis captures the non-deviant status of (22):

(22)   Why do you think $[t_{wh} C_{that}$ [John likes Mary $t_{wh}]$

Again, in constructing the embedded CP, the *wh*-element, *why* in this case, is never compelled to move to Spec, TP, instead moving directly to Spec, CP, and hence is never a derivational sister to {T, vP}, and hence *that* escapes (obligatory but Recoverability-violating) deletion. In fact, our analysis captures the notorious subject/adjunct asymmetry in γ-marking (see Huang 1982; Lasnik and Saito 1984, 1992) but without invoking any Surface Structure (SS) versus Logical Form (LF) asymmetry in the targets (arguments versus non-arguments) of the γ-marking algorithm.[7] All such descriptive technicalia are prohibited under minimalist analysis, rightly raising the bar on what can count as an explanation versus an unilluminating formal/technical redescription often more "complex" than the data described (as discussed by Chomsky 1995b). In addition, phenomena exhibited by data such as (23) (Lasnik and Saito 1984, 1992) are also accounted for.

(23)   Who do you think $[t_{wh} C_{that}$ [John said $[t_{wh} C_{null} [t_{wh}$ left]]]]

In (23), a *wh*-element "crosses" two CP phase cycles. In the lowest CP phase cycle, the *wh*-element moves to Spec, TP and Spec, CP, so the deletion rule applies to Spec, TP; hence, only C_{null} is permitted in the embedded C. In the next CP phase cycle, however, the *wh*-element moves directly to Spec, CP, not to Spec, TP, so the deletion rule does not apply to Spec, TP. Spec, TP is phonologically realized as /John/, and the local C, namely C_{that}, is phonologically realized as /that/.

4.3 Cross-Linguistic Variation of Complementizer-Trace Effects

As our deductive analysis now stands, there is a problem. As is well known, complementizer-trace effects are parameterized, i.e. allowed in some grammars. Our analysis, based on deep principles such as Recoverability and Minimal Computation, presumably un-parameterized, would seem overly restrictive, wrongly predicting that *that*-trace effects are universally barred. Here we attempt to address this problem of how *that*-trace can possibly ever be allowed.

To begin, consider the well-known *que-qui* alternation. Roussou (2010) notes that it is possible to analyze *qui* as *que* + *il* (Rooryck 2000) or as *que* followed by the clitic *-i* (Taraldsen 2002). Given these possibilities, consider the following contrast (Roussou 2010:108):

(24) Qui   penses-tu   qui/*que   est   venu?
     who   think-you   that   is   come
     "Who do you think has come?"

If a pronominal form (such as *il* or *-i*) counts as a phonologically realized Spec, TP at some point of a derivation, then there is no reason for the deletion rule to apply to Spec, TP, and C+Spec, TP is phonologically realized as complex /qui/.

If Spec, TP is literally absent, as argued in *pro-drop* languages, e.g. Italian, then the deletion rule, by definition, cannot apply to Spec, TP. If there is no deletion in Spec, TP, there will be no corresponding deletion of a C occupying the same position as Spec, TP. Given this, consider (25) (Roussou 2010:106):

(25) Chi   credi   che   abbia   telefonato?
     who   think-2s   that   has   telephoned
     "Who do you think has telephoned?"

If *chi* directly moves to (embedded) Spec, CP (Rizzi 1982), i.e. not through Spec, TP, then, in principle, nothing prevents C from being phonologically realized as /che/. But the literal absence of Spec, TP would circumvent the "two-peaked" analysis of phase-based application of Transfer. That is, under EKS (2012), "counter-cyclic" creation of Spec, TP is precisely what triggers Transfer (to resolve the "two-peaked" situation). One possible way for us to guarantee cyclic Transfer is to pursue the line of Alexiadou and Anagnostopoulou's (1998) analysis, where the inflection is understood to correspond to the morphological realization of EPP. Specifically, if there is

(EPP-satisfying) "counter-cyclic" verb movement to T with rich agreement forms {V, {T, vP}}, then it will induce a "two-peaked" or intersecting situation, thereby triggering Transfer, as desired for all "finite clauses" (even those lacking Spec, TP).

Finally, consider the following pair, which raises a paradoxical problem: Just as in (26), in (27) the deletion rule does apply to Spec, TP, but C_{that} is nonetheless allowed, and it is phonologically realized as /that/ (Culicover 1992; Browning 1996):

(26) *Robin met the man that Leslie said that was the mayor of the city.
(27) Robin met the man that Leslie said that [for all intents and purposes] was the mayor of the city.

In the derivation of (26), C_{that} must undergo deletion (together with Spec, TP), but C_{that} bears phonological features, and it is the sole copy. Thus, the required deletion of C_{that} violates Recoverability.[8] By contrast, in the derivation of (27), C_{that} is curiously allowed, given the adverbial. The obvious difference between (26) and (27) is that an adverbial expression *for all intents and purposes* appears between C_{that} and Spec, TP, but how does this difference receive a principled account?

Browning (1996) argues that (27) differs from (26) in the structure of the embedded CP. She assigns to (27) the following CP recursion structure, where crucially there is complementizer movement from C to C:

(28) $[_{CP} \ldots C [_{CP} [\text{for all intents and purposes}] [t_C \ldots]]]$

If Browning's independently motivated CP recursion (or C-movement) analysis is correct, then the observed contrast, we argue, naturally follows. Consider the relevant aspects of the CP recursion structure of (27), illustrated in (29):

(29) $[_{CP} t_{OP} C_{that} [_{CP} [\text{for all intents and purposes}] [t_C [_{TP} t_{OP} \text{ was the mayor of the city}]]]]$

In the derivation of (27), the merged sisters of the lower occurrences of the operator OP are all deleted. There are (at least) two lower occurrences of OP in the embedded CP: {T, vP} and {v, VP}. The merged sisters of these occurrences include two copies of OP and one copy of C_{that}. Recall that under the "two-peaked" or intersecting situation, the lower copy of C_{that} counts as a merged sister of {T, vP}, and it undergoes deletion (together with Spec, TP and Spec, vP). Recall, in the core, ungrammatical *that*-trace effect (11), this results in an obligatory but unrecoverable deletion of *that*. But notice, if the lower copy of C_{that} gets deleted in (29), the phonological features of C_{that} are recoverable, because the higher copy of C_{that} still remains. Thus, the deletion of the lower copy of C_{that}, forced by Minimal Computation, satisfies

Recoverability, predicting that if *that* moves to a higher position, there will be no *that*-trace effect involving the departure site, exactly as in the derivation of (27), informally represented as (29).

5   SUMMARY

We first reviewed simplest Merge and its generation of "doubly rooted" or set-intersection structure, and then how Minimal Computation simplifies transfer to SM in accord with Recoverability. Recoverability requires C_{that} to be phonologically realized as /that/, and Minimal Computation requires the lower copies of *who* to get deleted (since only one set of phonological features of *who* entered the derivation, so by Recoverability only one can appear at SM). These two (opposing) very general requirements, Minimal Computation (= "not too much") and Recoverability (= "not too little"), however, appear to yield the *that*-trace effect applying only when the deletion rule applies to the merged sisters of {T, vP}, which include both (local) C_{that} and Spec, TP. As we noted at the outset, our analysis is unique in incorporating binary simplest Merge, yet it generates multiple sisters of a single category, as discussed. A final oddity is that, surprisingly, under the "two-peaked" analysis, C_{that} and Spec, TP are not in fact syntactically related, as can be seen clearly in (12) and (14)/(15); i.e. C does not c-command local Spec, TP, nor does local Spec, TP c-command C. In current terms neither can minimally search the other; hence, we have provided an account of complementizer and subject-trace effects which recognizes no syntactic relation between the two positions. Hence, our account of *that*-trace makes no appeal to a syntactic relation from C to its local Spec, TP. However, (a local) C and Spec, TP each count as a merged sister of {T, vP}, under the "two-peaked" analysis, employing simplest Merge (3i) barring both replacement (Freidin 1999) and label projection (Chomsky 2013). Given this, we argued that the core *that*-trace contrast, exhibited by (10) and (11), was deducible from the two very general principles, Minimal Computation and Recoverability, neither of which appears to be specific to a particular construction or language, and which may be, in part or in full, not-specifically-linguistic principles with far more general application in computational (and/or biological and/or physical) systems of other types that (informally) bar "random deletion and insertion." That is, perhaps these are both good candidates for 3rd factor laws, hence linguistic deduction from more general non-linguistic principles. But that important, fascinating, and unavoidable property of all scientific inquiry—concerning the level at which explanation occurs (see Chomsky 1965:51, 2005 for bringing this aspect of science to linguistics)—awaits further, interdisciplinary collaboration, given our ignorance concerning the broader issues at hand. We then gave brief preliminary analyses of a cross-linguistically variant range of grammatical complementizer-trace phenomena including the *que-qui* alternation (Roussou 2010; Rooryck 2000;

Taraldsen 2002), *pro-drop* languages like Italian (Rizzi 1982), *adverb that-*trace phenomena (Culicover 1992; Browning 1996), and so-called Empty Category Principle asymmetries (Huang 1982; Lasnik and Saito 1984, 1992; Safir 1985; Chomsky 1991; Rizzi and Shlonsky 2007).

NOTES

We would like to thank especially Noam Chomsky for his interest in our work, and also Miki Obata and Mamoru Saito. All errors are, of course, our own. Part of the material in this paper was presented at GLOW in Asia IX, hosted by Mie University (September 5, 2012). We are grateful to the participants for clarifying remarks.

1. See Collins (2002) and Seely (2006) for discussion of the idea that such labels (and label projection) can be eliminated entirely from the grammar.
2. Chomsky (1995a, 1995b) assumes that either α or β may project (in principle), but if the wrong choice is made, deviance would result.
3. See Groat and O'Neil (1996) for an alternative approach to covert movement whereby covert movement applies cyclically in the syntax, but the chain-tail is pronounced, as if, in the eyes of Phonetic Form (PF), the movement has not applied (= the definition of "covert" movement).
4. In section 4, we suggest that simplest Merge is not only conceptually desirable but empirically adequate, and that, at least with respect to *that*-trace phenomena, notoriously resistant to explanation, the empirical coverage/explanatory power of the theory is in fact concomitantly increased.
5. Chomsky (2007, 2008) and EKS (2012) argue, and in fact attempt to deduce, that all instances of EM must take place before any instance of IM, and hence C must be merged to TP before any instance of IM (involving TP) can occur.
6. (8a,b) is the single representation of the output of "counter-cyclic" subject raising. That is, there aren't two "separate workspaces" denoted by (8a,b), but rather a single representation of intersecting sets, analogous to the single phrase structure representation in (7), which is correspondingly not interpreted as two "separate" trees.
7. Epstein (1987, 1991) sought to deduce this asymmetry from an independently motivated A versus A-bar asymmetry in indexing, independently proposed in Chomsky's (1982) analysis of parasitic gaps (which are licensed by A-bar but not A binding). Epstein's (1987, 1991) analysis nonetheless resorted to levels, binding, (asymmetric) indexing, γ-features, and stipulations regarding the phonological content of *that* versus C_{null}.
8. We take the deviance of (26) to mean that the deletion algorithm does not distinguish *wh*-elements such as *who* and a null operator OP.

REFERENCES

Abe, J. 2011. The EPP and Subject Extraction. Unpublished manuscript, Tohoku Gakuin University, Sendai, Japan.

Alexiadou, A. and Anagnostopoulou, E. 1998. Parameterizing Agr: Word Order, V-Movement and EPP Checking. *Natural Language and Linguistic Theory* 16: 491–539.

Browning, M.A. 1996. CP Recursion and That-t Effects. *Linguistic Inquiry* 27:237–255.

Chomsky, N. 1965. *Aspects of the Theory of Syntax*. Cambridge, MA: MIT Press.

Chomsky, N. 1981. *Lectures on Government and Binding*. Dordrecht: Foris.

Chomsky, N. 1982. *Some Concepts and Consequences of the Theory of Government and Binding*. Cambridge, MA: MIT Press.

Chomsky, N. 1986. *Knowledge of Language*. New York: Praeger.

Chomsky, N. 1991. Some Notes on Economy of Derivation and Representation. In Freidin, R. (ed.), *Principles and Parameters in Comparative Grammar*, 417–454. Cambridge, MA: MIT Press. [Reprinted in *The Minimalist Program*, 129–166. Cambridge, MA: MIT Press, 1995.]

Chomsky, N. 1993. A Minimalist Program for Linguistic Theory. In Hale, K. and Keyser, S. J. (eds.), *The View from Building 20: Essays in Linguistics in Honor of Sylvain Bromberger*, 1–52. Cambridge, MA: MIT Press. [Reprinted in *The Minimalist Program*, 167–217. Cambridge, MA: MIT Press, 1995.]

Chomsky, N. 1995a. Bare Phrase Structure. In Webelhuth, G. (ed.), *Government and Binding Theory and the Minimalist Program: Principles and Parameters in Syntactic Theory*, 385–439. Oxford: Blackwell.

Chomsky, N. 1995b. *The Minimalist Program*. Cambridge, MA: MIT Press.

Chomsky, N. 2000. Minimalist Inquiries: The Framework. In Martin, R., Michaels, D. and Uriagereka, J. (eds.), *Step by Step: Essays on Minimalist Syntax in Honor of Howard Lasnik*, 89–155. Cambridge, MA: MIT Press.

Chomsky, N. 2005. Three Factors in Language Design. *Linguistic Inquiry* 36:1–22.

Chomsky, N. 2007. Approaching UG from Below. In Sauerland, U. and Gärtner, H.-M. (eds.), *Interfaces + Recursion = Language?*, 1–29. Berlin: Mouton de Gruyter.

Chomsky, N. 2008. On Phases. In Freidin, R., Otero, C. P. and Zubizarreta, M. L. (eds.), *Foundational Issues in Linguistic Theory: Essays in Honor of Jean-Roger Vergnaud*, 133–166. Cambridge, MA: MIT Press.

Chomsky, N. 2013. Problems of Projection. *Lingua* 130:33–49.

Chomsky, N. and Lasnik, H. 1977. Filters and Control. *Linguistic Inquiry* 8:425–504.

Collins, C. 2002. Eliminating Labels. In Epstein, S. D. and Seely, T. D. (eds.), *Derivation and Explanation in the Minimalist Program*, 42–64. Oxford: Blackwell.

Culicover, P. 1992. The Adverb Effect: Evidence against ECP Accounts of the *That-t* Effect. In Schafer, A. (ed.), *Proceedings of the North Eastern Linguistics Society 23*, vol. 1, 97–111. Amherst, MA: Graduate Linguistic Student Association, University of Massachusetts.

Epstein, S. D. 1987. Empty Categories and Their Antecedents. Doctoral dissertation, University of Connecticut, Storrs.

Epstein, S. D. 1991. *Traces and Their Antecedents*. Oxford: Oxford University Press.

Epstein, S. D., Groat, E., Kawashima, R. and Kitahara, H. 1998. *A Derivational Approach to Syntactic Relations*. Oxford: Oxford University Press.

Epstein, S. D., Kitahara, H. and Seely, T. D. 2012. Structure Building That Can't Be! In Uribe-etxebarria, M. and Valmala, V. (eds.), *Ways of Structure Building*, 253–270. Oxford: Oxford University Press.

Freidin, R. 1999. Cyclicity and Minimalism. In Epstein, S. D. and Hornstein, N. (eds.), *Working Minimalism*, 95–126. Cambridge, MA: MIT Press.

Groat, E. and O'Neil, J. 1996. Spell-Out at the LF Interface. In Epstein, S. D., Thráinsson, H., Zwart, C. J.-W. and Abraham, W. (eds.), *Minimal Ideas*, 113–139. Amsterdam: John Benjamins.

Huang, C.-T. J. 1982. Logical Relations in Chinese and the Theory of Grammar. Doctoral dissertation, MIT, Cambridge, MA.

Ishii, T. 2004. The Phase Impenetrability Condition, the Vacuous Movement Hypothesis, and *That-t* Effects. *Lingua* 114:183–215.

Kitahara, H. 2011. Can Eagles That Fly Swim? Guaranteeing the Simplest Answer to a New Puzzle. In Otsu, Y. (ed.), *The Proceedings of the 12th Tokyo Conference on Psycholinguistics*, 1–15. Tokyo: Hituzi Siobo Publishing.

Lasnik, H. and Saito, M. 1984. On the Nature of Proper Government. *Linguistic Inquiry* 15:235–289.

Lasnik, H. and Saito, M. 1992. *Move α*. Cambridge, MA: MIT Press.

Perlmutter, D. 1971. *Deep and Surface Structure Constraints in Syntax*. New York: Holt, Rinehart and Winston.

Rizzi, L. 1982. *Issues in Italian Syntax*. Dordrecht: Foris.

Rizzi, L. and U. Shlonsky. 2007. Strategies of Subject Extraction. In Sauerland, U. and Gärtner, H.-M. (eds.), *Interfaces + Recursion = Language?*, 115–160. Berlin: Mouton de Gruyter.

Rooryck, J. 2000. *Configurations of Sentential Complementation: Perspectives from Romance Languages*. London: Routledge.

Roussou, A. 2010. Subjects on the Edge. In Panagiotidis, E. P. (ed.), *The Complementizer Phase: Subjects and Operators*, 76–116. Oxford: Oxford University Press.

Safir, K. 1985. *Syntactic Chains*. Cambridge: Cambridge University Press.

Seely, T. D. 2006. Merge, Derivational C-Command, and Subcategorization in a Label-Free Syntax. In Boeckx, C. (ed.), *Minimalist Essays*, 182–217. Amsterdam: John Benjamins.

Sobin, N. 1987. The Variable Status of Comp-trace Phenomena. *Natural Language and Linguistic Theory* 5:33–60.

Sobin, N. 2002. The Comp-trace Effect, the Adverb Effect and Minimal CP. *Journal of Linguistics* 38:527–560.

Taraldsen, T. 2002. The *Que/Qui* Alternation and the Distribution of Expletives. In Svenonius, P. (ed.), *Subjects, Expletives and the EPP*, 29–42. Oxford: Oxford University Press.

9 External Merge of Internal Argument DP to VP and Its Theoretical Implications

Hisatsugu Kitahara

1 INTRODUCTION

This paper concerns External Merge of internal argument DP to VP and its theoretical implications. I first show that External Merge of internal argument DP to VP poses a problem not only for Chomsky's (2008) labeling algorithm (section 1) but also for the Case-theoretic analysis of feature-inheritance, developed by Richards (2007) and Chomsky (2007, 2008) (section 2). I then outline a unified solution to these problems, in which head-movement plays a crucial role (section 3). Finally, I identify and discuss some implications of the proposed head-movement analysis for the notion "Spec" (section 4).

2 A PROBLEM FOR CHOMSKY'S (2008) LABELING ALGORITHM

Chomsky (2008:145) argues that "the label of [a syntactic object] SO must be identifiable with minimal search, by some simple algorithm," and he suggests the following labeling algorithm (where LI is a lexical item):

(1) a. In {H, α}, H an LI, H is the label.
    b. If α is internally merged to β, forming {α, β}, then the label of β is the label of {α, β}.

This two-part algorithm, which has been motivated on independent grounds (see Donati 2006), makes (at least) the following three predictions: (i) if External Merge (EM) merges H and XP, forming {H, XP}, then H will be the label of its outcome {H, XP}; (ii) if Internal Merge (IM) merges XP and YP, forming {XP, YP}, then the probe (finding a goal for IM) will be the label of its outcome {XP, YP}; and (iii) if EM merges XP and YP, forming {XP, YP}, then the label of its outcome {XP, YP} will not be determined. The last case, yielding a "no label" situation, is regarded as a problem.

With these three predictions (in particular, the last one) in mind, let us adopt the VP-shell analysis of three-place predicates (proposed by Larson 1988 and later modified by Chomsky 1995) and examine the derivation of "the boy put the book on the table," which involves EM of internal argument DP *the book* to VP, forming the following SO:

(2)   {{the, book}, {put, {on, {the, table}}}}

The SO in (2) illustrates type (iii) above, {XP, YP} formed by EM of XP and YP, the label of which cannot be determined by the algorithm in (1).

One potential problem posed by cases such as (2) is that if Narrow Syntax (NS) cannot access the label of SO in (2), it will not be able to find the edge feature that permits the SO in (2) to undergo Merge (see Chomsky 2007, 2008 for discussion on the edge feature).

3   A PROBLEM FOR THE CASE-THEORETIC ANALYSIS OF FEATURE-INHERITANCE

The SO in (2) gives rise to another problem even if it is allowed to undergo Merge. Recall the Case-theoretic analysis of feature-inheritance, developed by Richards (2007) and Chomsky (2007, 2008), and assume, for the sake of discussion, that NS has managed to continue the derivation of (2) and construct the following v^*P phase:

(3)   {{the, boy}, {v^*, {{the, book}, {put, {on, {the, table}}}}}}

Under the Case-theoretic analysis of feature-inheritance, T and V inherit unvalued phi from C and v^*, respectively, and these heads T and V (bearing unvalued phi) value Case in accord with the probe-goal theory of agreement, which limits "the goal of the probe to its complement, the smallest searchable domain" (Chomsky 2007:9).

Given this much, the problem posed by the SO in (3) becomes obvious. At the v^*P phase in (3), *put* (inheriting unvalued phi from v^*) is responsible for the valuation of Case on *the book*, but *the book*, occupying the specifier of *put*, is not in the search domain of *put*. Notice that the set containing *put* as a member is {put, {on, {the, table}}}, and *the book* is not contained in the smallest searchable domain of *put*, namely the complement of *put* {on, {the, table}}. Thus, neither the Case on *the book* nor the phi on *put* will get valued.

In short, EM of internal argument DP to VP (in a derivation with a three-place predicate) not only forms a "label-less" SO but also places internal argument DP outside the search domain of V, causing the derivation to crash (if that argument's Case remains unvalued).

4 A "LAST RESORT" IMPLEMENTATION OF HEAD-MOVEMENT

Accepting the two problems noted above, I would now like to outline a unified solution to them. First, recall that if *put* stays in situ, excluding *the book* from its search domain, then NS cannot value Case on *the book* and phi on *put*. Thus, one (and arguably the only) logical possibility is that *put* undergoes IM, expanding its search domain. This is essentially the idea of expanding the minimal domain by V-movement, proposed by Chomsky (1995). Pursuing this possibility, I propose a "last resort" implementation of head-movement, more specifically, IM of label L as a supplementary sub-operation internal to the application of EM merging XP and YP.

(4) In the application of EM forming K = {XP, YP}, IM, understood as a supplementary sub-operation internal to this application of EM, takes a label L of either XP or YP, and merges L to K, forming a new SO = {L, K}.

As stated in (4), IM of L to K is (by hypothesis) a supplementary sub-operation, which completes a single mapping, triggered by EM merging XP and YP. This "last resort" execution of IM of L to K (= {XP, YP}) may be regarded as a way of breaking a "symmetric" relation between the two members XP and YP—an instance of the "symmetry-breaking" operation in the sense of Moro (2000).

With this proposal, let us return to the derivation of *the boy put the book on the table*. Once again, consider EM of internal argument DP *the book* to VP and its outcome in (2). The SO in (2) does not have a label of its own, but (4) does kick in, and IM, understood as a supplementary sub-operation internal to this application of EM, merges *put* to the SO in (2), forming the following SO (where the search domain of *put* is, in effect, expanded):

(5) {put, {{the, book}, {put, {on, {the, table}}}}}

The SO in (5) has a label of its own, namely *put*, identifiable with minimal search. Thus, under (4), the "no label" situation does not arise, as desired. That is, given (4), the output of EM merging internal argument DP *the book* to VP is the SO in (5), not the SO in (2).

Another desirable consequence of (4) is that *the book* is now placed in the search domain of (raised) *put*, as shown in (5). Suppose that, in the subsequent derivation, (raised) *put* inherits unvalued phi from v^*. Then, NS can (in principle) value Case on *the book* and phi on (raised) *put*. Thus, under (4), the Case-theoretic problem is also resolved. That is, given (4), NS can find *the book* in the search domain of (raised) *put* and execute the valuation of Case on *the book* and phi on (raised) *put*.

Given these desirable consequences, let us return to the SO in (5) and examine how this derivation continues from here. To proceed, NS identifies the label of the SO in (5), accesses its edge feature (permitting the SO in (5) to undergo Merge), and executes EM of v* to the SO in (5), forming the following SO:

(6) {v*, {put, {{the, book}, {put, {on, {the, table}}}}}}

Subsequently, NS executes EM of external argument DP *the boy* to the SO in (6), forming the following SO:

(7) {{the, boy}, {v*, {put, {{the, book}, {put, {on, {the, table}}}}}}}

This application of EM poses a problem, but it gets resolved in exactly the same way as the one posed by EM of internal argument DP *the book* to VP. The SO in (7) does not have a label of its own, but (4) does kick in, and IM, understood as a supplementary sub-operation internal to this application of EM, merges v* to the SO in (7), forming the following SO:

(8) {v*, {{the, boy}, {v*, {put, {{the, book}, {put, {on, {the, table}}}}}}}}

The SO in (8) has a label of its own, namely v*, identifiable with minimal search.[1]

As shown above, the "last resort" implementation of head-movement, formulated in (4), resolves not only the problem confronting the Case-theoretic analysis of feature-inheritance but also the "no label" situation induced by the two applications of EM: EM of internal argument DP to VP and EM of external argument DP to v*P.

5   ON THE NOTION "SPEC"

As a final note, I would like to consider what the proposed implementation of head-movement implies with respect to the notion "Spec." Notice that, under the current assumptions, EM and IM yield different results concerning the status of so-called Spec.

Suppose that α and β are not lexical items, and that L is the label of β. Let us then examine the following two applications of Merge: IM of α to β and EM of α to β.

If α is internally merged to β (forming {α, β}, whose label is L under (1b)), then NS, in accord with (4), will not execute IM of L to {α, β}. As a result, α will be excluded from the search domain of L. Informally speaking, α is not part of the "complement" of L; α is a "Spec" of L.

If α is externally merged to β, then NS, in accord with (4), will execute IM of L to {α, β} as a supplementary sub-operation internal to this application of EM. As a result, α will be included in the search domain of (raised) L. Informally speaking, α is not a "Spec" of L; α is part of the (expanded) "complement" of L (see Epstein 1998 for exposition of a similar idea in an earlier framework).

Thus, informally speaking, IM of α to β can create a genuine "Spec" of L, excluded from the "complement" of L, while EM of α to β cannot.[2]

This EM-IM distinction—IM can create a genuine "Spec," while EM cannot—may correlate nicely with the duality of semantics: "EM yields generalized argument structure (theta-roles, the "cartographic" hierarchies, and similar properties); and IM yields discourse-related properties such as old information and specificity, along with scopal effects" (Chomsky 2008:140). I must leave exploration of this potential correlation for future research.

NOTES

I would like to thank Jun Abe, Noam Chomsky, Samuel D. Epstein, Ruriko Kawashima, Hirohisa Kiguchi, Roger Martin, Miki Obata, Masayuki Oishi, Mamoru Saito, T. Daniel Seely, Chris Tancredi, and Shigeo Tonoike for valuable comments and helpful discussion. All remaining errors are, or course, my own. Part of the material in this paper was presented at the ELSJ 3rd International Spring Forum 2010 (held at Aoyama Gakuin University on April 25, 2010) and at the international meeting of Biolinguistics Network: The Language Design (held at UQAM on May 28, 2010). I am grateful to the participants for clarifying remarks. The research reported here was supported in part by the Ministry of Education, Culture, Sports, Science and Technology (Grant-in-Aid for Scientific Research (C) #22520409).

1. The derivation in question continues, and the external argument DP *the boy* undergoes Case-valuation at the following CP phase:

   (i) {C, {T, {v*, {{the, boy}, {v*, {put, {{the, book}, {put, {on, {the, table}}}}}}}}}}

2. Note that, under the current assumptions, theta-theoretic "assigner-assignee" relations are arguably reducible to probe-goal relations. Recall the SO in (8), repeated in (i):

   (i) {v*, {{the, boy}, {v*, {put, {{the, book}, {put, {on, {the, table}}}}}}}}

   In (i), each theta assigner finds an argument in its search domain: (i) v* assigns AGENT to *the boy* in the search domain of (raised) v*, (ii) *put* assigns THEME to *the book* in the search domain of (raised) *put*, and (iii) *put* assigns LOCATION to *on the table* in the search domain of (in-situ) *put*. From this perspective, the probe-goal theory may be assigned a more active role in the determination of theta-theoretic interpretations.

REFERENCES

Chomsky, N. 1995. *The Minimalist Program.* Cambridge, MA: MIT Press.
Chomsky, N. 2007. Approaching UG from Below. In Sauerland, U. and Gärtner, H.-M. (eds.), *Interfaces + Recursion = Language?*, 1–29. Berlin: Mouton de Gruyter.

Chomsky, N. 2008. On Phases. In Freidin, R., Otero, C. P. and Zubizarreta, M. L. (eds.), *Foundational Issues in Linguistic Theory: Essays in Honor of Jean-Roger Vergnaud*, 133–166. Cambridge, MA: MIT Press.

Donati, C. 2006. On *Wh*-Head-Movement. In Cheng, L. and Corver, N. (eds.), *Wh-Movement on the Move*, 21–46. Cambridge, MA: MIT Press.

Epstein, S. D. 1998. Overt Scope Marking and Covert Verb-Second. *Linguistic Inquiry* 29:181–227.

Larson, R. 1988. On the Double Object Construction. *Linguistic Inquiry* 19:335–391.

Moro, A. 2000. *Dynamic Antisymmetry*. Cambridge, MA: MIT Press.

Richards, M. 2007. On Feature Inheritance: An Argument from the Phase Impenetrability Condition. *Linguistic Inquiry* 38:563–572.

10 Labeling by Minimal Search

Implications for Successive-Cyclic A-Movement and the Conception of the Postulate "Phase"

Samuel D. Epstein, Hisatsugu Kitahara, and T. Daniel Seely

1 SIMPLEST MERGE AND LABEL IDENTIFICATION BY MINIMAL SEARCH

One recent development in minimalist theory (Chomsky 2004, 2007, 2008, 2013) is that Merge, formulated in the simplest form, applies *freely*[1] (i.e. without "teleological purpose")[2] as long as it conforms to 3rd factor principles such as the No-Tampering Condition and the condition of inclusiveness. Merge, by hypothesis, is no longer operating *in order to* create a configuration that allows interface-illegitimate features to be checked; it is not "purposeful" in the sense of early Minimalism in that it is no longer driven by convergence conditions (e.g. the valuation of phi features or Case features). Concepts such as "derivational economy" no longer determine— internal to the narrow syntax (NS)—when Merge must apply and when it cannot.[3] Rather, Merge is free; it optionally applies (and so crashing happens; that is, the system is not crash-proof).[4]

What prompted the development from purposeful Merge to freely applying Merge? In large part, it was due to the unification of Internal Merge (IM) and External Merge (IM); that is, IM and EM have been re-analyzed as instantiations of the *single* operation Merge (with *internal* and *external* simply expositional mnemonics for *one* operation accessing different resources).[5] It follows that if IM and EM are but one operation, then what is true of "one" is true of the "other." Thus, since EM applications are by hypothesis not driven by convergence conditions (e.g. the valuation of phi features or Case features), IM cannot be driven by the quest for convergence. Similarly, EM was hypothesized to be "driven" (at least in part) by theta theory. But since IM is arguably not driven by θ-theory (but see Bošković 1994; O'Neil 1997; and Hornstein 1999 for important contrary views), and since IM and EM are two possible applications of the single operation Merge, then EM cannot be driven by theta theory either. If so, there is nothing left for Merge to be driven by (not for convergence and not for coherence). Consequently, it is not "driven" at all, which means that it is simply *available* to apply, and does so optionally and freely (similar, in its freedom, to the Move α operation within Government and Binding (GB) theory). It applies not because it must but because it can.

Under the simplest conception of unified Merge, Chomsky (2013) argues that Merge (α, β) yields {α, β} with no label projection or linear order, and independently of the character of α and β.[6] We call this *simplest Merge*.

(1) *Simplest Merge*
    Merge (α, β) → {α, β}

Given (1), a syntactic object SO constructed from α and β by Merge is just {α, β}. Merge puts the two objects α and β into a relation,[7] the output being represented as a two-membered set. Nothing more. Thus, unlike the output of Merge in Chomsky (1995a) and much subsequent work, the output of Merge in this conception does not overtly encode a label; contra Chomsky's (1995a) notation, there is no constructed set {δ, {α, β}}, where δ represents the label (as either H(α) or H(β)) identifying the relevant properties of {δ, {α, β}} (see Chomsky 1995a, 1995b). Rather, under simplest Merge there is just {α, β}.

For an SO to be interpreted, however, it is necessary to know what kind of object it is. Chomsky (2013) takes *labeling* to be the process of finding the relevant (object identification) information of {α, β} generated by simplest Merge. He proposes that such labeling is "just minimal search, presumably appropriating a third factor principle, as in Agree and other operations." There are two cases in question: {H, XP} and {XP, YP}.[8] Chomsky outlines how minimal search operates to find the label of each case, as follows:

(2) Suppose SO = {H, XP}, H a head and XP not a head. Then minimal search will select H as the label, and the usual procedures of interpretation at the interfaces can proceed.
(3) Suppose SO = {XP, YP}, neither a head. Here minimal search is ambiguous, locating the heads X, Y of XP, YP, respectively. There are, then, two ways in which SO can be labeled: (A) modify SO so that there is only one visible head, or (B) X and Y are identical in a relevant respect, providing the same label, which can be taken as the label of the SO.
    (Chomsky 2013:43)

In {H, XP}, minimal search immediately finds a lexical item H (a bundle of features, provided by the lexicon) and a two-membered set XP (a set-theoretic object constructed by Merge). The former, being a lexical item, makes available what matters to the interface systems, while the latter, being a set, does not; it requires further search. Thus, H is identified as the label of {H, XP}.[9]

In {XP, YP}, minimal search is ambiguous, locating (with equally minimal "depth of search") each of the two heads X and Y of XP, YP, respectively. It is assumed that such failure to identify a unique head in {XP, YP} prevents labeling, and since labels are required for interpretation at the conceptual-intentional interface (CI), if the object lacking the label appears at CI, it violates Full Interpretation. For Chomsky (2013), however, there are two ways in which unlabeled {XP, YP} can be salvaged: (a) This SO must be modified so that there is only one visible head (i.e. X or Y (not X and Y)), or (b) X and Y share some prominent features, and the shared features are taken as the relevant identifying information (i.e. as the label of {XP, YP}).[10]

To see how minimal search finds the label in each case, let's examine concrete instances. Take SO_i = {v, VP}. Here minimal search finds v as the label of SO_i since v is unambiguously identifiable by applying (2); in any {H, XP}, the head H is always found with "less search" than any feature-bearing (hence relevant information-bearing) element within XP.

Next, take SO_j = {NP, {v, VP}}. Here minimal search is ambiguous, locating two relevant heads, N and v. If the SO is left as is, labeling fails and Full Interpretation is violated at CI in that CI cannot find the information it needs to identify the categorial status of this object; such identification of status is hypothesized by Chomsky (2013) to be a necessary prerequisite to CI (properly) interpreting the object. As pointed out above, one way to label SO_j is to raise NP to a higher position (= strategy (3A)), which yields (after merger of T to SO_j and subsequent subject raising) SO_k = {NP, {T, {NP, {v, VP}}}}. Chomsky (2013) takes the single NP (call it α) in SO_k to be in the domain D (in this case, in the set SO_j now embedded within SO_k) if and only if every occurrence of α is a term of D.[11] Given this, NP is taken to be not in SO_j (a term of SO_k) because SO_j does not contain every occurrence of NP as its term; rather, NP is taken to be in SO_k because SO_k contains every occurrence of NP as its term. Informally, the lower copy of NP is "invisible" when minimal search conducts a search for the label of {NP, {v, VP}}; it therefore "sees" only {v, VP} when it "looks at" {NP, {v, VP}}.[12] Thus, the movement of NP makes the v unambiguously identifiable; that is, minimal search finds the only "visible" head v as the label of SO_j. Note that this is Chomsky's account of "EPP-driven" subject raising, but without any appeal to the EPP (Extended Projection Principle) in any of its mysterious incarnations (see, among many others, Epstein, Pires, and Seely 2005; Epstein and Seely 2006; Bošković 2007; and the references cited therein regarding the "oddity" of the EPP). Rather, if there is no movement (and no expletive), then there is labeling failure, which in turn creates a barrier to CI interpretation.[13]

Turning to SO_k, namely, {NP, {T, {NP, {v, VP}}}}, it is also of the form {XP, YP}. Can minimal search find the label of SO_k? Chomsky answers "yes," even though SO_k is a set containing two non-heads. Chomsky suggests that in such cases, the phi features shared by the two relevant heads N and T (in finite clauses) can be the label of SO_k (= strategy (3B)); that is, when there are some prominent features shared by X and Y, minimal search *can* identify the label for {XP, YP}—namely the features (in this case, the phi features) appearing on both heads X and Y. Chomsky (2013) takes Successive-Cyclic Ā-movement to support his analysis. Consider *wh*-movement in (4).[14] (We use *t(race)* only for expository purposes.)

(4) [$_\beta$ In which Texas city did they think [$_\alpha$ *t* [C [$_{TP}$ the man was assassinated *t*]]]]?

Immediately after the *wh*-phrase *in which Texas city* (hereafter, the *wh*-PP) is internally merged to the specifier (Spec) of the embedded C, the embedded clause α is of the form of {XP, YP}, where XP is the *wh*-PP and YP is {C, TP}, as shown in (5).

(5) . . . (think) [$_\alpha$ [$_{XP}$ in which Texas city] [$_{YP}$ C [$_{TP}$ the man was assassinated *t*]]]

Crucially, the embedded C (selected by *think*) bears no Q-feature, and as a result there is assumed to be no prominent feature shared by XP and (the Q-feature-lacking) YP. If XP remains in this intermediate position, minimal search cannot find a label for α, since there is no prominent feature (e.g. phi features or Q-feature) shared by X (the head of the *wh*-PP) and Y (the head of {C, TP}). However, if the *wh*-PP raises to a higher position (rendering the lower copy of the *wh*-PP "invisible" inside α), then minimal search can find a unique "visible" head—namely C—as the label of α. Notice that the matrix clause β of (4) is also of the form {XP, YP}, but there is a feature shared by X and Y (namely the Q-feature of the *wh*-PP and the Q-feature presumably borne by the interrogative mood–marked C of the matrix); hence, Q can be the label of β.[15]

Chomsky's (2013) analysis thus has the following property: The "obligatory exit" from an intermediate position of *wh*-movement (e.g. *They think in which Texas city the man was assassinated?*) is accounted for by a labeling failure (ultimately, a CI violation of Full Interpretation). The analysis makes no appeal to a mismatch of features between *think*, which selects a [–Q] C, and the [+Q] *wh*-PP occupying the Spec of this [–Q] C. It appeals neither to an explicit Spec-head relation (defined via m-command/government) in CP, nor to any of the technical devices that have been non-explanatorily invoked in past research like coindexing of Spec and head in CP, nor to an S-structure level of representation (as in important prior analyses; recall Rizzi's (1997) *Wh*-Criterion and Lasnik and Saito's (1984, 1992) S-structure condition that blocks a [+Q] *wh*-phrase from occupying the Spec of a [–Q] C in English). Nor does Chomsky's analysis appeal to the EPP (obligatory Spec, T or Spec, C), as noted above for A-movement. No such descriptive technicalia are invoked.

Chomsky (2013) further examines data such as (6a–b).

(6) a. They thought the man was assassinated in which Texas city?
    b. *They thought [α in which Texas city [C [$_{TP}$ the man was assassinated *t*]]]?

English allows *wh*-in-situ constructions in relevant contexts, such as quiz shows.[16] But if a *wh*-phrase raises to form the embedded clause α and remains there, as in (6b), minimal search cannot find a label for α, since α is of the form {XP, YP} and there is no prominent feature (e.g. phi features or Q-feature) shared by X and Y, as just discussed. The fact that α has no label bars (6b) at CI gives exactly the right result.

The same pattern can be observed in a multiple *wh*-question context. Consider (7a–b).

(7) a. Who thought the man was assassinated in which Texas city?
    b. *Who thought [α in which Texas city [C [$_{TP}$ the man was assassinated *t*]]]?

Here again, if a *wh*-phrase raises to form the embedded clause α and remains there at CI, minimal search cannot find the label of α because α is of the form {XP, YP} and there is no prominent feature (e.g. phi features or Q-feature) shared by X and Y. The fact that α has no label correctly bars (7b) at CI.

It is important to note that the "no-label" situation, observed in (6b) and (7b), arises as a consequence of simplest Merge and 3rd factor minimal search. Moreover, it accounts for the "obligatory exit" from intermediate landing sites in *wh*-movement with no representational projection of labels as in Chomsky (1995a), and with no GB-style representationally defined technicalia like Spec-head/government/m-command relations, coindexing, or an S-structure level of representation to which specifically syntactic filters (e.g. the Case Filter or the EPP) apply.

In what follows, we argue that such a "no-label" situation *also* arises in cases of (phase-internal) Successive-Cyclic A-movement, just as it does in cases of Successive-Cyclic Ā-movement, with welcome empirical results that in turn raise the possibility of eliminating the concept of "phase" itself.[17]

2   SUCCESSIVE-CYCLIC A-MOVEMENT: A SELECTIVE REVIEW

Chomsky (2000) defined Move as the composite operation that combines Merge and Agree, and he demonstrated that (an economy or 3rd factor) preference for simpler operations over more complex ones explained relevant phenomena, without appeal to an S-structure level at which the descriptive Case Filter applies. For example, consider (8a–b).

(8) a. *There is likely [$_{TP}$ a man to be *t* in the room].
    b. There is likely [$_{TP}$ *t* to be a man in the room].

Each derivation involves the derivational stage [T [be a man in the room]], where T requires that something occupy Spec, T (the so-called EPP).[18] At this point, Merge of *there* in Spec, T and Move of *a man* to Spec, T are (in principle) both available to NS, and (in principle) either could be applied in order to satisfy the EPP. Of course, however, (8a) is ungrammatical. What excludes it? Preference for simpler operations over more complex ones selects Merge of *there* in (what will be embedded) Spec, T over Move of *a man* to (what will be embedded) Spec, T precisely because Merge (of *there*) is simpler than Move consisting of both Merge and Agree (Chomsky 2000); hence, the derivation of (8b) is "selected" over that of (8a). Thus emerges the "last resort" character of movement, accounting for such so-called Merge over Move phenomena. Note of course that Merge of *there* is possible only if *there* is an item present in the lexical array (LA) available to Merge. So, the initial choice of LA is crucial, and this device (i.e. the LA) must be part of NS.

Postulation of LAs, however, turned out to be necessary but not sufficient, empirically. Consider (9a–b).[19]

(9) a. There is a possibility [$_{CP}$ that a man will be t in the room].
    b. A possibility is [$_{CP}$ that there will be a man in the room].

(9a) is now seemingly paradoxical. The derivation of (9a) contains *there* (and, recall, inserting *there* is less complex than moving *a man*; hence, it is required), yet Move of *a man* to Spec, T is also possible. But it should not be possible, given that insertion of *there* is a simpler operation filling Spec, T. So somehow, when the embedded CP is being built in (9a), in particular Spec, T, Move can be preferred over Merge—the exact opposite of what was motivated to exclude (8a), namely "Merge over Move." Thus, the theory of that era confronted a seeming contradiction.

Chomsky (2000) presented a solution to this problem. The basic idea is that structures are built bottom-up, cyclically, and—importantly—in chunks called "phases," each associated with its own separate lexical subarray (SA), extracted from the LA. So, in effect, first we form the SA containing all and only the lexical material needed to generate the embedded CP phase, which in the case of (9a) includes *that, will, be, a man, in, the, room*. When *a man* moves, insertion of *there* is not an option since (crucially) *there* is—during the independent generation of this phasal CP—absent from the SA. Thus, movement of *a man* in fact does not violate Merge over Move, since nothing was available to merge in Spec, T when movement to Spec, T took place. Merge over Move is thus maintained as a non-stipulated operational preference. It provides an account of (9a), overcoming the apparent contradiction, and with no construction- or language-specific mechanisms. Moreover, it follows in part from non-linguistic principles of complexity (applying X and Y (here, Merge and Agree) is more complex than applying X (here, Merge) alone); that is, appeal to Universal Grammar–specific axioms is minimized by (what are now called) 3rd factor principles that are by hypothesis not specific to Universal Grammar.

In short, given postulation of SAs (extracted from LAs), (9a–b) do not compete. In the derivation of (9a), the (embedded) CP is constructed from SA$_i$, which contains no expletive; hence, Move of *a man* to Spec, T is the only option available at the derivational stage generating the (embedded) CP. In the derivation of (9b), the (embedded) CP is constructed from SA$_j$, which contains an expletive; hence, Merge of *there* in Spec, T is selected over Move of *a man* to Spec, T at the corresponding stage, because Merge (of *there* in Spec, T) is simpler than Move (of *a man* to Spec, T).

3 SUCCESSIVE-CYCLIC A-MOVEMENT: A NEW ANALYSIS

As we have just shown, Chomsky (2000) provided a principled account of the "last resort" character of movement by implementing (10a–d).

(10) a. Postulating Move as the composite operation that combines Merge and Agree
   b. Postulating lexical array LA
   c. Postulating lexical subarray SA (extracted from LA)
   d. Postulating Merge over Move (deducibly)

In this section, we argue that (10a) loses its conceptual and empirical support under simplest Merge. In addition, (10b–d) lose their original empirical motivation if labeling is just minimal search. We argue that under the simplifying assumptions of minimal search, data such as (8a–b) and (9a–b) receive a principled explanation, one that is unified in a key respect with the corresponding cases of Ā-movement like (6b) and (7b), which Chomsky (2013) analyzes as labeling (hence CI) failures. Specifically, by showing that remaining in an intermediate landing site of A-movement also results in a failure of labeling, we provide a unified account at least for the core data presented here.[20]

First, recall simplest Merge, defined in (1) and repeated here.

(1) *Simplest Merge*
   Merge $(\alpha, \beta) \rightarrow \{\alpha, \beta\}$

Under the simplest conception of Merge, Chomsky (2004, 2005) argued that Merge and Move are unified; they are just two possible instances— EM and IM—of Merge $(\alpha, \beta) \rightarrow \{\alpha, \beta\}$. EM takes α and β, where α originates external to β. IM takes α and β, where α originates internal to β; and given the No-Tampering Condition, IM necessarily yields two copies of α, one external to β (the landing site) and the other internal to β (the departure site). Chomsky notes that both EM and IM come for free: It would require stipulation to bar either of them. Thus, Move can no longer be expressed as the composite operation that combines (external) Merge and Agree (10a), since (external) Merge and Move are the very same operation—namely Merge.[21] Consequently, "Merge over Move" (10d) is not maintainable. In effect, (10a) and (10d) are eliminated.

Turning now to (10b–c), let us reconsider the data motivating the postulation of LAs and SAs. First, consider (8a–b), repeated here, where TP is replaced by α (whose categorial status is to be determined by labeling, under minimal search). We take *there* to be a complex SO, not a simple head.[22]

(8) a. *There is likely [$_\alpha$ a man to be *t* in the room].
    b. There is likely [$_\alpha$ *t* to be a man in the room].

If, as in (8a), *a man* raises to form the embedded clause α and remains there at CI, minimal search cannot find the label of α, because α is of the form {XP, YP} and there is no prominent feature (e.g. phi features or Q-feature) shared by X and Y.[23] The fact that α has no label bars (8a) by Full Interpretation at CI. Now if *there* is inserted to form the embedded clause α, as in (8b), and *there* is in fact an XP (perhaps of the form {D, pro}; see Uriagereka 1988), then α is (once again) a label-less set {XP, YP}, where crucially *there* and infinitival raising T do not share phi features.

Thus, *there* cannot remain in this position if the derived representation is to survive Full Interpretation at CI. If *there* bears at least one phi feature and undergoes further movement, then minimal search finds the only visible head T as the label of α, and a completely labeled, hence Full Interpretation–compliant, CI representation is generated; that is, the "no-label" situation does not arise in the final complete representation (8b).[24] Notice that this analysis also predicts that the "no-label" situation arises if *there* is merged to form the embedded clause α and stays there at CI, as in *There is likely there to be a man in the room* or *It seems there to be a man in the room* (see Lasnik 1992).

As shown above, the contrast exhibited by (8a) and (8b) now arguably follows with no reference to the notions LA (10b), SA (10c), or "Merge over Move" (10d). Given this "labeling" analysis, let us now consider (9a–b), repeated here.

(9) a. There is a possibility [$_{CP}$ that a man will be *t* in the room].
    b. A possibility is [$_{CP}$ that there will be a man in the room].

Suppose we dispense with the notions LA, SA, and "Merge over Move." Then there is no competition between insertion of *there* and movement of *a man*. Each counts as an option available to NS. Thus, (9a–b) are both generable. There is no longer any need to postulate LAs (10b) or SAs (10c) to account for data such as (8a–b) and (9a–b).[25] Thus, it seems we can eliminate (10a–d), repeated here.

(10) a. Postulating Move as the composite operation that combines Merge and Agree
   b. Postulating lexical array LA
   c. Postulating lexical subarray SA (extracted from LA)
   d. Postulating Merge over Move (deducibly)

Summarizing, we suggest that Chomsky's (2013) analysis explains "obligatory exit" from intermediate positions, not only in Successive-Cyclic Ā-movement, but also in (phase-internal) Successive-Cyclic A-movement. Moreover, we suggest that it does so by employing simplest Merge (with no explicit additional label notation, as in Chomsky 1995a) and 3rd factor minimal search for labels (labels being arguably a natural requirement necessary for CI interpretation), without any appeal to an S-structure level, a Spec-head/government/m-command relation, coindexing, or S-structure filters such as the Case Filter or the EPP.

If this "labeling" analysis is on track, then LAs and SAs are eliminated from NS, thereby simplifying NS. But notice now that the elimination of LAs and SAs entails the elimination of the notion "phase" itself, where a "phase" of the derivation is defined as a SO derived from an SA, extracted from an LA. In the next section, we briefly discuss this issue and conclude our discussion.

4   A REMAINING QUESTION: INDUCING STRICT-CYCLIC DERIVATION WITHOUT THE CONCEPT "PHASE"?

If "obligatory exit" from intermediate landing sites of successive cyclic movement can in fact be accounted for by minimal search label identification, for both A- and Ā -movement, and without appeal to the notion "phase" defined in terms of SAs or LAs, what becomes of the motivated cyclic computation induced by phase-based analyses? Is there some other way to induce such cyclic derivation but without defining phases in terms of SAs or LAs, which we conjecture to be eliminable, under the "labeling" analysis? In Epstein, Kitahara, and Seely (EKS) (2012b), we suggest one possibility: Namely we seek to deduce the Phase Impenetrability Condition (PIC; i.e. the timing of Transfer (and also which SO undergoes Transfer)) from the necessity of eliminating anomalous (derivationally defined) syntactic relations, generated by Chomsky's (2007, 2008) proposed "countercyclic" application of IM.

The basic idea of the EKS (2012b) approach is this. Suppose we have built up the CP in (11).

(11) $\{C, \{T, \{DP, \{v, VP\}\}\}\}$

Following Chomsky (2007, 2008) and Richards (2007), in EKS (2012b) we assume that C transmits its (inherently borne) phi features to T, and T then probes for matching phi features of DP. Rejecting counter-cyclic "replacement/infixing" that requires an enrichment of Merge,[26] and maintaining instead simplest Merge, we argue that subject raising to Spec, T is achieved by Merge but yields the following structure, which we first represent in its technical, set-theoretic form:

(12) {DP, {T, {DP, {v, VP}}}}

In purely formal terms, merging DP to {T, {DP, {v, VP}}} embedded in (11) yields the output (12). The relationship between (11) and (12) can be difficult to fully appreciate when examining just the sets. In somewhat informal (though visually more perspicuous) quasi-graph-theoretic terms, what we have is this:

(13)

Note that in (13) T′ (i.e. the spec-less T′ = {T, {DP, {v, VP}}}) has both a C sister and a DP sister and thus is immediately dominated by both the CP and the newly created TP projection; that is, the operation Merge creates the new set (12) without destroying any properties of the input set (11).

In EKS (2012b), we proceed to argue on empirical grounds against the Chomsky–Richards timing-of-feature-valuation explanation of Transfer (see Chomsky 2007, 2008; Richards 2007), and we suggest instead that intersecting sets such as (11) and (12), represented informally as in (13), though generable by (simplest) Merge, either halt the NS derivation (since there is no unique accessible root for Merge to apply to) or else constitute insufficient instructions to the CI systems. The situation must be remedied, and the remedy is our explanation for the existence, timing, and target of Transfer. That is, Transfer resolves the illicit intersecting set representation(s) by transferring TP and leaving the "edge" of CP for further operations (the alternative—namely transferring CP and leaving TP—results in non-convergence).

Notice, however, that the EKS (2012b) analysis still makes crucial use of LAs/SAs and a form of "Merge over Move," which are the very constructs we are attempting to eliminate here under the conjecture that given the labeling analyses discussed above, these postulates—and the phase-defined derivation incorporating them—are no longer necessary. In the EKS (2012b) analysis, C must be merged *before* IM of DP to spec-less TP (i.e. raising of the Spec of vP to Spec, TP must be "counter-cyclic" IM). But this ordering is a form of "Merge over Move,"[27] and it is needed in the EKS (2012b) system in order to create the "double peak" structure (13), which in turn induces the desired application of Transfer.

So the question arises: Is it possible to modify the EKS (2012b) analysis and still *force* the "double peak" structure (and thereby induce Transfer) but without appealing to LAs/SAs and "Merge over Move"? We believe the answer is yes; in fact, there are at least two ways to derive cyclic Transfer within the EKS (2012b) analysis. We briefly sketch these alternative deductions of Transfer below (leaving detailed re-analyses, and their consequences, for future research).

4.1   Deriving the "Double Peak" Structure through "Chain Invisibility"

Suppose LAs/SAs are eliminated entirely; rather than drawing from an LA/SA, NS draws directly from the lexicon.[28] With Chomsky (2007, 2008), assume that there are dedicated phase heads (i.e. that C and v inherently bear phi features). Finally, assume as in the EKS (2012b) system that it is the complex of features [phi + tense] (for nominative) and [phi + transitive property] (for accusative) that checks/values structural Case (under probe-goal agreement).[29] With the above assumptions in mind, suppose a derivation has built up to the spec-less TP in (14).

(14) {T, {{the, man}, {v, VP}}}

Given free Merge as in Chomsky (2013) (and assuming that there is no "Merge (EM) over Move (IM)"), we could in principle merge the DP *the man* in Spec, v to the spec-less TP; that is, we could "raise" the subject from Spec, v to Spec, T, *before* merging C, yielding (15).

(15) {{the, man}, {T, {{the, man}, {v, VP}}}}

Next, we could merge C, yielding (16).

(16) {C, {{the, man}, {T, {{the, man}, {v, VP}}}}}

Note that in the creation of (16), with (15) as input, no "counter-cyclic" operations have applied; specifically, there was no "counter-cyclic" merger to Spec, TP (this Spec, TP had already been created before the merger of C).

At the derivational point represented by (16), the phi features of C must be transmitted to T; recall that in the EKS (2012b) system, Case of *the man* is valued by the feature complex [phi + tense]. Since C inherently bears phi features, and since T inherently bears the tense feature, the required feature complex must be created derivationally via feature-transmission from C to T.[30]

After feature-transmission, T bears the Case-valuing features [phi + tense], and hence T can probe (i.e. minimally search for the first matching goal). Now, at first glance, it would appear that Case/agreement feature valuation (between T and *the man*) could take place, and since there was no "counter-cyclic" movement to Spec, T, there is no "double peak"—with the undesired result that there now is no required Transfer, triggered in order to rectify the "double peak." In other words, it would appear at first glance that we have just lost the "double peak" deduction of cyclic Transfer. However, under Chomsky's (2013) conjecture, it follows that, in fact, T (now bearing [φ + tense]) cannot "see" or successfully probe *the man*, since *the man* has moved and its lower copy is invisible to T and hence is not Case-valuable by T; technically, *the man* is no longer in the minimal search "checking" domain of T since there is an occurrence of *the man* (in Spec, T) that is not in the minimal search domain of T. Stated informally, T does not c-command all occurrences of *the man* (see Chomsky 1995b for the definition of *occurrences*), and hence T cannot Case-value *the man*; or, in other words, T does not c-command *the man* since T does not c-command the entire "chain" of *the man*. Notice further that C cannot Case-value *the man* since C (after feature-transmission) does not have all the features necessary for Case checking (namely phi features *and* the tense feature).[31]

Overall, then, this (non-counter-)cyclic derivation, where the subject DP is raised to Spec, T *before* C is merged, fails to yield a convergent derivation. If this analysis is viable, then we do not need to appeal to "Merge over Move" in order to induce the "counter-cyclic," double peak–forming, Transfer-inducing derivation we desire.

The desired, convergent, "counter-cyclic" derivation is as follows. It starts with (14), repeated here.

(14) {T, {{the, man}, {v, VP}}}

Rather than "raise" the subject *the man* to Spec, T before merging C (a derivation that crashes, as we've just shown), suppose we first merge C to spec-less TP (i.e. merge C to (14)), yielding (17).

(17) {C, {T, {{the, man}, {v, VP}}}}

Suppose next that there is phi feature-transmission from C to T. T now has all features necessary for nominative Case checking. Thus, T probes, and finds the local DP *the man*. And in fact *the man* is in T's domain since all occurrences of *the man* (there is only one) are c-commanded by T. Feature checking/valuation can occur. But the derivation is not done yet. Assuming there is a need to create a Spec, TP position (see our earlier discussion of Chomsky's 2013 analysis of the EPP),[32] the DP *the man* must raise to Spec, TP. But note that such raising of *the man* is now necessarily "counter-cyclic." And it is precisely such "counter-cyclic" raising that will create the "double peak" structure (13) that in turn induces cyclic Transfer. This is just the desired result. So we have shown that there is an independently motivated modification of the EKS (2012b) system that will result in the "double peak" deduction of cyclic Spell Out (PIC) without any appeal to LAs/SAs or to any form of (the currently unstatable) "Merge over Move."

4.2 Another Deduction of Cyclic Transfer without Appeal to LAs/SAs or to "Merge over Move"

There is an alternative deduction of cyclic Transfer requiring neither LAs/ SAs nor "Merge over Move." We outline this alternative below and briefly explore implementations of it.

Suppose we have (18); that is, we have built TP and have not yet merged C.

(18) {T, {DP, {v, VP}}}

Next, suppose that DP raises to Spec, T (given the EPP and specifically Chomsky's 2013 account of the EPP effects based on the need to create a labeled SO; but see note 32). That is, suppose we raise DP to Spec, T before we merge C. Such raising will produce (19).

(19) {DP, {T, {DP, {v, VP}}}}

Interestingly, for Chomsky (2007, 2008), at the very point that DP merges via IM to spec-less TP, Transfer applies; that is, there is cyclic Transfer. Why? Chomsky's argument (as we understand it) is as follows: If Transfer waits until later in the derivation to apply, then it can't be determined whether (19) involves two separate DPs (as in, say, *He thinks he is smart*, where there are two separate DPs *he*) or just one DP (as in, say, *He was arrested* $t_{(he)}$, where there is exactly one DP *he*).[33] There is a critical identity issue that the derivation must keep track of. Only simultaneously with DP-raising can Transfer "see" that a single DP was the input to, and output of, Merge and hence that it is a single DP, as opposed to two separate DPs. We assume with Epstein and Seely (2002) that Transfer can see the structural description and the structural change of (i.e. the input to and the output of) one and only one rule application; this much look-back is necessary and, by hypothesis, sufficient. Assuming then that Transfer can look back *only* from output to input of a single rule, once the next instance of Merge applies to (19), it is too late for Transfer to "know" that there was just one DP; in short, Transfer must apply internal to the application of Merge that produces (19). But transferring in (19) is problematic: It requires TP transfer immediately after TP creation by IM, incorrectly predicting that no C projections are ever created by Merge of C with a TP that was created by subject raising, under the assumption that Transfer renders an object inaccessible to Merge. But if Transfer waits until after Merge (DP, spec-less TP), then Transfer will not have the information it needs to tell if one DP or two DPs are present, under Chomsky's proposal.[34] Thus, the cyclic derivation (i.e. build TP; IM Spec, v to Spec, T; merge C; transfer TP) is not generable.

What about the "counter-cyclic" derivation? That is, suppose C is merged before DP raises to Spec, T. Recall (11).

(11) {C, {T, {DP, {v, VP}}}}

Next, suppose DP raises to Spec, T. Recall (13).

(13) {$_{CP}$ C

                \

                {T, {DP, {v, VP}}}}

           /

      {$_{TP}$ DP

Notice that under the EKS (2012b) "double peak" analysis, cyclic transfer of TP is in effect required/forced (as this analysis seeks to deduce the PIC). However, interestingly, under Chomsky's (2013) identity approach just considered, under which, if IM applies, it must be the last operation in a phase, Transfer also takes place obligatorily at this point—immediately after IM— in order to "keep track of identity." But notice that now there is a redundancy in that "double peak" and "identity" each force cyclic TP Transfer. That is, assuming the "identity" analysis renders the "double peak" analysis of Transfer unnecessary.[35]

To sum up this exploratory section, we conjecture that given the extension of Chomsky's (2013) "labeling" analysis to A-chains, as explored here, there may no longer be any need to appeal to the standard notion of "phase" defined in terms of LAs/SAs and "Merge over Move."[36] In fact, if Chomsky (2013) is right that the only operation is unified simplest Merge, it is impossible to state a principle of the form "Merge (EM) over Move (IM)." We have explored two approaches here, which, if they are on the right track, allow us to deduce the timing of Transfer, as well as the category undergoing Transfer, but without independently stipulating either the PIC or which categories undergo Transfer.

NOTES

We are deeply indebted to Noam Chomsky for his interest in and countless contributions to our work, including to this article. We are grateful to Noam for coming to the LSA Summer Institute at the University of Michigan in 2013 and talking to the students in a course the three of us co-taught, entitled "Derivational Minimalism." In addition, we thank all the students in our Institute course for their interest, participation, and terrific questions and contributions to the class. Marlyse Baptista, Vicki Carstens, Norbert Hornstein, Acrisio Pires, and Rick Lewis were also kind enough to sit in on some of our classes, and their contributions were truly invaluable. We owe Erich Groat our sincere appreciation for a detailed, thoughtful, written "critique" of an earlier version of this article. We are also indebted to Ruriko Kawashima for extensive and incisive feedback on previous versions of this article. In addition, we thank Masashi Nomura for his valuable comments on the manuscript. We are also grateful to the following groups for listening to aspects of this research and providing important commentary: the Keio Study Group of Generative Grammar, the University of Michigan Syntax Research (aka "Syntax Support") Group, and Generative Linguistics in Musashino. Aspects of this research were presented at the 31st conference of the English Linguistic Society of Japan in a workshop entitled "Simplest Merge and Label Identification by Minimal Search." Finally, we thank the Program for the Advancement of Next Generation Research Projects, Keio University, for its support of this research.

1. See Boeckx (2010) and Ott (2010) for discussion.
2. See Epstein (2007) for extensive discussion of what he calls "internalist functional explanation" as it concerns the theory of "purposeful" application of Merge.
3. Note too that Chomsky (2007:22) eliminates the Activity Condition; with respect to raising to Spec,T ". . . no recourse to the activity condition is needed."
4. See Frampton and Gutmann (2002) for detailed discussion of what they call a crash-proof model of syntax. For recent discussion of crash-proof grammars, see also Putnam (2010).
5. See Kitahara (1997) for an earlier attempt to reformulate Merge and Move as consisting of more elementary operations. See also the important discussions in Nunes (2001, 2004).
6. To the best of our knowledge, Collins (2002) was the first within the generative tradition to argue for the elimination of labels. For extensive further discussion of the elimination of labels and of the "projection" component of Merge, see Seely (2006); for further important discussion, see Boeckx (2006), Jayaseelan (2008), and Hornstein (2009), among others.
7. See Epstein et al. (1998) for the proposal that Merge creates the only syntactically significant relations.
8. We leave aside the only other possibility, {H, H}. See Chomsky (2013) for discussion. We also leave aside (with Chomsky 2013) issues with adjunction. For recent discussion of "head-head" merger in a language without phi-feature agreement, see Saito (2012, 2013a, 2013b).
9. A question remains as to how the conceptual-intentional systems use the information that, say, {H, XP} is an H-type thing; but the idea is that they can't interpret {H, XP} without this information (see Chomsky 2013 for discussion).
10. Note that the featural intersection of X, Y is taken as the label of {XP, YP}. Interestingly, as a reviewer points out, Chomsky (1995b) proposed this idea but at the time rejected the existence of projection of an intersect of features borne by X and by Y since X, Y might not have intersecting features.
11. The notion "term-of" was originally defined as follows (Chomsky 1995a:399):

    (i) a. K is a term of K.
        b. If L is a term of K, then the members of the members of L are terms of K.

    Given simplest Merge, however, the definition (i) requires the following modification, as proposed by Seely (2006:201):

    (ii) a. K is a term of K.
         b. If L is a term of K, then the members of L are terms of K.

    In this article, we adopt this simplified definition of the notion "term-of." See Seely (2006), Chomsky (2008:158n.16), and Epstein, Kitahara, and Seely (2012b) for relevant discussion. For recent discussion of the possible importance of reducing (ib) to (iib), see Epstein (2013).

12. The invisibility of lower copies is supported by cases such as English *wh*-movement (i) (see Chomsky 2007, 2008) and Icelandic dative subjects (ii) (see Jónsson 1996, also cited in Bobaljik 2008). In each case, a lower copy of the moved element, occupying Spec,v, does not interfere with the minimal search of T.

   (i) What do they like?
        [wh [C [T [wh [Subj [v VP]]]]]]
   (ii) Jóni   líkuðu   Þessir   sokkar.
        Jon.$_{DAT}$ like.$_{PL}$ these   socks.$_{NOM}$
        "Jon likes these socks."
        [C [NP.$_{DAT}$ [T [NP.$_{DAT}$ [v [V NP.$_{NOM}$]]]]]]

   Given data such as (i) and (ii), Epstein, Kitahara, and Seely (2012b) propose that α (goal) is invisible to the minimal search of β (probe) if some occurrence of α is outside β's search domain.

13. It should be noted that with expletive insertion (as in *There is a man in the room*), the lower portion (in this case, [a man in the room]) will not have a label. It could be that there is "short movement" of *a man* to the "specifier" of some higher head, rendering the lower copy of *a man* invisible and hence allowing the lower portion in question to be labeled, as P. Now the question arises of how (i), with short movement of *a man*, is to be excluded within Chomsky's (2013) account of the EPP.

   (i) *— will be a man in the room.

   We leave the important questions of how such existentials with *there* are to be allowed, and how those without *there* are to be excluded, to future research regarding Chomsky's (2013) compelling reduction of EPP to labeling by minimal search.

14. We ignore a lower copy of *the man* here, since it is irrelevant to our discussion. (In response to a reviewer's comment, this is not to say that a lower copy is irrelevant to all phenomena, for example possible reconstruction.)

15. As a reviewer notes, Bošković (2007) similarly proposes an "attraction-free" account of movement (i.e. one not driven by properties of the target), and Bošković's arguments for a non-feature-checking system can extend to Chomsky (2013). See also Bošković (2008), which provides an analysis of "freezing" effects of movement (see Epstein 1992; Rizzi 1997). Under the proposals in Bošković (2008), feature checking has a freezing effect on movement, and it is not clear how these effects can be accounted for in a "free Merge" system, where feature checking does not constrain the application of Merge. We leave this question for future research (see Epstein, Kitahara, and Seely 2013 for relevant discussion).

16. See Pires and Taylor (2007) for extensive discussion of the licensing conditions on such *wh*-in-situ cases. As a reviewer points out, related issues are discussed in Vlachos (2012).

17. Like Chomsky (2013), we leave the status of head-movement aside; see also note 8.

18. We ignore *to* here, since it is not relevant for our main concerns; but see note 24.

19. Examples such as (9a–b) and their importance were, to the best of our (and a *Linguistic Inquiry* reviewer's) knowledge, independently noted (in personal communications to others) by both Alec Marantz and Juan Romero. For discussion of the possible elimination of "Merge over Move," see Castillo, Drury, and Grohmann (1999, 2009) and Epstein and Seely (1999, 2006).

20. Goto (2013) independently points out that the core data presented here result in labeling failure at CI.

21. In addition, composite operations are in general unwelcome as we search for the primitive, minimal, undecomposable operations of NS.

22. See Chomsky (2013:46) for relevant discussion of the complex status of what appears to be a head.

23. Note that there are languages (such as Modern Greek and Portuguese) where T lacking the tense feature bears phi features; the consequences of this for labeling await further research.

24. Notice that free Merge in fact allows one-fell-swoop A-movement, a type of derivation that Epstein and Seely (2006) propose—and that they in fact assume is forced given computationally efficient satisfaction of the interfaces (Strong Minimalist Thesis). However, unlike Epstein and Seely (2006), Chomsky (2008:153) assumes there is phase-internal Successive-Cyclic A-movement. Although the facts are not entirely clear to us (see Epstein and Seely 2006 for discussion), allowing phase-internal Successive-Cyclic A-movement may be preferable to the one-fell-swoop analysis in Epstein and Seely (2006), with respect to capturing reconstruction (e.g. anaphoric binding) effects in so-called A-chains (e.g. *John seems to Mary _____ to seem to himself _____ to be _____ happy*). Interestingly, the free-Merge analysis assumed here would allow both one-fell-swoop A-movement and Successive-Cyclic A-movement. For further discussion, specifically about reconstruction effects in A-chains, see, for example, Lasnik (1999), Bošković (2002), and references therein.

25. Similarly, there is no need to stipulate LAs, SAs, or "Merge over Move" to account for the following contrast noted (with syntactically parallel examples) in Chomsky (2000:104):

    (i)   a. I expected [TP someone to be $t_{someone}$ in the room].
          b. *I expected [TP tI to be someone in the room].

    Here, too, each derivation involves the stage [T [be someone in the room]], and two options—EM of *I* in Spec,T and IM of *someone* to Spec,T—are (by hypothesis) available to NS. However, if EM of *I* in Spec,T, merging an argument into a non-theta-position, creates an illegitimate CI object, violating Full Interpretation, then the observed contrast naturally follows, and Chomsky's (2000) theta-theoretic condition (i.e. pure Merge in a theta position is required of (and restricted to) arguments) can be eliminated. See also Epstein, Kitahara, and Seely (2012a) for relevant discussion.

26. See Freidin (1999) for independent important arguments against "replacement" on the grounds that it is a "complex" multifaceted operation not executable given a desirable theory allowing only transformational rules that perform basic primitive operations.

27. Actually, in EKS (2012b) we attempt to deduce "Merge over Move" from efficiency considerations; the idea is that Merge involving no search of merged items is preferred over any application of Merge involving search of merged items. Since EM involves no search, all instances of EM must be exhausted (relative to a given LA/SA) before any instance of IM.

28. Note that there are both empirical and conceptual arguments for LAs/SAs. Above, we have conjectured that the empirical evidence for LAs/SAs can be accounted for without LAs/SAs. But we do not address the conceptual argument in favor of LAs/SAs, based on efficiency considerations.

29. In the EKS (2012b) analysis, these feature complexes (e.g. [phi + tense]) do not exist on any category in the lexicon; rather, they are created in the course of a derivation via feature-transmission. We focus here just on nominative Case.

30. We assume that the phi features of C move down to T to create [phi + tense] (downward feature-transmission of phi features from C to T); the alternative

is for the tense feature of T to move up to C, which also creates [phi + tense] (upward feature-transmission of the tense feature from T to C). As we will show in a moment, the latter feature-transmission option must be prohibited.

31. Note that if the tense feature of T were to "raise" to C, then C (now bearing the feature complex [phi + tense]) could in principle Case-value *the man* since *the man* is in fact in the domain of C (all occurrences of *the man* are c-commanded by C). It is crucial, then, that feature-transmission is downward.

32. As we showed earlier, it follows from Chomsky (2013) that Spec,v must raise from vP (since vP has no label without such raising). Interestingly, the landing site of the raised DP does not follow from Chomsky's account; that is, it does not follow that DP must raise *to* Spec,T but only that DP must raise *from* Spec,v (so that vP can become labeled). Perhaps relevant to this issue, and supporting this analysis, is the derivation of sentences like *How many men do you think that there are outside?* (adapted from Chomsky 1991:445), in which it appears that the moved DP has exited Spec,v but has not moved to Spec,T of the embedded clause. Chomsky's (2013) analysis predicts that the subject ultimately lands where it will not induce a labeling failure. As a result, Spec,T is fine, but Spec,C is problematic if C lacks phi features. The subject can move to a potentially problematic place, as in *wh*-movement to intermediate C, as long as it moves on further. Under free Merge, IM can move the subject anywhere in principle, but if a labeling failure occurs, then the CI representation pays the price. So labeling indirectly determines the departure site as well as the landing site of the subject. We leave the details of such derivations to further research (see EKS 2013 for relevant discussion).

33. It thus appears to us that Chomsky's (2007, 2008) analysis assumes the following: (a) A pair ⟨X, X⟩ is identified as copies created by IM only immediately after IM; and (b) if ⟨X, X⟩ is not identified as two copies created by IM, then it must be identified as two separate arguments. A less stipulative algorithm would be this: Freely assume ⟨X, X⟩ to be two copies or assume them to be two separate arguments. This would arguably suffice empirically; that is, if *He was arrested t(he)* is taken to contain two arguments, there is a theta/Full Interpretation/gibberish problem at CI. If *He thinks he is smart* is taken to involve two copies created by IM, then, again, there is a theta/Full Interpretation/gibberish problem at CI. This alternative, "free interpretation" analysis seems worthy of detailed exploration but lies beyond the scope of the present article.

It should be noted that the identity problem is much more general. It goes beyond arguments: For example, in *The boy likes the girl*, it arises concerning *the*. Chomsky (2007, 2008) assumes the "default" is to treat the two identical elements as repetitions (two separate morphemes), and then he adds exceptions: If they are formed by IM, then they are not repetitions but copies (of a single entity).

34. This is similar to the Chomsky–Richards analysis seeking to explain cyclic Spell Out by appeal to the nature of feature valuation. Chomsky and Richards argue that spelling out a feature before valuation causes a crash (unvalued features appear at the interface). But spelling out a feature after that feature is valued is too late, since Transfer cannot tell whether the feature was inherently lexically valued (in which case it is interpretable and so is not to be transferred) or underwent syntactic valuation (in which case it is uninterpretable and must therefore be spelled out in order to avoid a crash). The solution (Epstein and Seely 2002) is to allow one-operation look-back; that is, Transfer can see the input to and output of a feature valuation operation, and so it can tell whether a valued feature underwent syntactic valuation or was inherently valued. The analysis here is similar: Only internal to IM can it be determined that ⟨X, X⟩ is

two copies. Thereafter, it's impossible to determine if it consists of one DP or two DPs since a "chain" of DPs is indistinguishable from two separate DPs. See Epstein and Seely (2002) for detailed discussion.

35. Chomsky's (2013) "identity" analysis of Transfer has another interesting consequence: It follows from the analysis that feature-inheritance operates downward. We noted in section 4.1 that the phi features of C (and analogously the phi features of v) are transmitted to T (and from v to V) and that it is the complex of features [phi + tense] that checks (nominative) Case. We noted further (see note 31) that it is crucial that the tense feature of T *not raise* to C (to create the [phi + tense] complex). If the tense feature *is* transmitted up to C bearing phi features, then a possible landing site for Subj is Spec,C, not Spec,T, because it is C that has phi features (for labeling). So, if Subj has a reason to move out of Spec,v, it will end up in Spec,C. Now, given the "identity" analysis, the newly created CP containing Subj in its Spec must undergo Transfer. As a result, there is no way to continue this derivation. Chomsky's (2013) analysis therefore provides a "labeling + identity" account for why features must be inherited downward.

36. This conclusion is reached on independent grounds by Frampton and Gutmann (2002), as well as by Epstein and Seely (2002, 2006).

REFERENCES

Bobaljik, J. D. 2008. Where's Phi? Agreement as a Postsyntactic Operation. In Harbour, D., Adger, D. and Bejar, S. (eds.), *Phi Theory: Phi-Features Across Modules and Interfaces*, 295–328. Oxford: Oxford University Press.

Boeckx, C. 2006. *Linguistic Minimalism: Origins, Concepts, Methods, and Aims.* Oxford: Oxford University Press.4

Boeckx, C. 2010. A Tale of Two Minimalisms: Reflections on the Plausibility of Crash-Proof Syntax, and Its Free-Merge Alternative. In Putnam, M. T. (ed.), *Exploring Crash-Proof Grammars*, 89–104. Amsterdam: John Benjamins.

Boskovic´, Ž. 1994. D-Structure, Theta-Criterion, and Movement Into Theta-Positions. *Linguistic Analysis* 24:247–286.

Boskovic´, Ž. 2002. A-Movement and the EPP. *Syntax* 5:167–218.

Boskovic´, Ž. 2007. On the Locality and Motivation of Move and Agree: An Even More Minimal Theory. *Linguistic Inquiry* 38:589–644.

Boskovic´, Ž. 2008. On the Operator Freezing Effect. *Natural Language and Linguistic Theory* 26:249–287.

Castillo, J. C., Drury, J. and Grohmann, K. K. 1999. Merge Over Move and the Extended Projection Principle. In Aoshima, S., Drury, J. and Neuvonen, T. (eds.), *University of Maryland Working Papers in Linguistics* 8, 63–103. College Park: University of Maryland, Department of Linguistics.

Castillo, J. C., Drury, J. and Grohmann, K. K. 2009. Merge Over Move and the Extended Projection Principle: MOM and the EPP Revisited. *Iberia: An International Journal of Theoretical Linguistics* 1:53–114.

Chomsky, N. 1991. Some Notes on Economy of Derivation and Representation. In Freidin, R. (ed.), *Principles and Parameters in Comparative Grammar*, 417–454. Cambridge, MA: MIT Press.

Chomsky, N. 1995a. Bare Phrase Structure. In Webelhuth, G. (ed.), *Government and Binding Theory and the Minimalist Program: Principles and Parameters in Syntactic Theory*, 385–439. Oxford: Blackwell.

Chomsky, N. 1995b. *The Minimalist Program.* Cambridge, MA: MIT Press.

Chomsky, N. 2000. Minimalist Inquiries: The Framework. In Martin, R., Michaels, D. and Uriagereka, J. (eds.), *Step by Step: Essays on Minimalist Syntax in Honor of Howard Lasnik*, 89–155. Cambridge, MA: MIT Press.

Chomsky, N. 2004. Beyond Explanatory Adequacy. In Belletti, A. (ed.), *Structures and Beyond: The Cartography of Syntactic Structures*, vol. 3, 104–131. Oxford: Oxford University Press.

Chomsky, N. 2005. Three Factors in Language Design. *Linguistic Inquiry* 36:1–22.

Chomsky, N. 2007. Approaching UG from Below. In Sauerland, U. and Gärtner, H.-M. (eds.), *Interfaces + Recursion = Language?*, 1–29. Berlin: Mouton de Gruyter.

Chomsky, N. 2008. On Phases. In Freidin, R., Otero, C. P. and Zubizarreta, M. L. (eds.), *Foundational Issues in Linguistic Theory: Essays in Honor of Jean-Roger Vergnaud*, 133–166. Cambridge, MA: MIT Press.

Chomsky, N. 2013. Problems of Projection. *Lingua* 130:33–49.

Collins, C. 2002. Eliminating Labels. In Epstein, S. D. and Seely, T. D. (eds.), *Derivation and Explanation in the Minimalist Program*, 42–64. Oxford: Blackwell.

Epstein, S. D. 1992. Derivational Constraints on Ā-Chain Formation. *Linguistic Inquiry* 23:235–259.

Epstein, S. D. 2007. On I(internalist)-Functional Explanation in Minimalism. *Linguistic Analysis* 33:20–53.

Epstein, S. D. 2013. Syntactic Representations Reduced to 3rd Factor Primitives of Set Theory? Manuscript, University of Michigan, Ann Arbor.

Epstein, S. D., Groat, E., Kawashima, R. and Kitahara, H. 1998. *A Derivational Approach to Syntactic Relations*. Oxford: Oxford University Press.

Epstein, S. D., Kitahara, H. and Seely, T. D. 2012a. Exploring Phase Based Implications Regarding Clausal Architecture. A Case Study: Why Structural Case Cannot Precede Theta. In Gallego, Á. J. (ed.), *Phases: Developing the Framework*, 103–124. Berlin: Mouton de Gruyter.

Epstein, S. D., Kitahara, H. and Seely, T. D. 2012b. Structure Building That Can't Be! In Uribe-Etxebarria, M. and Valmala, V. (eds.), *Ways of Structure Building*, 253–270. Oxford: Oxford University Press.

Epstein, S. D., Kitahara, H. and Seely, T. D. 2013. Criterial Freezing: Transformational Cessation vs. CI Interpretation. Manuscript, University of Michigan, Ann Arbor, Keio University, and Eastern Michigan University, Ypsilanti.

Epstein, S. D., Pires, A. and Seely, T. D. 2005. EPP in T: More Controversial Subjects. *Syntax* 8:65–80.

Epstein, S. D. and Seely, T. D. 1999. SPECifying the GF "Subject": Eliminating A-Chains and the EPP within a Derivational Model. Ms., University of Michigan, Ann Arbor, and Eastern Michigan University, Ypsilanti.

Epstein, S. D. and Seely, T. D. 2002. Rule Applications as Cycles in a Level-Free Syntax. In Epstein, S. D. and Seely, T. D. (eds.), *Derivation and Explanation in the Minimalist Program*, 65–90. Oxford: Blackwell.

Epstein, S. D. and Seely, T. D. 2006. *Derivations in Minimalism*. Cambridge: Cambridge University Press.

Frampton, J. and Gutmann, S. 2002. Crash Proof Syntax. In Epstein, S. D. and Seely, T. D. (eds.), *Derivation and Explanation in the Minimalist Program*, 90–105. Oxford: Blackwell.

Freidin, R. 1999. Cyclicity and Minimalism. In Epstein, S. D. and Hornstein, N. (eds.), *Working Minimalism*, 95–126. Cambridge, MA: MIT Press.

Goto, N. 2013. Labeling and Scrambling in Japanese. *Tohoku: Essays and Studies in English Language and Literature* 46:39–73.

Hornstein, N. 1999. Movement and Control. *Linguistic Inquiry* 30:69–96.

Hornstein, N. 2009. *A Theory of Syntax: Minimal Operations and Universal Grammar*. Cambridge: Cambridge University Press.

Jayaseelan, J. K. 2008. Bare Phrase Structure and Specifier-Less Syntax. *Biolinguistics* 2:87–106.

Jo´nsson, J. G. 1996. Clausal Architecture and Case in Icelandic. Doctoral dissertation, University of Massachusetts, Amherst.

Kitahara, H. 1997. *Elementary Operations and Optimal Derivations*. Cambridge, MA: MIT Press.

Lasnik, H. 1992. Case and Expletives: Notes toward a Parametric Account. *Linguistic Inquiry* 23:381–405.

Lasnik, H. 1999. Chains of Arguments. In Epstein, S. D. and Hornstein, N. (eds.), *Working Minimalism*, 189–215. Cambridge, MA: MIT Press.

Lasnik, H. and Saito, M. 1984. On the Nature of Proper Government. *Linguistic Inquiry* 15:235–289.

Lasnik, H. and Saito, M. 1992. *Move α: Conditions on Its Application and Output*. Cambridge, MA: MIT Press.

Nunes, J. 2001. Sideward Movement. *Linguistic Inquiry* 32:303–344.

Nunes, J. 2004. *Linearization of Chains and Sideward Movement*. Cambridge, MA: MIT Press.

O'Neil, J. 1997. Means of Control: Deriving the Properties of PRO in the Minimalist Program. Doctoral dissertation, Harvard University, Cambridge, MA.

Ott, D. 2010. Grammaticality, Interfaces, and UG. In Putnam, M. T. (ed.), *Exploring Crash-Proof Grammars*, 89–104. Amsterdam: John Benjamins.

Pires, A. and Taylor, H. L. 2007. The Syntax of *Wh*-in-Situ and Common Ground. In Elliott, M., Kirby, J., Sawada, O., Staraki, E. and Yoon, S. (eds.), *Proceedings from the Annual Meeting of the Chicago Linguistic Society 43*, 2:201–215. Chicago: University of Chicago, Chicago Linguistic Society.

Putnam, M. T. (ed.). 2010. *Exploring Crash-Proof Grammars*. Amsterdam: John Benjamins.

Richards, M. D. 2007. On Feature Inheritance: An Argument from the Phase Impenetrability Condition. *Linguistic Inquiry* 38:563–572.

Rizzi, L. 1997. The Fine Structure of the Left Periphery. In Haegeman, L. (ed.), *Elements of Grammar: Handbook of Generative Syntax*, 281–337. Dordrecht: Kluwer.

Saito, M. 2012. Case Checking/Valuation in Japanese: Move, Agree, or Merge? *Nanzan Linguistics* 8:109–127.

Saito, M. 2013a. Case and Labeling in a Language without Phi-Feature Agreement. Manuscript, Nanzan University, Nagoya, Japan.

Saito, M. 2013b. Conditions on Japanese Phrase Structure: From Morphology to Pragmatics. *Nanzan Linguistics* 9:119–145.

Seely, T. D. 2006. Merge, Derivational C-Command, and Subcategorization in a Label-Free Syntax. In Boeckx, C. (ed.), *Minimalist Essays*, 182–217. Amsterdam: John Benjamins.

Uriagereka, J. 1988. On Government. Doctoral dissertation, University of Connecticut, Storrs.

Vlachos, C. 2012. *Wh*-Constructions and the Division of Labour between Syntax and the Interfaces. Doctoral dissertation, University of Patras, Patras, Greece.

11 What Do We Wonder Is Not Syntactic?

Samuel D. Epstein, Hisatsugu Kitahara, and T. Daniel Seely

1 INTRODUCTION

This paper discusses the so-called halting aka criterial freezing phenomenon (Rizzi 1997, 2006, 2011, 2014) (analyzed in Epstein 1992 as an arguably deducible ("last resort") effect of Chomsky's Strong Minimalist Thesis (SMT), encapsulated as "computationally efficient satisfaction of bare output conditions"). Rizzi's (2014) insightful and attractive deduction-seeking analysis explains freezing phenomena—the inapplicability of movement to certain syntactic objects—by appeal to a particular (re-)formulation of the independently motivated hypothesis that X′ projections are invisible for movement, the so-called X′ invisibility hypothesis. Once a phrase moves to a criterial position, it is argued that given modifications (see below) of Chomsky's (2013) labeling-by-Minimal-Search analysis, movement halting can also be explained since a phrase moved to a criterial position becomes "an X′ projection," hence invisible to movement, thereby explaining criterial freezing. Despite the elegance of Rizzi's analysis, we present empirical and conceptual arguments disfavoring it. First, the possible empirical problem is that although the analysis prevents the Narrow Syntax (NS) from generating (a) *Which dog do you wonder John likes?* by appeal to independently motivated labeling theory and X′ invisibility, it nonetheless fails to exclude (b) *You wonder John likes this dog. We suggest (i) that (a) and (b) are the same phenomenon, hence are to be captured by the same law; (ii) that (b) is not excluded by label-based X′ invisibility; (iii) that morphophonological, conceptual-intentional (CI) requirements are independently needed to exclude (b); and (iv) that these requirements automatically exclude (a) as well, rendering label-based X′ invisibility unnecessary. If on track, this would suggest that halting of movement is in fact an illusion. Despite appearances, there is no syntactic prohibition on the application of successive cyclic movement that prevents (a) (contra Epstein 1992; Rizzi 1997, 2006, 2011, 2014). Rather, it is generated by an allowable movement (freely applied simplest Merge, as discussed below) but results in a violation of the independently needed morpho-phonological, CI requirements. As we will discuss, our re-analysis, shifting the burden from a Universal Grammar

(UG)-specific syntactic constraint on Internal Merge to independent interface conditions, allows us to maintain freely applied simplest Merge—Merge $(\alpha, \beta) \rightarrow \{\alpha, \beta\}$—subject only to 3rd factor laws (such as the No-Tampering Condition and inclusiveness). By contrast, enforcing syntactic halting in NS (movement inapplicability) necessitates in this case departure from (simplest) Merge in two important respects: (i) A dedicated syntactic (non-3rd factor, i.e. UG-specific) constraint is imposed on movement (a label-based incarnation of "X′ invisibility"); and (ii) this dedicated syntactic constraint must be applied only to Internal Merge (IM), not to External Merge (EM). This asymmetrical constraint prevents the adoption of Chomsky's important unification of EM and IM as simply two instantiations (which come for free) of the single rule (simplest) Merge. As Chomsky notes, this unification in turn (i) reduces the complexity of the object, namely UG, which must be evolutionarily explained (if indeed it is humanly explicable; see Chomsky 2013); (ii) for the first time renders the hitherto curious property of displacement unremarkable; and (iii) by intertwining IM and EM application, eliminates the long-standing two-stage, level-ordered model within which phrase structure representations are first generated and then undergo transformational rule application (see Epstein, Kitahara, and Seely (EKS) 2014b for further discussion).

The analysis we propose here seeks to eliminate a syntactic constraint and reassign its empirical effects to independently motivated interpretive constraints. In section 2, we review "obligatory exit" phenomena and the analysis of it presented in Chomsky (2013) and extended to new empirical domains in EKS (2014a). Section 3 reviews the reformulation of Chomsky's labeling analysis to obligatory halting or criterial freezing, as proposed by Rizzi (2014), and discusses potential problems with the syntactic-constraint-based analysis of halting/freezing. Section 4 presents our re-analysis of halting/freezing as illusory (i.e. movement from criterial positions is syntactically allowed, as in Chomsky 1995b:291), which we formulate in terms of independently necessary morpho-phonological, CI interpretive requirements. Section 5 discusses the potential relevance of aspects of scrambling in Japanese.

2 EXPLAINING "OBLIGATORY EXIT": A REVIEW

In this section, we review Chomsky's (2013) labeling analysis of A′-movement and EKS's (2014a) extension of it to A-movement. Each explains, informally speaking, "obligatory exit" from intermediate position as the result of labeling failure—ultimately, a CI violation of Full Interpretation (FI). More formally, we assume that simplest Merge applies freely; thus, an element may or may not move from a particular position, but in so-called non-criterial positions, if it does not move out, labeling failure results, and thus it appears that exit is obligatory.

In early Minimalism, Chomsky (1995a,b) proposed that Merge (α, β) yields a "labeled set" γ of the form $\{\delta, \{\alpha, \beta\}\}$, where δ identifies the relevant properties of γ. In effect, label projection was part of the definition of Merge. Collins (2002) and Seely (2006) argue that Merge (α, β) yields $\{\alpha, \beta\}$ with no label nor label projection. In recent work, Chomsky (2013) argues that Merge (α, β) yields $\{\alpha, \beta\}$ with no label projection or specification of linear order, and independently of the character of α and β. We call this *simplest* Merge:[1]

(1) Merge (α, β) $\rightarrow$ $\{\alpha, \beta\}$

Given (1), an object γ constructed from α and β by Merge is just $\{\alpha, \beta\}$, not a "labeled set" of the form $\{\delta, \{\alpha, \beta\}\}$ (where δ is taken to be the label of γ). The output of Merge does not overtly encode a label. In other words, there is neither stipulated endocentricity nor notationally represented projection. Strictly speaking, mental representations of syntactic form do not include the symbolic representation of a projected label.

For a syntactic object (SO) to be interpreted at CI, however, it is necessary to know what kind of SO it is (e.g. whether it is nominal or verbal). Chomsky (2013:43) takes *labeling* to be the process of finding the relevant (object identification) information of $\{\alpha, \beta\}$, ideally "just minimal search, presumably appropriating a third factor principle, as in Agree and other operations." He then outlines how Minimal Search[2] finds the label of each of the following two types of sets:

(2) Suppose SO = $\{H, XP\}$, H a head and XP not a head. Then Minimal Search will select H as the label, and the usual procedures of interpretation at the interfaces can proceed.

(3) Suppose SO = $\{XP, YP\}$, neither a head. Here Minimal Search is ambiguous, locating the heads X, Y of XP, YP, respectively. There are, then, two ways in which SO can be labeled: (A) modify SO so that there is only one visible head, or (B) X and Y are identical in a relevant respect, providing the same label, which can be taken as the label of the SO.

In $\{H, XP\}$ (see (2)), Minimal Search immediately finds a lexical item H (a bundle of features, provided by the lexicon) and a two-membered set XP (a set-theoretic object, constructed by Merge). The former, being a lexical item, makes available what matters to the interface systems, namely features, while the latter, being a set, does not; it requires further search. Thus, H is identified as the label of $\{H, XP\}$ unambiguously.

In $\{XP, YP\}$ (see (3)), Minimal Search is ambiguous, locating (with equally minimal "top-down depth of search") each of the two heads X and Y of XP, YP, respectively. It is assumed that such failure to identify a unique feature-bearing element in $\{XP, YP\}$ prevents labeling, and since labels are required at CI, if an object lacking an identified unique label appears at CI, it violates

FI.[3] For Chomsky (2013), however, there are two ways in which unlabeled {XP, YP} can be salvaged: (A) Modify this SO, so that there is only one "visible" head, i.e. X or Y (but not X and Y);[4] or (B) X and Y share (or, more accurately, agree in) some prominent feature, e.g. the Q-feature, and such shared features are taken as the relevant identifying information, i.e. as the identified label of {XP, YP}.

Chomsky (2013) takes A'-movement to support his labeling analysis. Consider (4) (where *t* is an abbreviation for full copies):

(4) [$_\beta$ In which Texas city did they think [$_\alpha$ *t* [C [$_{TP}$ the man was assassinated *t*]]?

Immediately after the *wh*-phrase *in which Texas city* (hereon, *wh*-PP) is raised to the specifier of the embedded C, the embedded clause α is of the form of {XP, YP}, where XP is the *wh*-PP and YP is {C, TP}, as shown in (5):

(5) . . . (think) [$_\alpha$ [$_{XP}$ in which Texas city] [$_{YP}$ C [$_{TP}$ the man was assassinated *t*]]

Crucially, the embedded C (selected by *think*) bears no Q-feature, and so there is assumed to be no prominent feature shared by the Q-bearing X and the Q-lacking Y in (5). If XP remains in this intermediate position, Minimal Search cannot find the label of α, and so FI will be violated at CI. But if XP raises to a higher position, as in (4), then Minimal Search can find a unique visible head, namely C as the label of α.[5] Notice the matrix clause β of (4) is also of the form of {XP, YP}, but in β there is a prominent feature shared by X and Y, namely the Q-feature of the *wh*-PP and the matrix C_Q; hence, the shared Q can be the label of β.

Chomsky (2013) also examines data such as (6a, b):

(6) a. They thought the man was assassinated in which Texas city?
    b. *They thought [$_\alpha$ in which Texas city [C [$_{TP}$ the man was assassinated *t*]]]?

English allows such *wh*-in-situ constructions in relevant contexts, e.g. a quiz show. But if a *wh*-phrase raises to form the embedded clause α and remains there, as in (6b), Minimal Search cannot find the label of α, since α is of the form {XP, YP}, and there is no prominent feature (such as Q) shared by X and Y, as just discussed. The fact that α has no label bars (6b) by FI at CI, as desired.

EKS (2014a) note the same pattern in a multiple *wh*-question context. Consider (7a, b):

(7) a. Who thought the man was assassinated in which Texas city?
    b. *Who thought [$_\alpha$ in which Texas city [C [$_{TP}$ the man was assassinated *t*]]]?

Here again, if a *wh*-phrase raises to form the embedded clause α and appears there at CI, Minimal Search cannot find the label of α because α is of the form {XP, YP}, and there is no prominent feature (e.g. Q) shared by X and Y. The fact that α has no label correctly bars (7b) by FI at CI.[6]

EKS (2014a) provide further evidence for Chomsky's (2013) labeling analysis, arguing that a labeling failure analogously arises in (phase-internal) successive cyclic A-movement, just as it does with (phase-crossing) successive cyclic A'-movement. Consider (8a,b):[7]

(8) a. *There is likely [$_\alpha$ a dog to be *t* in the room].
    b. There is likely [$_\alpha$ *t* to be a dog in the room].

If, as in (8a), *a dog* raises to form the embedded clause α and appears there at CI, Minimal Search cannot find the label of α, because α is of the form {XP, YP}, and there is no prominent feature, specifically no phi features, shared by X and Y (given that *a dog* and infinitival raising T do not share phi features, under the hypothesis that T = *to* is phi-less). The fact that α has no label bars (8a) by FI at CI. Thus, EKS extend the Q-based analysis of A'-movement to a phi-based analysis of A-movement. If *there* is instead inserted to form the embedded clause α, as in (8b), then α is (once again) a label-less set {XP, YP} (given that *there* and infinitival raising T do not share phi features). If *there* undergoes further movement, as in (8b), Minimal Search finds the only visible head T as the label of α. Thus, a labeling failure does not arise in the final complete matrix CP representation appearing at CI (8b).

To summarize, labeling failure, observed in (6b)/(7b)/(8a), unifies these phenomena arising as a consequence of freely applied simplest Merge and labeling-by-Minimal-Search, interacting with the independently motivated CI requirement that every SO appearing at CI must have an identifiable unique label.

Such interaction accounts for, informally speaking, the "obligatory exit" from intermediate position in (4)/(8b). It is important to note however that syntactic "exit" is not in fact obligatory, under freely applied simplest Merge. Rather, "exit" is syntactically optional—yet if exit from the intermediate position fails to apply in such cases, there is a CI interpretive problem (labeling failure) as a result.[8]

3   "OBLIGATORY HALT" IN CRITERIAL POSITION: A PROBLEM

In this section, we first review relevant aspects of Rizzi's (2014) labeling analysis of "obligatory syntactic halt" in criterial position, in which he proposes a particular formalization of labeling to explain "criterial freezing" phenomena (Rizzi 1997, 2006, 2011), earlier analyzed as a halting effect deducible from Chomsky's independently motivated SMT, i.e. computationally efficient satisfaction of the interface conditions (Epstein 1992). We then present arguments against Rizzi's labeling analysis of "criterial freezing."

Consider (9a,b), the standard kind of case traditionally used to motivate what is referred to as "criterial freezing":

(9) a. You wonder $[_\alpha$ $[_{XP}$ which dog] $[_{YP}$ C_Q $[_{TP}$ John likes t]]].
    b. *Which dog do you wonder $[_\alpha$ t $[C_Q$ $[_{TP}$ John likes t]]]?

In (9a), *which dog* raises to form the embedded clause α = {XP, YP}, where there is a feature Q, shared by the *wh*-element X (of *which* dog) and the Q-bearing Y (= C_Q); hence, the shared Q is the label of α in (9a). Rizzi's insightful analysis seeks to explain (9b) as blocked by a syntactic constraint disallowing further movement of *which dog*; i.e. the core assumption is that there exists a syntactic constraint on movement application that prevents exit from the specifier of the embedded C in (9b). This is done by appeal to the (movement-preventing) structure resulting from the Q-labeling in (9a). That is, Rizzi proposes that upon the creation of α in (9a), the label Q is assigned to XP, YP, and to α as well, as shown in (10):

(10) ... $[_Q$ $[_Q$ which dog] $[_Q$ C_Q $[_{TP}$ John likes t]]]

In (10), XP (= $[_{XP}$ which dog]), YP (= $[_{YP}$ C_Q $[_{TP}$ John likes t]]), and α (= $[_\alpha$ $[_{XP}$ which dog] $[_{YP}$ C_Q $[_{TP}$ John likes t]]]) are all Q-projections. Crucially, however, it is only α that counts as a maximal Q-projection.[9]

Given this Q-labeled structure, Rizzi reduces "criterial freezing" to an explicit syntactic ban on movement of non-maximal projections (in earlier work, adopting X-bar theory explicitly, it was called "the X′ invisibility hypothesis," incorporated by e.g. Chomsky 1995b and Epstein and Seely 2006). Thus, movement is barred by a syntactic constraint on IM application. Rizzi then generalizes the impossibility of movement of non-maximal projections as the following principle:

(11) Maximality: Only maximal objects with a given label can be moved.

Given (11), movement of non-maximal projections is systematically banned.[10] Rizzi's insight is that once $[_Q$ which dog] moves to form the embedded clause α, by Rizzi's formulation of Q-labeling, $[_Q$ which dog] no longer counts as a maximal object with the Q label. It is only α (= $[_Q$ $[_Q$ which dog] $[_Q$ C_Q $[_{TP}$ John likes t]]]) that now counts as a maximal object with the Q label. Thus, the maximality principle (11) explains "criterial freezing" effects as actual freezing; i.e. movement is formally prohibited.[11]

It is important to note that Rizzi's deduction incorporates (at least) the following three principles:

(12) a. Every SO appearing at CI must have a label.
   b. Labeling takes place in NS obligatorily and immediately when-ever applicable.
   c. Only maximal objects with a given label can be moved.

(12a), also assumed in Chomsky (2013), is taken to be part of FI at CI. (12b) is perhaps reducible to computational efficiency (Earliness, see note 12 below) and is apparently needed so as to enforce actual freez-ing (a movement ban) immediately upon creation of the relevant con-figuration.[12] But (12c) is crucially a dedicated syntactic constraint on movement.

Despite the elegance of Rizzi's attempted deduction, we argue that (12c) loses its conceptual support under freely applied simplest unified Merge; hence, it should be eliminated. That is, under freely applied sim-plest Merge, as formulated in (1), we suggest that nothing prevents Merge from applying to an SO occupying a criterial position. Simply put, {which, dog} is an SO in (10); hence, freely applied simplest Merge can apply to it.[13,14]

Recall the simplest conception of Merge formulated in (1), repeated below:

(1) Merge $(\alpha, \beta) \rightarrow \{\alpha, \beta\}$

Chomsky (2004, 2005, 2007, 2008, 2013) argues that (1) applies freely as long as it conforms to 3rd factor principles (such as the No-Tampering Condition and the condition of inclusiveness). If tenable, there are no syn-tactic constraints on the application of Merge. Furthermore, under (1), Merge and Move are unified; they are just two possible instantiations—EM and IM—of Merge $(\alpha, \beta) \rightarrow \{\alpha, \beta\}$.[15] Chomsky argues that Merge comes free, and since EM and IM are just instances of Merge, they come free as well. It would require stipulation to bar either type of applica-tion of Merge. Importantly, then, (12c) appears to be not only a specifi-cally syntactic constraint but one which applies only to IM—but not to EM—precluding unification. That is, (12c) cannot be generalized to con-strain all applications of Merge, because objects with no label (e.g. {EA, {v, VP}}) can be merged with T, under Chomsky's (2013) labeling analysis, as adapted by Rizzi.

To summarize, the account under review appeals to the dedicated uniquely syntactic constraint on transformational rule application, not cur-rently reducible to 3rd factor considerations, namely (11), which in turn entails the existence of two distinct structure building operations, EM and IM, the latter constrained by (11), but the former exempt.

4 EXPLAINING "OBLIGATORY HALT" AS A SYNTACTIC ILLUSION: A MORPHO-PHONOLOGICAL, CI ANALYSIS

In this section, we first identify independently motivated morpho-phonological, CI requirements for properly interpreting clauses whose labels are identified as the interrogative complementizer C_Q or the Q-feature shared by the two heads C_Q and WH_Q, and then explain "obligatory syntactic halt" in *wh* criterial position as the only way to circumvent a violation of these requirements. Crucially, under this analysis, there is in fact no syntactic "halting" constraint (contra Rizzi 1997, 2006, 2011, 2014; Epstein 1992); rather, *wh*-movement from *wh* criterial position (freely applied simplest Merge) is allowed to apply in NS, but if it does, independently motivated morpho-phonological, CI requirements are violated.

Let us begin with the following (minimum) assumptions concerning C_Q: (i) There is only one C_Q in the (English) lexicon, appearing in both *yes/no*- and *wh*-interrogatives (Chomsky 1995b);[16] (ii) every syntactic object must be labeled at CI (Chomsky 2013); (iii) a CP with the label C_Q, unaccompanied by a *wh*-specifier, is interpreted as a *yes/no*-question at CI; and (iv) a CP with the label Q, when Q is shared by the two heads C_Q and WH_Q (the latter being the head-feature of a *wh*-phrase in "Spec, CP"), is interpreted as a *wh*-question at CI (Chomsky 2013).

Given this much, consider (an "underlying" representation of) a matrix *yes/no*-question of the following form:

(13) $[_\alpha C_Q [_{TP}$ John likes this dog]]

Adopting the labeling analysis of Chomsky (2013), in (13), the label of α is the head C_Q since α is of the form {H, XP}, where the head H determines the label. However, as Noam Chomsky (personal communication) points out, the SM representation of (13) with neutral or falling intonation is not possible. More specifically, in English, matrix *yes/no*-questions require either T-to-C inversion or rising (question) sentential prosody.[17] Now, consider the following case in which (13) is embedded:

(14) *You wonder $[_\alpha C_Q [_{TP}$ John likes this dog]].

In (14), the label of α is C_Q, and this label C_Q is unaccompanied by a *wh*-specifier. As a result α is interpreted as a *yes/no*-question at CI. The morpho-phonological problem with (14) is that T-to-C is unavailable as is rising intonation in English embedded clauses. But, in addition, α in (14), though required to be interpreted as a *yes/no*-question, in fact cannot be interpreted as a *yes/no*-question. That is, Chomsky assumes that, when embedded, a *yes/no*-question, interpreted in concert with the structure above it, yields a composed representation that is "gibberish, crashing at CI" (Chomsky 2014; see also Chomsky 1995b).[18]

This morpho-phonological, CI analysis of (13) and (14)[19] sheds new light on the following contrast, exhibited by (15a,b) (where *t* is used only for expository purposes, representing a copy of the category that undergoes movement):

(15) a. You wonder [$_\alpha$ [which dog] [C_Q [$_{TP}$ John likes t]]].
     b. *Which dog do you wonder [$_\alpha$ t [C_Q [$_{TP}$ John likes t]]]?

Under the labeling analysis of Chomsky (2013), in (15a), the label of α is the Q-feature, shared by the two heads, namely C_Q and the operator WH_Q, and this label Q, accompanied by a *wh*-specifier, is interpreted as a *wh*-question (an indirect one in (15a)) at CI. In (15b), however, Minimal Search fails to identify the Q-feature (shared by the two heads C_Q and WH_Q) as the label of α, because the operator WH_Q (= t) in α is "invisible" to Minimal Search. That is, Chomsky (2013) takes WH_Q to be inside α if and only if every occurrence of WH_Q is a term of α. Thus, after *wh*-movement into the matrix clause, the copy of WH_Q in α is invisible to Minimal Search when it searches α for its label identification (see EKS 2012 for further empirical support of this analysis).

Notice that the analysis proposed here asserts that the embedded clause α in (15b) cannot be interpreted as a *wh*-question, because *which dog* in the specifier of the embedded C_Q is invisible to Minimal Search. It predicts that the label of α is the C_Q (recall that α appears to Minimal Search as [C_Q TP]), and although selection is thereby satisfied, as *wonder* selects C_Q, α cannot be interpreted as a *wh*-question. So what interpretation does (15b) receive?

We argue that α in (15b) receives a *yes/no*-question interpretation. Recall from above that a CP with the label C_Q, unaccompanied by a *wh*-specifier, is interpreted as a *yes/no*-question at CI. The hypothesized problems with (15b) are then that T-to-C is unavailable, as is rising intonation, in English embedded clauses, and when embedded a *yes/no*-question is gibberish (and perhaps crashing) at CI. Thus, contra Epstein (1992) and Rizzi (1997, 2006, 2011, 2014), we follow Chomsky (1995b) in proposing an unconstrained NS that allows the movement depicted in (15b), and we hypothesize that its anomaly is in fact due to peculiar aspects of overt English morpho-phonology and the universal CI requirement for interpreting a *yes/no*-question; (15b) is out for essentially the same reason as (14) is.[20] Thus, as noted in section 1, the analysis presented here unifies (15b) and (14) as "the same phenomenon," whereas Rizzi's "X′ invisibility" analysis of (15b) fails to exclude (14).

Similarly, this morpho-phonological, CI analysis captures the following contrast:

(16) a. ??Which dog do you wonder [$_\alpha$ [which picture of t] [C_Q [$_{TP}$ John likes t]]].
     b. *Which picture of which dog do you wonder [$_\alpha$ t [C_Q [$_{TP}$ John likes t]]]?

In (16a), the C_Q and the operator WH_Q of *which picture (of which dog)* determine the label Q of α.[21] In (16b), however, the C_Q fails to determine the label Q of α in conjunction with the operator WH_Q since the *wh*-phrase *which picture of which dog* in α is invisible to labeling.

If the labeling analysis of (15a,b) and (16a,b) is on track, it suggests that "obligatory syntactic halt" from *wh* criterial position is in fact an illusion. There is no prohibition against such movement; rather, free (and simplest) Merge can execute movement from a criterial position, but such movement necessarily leads to a violation of the independently needed morpho-phonological, CI requirements.

Recall that the morpho-phonological, CI analysis is independently necessary to rule out (14). That is, (14) crucially satisfies the requirement that every SO have a unique label at CI. In (14), the label of CP is simple C_Q, via the application of (2); i.e., there is no labeling failure in (14). Therefore, it appears that Rizzi's (2014) analysis also needs something additional, perhaps the morpho-phonological, CI analysis presented here, to exclude cases like (14). But if the morpho-phonological, CI analysis is postulated, notice that the maximality principle (11) is empirically dispensable, and conceptually the elimination of (11) is arguably attractive, given that, as noted, (11) is both a UG-specific syntactic constraint and, in addition, one that applies uniquely to IM, thereby precluding the unification of EM and IM as simply different instantiations of the single rule (simplest) Merge.[22]

Summarizing, we identified and appealed to the following assumptions concerning English C_Q:

(i)   There is only one C_Q in the (English) lexicon, appearing in both *yes/no-* and *wh*-interrogatives.

(ii)   Every SO must be labeled at CI.

(iii) An SO, the label of which is identified as the head C_Q, unaccompanied by a *wh*-specifier, is interpreted as a *yes/no*-question.

(iv) An SO, the label of which is identified as the Q-feature, shared by the two heads C_Q and WH_Q, is interpreted as a *wh*-question.

(v)   English *yes/no*-questions require T-to-C inversion or rising (question) sentential prosody, available only in matrix clauses, and when embedded, the resulting structure cannot be felicitously interpreted; such structures are gibberish (and perhaps crash) at CI.

(i)–(v) are all independently motivated, and to explain apparent "obligatory syntactic halt" in *wh* criterial position, nothing more seems to be needed. We argued that there is no need to invoke an NS-specific halting constraint; the "halting" effect, observed in (15b), naturally follows from the independently needed morpho-phonological, CI analysis.[23]

5   FREE MERGE + OVERT CASE = SCRAMBLING?

As demonstrated in the preceding sections, Chomsky's (2013) labeling analysis predicts that (in a derivation satisfying FI at CI) a category that undergoes movement ultimately lands where it won't induce a labeling failure. It can move to a potentially problematic place as in *wh*-movement to the intermediate specifier of C, as long as it further moves on. Under freely applied simplest Merge, "IM" can move it anywhere in principle,[24] but if a labeling failure occurs, then it pays the price at CI. This labeling analysis sheds new light on scrambling. It has been observed that overt Case particle languages like Japanese allow scrambling. In this section, we argue that this observation receives a principled account under the labeling analysis.

The intuition that we would like to pursue is that in Japanese, each overt Case particle constitutes an independent head, while in English, abstract Case is part of a nominal head. Given this much, prior to valuation, a Case-marked object in Japanese is schematically a set containing unvalued Case (*u*Case) and α, where *u*Case is a head and α is a complex object. In English, however, the nominal head inside α bears *u*Case. Recall that *u*Case bears a formal feature that must be valued in NS. But notice, after valuation, Japanese Case, unlike English Case, becomes a purely phonological head which has nothing to do with NS and CI (see Chomsky 2000; EKS 2010).

Given these assumptions, we would like to propose that such purely phonological heads, namely valued Case (*vl*Case) in Japanese, cannot serve as a label identifier at CI. Under this proposal, upon the valuation of Case, a Case-marked object in Japanese becomes ZP = {*vl*Case, XP}, in which the purely phonological head *vl*Case exists (as a head) but is ineligible as a label.[25] Thus, in {{vCase, XP}, {YP}}, Minimal Search finds vCase and Y (the heads of each set), but since *vl*Case is not a possible label, Minimal Search has not found two possible labels. Rather, in finding *vl*Case and Y, it has found a unique label (even though this is a {ZP, YP} structure without feature sharing/agreeing). The label is therefore Y.

This proposal immediately explains why Case-marked objects never project (see Saito 2013). Notice they are headed by the purely phonological head *vl*Case, and Minimal Search finds it, but such a phonological head, being "unqualified" for label identification for CI, will never be a candidate for a label of a newly formed object. This in turn entails that a Case-marked object will never induce the so-called {XP, YP} problem, given that one of the relevant heads can serve as a label. So, suppose one of the heads, say the head of the XP, turns out to be vacuous for labeling. Then the remaining head of the YP (if visible to labeling and qualified as a labeler) will be the label of this object.

Take concrete cases. Japanese allows an object NP to undergo scrambling to the sentence-initial position from within the same clause or out of an embedded clause (see, among others, Saito 1992):

(17) a. [Masao-ga   sono   hon-o   katta]   (koto)
      Masao-Nom   that   book-Acc   bought   (fact)
      "Masao bought that book"

    b. [**sono hon-o**   [Masao-ga *t*   katta]]   (koto)
        that   book-Acc   Masao-Nom   bought   (fact)

(18) a. [Hanako-ga [[Masao-ga   sono   hon-o   katta]   to]
       omotteiru]   (koto)
       Hanako-Nom   Masao-Nom   that   book-Acc   bought   that
       think   (fact)
       "Hanako thinks that Masao bought that book"

    b. [**sono hon-o**   [Hanako-ga   [[Masao-ga *t*   katta]   to]
       omotteiru]]   (koto)
       that   book-Acc   Hanako-Nom   Masao-Nom   bought   that
       think   (fact)

In (17b) and (18b), the Case-marked object XP *sono hon-o*, represented as {uCase, α}, where α is a complex object, is scrambled to a higher position, forming {{uCase, α}, YP}. But upon the valuation of Case, a Case-marked object, in effect, becomes {vCase, α}, in which the purely phonological head vCase is visible to the eyes of Minimal Search but is ineligible to serve as a label. Thus, it follows that the label of {{vCase, α}, YP} is the remaining head, i.e. the Y head of the YP. Under these assumptions, the scrambling of an overtly Case-marked object {vCase, α} never yields a labeling failure.

To summarize, Japanese-type languages with overt Case particles allow scrambling, because scrambling of an overtly Case-marked object never yields a labeling failure. When an NP headed by a valued Case is scrambled, such a head, being vacuous to labeling, will never be a candidate for the label of the newly formed object created by this application of scrambling. As a result, the label of the merged sister of this NP will always be the label of the newly formed object. That immediately explains why scrambling neither "projects" the mover nor induces a labeling failure.

Note, if the overt Case particle is "dropped" from NP, rendering Case part of a nominal head as in English-type languages, then the labeling analysis, developed here, predicts that scrambling of NP with no overt Case particle will be restricted to a very local domain where a labeling failure is circumvented by some prominent feature, shared by the relevant heads. There is an interesting observation, consistent with this prediction, reported by Kuroda (1988):

(19) a. [**nanika-o**   [Masao-ga *t*   katta]]   (koto)
       something-Acc   Masao-Nom   bought   (fact)
       "Masao bought something"

    b. *[**nanika**   [Masao-ga *t*   katta]]   (koto)
       something   Masao-Nom   bought   (fact)

(20) a. [**Hanako-o**   [Masao-ga   Taroo-ni *t*   syookai-sita]]   (no itu?)
       Hanako-Acc   Masao-Nom   Taroo-Dat   introduced   when
       "(When was it that) Masao introduced Hanako to Taroo(?)"

b. *[**Hanako** [Masao-ga Taroo-ni *t* syookai-sita]] (no itu?)
   Hanako Masao-Nom Taroo-Dat introduced when

As shown in (19b) and (20b), scrambling of NP with no overt Case particle is blocked. Under the labeling analysis presented here, each case is ruled out as a labeling failure. Needless to say, these data and many other interesting observations concerning scrambling require further investigation.[26]

6 SUMMARY

This paper argues that independently motivated morpho-phonological, CI requirements (for properly interpreting clauses whose labels are identified as the interrogative complementizer C_Q or as the Q-feature shared by the two heads C_Q and WH_Q) naturally account for certain "criterial freezing" effects. However, "freezing" is a misnomer under this analysis, which crucially permits movement from criterial positions (which invariably results in morpho-phonological, CI problems). No UG-specific syntactic constraints on (free and simplest) Merge or syntactic "filters" of any kind are required. Merge, formulated in the simplest form, is free to apply, conforming only to 3rd factor principles, yet effects of "criterial freezing" result. Thus, if a *wh-phrase* moves from a criterial position, interface anomaly results. Contra Rizzi, we have suggested that there is no NS constraint, applied to IM but not to EM, preventing the move by virtue of applying an Earliness principle to syntactically obligatory labeling with projected labels explicitly represented in NS (contra Chomsky 2013). If viable, this kind of minimalist (re-)analysis contributes to the overall program of eliminative or reductive analysis of UG and NS, allowing us to maintain freely applied, simplest Merge subject to constraints imposed only by Chomsky's (1965:59, 2005) "3rd factor," thereby yielding welcome and widespread prospects for deeper explanation of the formal content, and perhaps the very existence, of human knowledge of language.

ACKNOWLEDGMENT

We thank Luigi Rizzi for his assistance, and we are indebted to Noam Chomsky and Ezra Keshet for their very valuable discussion of key ideas presented here. For helpful comments we thank Jun Abe, Nobu Goto, Yoichi Miyamoto, and Masashi Nomura. We would also like to thank the audiences of the following conferences, where different portions of this material were presented: Workshop on Altaic Formal Linguistics 10, MIT, May 2–4, 2014; GLOW in Asia X, National Tsing Hua University, Taiwan, May 24–26, 2014; Labels and Roots workshop, Jahrestagung der Deutschen Gesellschaft für Sprachwissenschaft, Marburg, Germany, March 5–7, 2014.

NOTES

1. See Collins (2002) on the elimination of labels in representations, and see Seely (2006), who seeks to explain their representational absence as the result of eliminating the "projection phase" of Merge application. Both authors argue for "simplest Merge" on minimalist grounds.

2. Note that "minimal search" is not formally defined in Chomsky (2013). The intuitive idea is that minimal search finds the first lexical item (within a given set). See Rizzi (2014) for some discussion.

3. The assumption is that XP and YP are of the form {X, α}, {Y, β}, respectively, and X, Y are heads with "qualifying" features. In principle, we could have XP, YP, where XP is {X, α} but YP is itself {ZP, WP}; note that in this case there would not be equal minimal search into XP, YP finding heads X, Y; rather, the head X would be "found first." In this paper, we leave this possibility aside.

4. Chomsky (2013) takes α to be in the domain D if and only if every occurrence of α is a term of D.

5. In (5), once *wh*-PP raises to the "specifier" of the matrix C, the *wh*-PP copy in the intermediate position is no longer in the domain of the embedded CP; hence, this *wh*-PP in intermediate position is effectively "invisible" for label calculation. The embedded CP, with respect to what's in its domain, is {C, TP}, and thus it will have the label C. See note 3 for the relevant definition.

6. Notice there is no LF covert movement in the current framework. Rather, each phase-head complement is sent both to SM and CI at the derivational point of phasal completion. If there were covert LF movement, this could overgenerate (7b) by raising *in which Texas city* only in the LF component.

7. In (8a,b), we take *there* to be a complex syntactic object, not a simple head (see Chomsky 2013:46n.42, and the references cited therein).

8. EKS (2014a) also argue that under the proposed labeling analysis of (8), the (or perhaps one) central empirical motivation for the postulate "phase" and for the constraint "Merge over Move" (unstatable under unified simplest Merge) is eliminated. See EKS (2014a) for discussion.

9. Rizzi (2014) assigns the label Q to each relevant mother-node in the (non-bare) phrase structure tree representation he provides, corresponding to (10). It is not clear, however, how this label Q is represented (or, under strict adherence to Chomsky 2013, how it's identified) *in* the relevant bare phrase structure set-theoretic representations formed by simplest Merge. We leave open this potentially important issue regarding the degree to which Rizzi's freezing analysis is in fact *deduced* from precisely what is proposed in Chomsky's (2013) labeling theory (but for some relevant discussion, see EKS 2013). Another potential problem confronting this analysis is as follows: If labels are required only at CI, as assumed, then, without adding further stipulations, labeling could be delayed until CI, in which case we could move *which dog* in NS (as in (9b)) while it is still maximal and thus moveable, yielding the wrong result. That is, in order to work as desired, the syntactic freezing analysis requires Pesetsky-style Earliness (as Rizzi (2014) proposes) guaranteeing immediate and obligatory labeling in NS.

10. As Rizzi (2014) notes, this bars head movement as well as "X′ projections" from moving. As a possible solution, Rizzi suggests enriching syntactic representations so that heads, e.g. *kick*, are represented as [kick + lex]. We leave open the consequences of this.

11. The implementation of the labeling analysis is not clear in all cases. Notice that before *which dog* moves to the "specifier" of C, it's arguably a DP, since

minimal search finds the head *which*, a D. But then {which, dog} would be a maximal DP, perhaps also a non-maximal Q), even in the "specifier" of C, and hence should be able to move, as a maximal D, under (11). One possible route to a solution would be to analyze *which dog* as QP containing DP within it. Then the moved *which dog* in the "specifier" of C is not DP but rather only Q-bar and hence is frozen. Note that this raises the more general issue of the exact nature of the labeling algorithm of Chomsky (2013). (See also Rizzi 2014:38–39n.15.)

12. In this regard, Rizzi proposes an "earliness principle" governing his explicitly syntactic labeling. We leave open the question of whether this syntactic earliness is consistent with the assumption that labels are needed only at CI. See also note 9. In addition, if Earliness is not to be an operation-specific constraint applied only to obligatory NS labeling, then the empirical consequences of Earliness—construed as a 3rd factor constraint—applied to all operations need to be investigated.

13. The efficacy of Rizzi's (2014) deduction of freezing (from independently motivated principles) of course depends on the extent of the independent motivation for X′ invisibility, expressed via (11), without which the account of such freezing would be ad hoc. We do not address here the extent of the existing empirical motivation for, hence empirical adequacy of, the principle of X′ Invisibility, which (11) is presumed to subsume. See e.g. Chomsky (1995b) and Epstein and Seely (2006) for analyses adopting the X′ Invisibility principle.

14. The question then is, of course, how to prevent the result of such allowable movement, and whether simplification in one component (i.e. the transformational component is simplified by eliminating the non-3rd factor maximality constraint on Merge) leads to proliferation in another (CI interpretive laws). We address this question in section 4.

15. See Kitahara (1997) for an earlier unification.

16. Why would C_Q appear in both *yes/no*-questions and *wh*-questions? This might be explained under analyses of *wh*-questions in which they are interpreted as a family of *yes/no*-questions. So, for example, *what did you buy* is interpreted as something like: "Did you buy a car? Answer me yes or no. Did you buy a pen? Answer me yes or no," etc. We are indebted to Ezra Keshet for this idea and for valuable discussion of issues relevant here.

17. Presumably, one or the other is needed as an overt indicator of the otherwise undetectable presence of C_Q, as Chomsky (2013) notes.

18. Leaving aside whether it is "crashing," i.e. some yet-to-be-proposed unvalued feature appears at an interface, one possibility regarding its status as gibberish is as follows: The CP headed by C_Q is itself interpreted as a *yes/no*-question and so would be interpreted as: "Answer me this: Does John like this dog?" that is, a performative request made of the speaker's interlocutor for a specific kind of information As such, embedding it, as in *I wonder John left* yields an interpretation like: "I wonder, 'Answer me this, Did John leave?'" This is anomalous to the extent that one cannot wonder a request for information.

19. Notice that (13) violates only the English morpho-phonological requirement (if neither T-to-C raising nor rising intonation is applied), while (14) violates the morpho-phonological requirement *and* is gibberish at CI (see note 18). We leave the consequences of this for future research.

20. This labeling analysis of (15a,b), in which "criterial freezing" violations become a CI problem, was first suggested by Noam Chomsky in his class lecture at the University of Michigan 2013 LSA Summer Institute, on July 11, 2013.

21. The *wh*-extraction of *which dog* involves an extraction out of the edge of the lower phase, which might be a source of the observed deviance (see Chomsky 1986, 2008; Gallego 2009 for important discussion).

22. In Japanese, unlike English, raising from *wh* criterial position appears to be permissible. Consider (i) (from Takahashi 1993):

(i) Nani-o   Taroo-wa   [Hanako-ga *t*   katta ka]   siritagatteiru no
    what-ACC   Taroo-TOP   Hanako-NOM   bought Q   want-to-know Q
    "What does Taroo want to know whether Hanako bought?"

Given that (i) converges and is interpretable at CI, we suggest that the interrogative complementizer C_Q and the counterpart of "whether" are homophonous in Japanese; they are pronounced as *ka*. Thus, in (i), *ka* is not an interrogative complementizer C_Q; rather, it is the Japanese counterpart of "whether," as the translation indicates.

23. The labeling analysis, developed here, sheds new light on partial *wh*-movement. Consider the following German data (from Sabel 2000):

(i) a. [β Was [C_Q meinst du [α   wen [C Peter Hans *t* vorgestellt hat]]]?
       WH   think you$_{nom}$ who$_{acc}$ P$_{nom}$ H$_{dat}$ introduced has
       "Who do you think Peter has introduced to Hans?"
    b. [β Was [C_Q meinst du [α   wem [C Peter *t* die Leute   vorgestellt hat]]]?
       WH   think you$_{nom}$ who$_{dat}$ P$_{nom}$ the people$_{acc}$ introduced has
       "To whom do you think Peter has introduced the people?"

It is generally assumed that *was* is not a *wh*-phrase; it is a *wh*-expletive that functions as a scope marker; and the *wh*-phrase *wen/wem* "who$_{acc}$/who$_{dat}$" is interpreted at the matrix CP, thanks to this *wh*-expletive, even though the *wh*-phrase is located in the embedded CP. From the labeling point of view, however, if the *wh*-phrase headed by the WH_Q remained in α and appeared there at CI, a labeling failure would result, contrary to fact. So what is going on? One possibility is that even though the WH_Q (or the phrase containing it) can remain, violating FI at CI, in (ia,b) the WH_Q (or the phrase containing it) can choose an option of moving out, allowing α to be labeled. Pursuing this possibility, what is left behind by such movement may in fact be only the pronominal material of the *wh*-phrase, including phi and Case; it is no longer the *wh*-phrase headed by the WH_Q. One possible implementation of this might be to apply Obata and Epstein's (2011) "Feature Splitting Internal Merge" hypothesis.

In this regard, Dutch provides an interesting case. Instead of *wie* "who," the pronominal element *die* can appear in α, as in (ii) (from Boef 2013):

(ii) a. Ze   vroeg   wie   jij   denkt [α wie   het   gedaan   heeft]
        she   asked   who   you   think   who   it   done   has
        "She asked who you think has done it."
     b. Ze   vroeg   wie   jij   denkt [α die   het   gedaan   heeft]
        she   asked   who   you   think   DEM   it   done   has
        "She asked who you think has done it."

If the structure of this A′ pronoun is analyzed as "WH_Q + pronominal material," then the WH_Q (or a phrase containing it) moves out of α to form the label Q of the matrix clause, leaving its pronominal content behind, and such non-WH, non-Q pronominal content gets pronounced as *die* in Dutch, leaving the door open for a way to circumvent a labeling failure in the embedded clause.

24. See Chomsky and Lasnik (1977), Chomsky (1981), and Lasnik and Saito 1992 for "Move α" precursors of "freely applied Merge."

25. There is a precedent, in Chomsky (2013), for analyses in which a head does not count as a label, e.g. conjunction head *&*. So, in {{X, α}, {&, {{X, α}, {Y, β}}}}

(where {X, α} moves to the "specifier" of &), minimal search finds two heads X and &, but & does not count as a label, so the remaining head, namely X, serves as the label of {{X, α}, {&, {{X, α}, {Y, β}}}}. See Chomsky (2013:46) for more detailed discussion.

26. One such case involves free application of Merge (i.e. what is traditionally referred to as "scrambling") of a *wh*-phrase with no overt Case particle. Under the labeling analysis developed here, it should be possible if its landing site is a "specifier" of C bearing Q since then a labeling failure does not occur. The judgments about this prediction, however, are not clear. We leave this important and interesting issue for future research.

REFERENCES

Boef, E. 2013. Partial *Wh*-Movement Revisited: A Microcomparative Perspective. Paper presented at "Toward a Theory of Syntactic Variation," Bilbao, June 5–7, 2013.

Chomsky, N. 1965. *Aspects of the Theory of Syntax*. Cambridge, MA: MIT Press.

Chomsky. N. 1981. *Lectures on Government and Binding*. Dordrecht: Foris.

Chomsky, N. 1986. *Knowledge of Language: Its Nature, Origin, and Use*. New York: Praeger.

Chomsky, N. 1995a. Bare Phrase Structure. In Webelhuth, G. (ed.), *Government and Binding Theory and the Minimalist Program: Principles and Parameters in Syntactic Theory*, 385–439. Oxford: Blackwell.

Chomsky, N. 1995b. *The Minimalist Program*. Cambridge, MA: MIT Press.

Chomsky, N. 2000. Minimalist Inquiries: The Framework. In Martin, R., Michaels, D. and Uriagereka, J. (eds.), *Step by Step: Essays on Minimalist Syntax in Honor of Howard Lasnik*, 89–155. Cambridge, MA: MIT Press.

Chomsky, N. 2004. Beyond Explanatory Adequacy. In Belletti, A. (ed.), *Structures and Beyond*, 104–131. Oxford: Oxford University Press.

Chomsky, N. 2005. Three Factors in Language Design. *Linguistic Inquiry* 36:1–22.

Chomsky, N. 2007. Approaching UG from Below. In Sauerland, U. and Gärtner, H.-M. (eds.), *Interfaces + Recursion = Language?*, 1–29. Berlin: Mouton de Gruyter.

Chomsky, N. 2008. On Phases. In Freidin, R., Otero, C. P. and Zubizarreta, M. L. (eds.), *Foundational Issues in Linguistic Theory: Essays in Honor of Jean-Roger Vergnaud*, 133–166. Cambridge, MA: MIT Press.

Chomsky, N. 2013. Problems of Projection. *Lingua* 130:33–49.

Chomsky, N. 2014. Problems of Projection: Extensions. Manuscript, MIT, Cambridge, MA.

Chomsky, N. and Lasnik, H. 1977. Filters and Control. *Linguistic Inquiry* 8:425–504.

Collins, C. 2002. Eliminating Labels. In Epstein, S. D. and Seely, T. D. (eds.), *Derivation and Explanation in the Minimalist Program*, 42–64. Oxford: Blackwell.

Epstein, S. D. 1992. Derivational Constraints on A′-Chain Formation. *Linguistic Inquiry* 23:235–259.

Epstein, S. D., Kitahara, H. and Seely, T. D. 2010. Uninterpretable Features: What Are They and What Do They Do? In Putnam, M. (ed.), *Exploring Crash Proof Grammars*, 125–142. Philadelphia: John Benjamins.

Epstein, S. D., Kitahara, H. and Seely, T. D. 2012. Structure Building That Can't Be! In Uribe-etxebarria, M. and Valmala, V. (eds.), *Ways of Structure Building*, 253–270. Oxford: Oxford University Press.

Epstein, S.D., Kitahara, H. and Seely, T.D. 2013. Simplest Merge Generates Set Intersection: Implications for Complementizer-Trace Explanation. In Goto, N., Otaki, K., Sato, A. and Takita, K. (eds.), *The Proceedings of GLOW in Asia IX*, 77–92. Mie, Japan: Mie University.

Epstein, S. D., Kitahara, H. and Seely, T. D. 2014a. Labeling by Minimal Search: Implications for Successive-Cyclic A-Movement and the Conception of the Postulate "Phase." *Linguistic Inquiry* 45:463–481.

Epstein, S. D., Kitahara, H. and Seely, T. D. 2014b. From *Aspects* 'daughterless mothers' (aka delta nodes) to POP's 'motherless' sets (aka non-projection): a selective history of the evolution of Simplest Merge. Unpublished ms., University of Michigan, Ann Arbor, Eastern Michigan University, Ypsilanti, and Keio University, Minato, Japan.

Epstein, S.D. and Seely, T.D. 2006. *Derivations in Minimalism*. Cambridge: Cambridge University Press.

Gallego, A.J. 2009. On Freezing Effects. *Iberia* 1:33–51.

Kitahara, H. 1997. *Elementary Operations and Optimal Derivations*. Cambridge, MA: MIT Press.

Kuroda, S.-Y. 1988. Whether We Agree or Not. *Linguisticae Investigationes* 12:1–47.

Lasnik, H. and Saito, M. 1992. *Move α: Conditions on Its Application and Output*. Cambridge, MA: MIT Press.

Obata, M. and Epstein, S.D. 2011. Feature-Splitting Internal Merge: Improper Movement, Intervention and the A/A′ Distinction. *Syntax* 14:122–147.

Rizzi, L. 1997. The Fine Structure of the Left Periphery. In Haegeman, L. (ed.), *Elements of Grammar*, 281–337. Dordrecht: Kluwer.

Rizzi, L. 2006. On the Form of Chains: Criterial Positions and ECP Effects. In Cheng, L. and Corver, N. (eds.), *Wh-Movement on the Move*, 97–134. Cambridge, MA: MIT Press.

Rizzi, L. 2011. On Some Properties of Criterial Freezing. In Panagiotidis, E. P. (ed.), *The Complementizer Phrase*, 17–32. Oxford: Oxford University Press.

Rizzi, L. 2014. Cartography, Criteria and Labeling. Manuscript, University of Geneva, Geneva, Switzerland.

Sabel, J. 2000. Partial *Wh*-Movement and the Typology of *Wh*-Questions. In Lutz, U., Müller, G. and von Stechow, A. (eds.), *Wh-Scope Marking*, 409–446. Amsterdam: John Benjamins.

Saito, M. 1992. Long Distance Scrambling in Japanese. *Journal of East Asian Linguistics* 1:69–118.

Saito, M. 2013. Case and Labeling in a Language without φ-Feature Agreement. Manuscript, Nanzan University, Nagoya, Japan.

Seely, T.D. 2006. Merge, Derivational C-Command, and Subcategorization in a Label-Free Syntax. In Boeckx, C. (ed.), *Minimalist Essays*, 182–217. Amsterdam: John Benjamins.

Takahashi, D. 1993. Movement of Wh-Phrases in Japanese. *Natural Language and Linguistic Theory* 11:655–678.

Index